FINANCIAL CRISIS MANAGEMENT
IN REGIONAL BLOCS

FINANCIAL CRISIS MANAGEMENT IN REGIONAL BLOCS

edited by

Scheherazade S. Rehman
The George Washington University

KLUWER ACADEMIC PUBLISHERS
Boston/Dordrecht/London

Distributors for North America:
Kluwer Academic Publishers
101 Philip Drive
Assinippi Park
Norwell, Massachusetts 02061 USA

Distributors for all other countries:
Kluwer Academic Publishers Group
Distribution Centre
Post Office Box 322
3300 AH Dordrecht, THE NETHERLANDS

Library of Congress Cataloging-in-Publication Data

A C.I.P. Catalogue record for this book is available from
the Library of Congress.

Table of Contents

Acknowledgements

I dedicate this book to the special people in my life whose love and support made this possible: Liza, Richard and Roxolana and more specially to the little ones: Janana, Faazal, Shiva, Darya and more recently Jehaan.

I owe a debt of gratitude to the contributors who made time in their busy schedules to address the issues raised by regional financial crisis.

I would specially like to thank Professor Peter Gray (Rutgers University) for providing the idea for this publication and for his on-going support. I would also like to thank Professor Geza P. Lauter (George Washington University) whose continuous support has been indispensable and Professor Hossein Askari (George Washington University) for his advice.

Levent Ozbilgin's (George Washington University) editing assistance, research and technical support was extremely helpful as was Susen Rakibe Musal's (George Washington University) editing assistance.

I am indebted to Zachary Rolnik (Kluwer Academic Publishers) for his enthusiasm and support over the years.

Finally, I am grateful to the George Washington University, the School of Business and Public Management and the International Business Department for their support.

Contributors

ABOUT THE EDITOR

Dr. Scheherazade S. Rehman is Assistant Professor of International Finance and the Director of the Joint International MBA-MA Degree Programs at The George Washington University in Washington D.C. Prior to that she served as a foreign exchange and money market trader. She has served as an advisor to The World Bank, OPIC, USAID, numerous governments and multinational corporations. Dr. Rehman is also a senior partner/consultant of International Consultants Group, a Washington-based international financial/business management consulting company.

She has written several books, including, The Path To European Economic and Monetary Union (Boston: Kluwer Academic Publishers, 1997). She has also written extensively on central banking and global monetary systems, international trade and finance, financial sector development in transitional economies, and the euro.

ABOUT THE CONTRIBUTORS

Dr. Hossein Askari is currently Global Management Research Professor and Director of the Institute for Global Management Research at The George Washington University. He served on the IMF's Executive Board between 1979-81 and has advised a number of institutions including the United Nations, the OECD, The World Bank, The International Finance Corporation, the Ministry of Finance of Saudi Arabia, the Gulf Cooperation Council and various international oil companies.

Dr. Age F. P. Bakker is Deputy Director of the Central Bank of The Netherlands and Professor of Monetary Issues and Banking at the Vrije Universiteit of Amsterdam. He is a crown-appointed member of the Social and Economic Council in The Netherlands and is a member of a number of policy committees within the framework of the Bank for International Settlements (BIS), the European Monetary Institute (EMI) and the OECD. During his employment at the central bank (since 1976) he has worked on temporary leave at the International Monetary Fund.

Dr. Lajos Bokros is currently a Senior Adviser at Finance and Private Sector Development VP, The World Bank. Dr. Bokros was Minister of Finance of Hungary from 1995-96. He was also the Chairman and CEO of Budapest Bank, Ltd. from 1991-95 and Chairman of the Board of the Budapest Stock Exchange from 1990-95. Between 1990-91 he was a member of the Board of Directors of the State Property Agency (privatization agency). He also served as the Director of the Capital Markets Department and member of the Board of the National Bank of Hungary (NBH) (1989-91).

André de Lattre was Deputy Governor of the Bank of France from 1966 to 1974 and Chairman and Chief Executive Officer of Crédit National from 1974 to 1982. He became the World Bank Special Representative for IDA negotiations in 1983 and the Managing Director of The Institute of International Finance, Inc. from 1984 to 1986. From 1989-1996 he served as the Chairman of Banque Française de Service et de Crédit. Mr. De Lattre was Professor of Economics at the Ecole Nationale d'Administration (1955-56) and at the Institut d'Etudes Politiques de Paris (1958-83).

Dr. Roque B. Fernandez is the current Minister of Finance of Argentina. Previously, he has been the President of the Central Bank of Argentina (1991-1996). He also currently teaches macroeconomics at CEMA (Centro de Estudios Macroeconomicos de Argentina) and has taught in the Departments of Economics at the University of Southern California, Florida International University, and Universidad Catolica de Chile.

Dr. Daniel Gros is currently a Senior Research Fellow and Director of the Economic Policy Programme at the Centre for European Policy Studies (CEPS) in Brussels. He is also a Visiting Professor at the University of Frankfurt's Department of Economics. Dr. Gros has served as an Economist at the International Monetary Fund.

Dr. Arend J. Kapteyn is an economist at the Monetary and Economic Policy Department of the Central Bank of The Netherlands, particularly responsible for IMF-affairs. In his work, he has been actively involved in discussions on the expansion of the General Arrangements to Borrow and the resolution of sovereign liquidity crises. Prior to his employment at the central bank he worked for the Economic Strategy Institute in Washington D.C. and Fokker Aircraft in The Netherlands.

Dr. Philippe Maystadt is the current Vice-Prime Minister (since 1995), Minister of Finance (since 1988) and Minister of Foreign Trade of Belgium (since 1995) and Chairman of the Interim Committee of the IMF (since 1993). He is also currently a part-time Professor of Law at the Catholic University, Louvain (since 1989). He has previously served, among others, as the Chairman of the Council of Governors of the EBRD, the First Vice-Chairman of the Bureau of the Boards of Governors of the African Development Bank Group, Chairman of the Council of Ministers of Economy and Finance of the European Community, Chairman of the G-10 Ministers of Finance, and Belgium Minister of Economic Affairs. In September 1990, Vice-Prime Minister Maystadt was awarded the title of "Finance Minister of the Year" by Euromoney magazine.

Dr. Frederic S. Mishkin is currently the A. Barton Hepburn Professor of Economics at the Graduate School of Business, Columbia University and Research Associate at the National Bureau of Economic Research. He was formerly Executive Vice-President and Director of Research at the Federal Reserve Bank of New York and Associate Economist to the Federal Open Market Committee.

Dr. Franco Modigliani is Institute Professor Emeritus at the Massachusetts Institute of Technology (MIT). Professor Modigliani was the recipient of the 1985 Nobel Memorial Prize in Economic Science. Also in 1985, he received the James R. Killian Faculty Achievement Award from MIT. He is a member of the National Academy of Sciences and a member of the American Academy of Arts and Sciences. He is past president of the Econometric Society, the American Economic Association and the American Finance Association, and honorary President of the International Economic Association.

Jacob Nell was the former Assistant Editor of the Central Banking journal (U.K.) and is currently employed by H.M. Treasury. Mr. Nell has also served as a Consultant to the Economic Expert Group of the Russian Ministry of Finance. He has edited a credit rating presentation of the Russian Federation (summer 1996), organized and edited a special issue of Central Banking on the Central Bank of Russia, and written widely on central banking, monetary policy and financial regulation, including editing reference books on international financial institutions and financial regulators.

Dr. Howard Reed was the Special Counsel for Finance and Investment Policy to the United States Trade Representative (USTR), the Executive Office of the President during the 1st term of the Clinton Administration between 1993–1996. He has represented the USTR at the World Bank, IMF and on the Board of the US Export-Import Bank. Dr. Reed was previously a Professor at the University of Texas at Austin (1977-85).

Dr. Roberto Rinaldi is currently the Head of the Monetary Analysis Office in the Monetary and Financial Sector at the Bank of Italy. He joined the Bank of Italy in 1985. Dr. Rinaldi was a member of a working group at the Band of International Settlements (BIS) dealing with issues related to monetary policy coordination among EEC countries (1986-87) and has served as a monetary policy and research expert in the IMF programs providing technical assistance to East European Countries (1992-95).

Sheikh Salem Abdul Aziz Al-Sabah is the current Governor of the Central Bank of Kuwait (since 1986). He was internationally recognized for his leadership of the Central Bank of Kuwait (from exile) during the Iraqi occupation and was a central figure in the reconstruction of the banking and financial sector during the period following the liberation of Kuwait. In 1988, he was awarded the title of "Governor of the Year" by Euromoney magazine.

Dr. Carlo Santini is the Central Manager for Economic Research at the Bank of Italy. In addition, he also has supervision over the Foreign and the Money and Financial Markets Departments. He serves as Governor's Alternate on the Bank of International Settlements (BIS) Board and attends the Council of the European Monetary Institute. He is a member of the "Euro-currency Standing Committee" and of the Board of the Ufficio Italiano dei Cambi (Italian Exchange Office).

Dr. Liliana Schumacher, J.D. is Assistant Professor of International Finance and Banking at The George Washington University. She was previously Principal Economist in the Research Department at the Central Bank of Argentina where she was active in the study and design of financial regulations. She has written extensively on international banking; risk management, fiscal policy, Latin American banks and international financial markets.

Dr. Dr. h.c. Professor Hans Tietmeyer is the current President of the Deutsche Bundesbank. He is also the Chairman of the G-10 central bank governors, the Chairman of the EC Economic Policy Committee, Chairman of the OECD Working Party on Positive Adjustment Policies, Chairman of the EC Monetary Committee and Chairman of the Board of the "Deutsche Bundesstifung Umweit" (German Federal Foundation for the Environment). He is the bearer of the Knight Commander's Cross (Badge and Star) of the Order of Merit of the Federal Republic of Germany.

Dr. Josef Tošovský is the current Governor of Czech National Bank (since 1989). He is a member of the Academic Board of the Prague School of Economics, a member of the advisory body to the Rector of Charles University in Prague and a member of the CERGE Institute's Board of Directors. In 1993, Dr. Tošovský was awarded the title of "Central banker of the Year" by Euromoney magazine. In 1994, the European Business Press Federation elected him "European Manager of the Year." In addition, Dr. Tošovský received, as the first laureate at the Masaryk University in Brno, the Karl Englis Prize.

Kaspar Villiger is the current Minister of Finance (Head of the Federal Finance Department) of Switzerland (since 1995). In 1995, he was President of the Swiss Confederation. Prior to this, in 1989 he was elected Federal Councilor and conducted the Federal Military Department until 1995 and in 1987 was elected to the Council of States where he became member of the Ways and Means Committee and of the Transport Committee. As National Councilor, Minister Villiger, also served as a member of the defense committee from 1983 until 1987.

Sir Alan Walters was the chief economic advisor for Prime Minister (now Baroness) Margaret Thatcher from 1980-84 and 1989. He is currently Vice Chairman and Director of AIG Trading Group, Inc. (a subsidiary of the American International Group). He has been an advisor to the World Bank, various governments, central banks, and financial institutions. He has also held professorships at the Johns Hopkins University, University of Birmingham and the London School of Economics where he was the Sir Ernest Cassel Professor of Economics. He was knighted by Queen Elizabeth II in June 1983.

Introduction

SCHEHERAZADE S. REHMAN (editor)
Assistant Professor of International Finance and Director, Joint International MBA-MA Degree Programs, The George Washington University

Financial crises are not a new international economic phenomena. They have occurred throughout history resulting in the loss of national and international public and personal wealth, creating political uncertainty and shaking the foundations of the national, regional and international economic and social order.

Although in a general sense such crises are caused by either internal or external shocks or a combination thereof, the specific reasons triggering them vary. They range from inappropriate or failed domestic and international economic policies through unexpected or not fully understood international economic events to wars. Thus, there is no generally accepted definition or comprehensive explanation of what constitutes or causes such crises, although certain events such as, among others, excessive actions or reactions to political and/or economic developments by financial market participants, lack of reliable information, uncertainty, confusion and a degree of panic seem to be present wherever and whenever they occur.

This book presents a collection of articles providing answers to the basic questions of what could have caused some of the more recent regional financial crises, what their key characteristics were, how they could have been prevented, what lessons national governments, central bankers and the International Monetary Fund (IMF) have learned and how such crises could be prevented in the future.

The authors include current and former cabinet members of national governments, central bankers, IMF officials, scholars and practicing economists in both national and multilateral organizations, all of who have either participated in the management of the various types of financial crises they analyze and discuss and/or have made major contributions to their understanding, including recommendations of how they could be avoided in the future.

Part I of the book, *History and Background,* consists of one article, "Managing Financial Crises: Who Is in Charge?," by Dr. Howard Curtis Reed, Special Counsel for Finance & Investment Policy to the United States Trade Representative during 1993-1996. Dr. Reed explores the history, scope and varying international responses to past financial crises. He concludes that such crises can be caused by a combination of factors and that there is no global manager" to effectively deal with them.

Part II, *European Union and Other Regional Exchange Rate Arrangements,* includes six articles addressing the issues of regional exchange rate arrangements and their implications for national and regional economies and global financial markets. In the first article, "Monetary Unions in Europe," Sir Alan Walters, ex-chief economic advisor to Prime Minister (now Baroness) Margaret Thatcher between 1980-84 and 1989 and current Vice-Chairman and Director of AIG Trading Group, Inc., discusses the economic and political issues involved in the creation of the Economic and Monetary Union (EMU) of the European Union (EU) by 1999. Sir Alan takes a skeptical view of the project and argues that the U.K. should stay out of it.

In the second article, Dr. Dr. h.c. Professor Hans Tietmeyer, President of the Bundesbank of the Federal Republic of Germany explores the various aspects of "Financial Crisis Management in the EU/ERM." Dr. Tietmeyer concludes that the Exchange Rate Mechanism (ERM) crises involving most European Union (EU) currencies in 1992-1993 had occurred because the participating nations did not always observe the three basic ERM principles, namely the primacy of domestic price stability, the necessity of early central rate re-alignments and the need for flexibility. He also draws some important lessons concerning the stability requirements of regional exchange rate arrangements.

Dr. Tietmeyer's contribution is followed by a study looking at the same phenomenon from the viewpoint of one of the participating nations deeply involved in the crises. Authored by Dr. Roberto Rinaldi, Head of the Monetary Analysis Office in the Monetary and Financial Sector at the Bank of Italy and Dr. Carlo Santini, Central Manager for Economic Research at the Bank of Italy, the article "Italy: Two Foreign Exchange Crises" contains an analysis of the 1992 and 1995 lira crises. The authors argue that the globalization and liberalization of financial markets limit national sovereignty in setting and implementing economic policies. The smaller and more open a national economy is, the more stringent are the limitations. Dr. Rinaldi and Dr. Santini also present conclusions concerning the need to coordinate global economic policies over the medium-term.

Mr. André de Lattre, former Deputy Governor of the Bank of France, contributed the article on "The Single Currency as a Stabilizing Factor in International Relations: A French View." He believes that through the creation of the European single currency, the Euro, the quest for European and global financial stability may at last be rewarded. He recalls the steps on the road toward European monetary union, asks questions about what went wrong and reflects on the possible role of the new currency in Europe and the rest of the world.

Along the same lines but from the viewpoint of a small, open economy with a strong currency, the Minister of Finance of Switzerland, Kaspar Villiger, in the article "EMU and the Swiss Franc," looks into the future and explores the impact of four potential Economic Monetary Union (EMU) scenarios involving the Euro and the Swiss Franc. Minister Villiger does not foresee any financial crises emerging from any of the possible four scenarios he analyzes, although he points out that the Swiss currency and financial markets would be differently affected.

In the concluding article of this part, "Exchange Rate and Economic Policy in Three Regional Blocks: The EU, the GCC and the CFA," Dr. Franco Modigliani, Institute Professor Emeritus at the Massachusetts Institute of Technology, winner of the 1985 Nobel Price in Economics, and Dr. Hossein Askari, Global Management Research Professor and Director of the Institute of Global Management Research at The George Washington University in Washington D.C., take a historical look at the economic and financial performance of a group of countries with different fixed parity exchange rate systems. They discuss the nature, potential benefits and costs of the policy measure leading to the single currency arrangement in the European Union (EU), the informal pegging of the Gulf Cooperation Council (GCC) nations' currencies to the US dollar and the formal pegging of the West African Economic and Monetary Union (CFA) member nations' currencies to the French Franc. Professors Modigliani and Askari argue that while such regional currency exchange rate arrangements may generate economic benefits, their costs as, for example, the loss of output and rising unemployment, outweigh such benefits. They conclude by emphasizing that if the potential financial crises are not dealt with before they occur, financial disturbances could worsen the economic distortions already present in all three regions.

Part III, *The Mexican Crises and The Tequila Effect,* contains two contributions. In the first article, "The Mexican Financial Crisis of 1994-95: An Asymmetric Information Analysis," Dr. Frederic S. Mishkin, the former Executive Vice-President and Director of Research at the Federal Reserve Bank of New York and currently the A. Barton Hepburn Professor of Economics at Columbia University and Research Associate at the National Bureau of Economic Research, outlines his asymmetric information theory of financial crises in emerging market countries, focusing on the adverse selection and moral hazard implications of such information. He then uses the theory to explain why the Mexican financial crisis had occurred and why it had such a devastating effect on the economy. In the last part of his paper,

Professor Mishkin discusses the policy implications of the asymmetric information theory for emerging market countries.

The Mexican crisis analyzed by Professor Mishkin raised the specter of the so-called "Tequila Effect" (after-shock) in the global financial markets, particularly in the South American region. In their jointly authored paper "The Argentine Banking Panic After the "Tequila" Shock: Did "Convertibility" Help or Hurt ?," Dr. Roque B. Fernandez, Minister of Finance and former President of the Central Bank of Argentina together with Dr. Liliana Schumacher, former Principal Economist in the Research Department of the Central Bank of Argentina and currently Assistant Professor of International Finance and Banking at The George Washington University in Washington D.C., argue that while the Mexican events affected the Argentina banking sector, they did not create a crisis. Minister Fernandez and Professor Schumacher point out that the 1991 Argentine convertibility plan (currency board) restrained the forces generating budget deficits and, thus, inflation. Specific policies were put into place to manage moral hazard and to prevent panic in the banking sector. Although banks failed and merged, this was primarily due to structural and competitive changes prior to the 1994 Mexican crisis. The authors conclude that the convertibility plan was successful in maintaining internal and external equilibria.

Part IV, *The Transforming Economies*, shifts the focus of analysis from developed or developing market economies to nations undergoing a transformation from centrally planned to competitive market economies such as Russia, the Czech Republic and Hungary. In the first of three papers, Jacob Nell, former Assistant Editor of the <u>Central Banking</u> journal (U.K.) and currently with H.M. Treasury, analyzes the process through which the Russian government restructured the banking sector to avoid a financial crisis. "The Consolidation of Russian Banking" is focused on the policy measures of 1994 and 1996 which shook up the Russian banking industry yet, at the same time, probably prevented a major financial crisis from occurring.

Dr. Josef Tošovský, Governor of the Czech National Bank, in his article on "Managing Financial Turbulence: Czech Experience," discusses the 1990 and 1993 financial crises in the then still Czechoslovak Republic. The first crisis was caused by the introduction of the systemic transformation and macro-economic stabilization policies and the resulting currency speculation. The 1993 crisis resulted from the splitting of the country into the Czech and Slovak Republics, a move that initially involved an economic union and a common currency. However, such arrangements required macro-economic policy coordination at a time when the two countries were economically and politically growing apart. The resulting second wave of currency speculation raised the danger of a financial crisis in both countries. However, with the assistance of the IMF, the Czech National Bank took the necessary steps to prevent this from happening.

In the final contribution to this section, Dr. Lajos Bokros, former Hungarian Minister of Finance, discusses the economic conditions that had led up to and the policies that had to be implemented to prevent a major internal and external financial disequilibrium in his country. The article, "Stabilization Without Recession: The Success of a Long Awaited Financial Adjustment in Hungary," first describes the process of how Hungary, an early reforming economy, came to the brink of financial disaster as a transforming economy by 1994. He then describes the elements of the policy "package" named after him that eventually stabilized the nation's economy, prevented a major financial crisis but ran into strong public opposition due to the economic sacrifices the policies required.

Part V, *Special Topics: Public Debt and War,* contains two articles. The first addresses the potential for financial crises caused by high domestic debt, using European Union member nations as examples. The other raises the issue of what can be done to prevent a crisis in case of war. In the first paper, "Self-Fulfilling Public Debt Crises," Dr. Daniel Gros, Senior Research Fellow and Director, Economic Policy Programme, Centre for European Policy Studies (Brussels) and Professor at the University of Frankfurt develops a theoretical framework for understanding the implications of high public debt and argues that countries with such debt could end up in either of two model-consistent equilibria. Under the first equilibrium, the government has strong anti-inflationary credentials, thus, interest rates and the debt-service burden remain low. The other represents a "debt trap." If both equilibria are possible, the latter, if it occurs, is unstable.

In the second article, "The Impact of the Iraqi Invasion on the Kuwaiti Banking and Financial System: Lessons Learned from a Financial Crisis," Sheikh Salem Abdul Aziz Al-Sabah, the Governor of the Central Bank of Kuwait, discusses the policies implemented by his government and institution to prevent a major financial crisis that could have been generated by the 1990 Iraqi invasion and temporary occupation of Kuwait. In analyzing the lessons learned, he emphasizes the importance of a strong and flexible financial infrastructure.

Part VI, *The Role of the IMF,* presents two papers addressing the past and potential role of the International Monetary Fund (IMF) in managing financial crises. In the first contribution, "Financial Crisis Management and the Role of the IMF, 1970-1995," Dr. Professor Age F. P. Bakker, Deputy Director of the Central Bank of Netherlands and Dr. Arend J. Kapteyn, economist at the Monetary and Economic Policy Department of the Central Bank of The Netherlands, provide an overview of past IMF actions. Beginning with the breakdown of the Bretton Woods system in the early 1970s, they analyze global economic and financial events as well as the changing role of the IMF. Dr. Bakker and Dr. Kapteyn discuss the 1970s energy and the subsequent external debt crisis of the 1980s as well as the financial crises caused by the economic transformation process in the formerly centrally planned economies during the early 1990s as well as the Mexican events of 1994. They conclude that through the introduction of new programs and measures as needed, the IMF lived up to past challenges.

In the concluding article of the book, "The Role Of The International Monetary Fund In Promoting Stability In The Global Economy," Philippe Maystadt, Vice-Prime Minister and Minister of Finance and Foreign Trade of Belgium and Chairman of the Interim Committee of the International Monetary Fund, outlines a series of new programs and policy measures that the IMF has developed to prevent and, if necessary, manage future financial crises wherever they may occur. In doing so, Minister Maystadt also enumerates what additional IMF measures are needed to introduce more stability into the ever-changing, increasingly more complex, interdependent and competitive global financial markets.

Part VII, Summary and Conclusions, by Dr. Scheherazade S. Rehman (editor), Assistant Professor of International Finance and Director of the Joint International MBA-MA Degree Programs at The George Washington University in Washington D.C. brings together the key arguments of the various contributors as they pertain to the different types of actual or potential regional financial crises and their implications. She also offers a set of conclusions based on the lessons learned.

PART I

HISTORY AND
BACKGROUND

1

Managing Financial Crises: Who's In Charge?

HOWARD CURTIS REED
Special Counsel for Finance & Investment Policy to the United States Trade Representative, the Executive Office of the President during the 1st term of the Clinton Administration, 1993 - 1996

Financial crisis management is a topic that generates considerable interest typically in boon times when there is concern that speculation is displacing fundamentally sound investment principles, and again during the crisis when solutions are sought. Kindelberger (1989, p.3) observes that if few books on the subject appeared during the several decades after World War II, following the spate of the 1930's, it was because the industry producing them is anticyclical in character, and recessions from 1945 to 1973 were few, far between and exceptionally mild.

The quintessential financial crisis occurs when there exists a significantly high probability that the financial infrastructure of a system will collapse. The results of which will cause chaos, rebellion, and the destruction of a society and societal order. Of course there are degrees (or ranks) of a crisis. The degree or rank of a crisis is determined by the severity of the probable outcome if the direction of events is not slowed, stopped, or reversed. The causes of financial crises are many and most frequently are the result of excesses, i.e., excessive speculation, excessive monetary expansion, and excessive credit. Other causes may be classified as international propagation where the connection and linkages expanding and exacerbating crisis has included trade and capital markets activities; flows of hot money; changes in central bank reserves; fluctuations in prices of commodities, securities, and currencies; and changes in interest rates. The central issue pertaining to a crisis or crises is what to do? What should be done to prevent a crisis? And what should be done to induce recovery from a crisis? The general answer or response is quite simple--there are two choices (1) laissez-faire, or (2) management initiatives.

The laissez-faire or free market approach has a large and distinguished group of advocates. So does the group advocating government action (management) to prevent and resolve financial crises. The laissez-faire contingents believe that the market is rational, with sufficient resources and tools to extricate itself from crises. This view argues that recession, deflation, and bankruptcy at times are good for markets and economies. It clears the system of the excesses and the euphoria. The hands-off approach to macro financial management is irresponsible. Markets left alone to provide liquidity, direct the flow of capital, and regulate itself would not only be inefficient but would also fuel the cycles of booms and busts. These markets would surely create a state of dependency among developing countries, which would further raise the level of tension and confrontation between the developing and developed countries. It is necessary for governments to provide market oversight through supervision, regulation, and policy. Complementing these activities, governments should, and often do, engage in negotiations to secure agreements that will establish a stable framework in which the global political economy can function most efficiently.

THE WORLD DEPRESSION AND BRETTON WOODS

The history of the financial crisis dates back to at least the Fourteenth Century and the failure of the two largest banking houses in Florence. The failure of the House of Peruzzi in 1343, and the House of Bardi in 1346 was a severe blow to the Florentine economy that might well be compared to the stock market crash of 1929 in its effects (Veseth, p.30). These failures came about as the result of events that have the ring of Twentieth Century familiarity about them. In 1339 the Florentine government borrowed heavily from the banking community to pay for military activities and for imports of food during the famine of that year. In 1342 when revenues fell short of what was needed to service debt, the Lord of Florence suspended payments on the debt. The citizens of Florence were large holders of the debt. After payments were suspended, the debt holders drew down their deposits from the banking houses to offset the income lost from their investments in the public debt. The result was to drain liquidity from the banks.

Florentine banking liquidity was further weakened when the King of Naples and his court, large depositors in the banking houses of Florence, withdrew their assets. The withdrawal was precipitated by Naples' uncertainty of Florence's political allegiance in the power struggle between the Emperor Frederick II and the Vatican. The Florentine banks were also large lenders to England. The withdrawal of assets by the King of Naples prevented these banks from continuing to finance

England's military exploits. That action precipitated a chain of events that eventually caused England to default on its debts to the Florentine banking houses. The collapse of the banking houses, Peruzzi and Bardi, precipitated the failure of other banking houses and brought the economy to its knees, thus ending Florence's reign as a center of wealth, power, and greatness.

Charles Kindelberger (1990, pp.48-50) recounts a major Sixteenth Century crisis. The prominent and wealthy German banking families, the Fuggers and the Welsers, were crippled when their loans to the Habsburgs of Spain (Phillip II) were not repaid. As a result of mounting war debt and his inability to pay his troops, the King, Phillip II, in September 1575 declared himself bankrupt and canceled all licenses to export silver (specie). By 1576 his entire army had dissolved in mutiny and desertion. In 1596 Phillip II once again declared bankruptcy. Attempting to repair his finances, he signed asientos (notes) that he could not make good. He then revoked the licenses for exporting specie on all earlier asientos, and took over revenues that had been assigned as surety to creditors. These crises brought the Fuggers of Augsburg to the brink of bankruptcy and caused the collapse of Genoan credit.

The contemporary reference point for financial crisis is the World Depression (1929-39). When, as was the case in the years immediately preceding the stock market collapse of October 1929, euphoria is based on expectation that stock prices will continue to rise to record levels week after week and the market meanders and declines for a while, the tendency then is to convert to cash. When market forces are left to their own resources, as in 1929, much more often than not, a full blown "crisis" occurs.

Charles Kindelberger, perhaps the most ardent advocate of maintaining a hierarchical system (among countries) of global economic leadership, argues that the world needs a "leader," a "stabilizer," a "lender-of-the-last resort." In his book (The World in Depression, 1929-1939), Kindelberger cites five functions the leader/stabilizer should discharge: (1) provide an open market for traded commodities when there are gluts and/or acute shortages; (2) provide a steady flow of capital so as not to cut off loans suddenly; (3) lead the coordination of monetary and fiscal policies among the major nations; (4) maintain some coherent system of exchange rates; and (5) serve as a lender-of-last resort in a financial crisis, providing liquidity to halt liquidation, capital withdrawals, and bank collapse. Kindelberger calls these five functions "international public goods." He argues that these public goods do not emerge spontaneously from the market system, they are provided. In the absence of a world government, they must be provided by a country using its institutional infrastructure and resources. Political scientists have largely accepted the argument that world economic stability is a public good that has to be provided, if at all, by some country that takes charge, accepts responsibility, and acts as a leader. What Kindelberger called leadership, political scientists now call hegemony.

Much of the success of the post World War II Bretton Woods System of fixed exchange rates was due largely to the consensus view that the United States, committed to a policy of full employment, would be the "leader" (the stabilizer) of the world economy. During the July 1944 conference at the resort hotel in Bretton Woods, New Hampshire, it was agreed that demand was the key to economic growth. The mechanism to create (and sustain) this demand was the creation of a gold-exchange standard that permitted central banks to hold dollars that could be exchanged for gold. It was this arrangement, more than anything else, that established the dollar as the world's currency. It was the currency of settlement. The United States, as a result of these agreements became the world's greatest creditor nation, the engine of the world economic growth; it provided the liquidity that greased the wheels of commerce. United States funding was made available to the rest of the world through the Marshall Plan for the reconstruction of Europe, the IMF, the World Bank, and the private sector. This funding gave countries the resources with which to purchase U.S. produced products which in turn provided the capital goods needed to rebuild their economies and equally important it provided the resources to purchase consumer goods to satisfy the pent-up demand from the war years.

The dollar based gold-exchange standard was responsible for the success of, as well as the demise of, the Bretton Woods System. Several key elements characterized that system. As nations pegged their currencies to the dollar, a system of fixed exchange rates was achieved. Because the dollar was the world's principal reserve currency, international liquidity became a function of America's balance of payments. The linchpin of the system was the pledge of the United States to keep the dollar convertible into gold at US$35 per ounce. As long as the United States backed this pledge and other nations had confidence in the soundness of the U.S. economy, the system worked. The dollar was as good as gold. It became the principal medium of exchange, the unit of account, and the store of value for the world (Gilpin, p.134).

In March of 1973, the Bretton Woods System of fixed exchange rates officially came to an end with the decision to let exchange rates float. The system, however, had started to unravel as far back as 1958/59 when dollar holdings from Soviet Bloc countries were deposited with banks in London as earning assets. [This was the beginning of the eurodollar/eurocurrency market.] These dollar deposits, during the ensuing years, were joined by dollar deposits from European central banks. These central banks were being forced to hold dollars because the United States was refusing to convert dollars into gold as required by the Bretton Woods Agreements. European central bank dollar deposits increased significantly after the "gold pool" agreement in 1961, which relieved the United States of some of its responsibility for maintaining the price of gold at US$35 an ounce. European business firms also deposited dollars in London banks as a means of diversifying their liquidity by holding ready assets in the world's principal reserve currency, and because European central banks were discouraging dollar conversions into domestic currencies due to the dollar-gold convertibility impasse. Private citizens also were depositing dollars in London banks as a means of diversifying their asset holdings, insuring against uncertainty as the cold war was at its height, and because of the attitude of European central banks.

As time passed and United States trade deficits and inflation grew, these overseas dollar deposits grew. Because these deposits were in dollars and outside of the monetary control of the Federal Reserve, United States commercial banks during the late 1960's and early 1970's would borrow money from their London branches to breach the Federal Reserve's restrictive monetary policy. As other European financial centers (in addition to London) began to accept dollar deposits and as other currencies entered the deposit market, the eurodollar market became an unregulated supranational capital market that has, over the years, been the single most important factor in the economic growth and development of market oriented economies by providing unparalleled access to capital at lower costs for net users and greater liquidity for net suppliers of capital. The early growth and influence of the eurodollar market led to the unilateral renunciation by the United States in 1968 of its obligations to provide gold to private purchasers at US$35 an ounce, and in 1971 to officially close the gold window[1] to foreign governments.

The demise of the fixed (pegged) exchange rate system of Bretton Woods began with President Nixon's statement, in August 1971, which officially suspended dollar-gold convertibility; imposed a surcharge on U.S. imports in order to force the Europeans and the Japanese to revalue their currencies; and imposed wage and price controls to slow United States inflation. As a result of these events, a meeting was called for the G-10 countries[2] to meet in Washington at the Smithsonian in December to find a solution to the pending crisis. The main element of the Smithsonian agreement was to widen the band (margin) for exchange rate fluctuations from plus or minus 1 per cent to plus or minus 2.25 per cent. This wider band did not work and the Bretton Woods system of pegged exchange rates officially came to an end fifteen months later, when the G-10 finance ministers agreed to float their currencies.

THE POST BRETTON WOODS ERA

Seven months after the Smithsonian Agreements ended, the world was profoundly shocked by the quadrupling of the price of oil. The G-10 countries which viewed themselves as caretakers (overseers) of the world economy suddenly realized that their (and the world's) future depended largely on the price of, what West German Chancellor Helmut Schmidt would later call the "world product," oil. In an instant, it was realized that the single, most important, commodity to world economic prosperity was oil. The Organization of Arab Petroleum Exporting Countries (OAPEC) singled out the events leading up to and the outcome of the Arab-Israeli war of 1973 as the principal reason for the sudden and extraordinary increase in the price of oil. There may have been economic reasons for an increase but not sufficient to justify a fourfold increase.

As a result of the increase, oil importing countries encountered the twin devils--deflation and inflation. Deflation occurred as purchasing power was transferred from their economies to the economies of the oil exporting countries; and simultaneously inflation was increasing as the effects of sharply higher oil prices, which impacted virtually every sector of their economy, raised prices on commodities and services across the board. All of this resulted in a massive transfer of wealth to the oil exporting countries.

The wealth transfer problem was exacerbated by the mechanism used to transfer the wealth. The wealth that was transferred from the oil importing countries to the oil exporting countries was then used to finance (via loans) the oil importing countries purchase of oil. Somewhat ironically the mechanisms used to facilitate these financial flows were the financial institutions of the oil importing countries. The devastating impact of simultaneous deflation and inflation could have been significantly reduced if the intermediating institutions had done their part to keep the cost of capital low, very low. This could have been done by restraining their bids (i.e., interest rates offered) for deposits from oil exporting nations which, in turn, should have reduced the interest rate charged to the borrower thereby lowering the borrower's debt service (cost of capital). In their defense, the intermediating institutions were concerned, and rightfully so, that they would experience a severe liquidity crisis if they were alone (i.e., the only bank) in offering very low bids for oil exporting country deposits. This was a legitimate concern since significant amounts of their asset portfolios were in loans to developing countries. The irony is that these intermediating institutions were not only being forced to feed the twin devils of inflation and deflation, but they were also accepting the risk of financing the world's poorest countries during the crisis.

The twin devil crisis and the developing country debt crisis that resulted from the oil price increases of 1973/74 and 1978/79 were both prolonged and exacerbated by G-7 (or perhaps G-10) failure to coordinate their efforts by expanding their "lender-of-last resort" commitment to cover eurodollar/eurocurrency market activity for the intermediating institutions.

The combination of these events and the fact that oil prices and payments were denominated in United States dollars led to what many economists, central bankers, government officials, and some exporters called the dollar crisis, i.e., the overvalued dollar. Taking an almost exclusive "trade" perspective, United States Treasury Secretary, James Baker, convened a meeting of the G-5 countries[3] on September 22, 1985 at the Plaza Hotel in New York. The agreement reached declared that the dollar was too strong and no longer reflected "fundamental economic conditions." The Plaza agreement called for the "orderly appreciation" of other currencies against the dollar.

Was a crisis avoided as a result of the Plaza Accord? Not likely! This was an agreement to accommodate the United States and once again allow it to shrink from taking the financial initiatives required for economic and political leadership. United States policy makers were under the illusion that "consumer behavior" was determined almost exclusively by product price. If the dollar's value declined in relation to other currencies, particularly the Japanese yen and the West German Deutsche mark, they believed that United States imports of automobiles, machinery, and electronic products would decline accordingly, and that United States exports would increase accordingly. Neither happened! United States consumers valued quality and reliability over price and apparently so did foreign consumers because United States balance of payments did not improve even though the dollar's foreign exchange value against the yen and Deutsche mark had declined by more than 30 per cent three years after the Plaza Accords.

THE G-7 COUNTRIES

For more than twenty years the G-7 countries have made a valiant effort to function as a cohesive institution. The effort began in 1975 as the seven countries attempted to fill the void of leadership left by the United States following the end of the Bretton Woods system. The G-7 achieved early success at the Bonn summit in 1978, when the United States agreed to decontrol its domestic oil prices, and the West Germans and the Japanese agreed to expand their economies. The G-7 was instrumental also in resolving the developing country debt crisis of the 1980s. Other tangible successes are more difficult to identify. For those that are inclined to cite the Plaza Accords as a success, it should be noted that it was the G-5 countries not the G-7 that reached the agreement to lower the dollar's foreign exchange value.

In monetary and financial matters the G-7 countries rely primarily on their central banks to provide surveillance and analysis of global financial markets, and to manage (through market intervention) the foreign exchange value of their currencies. To a remarkable degree the actions of G-7 central banks are almost always well coordinated. The degree to which central bank activities are well coordinated and the effectiveness of their actions is due principally to their monthly meetings in Basle, Switzerland. One weekend each month, central bankers from the G-10 (plus one) countries[4] meet at the Bank for International Settlements to discuss policy, regulatory, and strategy issues such as -- market capitalization and supervision, international payment and settlement system rules and procedures, computer technology, money laundering, and market intervention. Central bank influence is derived principally from this power of coordination. Central banks, however, reserve their greatest power and influence for their knack of "jawboning" and coopting markets by "fiat." A fact that I find particularly disturbing and as threatening to the operations of free and orderly financial markets as would be the case if these markets were unsupervised and unregulated.

Look, for example, at the reaction of the world financial markets responding to a speech made by U.S. Federal Reserve Chairman, Alan Greenspan. As reported by the Financial Times (weekend, December 7/8, 1996, p.1.)

> World financial markets suffered a "frantic Friday" yesterday as comments by Mr. Alan Greenspan, the Federal Reserve chairman, about "irrational exuberance" in asset markets unsettled traders and investors.
> The implied threat behind the comments was that the Fed might, at some point, have to raise rates to cool such sentiments and to head off inflationary pressures.
> Asian markets were the first to take fright, with the Nikkei 225 average in Tokyo falling 667.2 points, or 3.2 per cent to 20,276.7, its biggest one-day decline since April 1995. Hong Kong, which because of its link to the US dollar is closely tied to US interest rates, also suffered, with the Hang Seng index dropping 2.9 per cent.
> Europe followed suit. At their worst, the German and French stock markets were down 4.7 per cent and 4.9 per cent respectively while Amsterdam dropped 6.2 per cent. In London, the FTSE 100 index was down 168.5 points, or 4.2 per cent, lower at its worst.
> The sell-off carried over into the US where, just after Wall Street opened, the Dow Jones Industrial Average shed more than 145 points. But US payroll data eased fears of inflationary pressures and the Dow closed the day 55.16 points lower at 6,381.95.
> Mr. Greenspan made his remarks in a speech on Thursday evening on developments in US monetary policy. He suggested the central bank was paying close attention to the recent surge in US equity markets. Assessing movements in asset prices, he said, had to be an "integral part" of monetary policy.
> "How do we know when irrational exuberance has unduly escalated asset values, which then become subject to unexpected and prolonged contractions?' he said.

In this regard, the impact of central bank activity on financial markets and the residual impact on economies must be clearly understood. Was consideration given to the thousands of owners of securities that, for whatever reason(s), must liquidate their holdings of securities on the day or days immediately following such a statement? Was consideration given to the impact that these liquidations, at amounts that are billions of dollars (in the aggregate) less than what they would have been, absent the chairman's comments, will have on the financial well-being of individuals and entities without the resources to mitigate the market's lost value? Not likely! In addition, there is no indication that chairman Greenspan's comments were coordinated with comments or actions of other central bankers and central banks.

Now to the issue of influence (or ruling) by fiat. As I have recounted elsewhere (Reed, 1995), in today's world, the policy tool to affect exchange rates and capital flows is the interest rate. The relationship between interest rates, inflation, and economic growth is not only complicated but is critical to providing some understanding of the complex relationship between interest rates, exchange rates, and capital flows. Governments, through their central banks, manipulate interest rates primarily with open market, discount, and/or reserve actions. The most prominent interest rate is, of course, the one prevailing in the United States by virtue of the dollar's role as the world's principal reserve and settlement currency, and the size of the U.S. economy. The other G-10 countries are also important players in this arena.

The conduits of central bank initiatives are the large internationally active financial institutions headquartered primarily in the G-10 countries. Typically these institutions are the commercial banks, investment banks, merchant banks, and the universal banks. These large internationally active institutions generate the overwhelming majority of their funding from financial markets, not from their respective central banks. [It should be noted that this has been so for nearly thirty years]. Central banks, traditionally, derive their influence from two sources. First, their greatest influence came from being the primary source of marginal funding for large international financially active institutions. Second, their influence is due to the market's perception of their influence in financial matters, i.e., setting interest rates. The influence of central banks today is derived more from the latter than the former since liberalization of capital movements has significantly eroded their control over the money supply.

There is a paradox in supposedly market-based economies throughout the world having their capital costs, capital flows, and exchange rates determined more by central bank fiat than by market forces. There are problems in having any authority exert influence in ways that negate overall "free" market objectives by disproportionately and artificially increasing or decreasing interest rates in ways that are counter to rational market behavior. The danger, for example, is that these authorities may -- in their efforts to choke off future inflation -- set a ceiling for a non-inflationary growth rate that is not high enough to fully and efficiently utilize the resources of an economy, thus stifling economic growth and typically causing unemployment to remain at unnecessarily high levels. Another danger, for example, is that increasing interest rates by fiat (and at odds with market behavior and expectations) may have the unintended effect of causing inflation rather than inhibiting it through the cascading effect on the markets.

The residual impact of a country's interest rate changes on other economies is generally directly proportional to the originating country's economic/financial influence on the world economy as a whole, for example: the role of its currency; and the size and structure of its economy. Many economists and financial market observers fear that the risk of official miscalculations of the impact of interest rate changes is increasing. Their argument is that present day economies can sustain higher rates of non inflationary growth than in years past. Some of the reasons given for this are the growing importance of international trade; significant (and continual) increases in productivity and capital investments; increases in the efficiency of capital utilization; and the growing impact of communications and information technology.

In addition to the importance of the large internationally active banks, it is also necessary to consider the maze of professionally managed money funds (e.g., bond funds, hedge funds, mutual funds, etc.), which total more than US$20 trillion, with approximately one-third of that total being managed from the United States. It is the growth of these managed funds over the past twenty-five years and their propensity to invest in securities and in other financial assets, largely at the expense of investments in capital equipment and facilities (i.e., "real" asset investment), that has significantly undermined the effectiveness of monetary policy as an instrument of control[5]. These types of funds can appear, disappear, and reappear in various markets within the span of the same trading day. The strategy of the fund manager is to enhance returns through mobility, so the geographic location and the investment vehicle are inevitably transitory and subject to sudden change. These funds are the personification of the "gypsy" way of life.

If the operational objective of governments throughout the world is to continue the present free market structure of international financial activity, government authorities and central bankers must come to recognize the short comings of manipulating financial markets by central bank fiat. The official reserves of the G-7 countries, Switzerland, and the Fund collectively are less than one trillion dollars. This is less than one-twentieth of the amount of funds under management. Granted this does oversimplify the issue since governments have other tools in their arsenal (i.e., fiscal policy, regulatory authority, and of course seigniorage through control of the printing presses). Nonetheless, it clearly illustrates the point. With more than US$20 trillion under professional funds management, and an average daily cross-border capital flow ranging between US$1 trillion and US$1.5 trillion together with foreign exchange trading of US$4 trillion daily, it appears that short of sustained coordinated actions the industrial country governments are and will continue to be overwhelmed.

The critical issue for the G-7 countries is coordination. It is not an issue of leadership, it is one of being willing to accept the responsibility of being a member of the governing hierarchy. Members of this hierarchy are not elected nor are they chosen on the basis of arbitrary criteria. These countries represent the largest and most influential political economies in the world. Preserving and enhancing this well-being requires leadership. Since no country is willing, nor capable if it were willing, to act as "the" leader, then a well orchestrated plan, strategy, and implementation of policy initiatives is required of the hierarchy. Without coordination there is no leadership and events will continue to proceed with great volatility and thereby arrogating virtually all efforts to prevent financial crises from developing.

Another concern emanating from the issue is the process and the manner in which the financial affairs of the global economy will be governed. Will it continue to be the present ad hoc approach? Or, will specific, in depth, attention be given to examining the capability and infrastructure of existing multilateral institutions to oversee these affairs? The two obvious candidates are the International Monetary Fund and the World Trade Organization.

INTERNATIONAL MONETARY FUND

The International Monetary Fund (the Fund or IMF) was established to supervise the Bretton Woods system of fixed but adjustable exchange rates and to serve as a lender of last resort. The system worked remarkably well for more than twenty-five years. For reasons already documented, the system was discarded in 1973 by the world's principal economies. The present floating exchange rate regime and capital markets free of exchange controls has brought about prodigious growth in the cross border flows of private capital. These events have rendered the Fund's role as lender of last resort, a vestige of the past for all but the poorest countries.

The fact that the Fund's role is diminished requires that it rethink, in this new role, the scope of its mission, not necessarily the mission itself. Its mission today is threefold: (1) surveillance of economic policies and exchange rate regimes; (2) giving macroeconomic advice and guidance; and (3) providing funding for the lesser developed countries and countries in transition. A number of speakers, mostly from non G-7 countries, at the 1994 IMF/World Bank meetings in Madrid argued passionately for the industrial countries to use the Fund as the principal forum for multilateral surveillance and coordination of national fiscal and monetary policies. The point was made, and rightly so, that developing countries have the most to gain from such a forum. It is only in a multilateral forum that coordination of industrial countries' policies will have the necessary influence to warrant adherence to the resulting policies and actions from the rest of the world community. The probability that the G-7 countries will submit their economies to Fund surveillance and coordination, in the foreseeable future, is zero. It just is not going to happen.

The Fund's overall status and role as a significant player in international finance will depend on its willingness to recognize and accept a role that focuses on lesser developed countries and economies in transition. The scope of the Fund's mission will be limited to surveillance, providing advice and guidance, and to providing bridge financing to give these countries time for their markets to be sufficiently integrated into the global financial markets. Sustained economic growth and development in today's world require access to the capital provided by these global financial markets.

If the Mexican peso crisis of 1994/1995 had not occurred, the Fund's role would be more restrictive than it is today. It was apparent at the 1994 IMF/World Bank annual meetings in Madrid that the G-7 finance ministers envisioned a considerably less prominent future role for the Fund. There was a serious rift between the G-7 ministers and the IMF Managing Director Camdessus over proposed SDR allocations, but the allocation disagreement was only incremental in its impact. It was during the meetings celebrating the fiftieth anniversary of Bretton Woods (September 28 and 29) that the G-7 ministers made clear their views of a more constrained and narrowly focused IMF. The tone and the intent were clear. The role and responsibility of the IMF must shrink.

The peso crisis in Mexico strengthened the Fund's hand and gave it leverage, not only to remain a major player but to enhance its role in providing the guidance and incentive for countries to pursue the policies that are necessary for financial and economic stability. As a hangover from the Madrid meetings, observers, at first, did not believe that the Fund would play a significant role in resolving Mexico's financial crisis. It was at first thought that the United States would provide more than 90 per cent of the required financial package for Mexico. The Fund's initial proposal was a modest loan package of US$2 to US$3 billion. As conditions worsened, due largely to G-7 inaction, the Fund's loan proposal was increased to US$7.8 billion. Due to Congressional opposition, in the end the United States funding was reduced to US$20 billion, from US$40 billion, and IMF funding was increased to US$18 billion.

The Fund's return as a major player so soon after the Madrid meetings came about primarily because of Mexico and the inactivity of the G-7 countries. The G-7 ignored, for more than a year, warnings from a number of respected private economists and market specialists that Mexico's current account deficit was not sustainable and that a significant devaluation was needed. For the United States and Mexico, the politics of NAFTA was such that it made devaluation unacceptable regardless of the merits. The other G-7 countries were indifferent. They either did not fully understand the problem, did not realize the significance of the problem, or saw it as an America (NAFTA) problem. Perhaps it was some combination of all three. Clearly the consequences of Mexico's financial problems were global and early coordinated G-7 action would have avoided the crisis. Countries throughout South America as well as the dynamic economies of East and Southeast Asia saw capital inflows decline, and capital costs increase in the days and weeks following the recognition of Mexico's financial difficulties.

The Fund's resiliency as a result of the peso crisis is likely to have little impact on any decision that the G-7 may undertake regarding overseeing the financial affairs of the global economy for the reasons discussed previously, and for two others. First, in government, finance is one of those preserves that is guarded by those in charge with the passion and tenacity of a "mad jealous lover." Given this culture, the G-7, as they see it, are not about to compromise their sovereignty on finance matters. Another inhibiting factor for the IMF is that trade and trade issues are clearly overtaking (perhaps they have overtaken) finance as the preeminent international concern of government officials and non-financial business entities.

THE WORLD TRADE ORGANIZATION

A number of factors have contributed to the world's economic success of the past fifty years. The single most important factor accounting for the success of the postwar world economy is the sustained expansion of world trade. The continual growth in world trade has brought about a global economy that is characterized as much by its dynamics as it is by its growth. Financial markets are another factor. These markets have been integrated to the point that the concept of a national market or a national currency is becoming an anachronism. Currencies, for example, are no longer symbols of national sovereignty but are international commodities traded like precious metals, oil, and pork bellies. Other notable changes taking place within the world economy are the rising number of developing countries being transformed into industrial, high technology, service oriented economies. These newly industrialized countries are significant exporters of first generation technology and products. And some of these countries are becoming net exporters of direct investment capital. Regional integration also has been a significant factor in this postwar economic success particularly in Western Europe where the European Union is on the verge of establishing a single currency, and in southeast Asia where the less formal Association of South East Asian Nations (ASEAN) has nonetheless been very effective. In recent years the pace to integrate has quickened with the establishment of the North American Free Trade Agreement (NAFTA), the informal but increasingly effective Asia Pacific Economic Forum (APEC), and the encouraging progress that is being made in southern Africa with the Southern African Development Community (SADC).

Changes such as these produce greater economic interdependence between nations and increase the need to identify and organize a hierarchical institutional structure that will provide credible assurances that the trade rivalries among Japan, the United States, and the European Union will not be permitted to undermine the open-multilateral trading system that has worked so well since the end of World War II. The World Trade Organization was created to preserve and enhance this open multilateral trading system.

The World Trade Organization (WTO) is an impartial institution that provides a forum for: (1) negotiating and resolving trade disputes; (2) designing a global trade framework; and (3) establishing the rules and regulations that govern international trade. The WTO's institutional infrastructure functions as a surveillance and governance mechanism for the global multilateral trading system. The establishment of the WTO was the result of provisions included in the "Final Act" of the Uruguay Round Multilateral Trade Negotiations. The Final Act significantly expands the regulatory framework for international trade beyond that of the General Agreement on Tariffs and Trade (GATT). In addition to establishing the WTO, the expanded framework establishes a more liberalized set of rules governing international trade in goods, intellectual property rights, and for the first time services (including financial services). It also codified and perfected the rules governing multilateral dispute resolutions and trade surveillance.

In terms of financial management of the international monetary system, perhaps the most significant provision of the Final Act is the requirement that the WTO cooperate with the Fund and the World Bank to achieve greater coherence in global economic policy making. The operative set of WTO rules governing this requirement is the newly created General Agreement on Trade in Services (GATS). Included in the GATS are a number of provisions pertaining to foreign exchange restrictions. There were no provisions under the previous GATT framework to address foreign exchange restrictions. These issues were largely left to the Fund. The WTO is now required to develop greater cooperation with official international organizations responsible for monetary and financial matters, particularly the International Monetary Fund. This cooperation is to be carried out while at the same time respecting the mandate, confidentiality requirements, decision-making autonomy of each institution, and avoiding the imposition on governments of cross-conditionality and other conditions. The provision also requires the WTO's Director-General to review, with the heads of the Fund and the Bank, the implications of the WTO's responsibilities for cooperation and the forms that such cooperation would take.

The extent of the WTO's influence is not readily seen but it is there. Article XII [5(e)] of the Final Act requires that "...all findings of the statistical and other facts presented by the Fund relating to foreign exchange, monetary reserves and balance of payments, shall be accepted and conclusions shall be based on the assessment by the Fund of the balance-of-payments and the external financial situation of the consulting member." Even though the WTO has to accept the Fund's statistics, conclusions, assessments, etc., it is left to the WTO **alone** to decide whether a country is entitled to a *safeguard* action under Article XII.[6] In addition, where a safeguard action is authorized, it is the responsibility of the WTO to establish the conditions under which the *safeguard* action is taken. The WTO structure was, in part, designed to provide for a coalescing of trade, investment, and financial issues in a way that provides for better coordination and increased sensitivity among these three issues in instances where adjustments are required.

The WTO's attraction as an institution with the appropriate infrastructure to oversee the financial affairs of the global economy is further enhanced by the fact that "financial services" (banking, insurance, and securities) are now a trade sector within the WTO's framework. The WTO in providing the framework for negotiating financial service agreements gives it the opportunity to now impact financial market efficiency and capital costs. Financial service issues being negotiated cover a comprehensive range of activities -- retail and wholesale banking, funds' management, underwriting, brokerage, insurance and reinsurance, and equity ownership. The objective is to obtain full market access on the basis of national treatment and the most-favored-nation principle.

Another tool of the WTO that enhances its attraction is the dispute settlement understanding (DSU) mechanism. The DSU gives the WTO a working remedy to enforce agreements that are not available to the IMF. The DSU has strict time limits (16 months) for rulings;[7] it has an appellate review process; and it has increased transparency. The establishment of dispute principles and procedures regularizes and improves the environment for cross border flow of goods, services, and investments.

WHO'S IN CHARGE?

Orderly economic management in a world of floating exchange rates and large volatile capital markets free of exchange controls is immensely difficult. Complicating the task is the increased role of private capital flows and the volatility and unpredictability of portfolio capital. The world needs credible international safety nets which, while preserving the freedom of capital markets, will ensure that "enterprise does not become a bubble in the whirlpool of speculation."[8]

Orderly capital flows and minimal speculation occur when portfolio capital follows the flow of goods, services, and direct investment capital. Even though the world's money and capital markets are highly integrated and tend to seek out (daily and in some instances hourly) opportunities that provide the greatest return, there is still great value in the pattern of "capital flow discrimination." Local and regional financial centers, as opposed to international and global financial centers, are not very different today from what they were in years past. In large geographically diverse countries the borrowing, lending, and investing pattern still starts locally, extends to the national level, then beyond the country's borders to the region, and finally international (or global). In geographically confined countries the pattern is abbreviated primarily because the financial center and the industrial center is usually the same. In addition, "regional" does not mean "domestic regional" because of the country's small size it means the geographic and cultural region in which the country is located. In these instances, the lending, borrowing, and investing pattern starts locally, extends to the region, and finally global. Such patterns discriminate on the basis of geography and culture. In other words it discriminates in favor of the lender's knowledge and familiarity with the borrower and with the borrower's geographic area.

The success, over the past twenty years, of the economies of East and Southeast Asia are tied closely to the emergence of Hong Kong and Singapore as regional financial centers. A review of the lending and investing patterns of these centers during the past twenty years tracks closely with the pattern for financial centers located in geographically confined countries. Clearly Hong Kong and Singapore discriminated in favor of their region. The region's economies were assured of continual access to capital at reasonable costs. This, in turn, instilled confidence which attracted additional longer term capital which increased employment, wages, the standard of living and all of the other residual benefits that followed from a growing and dynamic economic environment.

In recent years much has been said and written about the beneficial role that the global capital markets have played in bringing about the economic successes in East and Southeast Asia, Southern Europe, and selected countries in South America and South Asia. Portfolio money managers readily admit that when consideration is given to investing funds in foreign countries, the economic history and contemporary environment of the region is actually more important than the individual country where the investment is being considered. Islands of success are usually short-lived unless other neighboring countries also become strong economically.[9] These considerations help explain why East and Southeast Asia still receive the greatest amount of investment capital and why Sub-Saharan Africa receives the least amount.

The debate over which trade policy arrangements will provide the greatest benefits to the global economy is moving more and more in the direction of regionalism. The 1994 and 1995 Economic Reports of the President clearly and forcefully outline the Clinton administration's policy supporting regional trading arrangements as building blocks for multilateral free trade. Several relevant passages from the 1995 Economic Report of the President give the Administration's position clearly and succinctly.

> Traditionally, economists have voiced concerns that an increased emphasis on plurilateralism might divert attention and energy away from multilateralism and result in harmful trade diversion. And indeed, certain types of preferential trade agreements can undermine the multilateral system.

> In general, preferential trade agreements that reduce the discretion of member countries to pursue trade liberalization with nonmembers are more likely to become stumbling blocks...

When structures according to principles of openness and inclusiveness, regional blocks can be building blocks rather than stumbling blocks for global free trade and investment. Seen in this light, carefully structured plurilateralism is a complement rather than an alternative to U.S. multilateral efforts.

There are a variety of ways in which plurilateral agreements can serve as building blocks for multilateral market opening. First, plurilateral accords may achieve deeper economic integration among members than do multilateral accords because the commonality of interests is greater and the negotiating process simpler...

Regionalism has recently received another major endorser. At the conclusion of the October 1995 quadrilateral meeting of the trade ministers from the United States, European Union, Canada, and Japan, EU Trade Commissioner Leon Brittan said that "trade liberalization is now more likely to move forward through regional arrangements than through another multilateral round."

Another major step in support of regional trade arrangements was taken on February 6, 1996 when the WTO General Council established a committee on "Regional Trading Arrangements." The Committee will conduct reviews of all trading agreements. The core axiom of the WTO is the most-favored-nation (MFN) principle. WTO members must extend to all other members the best treatment, in terms of customs duties, charges, rules and procedures, that it gives to products originating or destined for any other country. Regional integration arrangements are an exception -- the major exception -- to this principle.

These arrangements, establishing free trade areas and customs unions, are covered in the WTO by two main provisions; (1) Article XXIV of the GATT 1994 and the related Understanding on the Interpretation of Article XXIV which applies to trade in goods; and (2) Article V of the General Agreement on Trade in Services (GATS) which applies to trade in services. While GATS Article V came into force with the WTO, Article XXIV of GATT 1994 is identical to the provision in GATT 1947. These rules reflect the desire of the GATT's drafters to provide for free trade areas and customs unions, while at the same time ensuring that the trading interests of third countries are respected, and, more generally, that such arrangements are compatible with a rules-based and progressively more open world trading system. For this reason, GATT Article XXIV and GATS Article V establish a number of conditions which the arrangements must satisfy, as well as transparency requirements to monitor whether those conditions are being met.

In a more specific but less dramatic way, the events of November and December of 1996 may be a more definitive statement on the emerging influence of regional arrangements on multilateral issues. In November at the annual APEC meeting (in Manila), President Clinton, to the surprise of virtually everyone, managed to get the other Heads of State to commit to substantial abolishment of all import duties on information-technology products by the year 2000. [Annual global sales in this sector exceed US$500 billion dollars.] Prior to the December WTO ministerial meeting in Singapore, no official in Washington or in Geneva (at the WTO) was confident that the ministerial meetings would get a WTO agreement to match the APEC action. It did happen, the ministers agreed to abolish all import duties on these products by the year 2000. Before the ministerial meetings, the word out of Geneva was that the Malaysians would object on sovereignty grounds and that the EU was not in favor of an agreement because they are not strong in this sector and their objective was to protect their domestic markets.

It should be noted that at this early stage in APEC's development, its primary objective is to be a forum for building momentum for trade liberalization. APEC is not a formal regional arrangement, so if the WTO ministers had not gone along with the APEC announced tariff reductions, the members of APEC would have had to proceed by unilateral means -- passing laws, issuing proclamations, etc. The process would have been slow and cumbersome and would have surely run afoul of WTO principles. Apache's strategy in Manila was to endorse the tariff reductions politically but initiate the actual reductions through the WTO. Once you change your tariff schedules in the WTO, a country is "bound" to the change. If a country backslides on that commitment, it will trigger the DSU enforcement mechanism.

The irony in all of this as it relates to managing the financial affairs of the global economy is that no one (country or group of countries) is in charge, but no one should doubt the power of the G-7 to be in charge if and when it chooses to do so. Events are moving along without guidance and real direction. The tepid leadership that appears from time-to-time is ad hoc at best. What is clearly emerging is broad based support for formal regional arrangements that will drive the process of trade liberalization. The WTO will then implement and enforce the agreements. This arrangement may, in fact, be the catalyst that will bring about greater coordinated G-7 participation in managing the global economy and by encouraging the G-7 countries to take a more active and forceful role through the structure of formal regional agreements.

NOTES

[1] It should be noted that the "gold window" had in fact been closed since 1964 when the United States began refusing conversions requests of foreign central banks.

[2] Belgium, Canada, France, Germany, Italy, Japan, Netherlands, Sweden, United Kingdom, and the United States.

[3] France, Germany, Japan, United Kingdom, and the United States

[4] G-7 countries plus Belgium, Netherlands, Sweden, and Switzerland. When G-10 is used it will always refer to these eleven countries.

[5] It could be argued that this behavior is the natural process of intermediation, by which savings are channeled eventually into real assets. Perhaps, but the evidence does not support this view. Theoretically however, this view seems reasonable, but over what period of time?

[6] In the event of serious balance-of-payments and external financial difficulties or threat thereof, a Member may adopt or maintain restrictions on trade in services on which it has undertaken specific commitments, including on payments or transfers for transactions related to such commitments. It is recognized that particular pressures on the balance of payments of a Member in the process of economic development or economic transition may necessitate the use of restrictions to ensure, *inter alia*, the maintenance of a level of financial reserves adequate for the implementation of its program of economic development or economic transition.

[7] There must be a consensus of the panel to reject a panel's recommendation.

[8] Comments of Dr. Manmohan Singh, Finance Minister of India, IMF/World Bank Meetings, afternoon session (September 29, 1994), Madrid.

[9] There are, of course, exceptions, particularly when natural resources are involved.

REFERENCES

Gilpin, Robert. The Political Economy of International Relations, Princeton: Princeton University Press, 1987.

Kindelberger, Charles P. Historical Economics, Berkeley: University of California Press, 1990.

Kindelberger, Charles P. Monies, Panics, and Crashes, New York: Basic Books, Inc., 1989.

Kindelberger, Charles P. The International Economic Order, Cambridge: MIT Press, 1988.

Reed, Howard Curtis, "Restructuring the International Financial System," The Brown Journal of World Affairs, Providence: Summer 1995, Vol. II, Issue 2, pp.263-273.

Reed, Howard Curtis, The Preeminence of International Financial Centers, New York: Prager Publishers, 1981.

Simmel, George, The Philosophy of Money, London: Routledge Press, 2nd Edition, 1990.

Veseth, Michael, Mountains of Debt, Oxford: Oxford University Press, 1990.

PART II

EUROPEAN UNION AND OTHER REGIONAL EXCHANGE RATE ARRANGEMENTS

2

Monetary Unions In Europe

SIR ALAN WALTERS
Ex-Chief Economic Advisor to Prime Minister Margaret Thatcher and Vice-Chairman and Director of AIG Trading Group, Inc.

MONETARY UNIONS AND SINGLE CURRENCY

Monetary unions essentially require either one currency or absolute fixity of exchange rates for the union's member currencies with respect to one another. There is no substantive economic difference (apart from the profits of seigniorage) between the case of a single currency and absolutely fixed (or to use the Maastricht formula "irrevocable") exchange rates. Thus both Panama and Hong Kong are in the dollar monetary union, but the former has the greenback as its currency whereas Honk Kong's own currency, the Hong Kong dollar, circulates and exchanges at a fixed parity of 7.8 to the greenback. But in both cases the Federal Reserve Board in Washington D.C. determines monetary policy. And of course the Fed never mentions Hong Kong, let alone Panama, in determining monetary policy. Clearly interest rate and open market policy are attuned to domestic economic conditions in the United States. If Hong Kong and Panama find this policy damaging to their interests, then, say the Fed, they are at liberty to break the fix. If they don't like it they can "lump it."

TRANSMISSION AND TRANSITION PROBLEMS

In Europe, the path to Monetary Union (MU) began in 1979 with the Exchange Rate Mechanism (ERM), the brainchild of Valerie Giscard d'Estaing and Helmut Schmidt. A grand "convergence" of European inflation rates on the low rate in the Federal Republic was sought using the exchange rate as the principle instrument. The proximate purpose was to create "a sea of stability" in European exchange rates: the underlying objective was a monetary union.

The stages were first a system of pegged (note, not fixed) exchange rates. Pegged exchange rates could wobble around a central value, and more important, when there was a "fundamental disequilibrium" (or in reality when the market decided it would be toppled) the peg could be moved. But this pegged system contained a fatal flaw: market speculators and fund managers were able to guess when a particular rate, such as sterling's 2.90 Deutsche mark in September 1992, was going to be moved. So they went short on sterling. This ran down the reserves of the Bank of England and so made it even more urgent to unpeg and stop the drain. In fact it did not matter whether there was a "fundamental disequilibrium" or not, when the speculators took against a currency, the weight of such funds would sink it.

Such experience - culminating in the debacle of August 1993 when in all but name, the pegged system completely collapsed - has convinced much influential opinion that pegged systems are not viable in this world of free capital movement. They invite massive speculation and cannot command the confidence needed to build Monetary Union.

A NOT SO QUICK FIX

Absolutely fixed exchange rates, as distinct from pegged exchange rates, are not susceptible to such disequilibriating capital flows. And it is natural that the architects of Monetary Union should look to a jump to absolutely and irrevocably fixed parities. Then there is no room for George Soros to take the Bank of England to the cleaners. Thus they could get on with the business of planning one money for Europe and one European Central Bank (ECB) to manage that currency.

To some considerable extent the fixed exchange rates have been achieved. The Dutch guilder, for example, has not changed its actual parity (1.18 guilder to 1 DM) against the Deutsche mark for almost a decade. The guilder has passed the critical test of market credibility. No-one believes that the guilder will devalue or revalue. It is truly fixed. Similar arguments apply to the other Benelux countries. And we are all aware of the battle for the "Franc-fort" (around 3.5 franks to 1 DM) where, not withstanding the massive cost in terms of lost output and unemployment, the commitment of French authorities is complete. Denmark is perhaps even closer to a fixed parity. The other countries are not so near. Spain, still nominally in the ERM with 15 per cent bands, staggers along after its recent devaluation and one can foresee it pegging again for a run at the Union. Italy, anxious as always to distill some credibility from its chaotic political economy, returned to a peg at the end of 1996. The other countries that make up the 15 country union will vary in their fixity from Austria, whose schilling is rigidly fixed to the mark to Sweden with a sad history of unhinged pegs to Greece, the joker.

A motley crew for the voyage of SS-Maastricht. It will not be smooth sailing. Mutiny, if not exactly on the cards, cannot be dismissed. Yet there is a prospect of a solid loyalty, albeit of the "opt in/out" variety in Britain and Denmark, among the upper ranks which may hold the lower decks in awe if not subjugation. We all look to the core of loyalists to keep the ship afloat. Recently, however, it seems as though the captain and first mate are, like a latter day Captain Bligh, to be helped over the side and bid farewell.

The original date for the first congealing of exchange rates, 1997, has quietly sunk in the mud of Flanders. Now 1999 is the date it is all supposed to start. Any country in the Union that satisfies the Maastricht conditions - basically a budget deficit less then 3 per cent of GNP, a history of stable exchange rates and low interest rates and a public debt of less than 60 per cent of GNP - is automatically chosen as a participating member of the monetary union.

But then there is a crucial delay - probably more than a year - between being nominated as member and the "irrevocable fixing" of exchange rates. This delay is needed on order to get the ECB up and running as an autonomous entity. It is likely that the unionized countries will find this a chaotic period as the markets speculate on the parities of the ultimate fix. Much will depend on whether the Bundesbank as lender of last resort to the Union will support currencies that come under pressure. Will they ruin their domestic monetary policy and erode the reputation of the Deutsche mark for the greater good of the EU and its Euro? Yet even if the Union members successfully weather the storm before the irrevocable fix, will they be able to maintain such irrevocable fixes to form a de facto union?

I cannot find comforting answers to these searching questions. But suppose the improbable and that, up to the "fixed and irrevocable" stage, everything goes swimmingly. Then to achieve a single currency by the scheduled date of 2002 would require immense changes in all the participating countries. This will have to be carried out when there is the most enormous pressure on computer expertise as we all reprogram for the year 2,000 problem. In addition, there are many knotty legal issues to be faced; for example the translation of interest and other contractual payments from individual currencies to the single currency. In my view it is virtually certain that the single currency could never be introduced "at a stroke;" on the contrary public acceptance would require the new single currency to circulate with the old currencies – a source for considerable confusion. Granted the lugubrious nature of decision making in the Union, the gradual translation to the single currency will hardly be smooth sailing.

THE POLITICS OF MONETARY UNION

All this suggests that a single currency for Europe is, at most, still conjectural. Yet, Mr. De Silguy, the European Commissioner for Monetary Affairs, announced on June 9th that "A single currency is a political necessity for Europe" and for "the Single Market." Does this mean, therefore, that the "Single Market" is doomed if there is no single currency? Is it a political necessity because the "Single Market" will fall apart?

Before such ex cathedra statements from the highest circles in Brussels, one quakes. But clearly it is arrant nonsense. There have been many single markets, common markets and customs unions among countries which have not had the same currency and even among countries which have not pegged their exchange rates. For example, from 1716 to the Bank Charter Act of 1844 there was a single market between England and Scotland, yet each had their separate currencies – indeed Scotland had a variety of currencies quite unrelated to the notes circulating south of the border. There are numerous other counter examples of single markets coexisting with monetary diversity. Indeed, one may stand de Silguy's statements on their head and argue that monetary diversity is necessary for a single market since it gives a critical degree of freedom in adjusting to the shocks and storms that economies are heir to.

The real reason for the urgency of monetary union is that Brussels sees it as the soft underbelly of full political union – a federal United States of Europe. Once a European Central Bank and a single currency rule, then this enormous power of the ECB must have its counterbalance in the very large budget that would be needed to pursue the central political aims of the Union. The German government has emphasized that a monetary union requires political union with democratic control of the highly centralized economic policy that would be implied.

The disposition of power and interests in Europe has always shaped the approach to a Monetary Union, often in curious ways. The French, who have largely fashioned the Community and to a lesser degree the Union in their own image, have always seen the Monetary Union as one way in which they could influence, perhaps even control, German monetary policy. They would hope to repeat the success with which their most able civil servants have largely controlled the European agenda in so many European and even international bodies. Yet, although the wish to have substantial influence over German monetary policy, they are averse to the political centralization of power, particularly, as one of the few atomic powers, over defense and foreign policy.

Per contra, Germany is unwilling to countenance a move to Monetary Union except in so far as there is a parallel progress in political union and in the development of greater democratic control.

THE MARK AS EUROPE'S MONEY

Even more pertinently, Germany has averred that there will be no single European currency or European Central Bank unless the currency is as sound as the Deutsche mark and the ECB has a reputation equal to that of the Bundesbank. Furthermore, the Bundesbank has repeatedly emphasized that the Maastricht conditionality for joining the Monetary Union was too lax and certainly should not be compromised any further. (As a matter of record, only Luxembourg, Finland, and Ireland satisfy the conditions today)

All this maneuvering is, in part, simply an episode in the grand play for power that is the essence of the European Union. But underlying it all is the reluctance, even determination, not to give up the symbol of their stability and success – the Deutsche mark and the Bundesbank. They know very well that if the immense monetary power of Europe passes to the European Central Bank, there is every likelihood that they would lose control to some French-led coalition, especially if Britain elects to opt out.

And for Germany there is another more attractive solution. Why go to all the trouble and terrors of creating a single currency and ECB? In Stage III of the journey to Maastricht, "fixed and irrevocable" rates of exchange mean that we shall already have a monetary union. Indeed we have a de facto central bank and a European currency – the Bundesbank and Deutsche mark, respectively. Why not stop at that comfortable state? The EMS was born in order to "borrow credibility" from the Bundesbank, and with fixed and irrevocable rates credibility is finally established.

This solution seems to me to be the most likely one to emerge from the Maastricht process. In terms of economics, it is not a bad solution, provided the Bundesbank pursues stable low-inflation monetary policies – and it has done quite a good job on those lines in the past. Of course the Bundesbank will ensure that the policies are good for Germany, and, as we have seen in the recent reunification of West and East Germany, such policies may not be the best for France, Italy, etc., such, however, is the cost of stability.

Politically, however, this German-dominated solution will not appeal to the French or the British, for that matter. All fond French plans of controlling Germany monetary policy will have come to naught. Of course, the ever sensitive Germans would be happy to consider more and more consultation on policy, through the European Monetary Institute, ECOFIN, etc. but they would never hand over the central levers of power of the Bundesbank.

It might be thought that the 14 other members of the Union will find this all most unsatisfactory. I am not so sure. The small countries of the Union, such as Benelux, Denmark, Austria, etc. cannot realistically expect to influence European monetary policy; they remain tied to Germany's apron strings... and they may well concede that Germany apron strings are more reliable than any the French could produce. And France has to face the fact that, if there were a leap to a single currency (a Frankenstein?), Germany would demand a loss of sovereignty which is quite unacceptable to Paris, even more so as the socialist/communist coalition outlines its policies.

Of course, a Monetary Union on the Deutsche mark and Bundesbank is a Euro-fudge, and contrary to the aims of Maastricht. But what else is new in Europe.

A PERSONAL VIEW

Supposing that from now on things go swimmingly for the Euro, the question remains "Should Britain join the Euro-bloc?" Taking on board all the reservations, I would say "No." With all the efficiencies of one currency counted, I believe it would be vastly offset by the changes of systems, laws and governmental environment that would be inevitably involved in such a high degree of political and economic integration.

The European Union countries are much more corporatist than post-Thatcher Britain. The emphasis on competition in Britain has a corresponding commitment to cooperation in the other 14. The typical decision-making in the corporations of the 14 consists of collaborations between employers (or their federations), bureaucrats and trade union bosses. The typical result of these policies has been to massively expand welfare, taxes, and the unit cost of labor... with the sad results that we see today in France, Germany, Spain, etc. Management, free from fears of hostile takeover bids, is entrenched and as unresponsive as the unions. Government intervenes extensively – as, for example, in the Thyssen/Krupp takeover affair, where the government intervened within 24 hours, or another example is the coal miners' strike to save their jobs in which they produce coal at five times the world price. The examples in France are even more numerous – from Credit Lyonais to Air France. Recourse to the pubic purse is par for the course.

In Britain we tried corporatism, with varying degrees of intensity, from 1945 through to 1979. It did not work. It took many years of painful Thatcher reforms for Britain to convert the crisis-stricken sclerotic systems under Wilson, Heath and Callaghan to the flexible economy that the British enjoy today.

Why should we throw this away for the dubious benefits of the benighted Euro?

3

Financial Crisis Management In The EU/ERM

HANS TIETMEYER
President, Deutsche Bundesbank

The Greek word "krisis" originally meant a "decisive turning point." The term was hence a neutral one and by no means implied a turn for the better or a turn for the worse. Over time, the word acquired negative connotations. In the course of business activity, crisis refers to the point where buoyant economic conditions go into reverse and a phase of economic failures and depression sets in. Schumpeter referred to the significant role that crisis plays in the process of "creative destruction," qualifying, in turn, the negative connotations which the word has.

Irrespective of whether it is a turn for the better or for the worse, crises always present a challenge to those who are, either directly or indirectly, affected by them. Crisis prevention is rightly considered to be the greatest skill in crisis management. However, this anticipatory form of overcoming a crisis is difficult in practice, if only because no crisis is completely identical to the previous one. Even if the basic patterns of causality and of the course they take are often similar, crises are, in most cases, unforeseeable. This is particularly true of the precise time of their emergence and, not infrequently, of their intensity too. Under the conditions imposed nowadays by globally integrated financial markets, the short-term trends in the exchange rates are especially difficult to forecast. If there is a change in the assessment of how appropriate the respective exchange rates are (changes which are often reinforced by the media), considerable exaggerations may arise, particularly over the short term. Along with trends in the current fundamentals and expectations concerning the future economic performance of the countries, this often also owes a great deal to crises of credibility at the political level.

SECTION 1

It was a crisis, too, that provided the crucial incentive and stimulus for the intensified efforts towards monetary integration within the European Community since the late sixties - the crisis in the global system of fixed exchange rates of Bretton Woods, which was becoming increasingly apparent at that time. As early as in the second half of the sixties, the disruptions in the Bretton Woods system were also affecting monetary conditions within the European Community. Tensions arose not only vis-à-vis the US dollar but also between certain European currencies. Some countries proceeded to reverse the liberalization of capital and payment transactions, which had already been started cautiously within the Community. This jeopardized the level of integration achieved in Europe and made further progress difficult.

Against the backdrop of worldwide turmoil in the foreign exchange markets, there was increasing discussion on whether and how far monetary integration would have to be accelerated within the European Economic Community. In 1970 a working group headed by Luxembourg's Prime Minister Pierre Werner submitted a report which outlined the path leading to a gradual implementation of an economic and monetary union (Werner plan) by 1980. But in 1971 the European governments actually only agreed on the terms and conditions of the first stage, and not on the more extensive proposals contained in the Werner plan, which, for example, envisaged the transfer of substantial elements of national policy to the Community level and the establishment of matching supranational institutions. Thus, only a European exchange rate mechanism was created, which limited the fluctuation margins between the EC currencies to +/- 2.25 % by providing for interventions on the basis of bilateral central rates. Up to the general floating of the exchange rates in March 1973, the buying and selling rates for the US dollar (tunnel) limited the Community's exchange rate band (the so-called "snake in the tunnel"). Subsequently, the structure of the tunnel weakened, and the members of the narrower margins arrangement operated a group floating vis-à-vis the US dollar.

The experience gained with the "snake" showed that a system of fixed exchange rates - even if it is limited regionally - can work only between countries whose economic development is sufficiently convergent and whose balances of payments are not exposed to especially severe longer-term tensions. However, since these prerequisites were met in the European Community only partly, the financial markets were repeatedly able to attack different currencies taking part in the "snake" arrangement. Consequently, France, the United Kingdom and Italy left the "snake."

In retrospect, it seems hardly surprising that the "snake" plunged into several crises: there was, after all, no sufficient stability consensus between the partners at that time. Above all, the members of the "snake" reacted in different ways to the economic and monetary policy challenges posed by the first worldwide oil price crisis. Whereas one group - including Germany - oriented itself more strongly towards the objective of internal stability and principally attempted to restore it, other countries responded by pursuing a more expansionary monetary policy, hoping that they would be able to reduce the pressure to adjust to the oil price shock, and influenced no doubt also by the highly problematic idea (which at that time was still prevalent) of an exploitable trade-off between unemployment and inflation. Major countries were hence not prepared to pursue a domestic economic policy that was compatible with exchange rate stability in a fixed exchange rate system, the stability standard of which was predefined by the most stable currency - the Deutsche mark. This resulted in considerable exchange-rate-related tensions within the European Community. The objective formulated on the basis of the Werner plan, namely the creation of an economic and monetary union within one decade, proved to be unrealistic, given the prevailing structures and circumstances of that time.

SECTION 2

At the end of 1978 the Community was divided into two blocks in terms of exchange rate policy: a hard currency block around the Deutsche mark, including the currencies of the Benelux countries and the Danish krone - the "small snake" - on the one hand, and the other currencies of the Community countries, on the other. This was the basic situation in 1979 when the EC partner countries, by introducing the European Monetary System (EMS), made a renewed attempt to accelerate and intensify the monetary policy integration of the Community.

In order to achieve greater exchange rate stability through the EMS, according to the original ideas put forward by its architects, Giscard d'Estaing and Helmut Schmidt, the central banks of countries with strong currencies - particularly the Bundesbank - were to support the weaker currencies in the "snake" to a larger extent than before. The linking of the system to the ECU was intended as a vehicle for this - the ECU being an artificial accounting unit calculated on the basis of a basket of all the EC currencies, consisting of fixed monetary amounts of the individual EMS currencies. Their value thus depends on the value of all the currencies contained in the basket. It is thus a kind of weighted average value. Intervention rules which were linked to ECU-oriented central rates could have placed the strong currency countries in a position of having to sell weak currencies unilaterally - in other words without the central banks of the weaker currencies being under a simultaneous obligation to intervene. However, purchasing foreign currencies increases the domestic money stock, and hence sooner or later leads to a higher rate of inflation. There would have been the possibility of the currencies that were originally sound becoming infected with the virus of inflation if their orientation had been towards the ECU.

However, this concept did not prevail in the negotiations - which owed much to the influence exercised by the Bundesbank. It is true that ECU central rates were established in a formal sense. The intervention rules were based on bilaterally defined central rates (parity grid), however, as they had been before in the case of the "snake." As a result, in practical terms the ECU was merely given the role of an accounting unit. The parity grid mechanism, with bilaterally defined central rates, thus made it possible for the most stable currency in the system to set the standard.

The maximum band, within which the exchange rates may fluctuate around the bilateral central rates, was limited to +/- 2.25 % in normal cases. However, until the late eighties the fluctuation margin for Italy was +/- 6 %. At first, the United Kingdom as well as the newly acceded Mediterranean countries Spain and Portugal did not take part at all in the EMS exchange rate mechanism. It was only in the late eighties and early nineties that they joined the EMS, and Greece has still not joined the system. In the wake of the turmoil in the European foreign exchange markets in 1992-3, after several critical escalations, the EMS band was generally expanded to +/- 15 %. Only Germany and the Netherlands still have a bilateral fluctuation band of +/- 2.25 %, which, owing to the high degree of convergence of economic trends and policies pursued by both countries, has proved to be possible without causing problems. The United Kingdom and Italy, however, have been outside the system since 1992, as are Sweden and Finland, which, in spite of their accession to the EU, have so far not joined the EMS exchange rate mechanism. By contrast, Austria joined the exchange rate mechanism at the beginning of 1995 within the enlarged fluctuation bands. But it has pegged its exchange rate to the Deutsche mark on its own initiative for a long time.

Responsibility for fixing and adjusting of the parities rests with the governments. For the central banks, a system of fixed exchange rates becomes problematical if it triggers intervention obligations that undermine the central bank's ability to pursue a stability-oriented monetary policy. This potential conflict became obvious, particularly for the Deutsche Bundesbank, in the 1992 currency crisis. However, since the creation of the EMS, there has been an informal agreement with the Federal Government by which the Bundesbank is entitled to refrain from buying foreign currencies in cases of emergency if the intervention obligations jeopardize its stability policy. The mere existence of this regulation has proved to have a beneficial effect.

The rules of the exchange rate mechanism explicitly provide for the possibility of the central rates being realigned in the event of sustained divergences. However, a realignment is subject to the agreement of all the participating governments. The key factor in the situation of the European currency markets assuming crisis-like proportions in 1992-3 was that the political bodies were not prepared to undertake the necessary adjustment of the parities in good time, but only when they were put under sometimes extreme pressure by the markets.

Overall, the following should be noted: the exchange rate mechanism of the EMS has elements of flexibility, even though it is a fixed exchange rate system. Elements of this kind are indispensable for being able to react to sustained divergences in the economic trends in the partner countries. Central rate adjustments, in particular, constitute one element of this flexibility. Above and beyond that, some regulations, which differ according to the country concerned, also contribute to the flexibility of the system to a certain extent.

In contrast to the Bretton Woods system, the European Monetary System does not, in legal terms, place particular emphasis on any one national currency. The role of the *de facto* anchor currency has been acquired by the Deutsche mark in an evolutionary market process. However, this is a position which has to be abandoned as soon as the currency ceases to fulfil its anchor function. Today, there are, in principle, four factors which make the EMS the "modern-day gold standard with the Deutsche mark as the anchor" - as the British Prime Minister John Major once described the EMS at the beginning of the nineties:

- first, the concept of the EMS as a system of bilateral - not ECU-oriented - central rates,

- second, the *de facto* anchor role of the Deutsche mark as the most important European currency,

- third, the strict anti-inflationary monetary policy pursued by the Deutsche Bundesbank, as a guarantor of the Deutsche mark's stability, and

- fourth, the decision of the partners to orient themselves towards the stability standard of the anchor currency and to pursue an anti-inflationary policy of their own.

SECTION 3

It is true that the three principles - primacy of domestic stability policy, early central rate adjustments, and flexibility of the system - are components of the EMS. In practice, however, these principles have not always been sufficiently observed. This also provided the starting point of the various crises in the EMS. Above all, the realization that exchange rate stability has to be achieved by domestic stability efforts - even if one links one's own currency to a stable anchor - had to gain ground in political practice in some countries - something which became apparent particularly in the initial phase of the EMS.

Seven realignments took place between the spring of 1979 and the spring of 1983. The appreciation of the Deutsche mark vis-à-vis the weighted average in the partner countries came to about 27 % in that period. If one considers the inflation rates in that period, the root causes become apparent. The average rates of inflation between 1979 and 1983 ranged from 4.9 % in Germany to 17 % in Italy (Belgium 7 %, Denmark 10.1 %, France 11.8 %, Ireland 15.8 %, the Netherlands 5.2 %). The second oil price shock at the end of the seventies doubtless made the start of the EMS more difficult and increased inflationary pressures in all countries. But the distinct differences in inflation rates at the beginning of the eighties also show that the partners - as had happened already during the first oil price shock in the seventies - again reacted quite differently to the economic policy challenges. Particularly in the partner country France, there was a prevailing conviction before the change in economic policy strategy in the spring of 1983 that it would be possible to counter the oil price shock and the recession by pursuing an expansionary monetary and fiscal policy. By contrast, in Germany, monetary policy has always been geared towards stability, and the Federal Government increasingly emphasized the importance of consolidating the budget - particularly after the change of government in 1982. Thus, the currency crises in the first few years following the establishment of the EMS mirrored these differences in stability orientation and in the economic policy strategies of the partner countries.

In the first few years of the EMS the situation was similar in some respects to the crises in the former "snake" following the first oil price shock, even though, in contrast to the seventies, the countries concerned did not leave the exchange rate mechanism. Given the continued significant differences in inflation rates and the underlying divergences in domestic stability policies, this was only made possible by a series of central rate adjustments, which were repeatedly preceded by tensions and volatility.

SECTION 4

The picture began to change gradually only when France, following dramatic controversies within the government, introduced a new stability policy in the spring of 1983 - a policy influenced by the Minister of Finance, Jacques Delors - and proceeded to adhere to that policy in the years that followed despite all difficulties. The decision made at that time, namely not to leave the EMS but, instead, to initiate a convincing internal stability policy by adjusting the parity of the Franc, was probably one of the most important events in the history of the EMS. In fact, as the eighties progressed, this decision prompted other EMS countries to intensify their internal stability efforts, too.

Between mid-1983 and 1987, only four realignments were necessary - significantly fewer than in the turbulent initial years. If one considers the inflation rates of this period, the progress achieved by the partner countries in combating inflation is striking. Thus, the average rates of inflation in 1984-8 ranged from 1.1 % in the Netherlands and Germany to 7.1 % in Italy (Belgium 3.0 %, Denmark 4.6 %, France 4.3 %, Ireland 4.6 %). The appreciation of the Deutsche mark vis-à-vis the weighted average of the EMS currencies up to the beginning of 1987, at 8 %, was considerably lower than in the first few years (27 %). This shows clearly that success in terms of domestic stability policy may itself lead to a stabilization of the exchange rates. The decline in oil prices was an additional factor which made inflation combating easier in all countries in that period. The appreciation of the US dollar in the eighties likewise took pressure off the EMS at times.

Admittedly, the fact that changes in the central rates had become less frequent also increased some partner countries' awareness of the pressure towards internal adjustment associated with the exchange rate mechanism of the EMS. It is true that internal adjustment was, at first, largely accepted as a consequence of the necessary catching-up process in stability policy. However, over the long term, domestic adjustment to the best performer in stability policy appeared to some countries to be increasingly difficult to sustain. France, in particular, again proposed that the EMS should be developed in the direction of greater "symmetry." The vehicle for achieving such symmetry was, in this instance, to consist of an expansion of the intra-marginal interventions and the inclusion of at least part of the foreign exchange purchased in the monetary reserves of those countries with strong currencies. In contrast to compulsory interventions, intra-marginal interventions imply that the central banks take action even before the extreme buying and selling rates are arrived at. Such interventions have to be agreed among the central banks, since, under the rules of the system, they require the approval of the central bank issuing the intervention currency.

The discussion triggered by France led to the conclusion of the Basle-Nyborg Agreement of 1987. In this agreement, the partner countries changed the repayment conditions arising from the intervention obligations. The basic structure of the EMS and the original intervention rules were retained, however. In addition, the agreement made it clear that an active exchange rate policy includes, beside interventions, the utilization of the fluctuation margins and interest rate policy measures in the currencies that have come under pressure. Nevertheless, the nagging accusation of asymmetry remained.

SECTION 5

Between January 1987 and September 1992 the EMS experienced a period of nominal exchange rate stability, and no realignment took place. Fundamentally, there were three reasons for this. First, since the mid-eighties some countries had achieved marked progress in reducing inflation rates. However, there were still some inflation-related differences between EMS countries, which over the longer term led to the gradual emergence of a need for corrections to the exchange rate. Second, a remarkable change had taken place in respect of the assessment of the exchange rate policy. The long-prevalent notion that a depreciation would procure competitive advantages met with less and less approval. This was due to bitter lessons learned from the past. In fact, the hoped-for-advantage brought about by a depreciation disappears quite quickly if rising import prices set a wage-price spiral in motion. In the end, the artificial competitive advantage has mostly vanished. What remains, however, is higher domestic inflation and a risk premium in respect of interest rates, since the markets expect the risk of depreciation to exist in future, too. And, third, the European Community took important steps in that period for intensifying economic integration. The road to a monetary union was discussed, and its basic features were laid down in the Maastricht Treaty. All the countries of the Community declared their willingness to grant independent status to the future European Central Bank and to set themselves more stringent stability targets in the future. It was partly owing to this success in negotiation that the harmful impression - as it later turned out - arose within the general public and in the financial markets that the EMS already constituted a *de facto* monetary union for the Community.

The EMS became increasingly attractive, and a number of countries expected the pegging of their exchange rates to the hard core, with the Deutsche mark as the anchor currency, to support their own stability policy. Thus, the peseta, the pound sterling and the escudo were introduced into the exchange rate mechanism. Italy forwent the extended fluctuation band and adopted the normal +/- 2.25 % fluctuation band arrangement of that time. Even some North European countries, which were not members of the Community at the beginning of the nineties, perceived advantages for their own stability policy in a unilateral link to the exchange rate mechanism of the EMS.

The strategy of pegging the exchange rates was probably largely motivated by the possibility of importing some of the credibility that the core group's stability policy had gained in the markets. Some countries thought it appropriate to pursue an exchange rate target vis-à-vis a currency or group of currencies recognized as stable by the markets in order to reduce inflation expectations at lower costs. For that reason, they endeavored to link their currencies as far as possible to the internal core, particularly the Deutsche mark. Admittedly, the rationale of such a strategy requires allowing the external disciplining stability constraints to have an impact on the domestic stability efforts of the countries concerned. In this way, the country has to pay back the credibility it has borrowed. As desirable as stable exchange rates may be - they must be based on sound economic conditions. Maintaining the existing parity over the long term, in particular, will not be possible if sizeable inflation differences exist for a lengthy period of time.

Unfortunately, however, some European countries did not heed this lesson, especially at the beginning of the nineties. Diverging prices and costs were not sufficiently reduced, whereas exchange rates remained nominally stable. Such differences largely continued to exist, meaning that the currencies of countries with lower inflation rates depreciated in real terms, whereas the currencies of less stability-conscious countries in some cases appreciated sharply in real terms. The average inflation rates between 1987 and 1992 in the countries with the most stable prices, i.e. the Netherlands and Germany, were 1.9 % and 2.4 %, respectively, whereas the United Kingdom, Italy, Spain and Portugal, for example, had rates of 6.0 %, 5.7 %, 5.9 % and 10.8 %. The countries with more stable prices were hence able to strengthen their competitive position in the Community markets, whereas the weaker countries began to lag behind.

Nevertheless, the currencies with less stable prices tended to be strong at times in the foreign exchange markets. Under the illusion (fostered by the conclusion of the Maastricht Treaty) that there was a *de facto* monetary union in which, according to prevailing opinion, there would be no more parity changes, even slight nominal interest rate premiums were sufficient for those countries to attract capital inflows. Thus, in the final analysis it was too easy for countries with less price stability to finance their growing current account deficits. The illusion of the external strength of the currencies with less price stability was accompanied for some time by an illusion concerning the internal competitive strength of the economies with a more stable currency - particularly Germany. This undesirable development, which was compounded by the temporary undervaluation of the Deutsche mark, also played a part in significant wage increases being agreed to in Germany at that time which exceeded growth in productivity.

The Bundesbank pointed to the continuing divergences at a very early stage and took a stand against the illusion of the *de facto* monetary union. In its 1990 Annual Report it said (page 66):

> "To the extent that the stability of exchange rates or even the pronounced strength of a number of partner currencies that do not belong to the "hard core" of the EMS can be explained essentially by inflation-induced higher rates of interest, it can basically be justified only if it is consolidated by a domestic economic policy that is durably geared to stability. If success is not achieved in coping with the

structural causes of inflation within a reasonable period of time, it will probably become increasingly difficult over the long term to avoid having recourse to exchange rate adjustments. ... This explains why a currency union that is not based on durable progress in the direction of convergence will remain under the threat of tensions. For this reason, changes in central rates within the 'EMS should not be excluded in principle during the transitional stages towards bringing about economic and monetary union."

SECTION 6

In this situation of external calm and pent-up problems of divergence, German reunification faced economic and monetary policy makers in the anchor currency country with a completely new and gargantuan challenge. In 1989 the German current account - owing not least to the real depreciation of the Deutsche mark - still recorded a record surplus of DM 108 billion or 5 % of the gross domestic product. At the same time, this was the highest current account surplus among the industrial countries. However, the reversal in external economic trends after reunification was just as striking. Within no more than two years, this record surplus was transformed in 1991 into a deficit of DM 30 billion or 1 % of the GDP. This change in the situation was caused by the unification-induced strong expansion of domestic demand, triggered by increased public expenditure on transfers to the East and by the pent-up consumption and investment demand in eastern Germany itself. The task of reconstructing eastern Germany entailed very high capital requirements. Moreover, the fast rise in public expenditure was largely financed at first not by higher taxation but by additional borrowing in the capital market.

On a macroeconomic analysis, the German economy, with its previously accumulated external assets, had a comfortable cushion for temporarily financing the external reversal. At the same time, the additional domestic demand was satisfied from abroad, too. This supported the economy in the European partner countries and more or less offset the restraining effects which the rise in interest rates in Germany had on economic activity in those countries. However, the sharply expansionary German financial policy and the wage increases in excess of productivity jeopardized internal monetary stability and compelled the Bundesbank to take monetary policy countermeasures. It was only in this way that the Bundesbank was able to keep the emerging risks of inflation within bounds and prevent the expansion and the growth of persistent inflationary expectations. But this policy mix contributed to the undesirable developments in the EMS exchange rates, which had been accumulating up to that time, making themselves felt to an increasing extent. The burdens arising from German unity thus aggravated the divergences which had built up previously. They were not, however, their real cause. In fact, even before German unification and the associated problematic policy mix in Germany, the EMS had experienced an increasing disparity between competitive positions. Both factors, taken together, led to an increasing need to adjust the exchange rates.

SECTION 7

The Danish referendum on the Maastricht Treaty in mid-1992, in which the majority of the Danish population rejected the European Monetary Union, suddenly made the markets aware of the pent-up problems of divergence. The markets at once started to question again the supposedly smooth transition from the existing parities to a monetary union. To this were added growing doubts concerning the willingness of some countries to preserve with the strict monetary policy necessary for defending the parities in an environment which had become more difficult in cyclical terms.

The main effect of the "rediscovery" of the exchange rate risk was that it generated a massive demand for Deutsche mark investment. The simultaneous interest-rate-induced decline of the US dollar rate increased the tensions. Whereas the markets rediscovered the exchange rate risk, the political bodies of most countries initially wished to retain the parities, which in the meantime had become unrealistic. Regrettably, the parity issue was sometimes even raised to the status of question of national honor and political prestige. At the beginning of the nineties, the instrument of central rate adjustments, which was to ensure the necessary degree of flexibility, was at first relegated completely into the background. At the same time, some member countries were faced with the dilemma (easily seen through by the markets) of having to counter the exchange rate tensions with rises in interest rates that were not consistent with the economic environment. It was only following dramatic series of critical developments in the financial markets and large-scale losses in monetary reserves that Italy and the United Kingdom yielded to the pressure of the markets and in 1992 made the decision to leave the exchange rate mechanism - at least for the time being. Other countries, such as Spain, Portugal and Ireland, made the exchange rates of their currencies more consistent with international price and cost relations by means of an - albeit belated - depreciation.

However, this did not restore calm in the foreign exchange markets. Instead, in mid-1993 the EMS was once again exposed to massive speculative attacks by the markets, which even large intervention volumes could not counteract. This new currency crisis showed that the credibility of the entire EMS had suffered considerably from the delayed corrections. As a result of this credibility crisis, even currencies which were fundamentally sound - like the French franc - were put under pressure. In the eyes of the markets, simple affirmations of the existing rules of the EMS on the part of the governments and the central banks were not able to restore the credibility of the EMS within its narrow fluctuation margins. The situation was also difficult because, on the one hand, the markets, in view of the general deterioration in the economic situation, assumed that individual countries - which in the meantime had achieved considerable progress in combating inflation - would unilaterally lower their interest rates even if this meant their own currencies having to depreciate. The slightest doubts concerning the permanence of the exchange-rate-oriented stability policy of individual EMS partners was enough to prompt investors to take flight from those currencies. On the other hand, in Germany, whose currency performed the function of the anchor currency, the scope for monetary policy action was tightly restricted. In the light of the growing public sector budget deficits and the sustained labor cost pressure, any accelerated interest rate reductions would have jeopardized domestic price stability.

Even foreign exchange market interventions cannot accomplish much in a conflict situation of this kind. In fact, the monetary reserves of a country which has come under pressure are quickly exhausted, as was shown, for example, by the trends in the French and Danish reserves during the July 1993 crisis. For that reason, various observers proposed that the central banks' mutual assistance should be substantially expanded. However, such demands ignored the monetary policy effects on the country with a strong currency. In fact, irrespective of whether the central bank intervenes itself or makes its own currency available to other countries for intervention purposes - bank liquidity is expanded by such measures and controlling monetary expansion is therefore made more difficult. Of the official DEUTSCHE MARK sales in the EMS, which came to DM 107 billion in July 1993, about DM 59 billion were reflected in an increase in German bank liquidity.

The finance ministers and the central bank governors, after internal and sometimes animated deliberation, therefore decided to extend the fluctuation margins from +/- 2.25 % to +/- 15 %, with effect from August 2, 1993. This was an approach that had been advocated by Germany on several occasions - albeit for a long time to no avail. The extension of the fluctuation margins which was then finally agreed was, in the final analysis, inescapable and produced a number of advantages. First, wider fluctuation margins can shield the monetary policy of countries with a strong currency more efficiently from disturbing inflows of money. Second, they make currency speculations more risk-prone, since now a potential reversal of exchange rate movements has to be allowed for. Riskless one-way bets have now been largely ruled out. The two-way bets associated with the extension doubtless ensure a more equitable distribution of opportunities and risks. Finally, extended fluctuation margins sharpen awareness of the stability policy responsibility to be borne by the countries themselves. Convergence deficits in the member countries become manifest more easily, since wide fluctuation margins restrain political influence in favor of the market forces.

In addition, the wider fluctuation margins are more consistent with the globalization of the financial markets. Given the freedom of capital transactions, a system of fixed - albeit adjustable - exchange rates is always exposed to the danger that it will be tested by the markets. Some observers even consider the increasing freedom of financial transactions in Europe to be the real cause of the crises experienced in 1992 and 1993. However, this argument confuses the cause of the crisis with its symptoms. The freedom of movement for capital is not in itself a source of disruption in what happens to the exchange rates but, rather, the catalyst for necessary adjustments to economic, financial and wage policies in the countries concerned. On the contrary, the freedom of capital transactions is a precondition for an optimum utilization of capital. A return to capital transaction controls would, in any case, have no prospect of success in a globalized world of integrated financial markets. However, the turmoil in the foreign exchange markets in 1992 and 1993 triggered an intense discussion on the lessons to be learnt from the crisis. Again, there were calls for the EMS to be organized more symmetrically. Basically, this was merely a new version of the discussions on the distribution of adjustment burdens which had preceded the creation of the EMS and the Basle-Nyborg Agreement. As before, this argument ignored the fact that a system of fixed exchange rates can be made symmetrical only if safeguarding internal monetary stability recedes into the background. In the case of "asymmetrical mechanisms," the country whose currency is put under pressure either has to raise its interest rates or to devalue its currency. Under symmetrical conditions, an expansionary impulse is generated in the countries with a strong currency either as a result of interventions or because the central bank has to lower its interest rates. In both cases alike, monetary stability is jeopardized - and that applies to the entire Community. A currency is able to become - and remain - a stable anchor only if the asymmetry which this necessarily entails is maintained, even, and precisely, in times of crisis. Such an asymmetry is the basis for ensuring that the strongest currency can fulfil its anchor function, and is therefore in the whole system's own best interest.

SECTION 8

The monetary union envisaged by the European Union will constitute a qualitative jump in Europe's monetary policy integration. Under the terms of the Treaty, the exchange rates of the partner countries which fulfil the entry criteria laid down in the Treaty are to be fixed irrevocably on January 1, 1999, at the latest. From that date onwards, the European Central Bank, which is to be established in 1998 and to be independent of instructions, will have sole responsibility for monetary policy in the Euro currency area. The national central banks will then become part of the new European System of Central Banks. In all probability, however, not all EU countries will be able to participate in the monetary union from the outset. This gives rise to a number of questions. How are the currency relationships between the Euro currency area and the other EU countries to be arranged? Any system which regulates the relations between what are known as "ins" and "outs" must take due account of the experience gained with the EMS. To what extent has the EMS proved to be successful? To what extent have shortcomings become apparent that can now be remedied? Is it possible to make the new system more resistant to crises?

The EMS has not explicitly given special prominence, in legal terms, to any particular currency. The anchor function of the Deutsche mark resulted from its better performance in the markets. However, this does not apply to a new European exchange rate system. The Euro is to become the anchor currency in Europe, according to the declared intention of all the member countries. The currencies of the countries which will participate in the monetary union will ultimately be absorbed by it. The Euro is thus to become the monetary policy center of gravity in Europe. If the calls for more "symmetry" were not justified in the case of the old EMS, this applies all the more to an exchange rate system which explicitly grants to the Euro the function of the anchor currency. The new exchange rate system, therefore, has to be asymmetrical, since the countries which join the monetary union at a later date will, as a rule, have to make up arrears in convergence. This also implies that the intervention burdens ought to be borne mainly by the "outs." If the European Central Bank is obliged to make interventions, it should in all cases have the right to suspend its intervention obligations, if its internal stability policy were otherwise to be put at risk.

Overall, the crises in the EMS show that even the most sophisticated exchange rate mechanism cannot be a substitute for internal stability efforts undertaken by the countries themselves. Quite the opposite: permanent stability success can by itself bring about a stabilization of the exchange rates. For that reason, an exchange rate system should clearly indicate the stability policy responsibility of the countries themselves. Appropriately wide exchange rate bands are better suited to fulfilling this requirement than bands that are too narrow. Maintaining unrealistic central rates for too long proved to be the Achilles' heel of the EMS. Thinking in terms of political prestige and national honor played a thoroughly significant role in this.

A new exchange rate mechanism in Europe should therefore include rules which, as far as possible, prevent parity changes from becoming politicized. Political pressure could be taken off the debate if the European Central Bank were given the right to initiate parity changes. As a supranational institution which is independent of instructions, its judgement is not geared to the special interests of individual countries or to what is politically opportune. Instead, its judgement is likely to be determined mainly by the economic fundamentals. Above all, it would be possible, in this way to generate a discussion on parity changes in good time.

Overall, this is a possibility of integrating elements of flexibility into the new exchange rate system, which are indispensable for its smooth operation in a heterogeneous Europe. Such elements are also likely to include different forms of exchange-rate and monetary-policy cooperation between the countries. The arrangements that will have to be made could be geared to the degree of convergence achieved in the countries - for example, narrow bands in the case of relatively substantial progress in convergence, and wide bands in the case of convergence backlogs. That would also generate incentives to pursue an internal stability policy. In fact, the bands concerned do not have to apply indefinitely, but, instead, could be adjusted to the degree of convergence achieved.

In my opinion, these principles are the main lessons to be learnt from the various currency crises in Europe. If these principles are observed, Europe will have a fair chance of avoiding future currency crises between the single currency, i.e. the Euro, and the currencies of the other EU countries which for the time being remain outside the union.

SECTION 9

Given the present globalization of the financial markets, the fixing of exchange rates has become more difficult than ever. Such a fixing, in fact, presupposes either a sustained congruity of underlying national trends and policies or the subordination of substantial parts of national policy to a supranational decision. The experience gained with the European Monetary System have shown how difficult it is to achieve such an integration or subordination on a lasting basis - even within a single region. In today's multi-polar world of big industrial countries and regions, it will be all the more difficult to achieve the necessary convergence at a global level - let alone to ensure it over the long term.

The future exchange rate movements of the Euro vis-à-vis the non-EU countries will depend on the monetary union's internal stability and on how they are assessed by the markets as well as on trends in the third countries themselves. At least under the present conditions, we cannot return to a system of globally fixed exchange rates on the model of the Bretton Woods system. At a global level, an increased international coordination of national policies, or the establishment of a so-called target zone system, is often seen as a means of preventing incorrect exchange rates. The experience gained with the Plaza (1985) and Louvre (1987) agreements, however, shows that international cooperation in the field of exchange rates can be successful only if it is based on credible measures to rectify undesirable developments in the participating economies; however, this also raises the question of the extent to which such cooperation is necessary in these circumstances. Concerted intervention in the form of purchases and sales of foreign exchange by central banks can impart supplementary signals to the foreign exchange markets in certain situations, but they can be no substitute for the elimination of undesirable economic trends in the participating countries.

All this does not imply that efforts at more international cooperation - especially those between the major industrial countries - fail to make sense. Quite the opposite, in fact. It is important, however, to focus on the international compatibility and inner consistency of national policy, and not to succumb to the illusion that exchange rates can be fine-tuned in isolation from that.

4

Italy: Two Foreign Exchange Crises

ROBERTO RINALDI
Head of the Monetary Analysis Office in the Monetary and Financial Sector, Bank of Italy
CARLO SANTINI
Central Manager for Economic Research, Bank of Italy

INTRODUCTION

The present paper aims to analyze the two foreign exchange crises that struck Italy, with serious repercussions for the financial markets in the summer of 1992 and the early months of 1995. Both episodes, described in sections 1 and 2 respectively, will be set against the international context, which was not uninfluential in triggering them and determining their course. Section 1 focuses on the signs of financial stress that emerged after the lira was suspended from the ERM and on the authorities' actions undertaken to preserve the stability of the financial system while countering the inflationary pressures caused by the exchange rate depreciation. Section 2 highlights the positive interaction between economic fundamentals and policy actions in contributing to overcome the crisis. Finally, in the conclusions, an attempt will be made to identify the lessons to be learnt from these turbulent episodes.

The paper contains two Appendices. The first deals with the issue of whether dollar shocks influenced the lira/Deutsche mark rate within the ERM band; to this aim two different methods to empirically identify dollar shocks are proposed (one method being based on a measure of the "financial" effective exchange rate of the dollar and the other method on principal component analysis). The second appendix aims at evaluating, through the information offered by implicit forward exchange rates, whether expectations and probabilities of a lira devaluation were relevant well in advance of the summer months of 1992, when adverse international events acted as catalysts of markets' expectations.

The Crisis Of The Summer Of 1992

The International Context

The lira crisis of the summer of 1992 was a particularly acute expression of a wider crisis that had emerged within the European Monetary System (EMS) against a background of imbalances in the competitive positions of its member countries, at a time of uncertainty concerning the ratification of the Maastricht Treaty, and of the conflict between internal and external policy objectives that pitted German monetary policies against those of the other major EU countries.[1]

The spark that lit the turbulence at the beginning of June was the negative result of the Danish referendum on the Treaty of Maastricht; on the assumption that the Treaty would be rejected, this fueled doubts regarding the maintenance of converging economic policies and of the objective of stable exchange rates within the Community. Expectations of tension were exacerbated by the French decision to hold a referendum on the Treaty on 20 September and the immediate perception of its uncertain outcome. Public opinion was unanimous in its conviction that a victory for the opponents of ratification would mean the definitive abandonment of plans for Economic and Monetary Union (EMU) and, therefore, variations in central rates. Several commentators questioned the very survival of the European Single Market.[2]

Political and economic issues in Europe were closely entwined. Germany was grappling with the problems of domestic stability posed by unification; inflation had been rising since mid-1990 and peaked at 6.3 per cent in April 1992 (Figure 1). On the foreign front, the expansionary impulse of unification was affecting the balance of payments: whereas in 1990 the current account had recorded a substantial surplus (US$49 billion, or 3.3 per cent of GDP), the years 1991 and 1992 showed large deficits, on the order of US$20 billion, or 1 per cent of GDP.

The Bundesbank was pursuing a decidedly tight monetary policy aimed at suffocating inflationary pressures through curbs on domestic demand, the appreciation of the Deutsche mark and inflows of cheap imports to satisfy excess demand from the eastern regions; net capital inflows triggered by the high level of domestic interest rates would have financed the resulting current account deficit. The Bundesbank first increased the discount rate from 6 to 6.5 per cent at the start of 1991; a series of further raises followed that took the official rates to postwar peak levels in the summer of 1992 (8.75 per cent for the discount rate and 10 per cent for the Lombard rate).

Figure 1
Consumer Prices
(percentage change on year-earlier month)

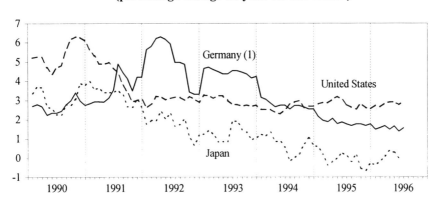

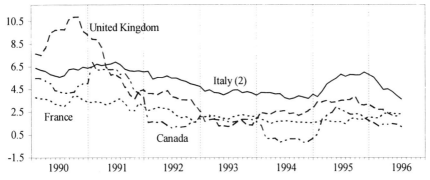

(1) Through 1991, western Länder only; (2) Cost-of-living index.
Sources: OECD and national statistics.

Despite the contribution of exports to Germany, growth in the other European countries remained modest (Figure 2). The latter, and France in particular, faced a dilemma: to give priority to the stability of exchange rates with the Deutsche mark by raising interest rates at a time of falling inflation, stagnation and growing unemployment; or to concentrate on a recovery of economic activity by relaxing monetary policy and devaluing.

Figure 2
Gross Domestic Product
(percentage change on year-earlier quarter)

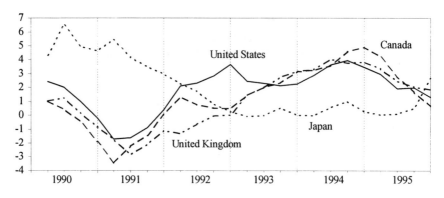

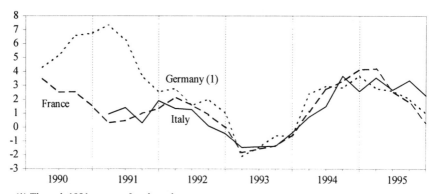

(1) Through 1991, western Länder only.
Sources: national statistics.

The simultaneous relaxation of US monetary policy aimed at fostering economic recovery was an added element of tension. At the beginning of 1991 the US economic downswing that had started at the end of 1989 bottomed out. The discount rate was lowered initially at the end of 1990, and further reductions brought the cost of borrowing from the Federal Reserve to a record low of 3 per cent. At that date the spread between German and US official rates, which had been negative by 1 percentage point in 1990, was 6 percentage points (Figure 3). The expansionary stance in the United States put pressure on the European exchange rate system on top of that caused by Germany's tight monetary policy.[3] The dollar fell to a minimum of 1.4 Deutsche marks in September 1992.

Figure 3
Official Discount Rates

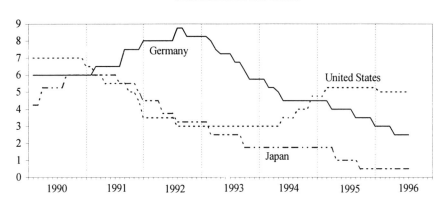

The restrictive monetary stance in Germany and the dollar's weakness were a challenge to the stability of central rates within the EMS. In fact, much more was at stake: if the French franc/Deutsche mark exchange rate had yielded, it would not have been just one more in the series of realignments that dotted the history of the EMS from 1979 to 1987; it would have signaled the abandonment of French aspirations to make the franc as stable as the Deutsche mark and, probably, of the ambitious design for the economic and monetary unification of Europe.

In the five years following the previous ERM realignment in 1987, exchange rate stability had not been accompanied in some countries -- notably Italy -- by significant progress particularly in the adjustment of public finances but also in the abatement of inflation. As the Committee of Governors emphasized in 1993, while nominal exchange rates were stable, "incomplete convergence towards low levels of inflation" had "brought significant changes in international competitiveness." This inadequate convergence, in the Governors' opinion, was chiefly caused by the persistence of substantial budget deficits, which in turn was leading to an unbalanced economic policy mix and the placing of too great a burden on monetary policy as a means of reducing inflation.

When the crisis broke, the conflict between internal and external policy objectives posed an obstacle to coordinated monetary policy action. The markets' perception that monetary cooperation in the EMS was under strain fueled speculative forays, first against the weaker currencies and later extending to the entire System and even to non-EMS European currencies. As Tommaso Padoa-Schioppa emphasized, the primary cause of the EMS crisis was "coordination failure." In a region in which the circulation of goods, services and capital have been liberalized, exchange rate stability could only be insured by coordinated monetary policies or, eventually, by a single policy[4].

The factors that combined to produce the "failure" were many: the divergence of German and US monetary policies already mentioned; an inadequate degree of economic convergence; official declarations that tended to fuel rather than to dampen unfavorable expectations; the refusal to adopt a general realignment of central rates; and the scant credibility of the new grid of central rates agreed on September 12th by the EMS countries. The failure was, in substance, the result of inability to solve the problem of the "nth currency" within a system of fixed but adjustable exchange rates either by hegemony or by cooperation.

During this delicate phase in the history of economic and political relations in Europe, Italy's position was one of pronounced weakness; it was the victim of events with little chance of determining their course, oppressed as it was by long-standing economic disequilibria -- in particular, high budget deficits and high relative inflation -- and by the moral and political crisis of a ruling class that was leaving the stage in shameful circumstances.

At this point a summary history of Italy's participation in the EMS and its Exchange Rate Mechanism (ERM) will be useful.

Italy and the EMS

Italy joined the EMS in keeping with a foreign policy stance under which Italy has played a leading role in European cooperation since the earliest postwar years.[5] Concern had been voiced over the risks involved in the commitment to hold fluctuations of the lira on the foreign exchange markets within the limit of 2.25 per cent. That margin could have proved too narrow for a country that still had extensive exchange controls -- albeit destined for gradual dismantling -- and an inflationary drift that undermined competitiveness and, accordingly, needed to be offset by recurrent devaluation. The drift was largely the result of a high and increasing level of wage indexation to offset all kinds of inflationary shocks.

From the technical standpoint, the solution eventually agreed on with Italy's partners was to allow a transitional period in which the lira would enjoy a broader fluctuation band of 6 per cent.[6] The country thus obtained greater freedom to use exchange rate policy as an instrument for the gradual correction of the disequilibria that undermined the Italian economy, notably higher inflation and precarious public finances, without risking repeated foreign exchange crises. In turn, the exchange rate constraint, although less stringent than for the other EMS currencies, was expected to exert the necessary pressure on costs and prices, shifting the emphasis, in safeguarding competitiveness, from periodic devaluation to productivity gains and cost controls.

Italy's participation in the EMS also marked the beginning of a phase that lasted several years with alternating periods of easing and tightening in which Italian monetary policy dropped the administrative instruments that had been employed sweepingly over the two previous decades to rely primarily on market instruments for indirect control of the aggregates.[7] On the operational level, the lira's position within the EMS band became the crucial indicator for monetary policy. As inflation gradually abated and the differential with Italy's European partners narrowed, the loss of competitiveness that nonetheless occurred was offset, only in part and with a lag, at a time when broad restrictions on capital movements were still in place, by exchange rate realignments, thus keeping the productive economy under continuing pressure to increase productivity through stricter control of costs, above all labor costs, and more intensive restructuring.[8]

Policymakers were cognizant from the outset of the limitations and risks of this approach to monetary and exchange rate policy. In his concluding remarks to the Annual Report for 1979, the Governor of the Bank of Italy called Italy's joining the EMS a "courageous decision" but added that it "implied consistent action, at the risk of degenerating into an empty ambition."

With the years, the isolation of monetary policy and its overburdening with diverse tasks grew increasingly manifest. On the political plane, Italy kept pace with its European partners in the construction of an increasingly integrated Community[9]; but fiscal and budgetary targets were almost never achieved, public financial adjustment being systematically postponed from one year to the next with a constant increase in the public debt both in absolute terms and in proportion to GDP. Whereas the average ratio of the Treasury's borrowing requirement to GDP in the sixties had remained around 2-3 per cent, it rose to around 10 per cent in the seventies, increased by another 2 points in the eighties and peaked at 13.2 in 1985. Public debt, which fluctuated around 40 per cent of GDP between the late sixties and late seventies, then started to increase steadily, growing by 20 points in the seventies, almost 40 in the eighties and exceeding the 100 per cent threshold in the early nineties (Table 1).

Table 1
Italian Treasury Borrowing Requirement And Public Debt
(as a percentage of GDP)

	Treasury borrowing requirement	Primary deficit	Interest payments	General government debt
1986	12.1	4.1	8.0	86.6
1987	11.3	3.7	7.6	90.7
1988	11.1	3.2	7.9	92.8
1989	10.7	1.9	8.8	95.8
1990	10.1	0.6	9.5	97.9
1991	10.4	0.4	10.0	101.4
1992	10.4	-0.8	11.2	108.5
1993	10.0	-1.7	11.7	199.3
1994	9.5	-1.1	10.6	125.5
1995	7.4	-3.6	11.0	124.9

The lira tended to appreciate n real terms, as gauged either by unit labor costs or producer prices (Figure 4). The balance of trade and the current account balance suffered, with regular deficits (Table 2)

Figure 4
Real Effective Exchange Rate Of The Lira,
Overall And Intra-EU
(1979=100)

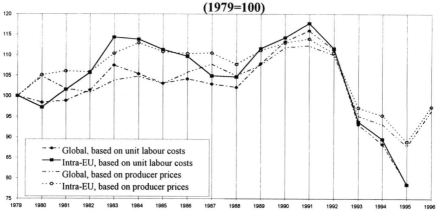

Source: Based on Bank of Italy, Istat and OECD data.

Table 2
Balance Of Trade, Balance On Current Account,
Italy's Market Share

	Trade balance (cif-fob) (1)	Current account balance (1)	Italian exports/world exports
1979	-1.5	1.6	4.8
1980	-5.0	-2.3	4.4
1981	-4.1	-2.4	4.6
1982	-3.4	-1.7	4.6
1983	-1.7	0.2	4.6
1984	-2.6	-0.7	4.6
1985	-2.6	-0.9	4.6
1986	-0.4	0.3	4.6
1987	-1.2	-0.3	4.4
1988	-1.3	-0.8	4.2
1989	-1.4	-1.4	4.3
1990	-1.1	-1.6	4.2
1991	-1.1	-2.1	4.1
1992	-0.8	-2.3	4.0
1993	2.1	1.2	4.2
1994	2.2	1.5	4.3
1995	2.5	2.5	4.4

(1) As percentage of GDP.
Source: based on Istat and IMF data.

The risk that Italy's increasingly precarious position in Europe might prove unsustainable was emphasized, clearly and with growing concern, by the Governor of the Bank of Italy from the mid-eighties. [10] Episodic crises in the foreign exchange and securities markets, though brief and relatively easily controlled, sounded the alarm over Italy's financial vulnerability. Speculation against the lira was particularly intense in the summer of 1987 and was countered not only by raising the discount rate and intervening in the financial and exchange markets but also by reinstituting some foreign exchange controls and setting a ceiling on bank lending. This, however, was the last time Italy resorted to administrative credit and exchange controls to deal with a foreign exchange crisis.

In his concluding remarks to the Bank of Italy's shareholders in May 1992, Governor Carlo Azeglio Ciampi issued a new warning of the unsustainability of the nation's public finance situation and even presented an econometric simulation of the Research Department covering the period 1992-1996 and tracing possible lines of action to redress the fiscal imbalance. A few months later, on the morrow of Italy's withdrawal from the EMS Exchange Rate Mechanism, Governor Ciampi recalled that action hinging on the exchange rate should have involved "not only consistent monetary policy but also a budgetary policy of reducing the deficit and an anti-inflationary incomes policy in the public sector with repercussions throughout the private sector."[11] But stable incomes policy arrangements and effective fiscal policy measures were not instituted until after the devaluation of the lira and Italy's subsequent withdrawal from the ERM in September of 1992.

The liberalization of capital movements, which Italy completed in 1990, the globalization of markets and financial innovation enhanced the capacity of the markets to monitor economic policy consistency and amplified the power of their reaction to expectations that the authorities would fail to achieve stability and financial equilibrium. Earlier, the restrictions on capital movements had partially isolated Italy and buffered the pressures, giving the authorities time to respond to speculative attacks.[12] Over the years, however, the very development of the international financial markets provided ample opportunities to circumvent exchange controls, which moreover turned out to be costly for the country introducing them insofar as they deprived the domestic financial market and banking system of the benefits of external openness and competition.

The inadequacy of monetary policy coordination emerged when the asymmetric shock of German unification struck the system's leading country. This called for fully concerted and coordinated adjustments in monetary policy stances and exchange rate parities. However, the countries of Europe failed to respond to this need.[13]

The Lira In The ERM In The Early Nineties And The Events Of Summer 1992

Between its accession to the narrow fluctuation band of the EMS in January 1990 and May 1992, the lira had been substantially stable within the ERM, despite occasionally being affected by the weakness of the dollar caused by the increasing divergence of German and US monetary policies. When tensions broke out at the end of 1990 (during the Gulf crisis) and 1991 the Bank of Italy reacted by using all the market instruments envisaged in the Basle-Nyborg agreements:[14] changes in interest rates, intervention in the foreign exchange markets and exchange rate movements within the fluctuation band. In November 1991 the Bank of Italy had placed a surcharge of half a percentage point on fixed-term advances, which had risen to 12 per cent; in December, in the wake of a similar move by the Bundesbank, the discount rate was raised by half a point to 12 per cent and the rate on fixed-term advances to 12.5 per cent.[15]

From the second week of May 1992, simultaneously with another dollar crisis, the lira's weakness became more pronounced (Figure 5). Following the result of the Danish referendum of June 2nd, which rejected the Treaty on European Union, it became acute and remained that way until the middle of July, during which time the monetary policies of Germany and the United States diverged still further.[16] The Bank of Italy regulated the lira's slide within the fluctuation band through massive interventions in the foreign exchange market, totaling US$13 billion in June and July. Official interest rates were repeatedly raised: on July 17th the discount rate stood at 13.75 per cent and the rate on advances at 15.25 per cent. As well as maneuvering official rates, the Bank acted decisively to tighten liquidity in the money market by severely limiting the supply of monetary base through repurchase agreements and rationing fixed-term advances. The rate on repos rose from 12.5 per cent at the end of May to a peak of 17.6 per cent on July 22nd (Figure 6); on the same date overnight interbank rates and three-month rates reached 18.7 and 17.3 per cent respectively -- increases of 6 and 5 points since the end of May. The interest rate differential vis-à-vis the mark widened with the three-month differential reaching 8 percentage points compared to 3 points at the end of May (Figure 7). On July 20th, the lira dropped to 761 against the Deutsche mark compared to 750 at the end of May.

Figure 5
The Lira's Position Within The EMS Band, The Dollar Effective Exchange Rate And Bank Of Italy Foreign Exchange Interventions

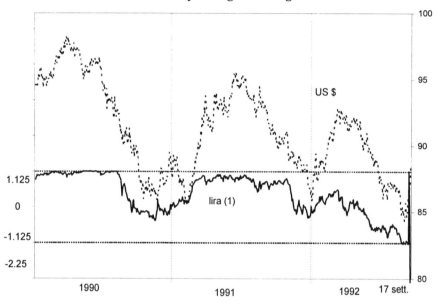

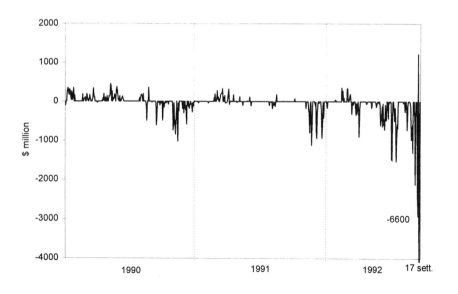

(1) Left scale.

Figure 6
Interest Rates In Italy

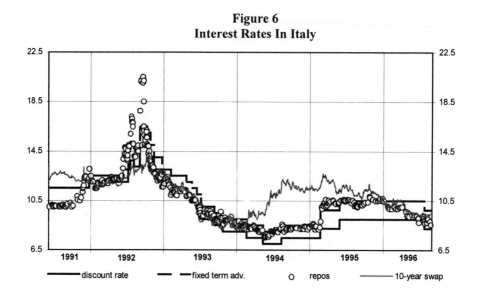

discount rate   fixed term adv.   O   repos   10-year swap

Figure 7
Ex-Coupon Prices Of Treasury Credit Certificates (CCT) And Bonds
(BTP) and Average Bid-Offer Spreads
(indices: 31 December=100; spreads in percentage points)

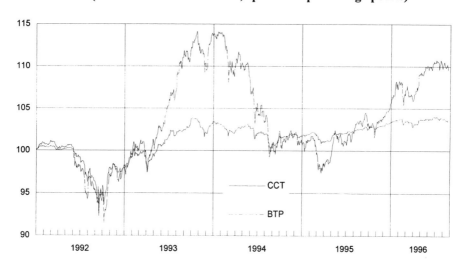

Figure 7 continued

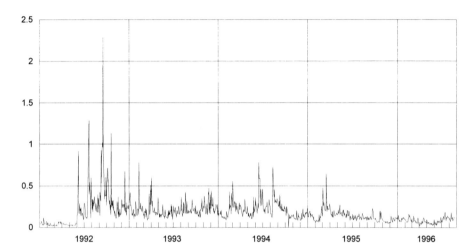

There was a pronounced fall in demand for government securities, both at issue and on the secondary market. At the Treasury bill auction in the second half of July, the supply of 12-month T-bills outstripped demand and average tender rates rose to 15.4 per cent. On the secondary market, the Bank of Italy made massive net outright purchases, amounting to 11.5 trillion lira in the months of June and July, 9.6 trillion lira of which were fixed-rate securities. Budget-cutting measures announced on 10 July by the new Government, which were intended to reduce the Treasury's borrowing requirement for 1992 by 30 trillion lira or 2 per cent of GDP, had a limited effect.[17] It was not until July 20th that foreign exchange and financial conditions showed some recovery, although this turned out to be only temporary. A number of factors contributed to the improvement: the central bank's restrictive action; concerted intervention in support of the dollar; the agreement of 31 July between employers and unions on incomes policy, disinflation and the cost of labor, which abolished all forms of wage indexation and guaranteed wage moderation for the following year by suspending company-level bargaining; Parliamentary approval at the beginning of August of the corrective budgetary measures for 1992, and announcement of a go-ahead for plans to privatize a number of public companies. On 4 August, in a moment of calm on the foreign exchange market, the Bank of Italy signaled approval of the measures adopted by reducing the discount rate by half a point, to 13.25 per cent. Until August 21st the lira remained fairly stable against the Deutsche mark, which was quoted at around 756. At the end of the second ten days of August the rates on repurchase agreements fell to around 15 per cent and interbank rates dipped to about 16 per cent.

Events continued to threaten the lira's basic stability, however, by fueling growing doubts about Italy's ability to control the economy and the financial aggregates. The liquidation of Efim, an insolvent state holding company, on July 17th generated strong negative reactions from foreign creditors. On August 13th, Moody's downgraded the Italian Republic from AA1 to AA3, and the general political climate worsened with the spread of accusations of corruption against major political figures.

Tension erupted again on August 24th. This was triggered by another sudden depreciation of the dollar which the leading countries were unable to stem despite further concerted interventions. International speculation was stimulated by unfavorable polls regarding the French referendum on the Treaty of Maastricht scheduled for September 20th. That date had formed a point of convergence for expectations of a realignment in the EMS, whose negative repercussions affected the lira in particular. On August 28th, the lira's exchange rate against the Deutsche mark hit the lower limit of the fluctuation band (765.4): the Bank of Italy and the Bundesbank were obliged to intervene in the exchange market and the official credit lines were activated.

On September 4th the discount rate was raised by 1.75 points to 15 per cent, and the rate on fixed-term advances was raised to 16.5 per cent. However, the Italian monetary authorities were aware that, with expectations of an imminent devaluation gaining in strength, changes to Italian interest rates alone would be ineffective unless concerted action was taken by all the ERM countries. More drastic measures, setting interest rates at the astronomical levels needed to compensate expectations of an imminent devaluation, would have been judged unsustainable in an economy whose burgeoning public debt was represented largely by short-term or short-term-linked securities. [18] But even leaving aside the public debt constraints on monetary policy, the level of interest rates deemed necessary to offset the expected devaluation would have been so high that it would per se have been seen as a symptom of crisis and, as such, have had perverse effects on expectations.

Around the end of August, the Italian authorities' main objective was to reach a concerted solution and advocate a revaluation of the Deutsche mark vis-à-vis all the ERM currencies (while not excluding a larger devaluation for the lira) and the simultaneous lowering of German interest rates. There was a clear perception that a devaluation of the lira alone would not have put an end to the crisis within the EMS. [19]

At the meeting of the Monetary Committee on August 28th the difficulty of defining a concerted solution became manifest: the meeting ended with a joint communiqué reaffirming the general desire to keep exchange rates stable. Neither did the EEC Finance Ministers meeting of 5 September in Bath lead to agreement. The positions of the different countries remained irreconcilable, with the result that no official measures were taken. This manifest inability to come up with a coordinated solution intensified speculation against the lira. When the Bundesbank's interventions in support of the lira reached, between September 7th and 11th, amounts that the German central bank considered as having a substantial effect on the money supply, it had to decide whether or not to continue helping out the Italian currency. At this point the Bundesbank was able to fall back on an agreement with the German government more than ten years previously that exempted it, in exceptional circumstances, from its internationally fixed obligations to intervene.

This was the background against which, on Saturday September 12th, Italy and Germany proposed to their European partners modifying the EMS central rates as follows: revaluation of the Deutsche mark by 3.5 per cent vis-à-vis all currencies and simultaneous devaluation of the lira by the same amount; reduction of German interest rates commensurate with the extent of the Deutsche mark's overall appreciation. The proposal was rejected by the other countries; the French authorities, in particular, feared that a depreciation of the franc would have negative repercussions on the now imminent Treaty referendum, while the British authorities saw no reason to alter the central rate of sterling. In the end, the initiative was merely a 7 per cent devaluation of the lira and a very minor reduction of German official rates. The inadequacy of these measures became abundantly clear in the days following the realignment of 12 September. On September 16th, the pound abandoned the ERM and the peseta devalued by 5 per cent; on September 17th, Italy suspended official intervention in the foreign exchange market. Pressure within the EMS continued unabated, even after the French referendum marginally sanctioned the Maastricht Treaty, affecting not only the lira but numerous other currencies including the French franc. Towards the end of September, the Deutsche mark was quoted at 840 against the lira, a depreciation of 11 per cent compared with the end of May. Short-term interest rates had climbed back to around 17 per cent[20].

Symptoms Of Financial Crisis

Over the four months between June and September 1992 the Italian balance of payments was visibly affected by the change in expectations. Capital movements registered substantial variations in comparison with trends over previous years. Inflows of foreign capital, though continuing, dwindled rapidly; in September, movements of bank capital turned around to record substantial outflows, for the first time since 1985. Outflows of Italian capital continued to be strong, reflecting both a trend to portfolio diversification made possible by the liberalization of foreign financial transactions and expectations of a realignment of EMS central rates. As the Bank of Italy's *Economic Bulletin* of February 1993 emphasized, Italian banks did not directly take up positions against the lira; the outflows of bank capital were more the result of the demand for lira by foreign operators, presumably for speculative reasons, which the Italian banks found it convenient to satisfy on account of the high lending rates that the international interbank market enabled them to apply.

The devaluation of the lira and its suspension from the ERM had negative repercussions on the financial markets. Both Italian and foreign operators were distrustful of lira-denominated financial instruments. Several factors combined to overcome the crisis, which was particularly acute from the time the lira began to float until the end of October 1992. The Government's declared intention, despite the uncertain political situation, was to give priority to tackling the disequilibria in public finances. The 1993 budget, outlined in the Government's Forecasting and Planning Report at the end of September 1992, envisaged drastically reducing the borrowing requirement by 93 trillion lira, or 6 per cent of GDP. By carefully graduating the lowering of interest rates from the extreme crisis levels, monetary policy aimed to attenuate expectations of inflation, which were fostered by the absence of exchange rate constraints as well as by the very extent of the lira's depreciation.[21] Market intervention and measures by the authorities to reassure the markets helped to overcome the difficulties; the solidity and efficiency of the money market and of the secondary market in government securities also played an important role.

The market for government securities reacted to the climate of uncertainty with a contraction in demand and a shift towards the shorter term, while the chances of attracting funds through net issues of medium and long-term paper virtually disappeared. Given the Treasury's high borrowing requirement, the supply of securities at issue had to adapt to investors preferences. In the two months of September and October 1992, the Treasury's borrowing requirement was financed exclusively through virtually equal volumes of net short-term issues and creation of monetary base. The Bank of Italy, however, continued to keep the overall creation of monetary base under tight control through open market repurchase agreements. In the second half of the year, monetary base grew at an annual rate of 3 per cent.

The Treasury nonetheless encountered difficulties in its issues of short-term paper. As with the Treasury bill auction at the end of August, demand was weak at the end of September: while just exceeding the supply of three-month and six-month bills, it did not cover the 12-month bills on offer and the Bank of Italy took up a total of 1 trillion lira. Interest rates continued to rise and the six-month rate touched 19 per cent. The climate of uncertainty was also visible in the greater-than-usual dispersion of rates at Italy's competitive bid T-bill auctions.[22]

Meanwhile, the Bank of Italy intervened repeatedly on the secondary market for government securities, with a view less to engineering appropriate rates than to limiting the wide fluctuations in the prices of government paper ensuring orderly trading.[23] In September and October, the Bank's net purchases of government paper on the secondary market, net of repos, exceeded 9 trillion lira, almost all in fixed rate securities; the increase in the Bank of Italy's portfolios of government paper was of more than 23 trillion lira in the five months between June and October (19.6 trillion lira of fixed rate bonds).

Between the end of May and mid-September, the price of Treasury bonds had fallen significantly; it rallied briefly but collapsed at the beginning of October. On October 6th, the Treasury bond index bottomed out at around 92, a loss of 10 points since the end of May, and on the same day the yield on ten-year Treasury bonds reached 13 per cent. Prices of Treasury credit certificates behaved similarly (Figure 7), despite the fact that they are indexed to short-term rates and therefore less susceptible, in principle, to variations in the latter. It has been estimated that about 50 per cent of the overall fluctuation in the prices of Treasury credit certificates in this period was attributable to factors other than the lag in adjusting coupon rates to short-term rates. One of the major factors was presumably issuer risk, which was also shown as increasing by other indicators of the specific risk attaching to Italian Treasury issues in foreign currency (Figure 8).

Figure 8
Yield Differentials Between Italian Treasury Issues
And Those Of Other Official Issuers

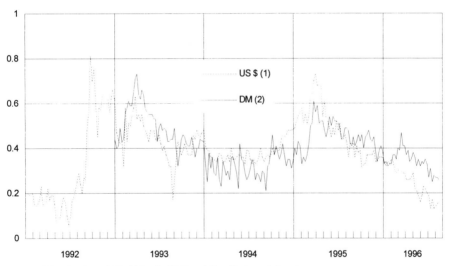

(1) Republic of Italy and World Bank; (2) Republic of Italy and Bund.

The solidity and efficiency achieved by the secondary market for government securities guaranteed the continuation of trading at times of extreme turbulence. This result was helped by the fact that the authorities proceeded with the process of reform and modernization of the Italian financial market even during such an acute crisis as that under examination. On September 11th, trading in 10-year Treasury bonds was launched on the Italian Futures Market (MIF). In the same month, trading in the screen-based market recorded fairly high daily volumes (on average 4-6 trillion per day), despite a widening bid-offer spread: for September the latter averaged 124 basis points for Treasury bonds and 158 basis points for credit certificates, compared with averages of only 6 and 8 basis points respectively between January and May.

The troubles that afflicted the government securities market were also fueled
by rumors of impending extraordinary measures affecting bonds in circulation. Bank
deposits also showed signs of instability with unusually heavy withdrawals. In
contrast, the circulation of banknotes recorded anomalous growth (Figure 9). Given
these circumstances, Governor Ciampi wrote a letter on September 30th to the
chairmen of the leading 30 Italian banks in which he not only denied the rumors
regarding extraordinary measures affecting securities or deposits, but also invited the
banks to "offer information and reassurance to their customers."[24]

Figure 9
Currency In Circulation [1]

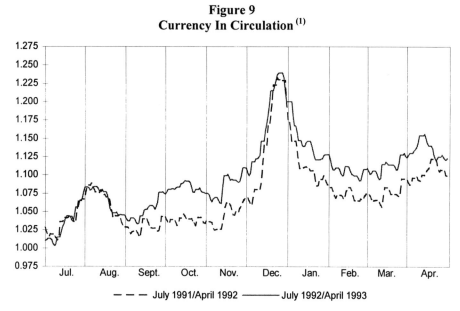

[1] Ratio to average stock for March-June.

From mid-October the monetary and financial situation began to show signs
of improving, but the tensions only really started to ease at the end of the month. The
Government's public finance interventions and the central bank's actions were crucial.
On October 22nd, Parliament approved the enabling Act submitted in July, which
delegated the Government to rationalize and review regulations aimed at curbing the
expansion of public spending in the medium term concerning health, public
employment, social security and the financing of local authorities. As already noted,
the Bank of Italy brought interest rates down cautiously and gradually, waiting until
October 23rd before first lowering the discount rate from 15 to 14 per cent. This
easing of conditions was nonetheless flanked by careful monitoring of the growth of

bank lending in lira, including guidelines for it until March 1993. The purpose of monitoring was principally anti-inflationary, to avoid any acceleration in lending that, at a time of falling interest rates, might offer scope to price increases in excess of the impact effect of devaluation. The central bank's prudent approach was aimed at reconciling the need not to exacerbate the already unfavorable cyclical conditions - to prevent devaluation from ratcheting up the rate of inflation. Although the effect of depreciation on prices would tend to be one-off a rise in the price level, by contracting real disposable income in the immediate term, it would heighten the risk that firms and wage-earners might try to pass on their loss of purchasing power, with a permanent impact on inflation -- particularly if the whole process were fueled by a faster pace of money creation and lending. The agreement of July 1992, which finally abolished the "scala mobile" wage indexation mechanism and guaranteed wage moderation for a year, was decisive in damping expectations of inflation and in containing it.

This caution in lowering interest rates was flanked by extreme downward stickiness of yields at the longer end of the market. The Bank of Italy's easing of conditions in the money market encountered resistance as regards longer-term yields. A further reduction of official rates by 1 percentage point on November 12th pushed very short-term interbank rates downwards but had little effect on longer-term yields, which remained where they had been. At the end of November, the differential between three-month interbank and overnight rates was 2 percentage points, and it remained above 1 point until the second ten days of December. The authorities interpreted these factors as reflecting uncertainty concerning the future of the lira and fears of a resurgence of inflation. It was only after the discount rate was lowered to 12 per cent on December 22nd, following Parliamentary approval of the 1993 Finance Law, that the interest rate differential returned to its usual levels. The climate of uncertainty was reflected strongly in longer-term yields. In October 1992, the 1 year-maturity rate 9 years forward showed a sharp increase, reaching the level of 13 per cent at the beginning of that month; the corresponding differential vis-à-vis the Deutsche mark almost reached 6 per cent. Long-term forward rates stood above the 12 per cent level till the beginning of March 1993 (Figure 10).

Figure 10
Long-Term Forward Rates In Italy And In Germany

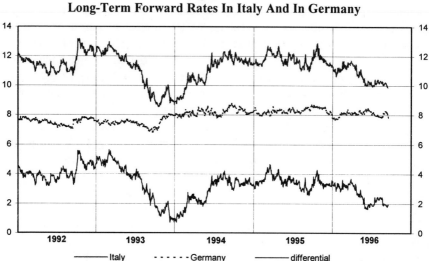

Yields to maturity on 10-year BTP were in January still around 1 percentage point above those of May 1992 (of about 12.5 per cent). It was only in the late spring of 1993 that long-term yields fell below the levels observed before June 1992, thanks also to the continued easing of inflation. In May 1993 inflation fell to 4.4 per cent, more than half a percentage point less than a year earlier. Interest rates continued to fall in the following months and the long-term differential between Italian and German rates narrowed to 2.5 percentage points in mid-May 1994. Nonetheless in June the spread vis-à-vis Bunds began to widen again: expectations of inflation showed clear signs of increasing, while aggregate demand was accelerating. To combat inflationary pressures, the Bank of Italy began to tighten monetary conditions already in mid-1994, raising the rate on repos. This was the start of the central bank's anti-inflationary strategy that led to the increases in the official rates of August 1994 and of February and May 1995.

The Episode Of February-March 1995

The crisis that struck the Italian financial and foreign exchange market early in 1995 was relatively short but extremely sharp. Here again, events originating elsewhere impacted on Italian markets already weakened by persistent financial imbalance, and by a protracted political crisis that raised doubts as to the ability of government to lead the country towards stability.

The foreign event forming the backdrop to this new Italian crisis was the financial turmoil that developed in Mexico towards the end of 1994. Statements by many observers, economists and the IMF itself cited the risk of a domino effect, with capital outflows from countries with large public debts, whether domestically or externally held. The flight to strong currencies resulted in a steep depreciation of the dollar and a parallel appreciation of the yen and the Deutsche mark. Intervention by the IMF, the U.S. and other industrial countries together with corrective action by the Mexican government succeeded relatively quickly in restoring more orderly market conditions, preventing the feared chain reaction.

The shock wave provoked by the Mexican crisis and the weakness of the dollar caught Italy at a time of political difficulty. A new government was being formed, but its parliamentary majority was considered to be too weak and too heterogeneous, in the prevailing assessment of the markets, undermining its ability to proceed with public finance adjustment. As a consequence, the expectation was for increased Treasury resort to the financial markets to cover a rising borrowing requirement and roll over the paper maturing in the first half of the year, whose volume was thought to be so large as to give rise to fears of default. Actually, as the Bank of Italy's *Economic Bulletin* indicated, the amounts maturing were not unusually large for the Italian market, either on an average annual basis or in relation to GDP.[25] But such considerations had little influence on these Cassandras, whose analyses were poorly documented to say the least.

The sequence of events was not dissimilar to that experienced in the summer of 1992 or in the course of other, less severe crises. There was an increase in capital outflows, taking the form both of Italian investment abroad and foreign disinvestment in Italy, especially in government securities. In the first quarter of the year the outflow totaled some 10 trillion lira (approximately US$6 billion). Rates on 10 year Treasury bonds rose to nearly 14 per cent, the spread vis-à-vis Bunds widening to a maximum of 658 basis points (Figure 11). These factors caused strong pressures on the lira, which depreciated rapidly, especially vis-à-vis the Deutsche mark whose quotation rose from 1,048 lira at the beginning of the year to 1,272 on March 17th, a loss of 18 per cent. In the same period, the dollar climbed from 1,710 to 1,764, a depreciation of 3 per cent for the lira; the loss in the lira's effective exchange rate was 15 per cent. No longer subject to the constraints of the ERM, the Bank of Italy made only modest foreign exchange market interventions and only in particularly disorderly market conditions. In any case the interventions did attain the desired effect, namely to restore more orderly conditions. As part of the Bank of Italy's anti-inflationary drive launched in mid-1994, bank liquidity and money market conditions were kept firmly under control. Following an increase in the official discount rate from 7.50 to 8.25 per cent and in that on advances from 8.50 to 9.75 per cent at the end of February, money market rates rose. The central bank provided refinancing through repos at rates that rose progressively from about 8.50 per cent at the beginning of February to around 10.75 per cent in March and April.

Figure 11
Interest Rate Differentials With Germany

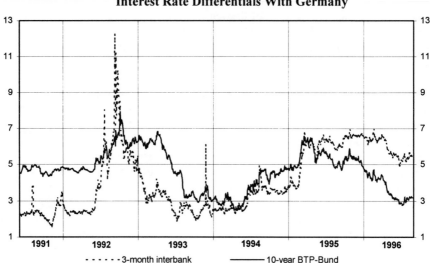

------- 3-month interbank   ———— 10-year BTP-Bund

Immediately upon its formation, the new Government approved a package of fiscal measures designed to bring the borrowing requirement for 1995 back under the target figure of 130 trillion lira, or 7.4 per cent of GDP (compared with 9.5 per cent in 1994); the target would in fact be achieved. Also, a plan for the reform of the public pension system was drafted which, though considered not entirely satisfactory by many observers, represented a significant turning point and a step in the right direction. The stringency of monetary policy, the enactment of the budget package and the orderly functioning of the primary and secondary markets in government securities all helped to overcome the acute phase of the crisis. In April the lira initiated a recovery on the foreign exchange markets that would proceed, albeit with frequent oscillations, for the rest of the year and into 1996 (Figure 12). By March of this year, the effective exchange rate had returned to the levels registered at the start of 1995, before the crisis. At the same time long-term rates declined and the spread between BTPs and Bunds narrowed, by March 1996, to just over 4 percentage points. The lira continued to strengthen in the months that followed, climbing back in August to the levels of two years earlier, and long-term rates continued their downward course, falling almost to 9 per cent, while the differential vis-à-vis the mark diminished to about 3 points.

Figure 12
Nominal Effective Exchange Rate Of The Lira
(monthly data; base 1979=100)

The underlying factor was a degree of monetary restriction that, after a further tightening in May 1995 by another increase in the official rates, was kept constant over the subsequent months in order to counter a resurgence of inflation and of inflationary expectations, fueled by the depreciation of the lira and even by the Government's fiscal package, which included increases in VAT rates, with fears of a cost-price spiral. The inflation rate peaked towards the end of 1995 at nearly 6 per cent; it then began to come down, albeit slowly, falling to about 3.5 per cent in the summer of 1996.

Serious though it was, the Italian foreign exchange crisis of 1995 is simply not comparable to that of Mexico either in dimension or in characteristics. Nevertheless, at the time there was no lack of analyses from commentators and economists in which the two experiences were linked.

The Italian crisis was limited in duration and, on the whole, circumscribed to the foreign exchange market. The government securities market, though subjected to strong pressures, showed no signs of lack of confidence on the part of investors, as the good performance of demand at Treasury auctions attests. The crisis was successfully defused thanks to the prompt adoption of fiscal and monetary measures. Underlying the situation were the structural factors that make the Italian economy robust enough to withstand financial shocks.

At the time of the 1995 crisis Italy had already achieved a stable balance-of-payments surplus on current account. The uninterrupted series of deficits recorded from 1987 to 1992 had been transformed into a very sizable surplus that swiftly cut the country's net external debt from 11 per cent of GDP in 1992 to 5 per cent in 1995. This radical reversal of Italy's external accounts was achieved thanks to the flexibility of Italian manufacturing, which quickly exploited the opportunities offered by depreciation. Between 1993 and 1995 Italian exports grew at an average annual rate of 8.5 per cent, compared with an increase in world trade of 7 per cent. A second factor in the soundness of the economy is the high rate of household financial saving, which has enabled the country to fund its large budget deficits and, since 1993, also produced net outward investment. As was noted by Governor Antonio Fazio (1994), the "financial deepening" of the Italian economy -- that is, the ratio of total financial assets to real wealth -- is lower in Italy than in the other leading industrial countries (Table 3). Despite a rise in the share held abroad in recent years, the bulk of Italy's public debt is held by resident households. The financial structure is also characterized, by international standards, by low gross household liabilities. The composition of firms' liabilities, while reflecting a certain backwardness of the financial system (above all of the private capital markets), also helps to attenuate the impact of financial turmoil on the private sector economy.[26]

Table 3
Gross Financial Assets As A Ratio To Real Wealth

	1965	1978	1989	1991	1993	1994
Italy	0.85	1.04	0.87	0.89	0.96	0.97
France	1.24	0.83	1.16	1.06	1.28	1.21
Germany [1]	0.92	0.89	1.01	1.12	1.16	1.16
U.K.	1.50	1.11	1.68	1.82	2.45	2.51
US	1.28	0.99	1.27	1.45	1.64	1.65
Japan	0.81	1.02	1.10	1.06	1.13	1.18

Source: Bianco and Massaro (1996).
[1] Through 1989, western Länder only.

CONCLUSIONS

The crises of 1992 and 1995 offer lessons that go well beyond our specific Italian experience, bearing above all on the role of the markets in relation to that of the authorities in determining a nation's economic policy strategy, and also on the effectiveness of the traditional instruments of direct and indirect intervention and on the extent and the procedures of international cooperation.

The liberalization of international trading and the globalization of markets place limits on national sovereignty in setting and implementing economic policy.

The more stringent the limits, the smaller a country is and the greater its degree of external openness. In this regard, some commentators have alluded to the "end of geography" in connection with the ability of the world market to punish economic policy errors swiftly.[27] Decisive factors in the market's assessment of a country's general reliability are its history, the prospects for inflation control, financial equilibrium (itself largely dependent on the state of the public finances), and its net position with the rest of the world. It is as if the global market had constructed a theoretical "model" or "benchmark" country against which to evaluate real countries. Perceived or merely expected divergence from the "benchmark" prompts international disinvestment, the taking of adverse positions, which drives down securities prices, depreciates the currency and tends to perpetuate long-term interest rate differentials, which can be described as the "premium" for country risk. When several adverse factors coincide, the course of events can turn into a financial and/or foreign exchange crisis.

In the short-run, whether such an assessment is right or wrong may be practically irrelevant. If the market's beliefs and reactions are sufficiently firm and widely held, they will tend to be self-fulfilling. The response of the authorities must rely on actions that can modify the beliefs, curb the reactions and guide expectations. A country with credibility can sustain the speculative pressure and weather its impact with just a mix of financial interventions and a temporary tightening of the monetary policy stance. A country that lacks credibility will have to earn it through appropriate monetary and fiscal policy measures for the medium-term.

The summer of 1992 represented the first time that Italy managed and overcame a foreign exchange crisis without resort to direct exchange or credit controls. Presumably such controls would only have aggravated the situation by feeding the market's belief that the authorities were incapable of achieving a stable equilibrium for the country in line with its EU partners. Instead, the irreversibility of the decision for complete liberalization was confirmed, which the market appreciated. That year, vigorous action towards the structural adjustment of the public finances was begun.

A model of price stability and financial equilibrium has been enshrined in the Treaty of Maastricht, which makes compliance with a set of "convergence criteria" a requisite for EU member countries' participation in the final stage of monetary union, with the adoption of the single currency.

For Italy in particular, owing to the greater divergence of the initial conditions, the consistency of economic policy measures with the Maastricht objectives has become the acid test for the confidence the markets are disposed to concede. In these circumstances national sovereignty is exercised in the choice of the ways and means for achieving given objectives rather than in deciding the objectives themselves. The financial and foreign exchange crises recounted in this paper occurred in conjunction with political situations in which the prevailing opinion among market operators was that Italy would fail to adopt a lasting policy of public financial readjustment and financial and price stability. Compliance with the Maastricht criteria is no more than a benchmark. Italy must continue its financial adjustment regardless; and it is to the country's progress on this course that the market has directed and will direct its scrutiny.

The globalization of the market would have been impossible without the extraordinary development of information technology. Globalization and the development of the financial and investment industry have influenced one another in an upward-spiraling process. Competition in the financial services industry has refined the techniques of portfolio management, risk control and hedging, but it has also spawned pressures for better performance, which may lead to risk-taking and which heighten the importance of expectations in decision-making.[28] The speed with which information circulates amplifies the effect of certain events on securities prices and exchange rates by concentrating a given type of market behavior in a brief period. Technical market analysis outweighs the economic fundamentals, at least in the very short- and the short-term; the "chartists" have the upper hand. Nor are we totally free of operators who, setting professional ethics aside, float untrue rumors that may endure and affect the market only transiently, but still long enough to generate price fluctuations that are profitable for those ready to exploit them.

The consequence has been more volatile securities and foreign exchange markets. This means opportunities for profit for large-scale investors, bank and corporate treasury managers; but it also entails comparable risks of loss, which need to be evaluated and controlled by supervisors and markets participants working together. All of us, from central bankers to dealers in the markets for goods, services and capital, have to learn to live with this heightened volatility. The widening of the fluctuation bands for ERM currencies from 2.25 to 15 per cent in August 1993 should be viewed in this framework.[29] The smallness of official reserves by comparison with the flow of funds mobilized by the international markets has convinced the central banks of the EU member countries of the need to ensure sufficient flexibility of exchange rates. In the end, an overstrict constraint prompts speculation and may, paradoxically, itself be the cause of tensions and increased volatility of exchange rates and interest rates. The development of instruments for hedging interest rate and exchange risk through the derivatives markets is a further manifestation of the drive for protection against unpredictable and uncontrollable risks.

Market globalization poses new challenges for international cooperation. As it is beyond the scope of these concluding observations to treat such a complex theme, we will offer only a few brief considerations.[30]

International cooperation, both worldwide (with the International Monetary Fund as the key institution) and regional (the most advanced instance now being the European Union) must focus on the design and execution of economic policies aimed at medium-term stability rather than on how to raise and use financial resources, however necessary, to deal with foreign exchange and financial crises. Here too, preventing crises is far more effective than defusing them once they have broken out.[31]

In especially severe disturbances, swift and correct analysis of the causes is crucial. If the crisis is rooted in economic fundamentals, the response cannot be solely financial. Exchange market interventions will never succeed in maintaining an unrealistic exchange rate; at most they may prevent cases of wild disorder. Only new monetary and fiscal policies embodying the credible pursuit of medium-term equilibrium can restore domestic and international investors' confidence in a currency. However, unforeseen events, including non-economic events, may trigger speculative attacks against the currency of a country whose economic fundamentals are basically sound. In such cases, resort to support interventions, possibly massive ones, can be effective; preferably, they should be coordinated internationally. Experience confirms the effectiveness of this approach.

In today's intercommunicating and rapidly changing world, economic policy makers cannot rely on prepackaged recipes. What is required, rather, is analytical continuity in order to pick up changes as they occur and adjust responses promptly.

APPENDIX 1

THE INFLUENCE OF THE US DOLLAR ON THE LIRA WITHIN THE ERM BAND

As pointed out in the section titled "The International Context," movements in the dollar seem to have placed added pressures on the grid of central rates within the ERM, on the lira in particular. Two issues are relevant in this context. First, it is necessary to verify whether the asymmetric influence of the US dollar on European cross rates was indeed relevant. Second, it is necessary, from a theoretical viewpoint, to point out the causes of this asymmetry (if empirically relevant).[32] In this Appendix we tackle the first issue, i.e. the problem of assessing the quantitative relevance of autonomous shocks to the dollar on the ERM grid.

The main difficulty in the empirical analysis is how to identify dollar shocks. For example, the analysis cannot exclusively rely on the observed link between movements in the Deutsche mark/dollar and those in the lira/Deutsche mark rate: the former rate, indeed, is influenced also by shocks to the Deutsche mark itself (for example, by policy changes in Germany). The observed correlation between the bilateral rates might be the result of a "truism": if the Deutsche mark is strong, it is strong vis-à-vis all currencies.

One way to overcome the identification problem is to make reference to "exogenous" information, such as political or economic news, and tracing its effects on exchange rates. Another route is to make use of an appropriate measure of the global "value" of the dollar, such as the effective exchange rate (Figure A1).[33]

Figure A1
The Trade-Weighted Effective Exchange Rate Of The Dollar
(1991=1)

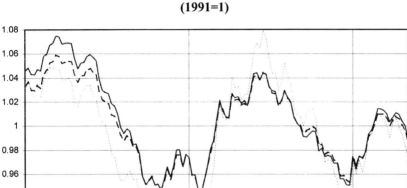

As suggested by Giavazzi and Giovannini (1989), the trade-weighted effective exchange rate might not be the appropriate one for the issue under investigation; a "financial" effective exchange rate, computed in relation to the importance of the different currencies in international financial markets, might be more suitable.[34] In this appendix, we construct two measures of the "financial" effective exchange rate of the dollar in the period January 1990-May 1992. They are calculated using two sets of weights: (a) the currency breakdown of cross border deposits of BIS reporting banks; (b) the transactions that takes place on average in each day between the US dollar and the other main currencies (Table A1 and Figure A2).

Table A1
Currency Weights In The "Financial" Effective Exchange Rate Of The Dollar

Currency	Weights [(1)]	Weights [(2)]
DM	0.34	0.37
YEN	0.32	0.30
SWF	0.12	0.10
£	0.10	0.15
CA$	n.a.	0.05
FFR	0.08	0.04
Lira	0.04	n.a.

[(1)] Calculated on the basis of the currency breakdown of cross border deposits of BIS reporting banks (1989-1992).
[(2)] Calculated on the basis of the 1992 average daily transactions on foreign exchange markets between the US dollar and the currencies reported in the table.

Figure A2
The "Financial" Effective Exchange Rate Of The Dollar
(1991=1)

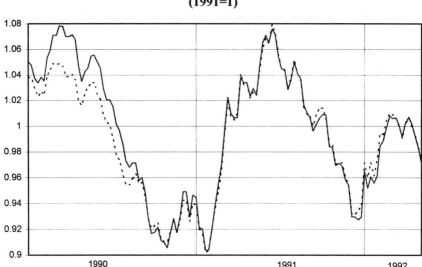

(1) The weights are those reported in the first column of table A1.

To identify dollar shocks we follow also a second methodology: it is assumed that they are identified by the first principal component of the log-changes of the price of the dollar in terms of the currencies indicated in Table A1. The first principal component (the common factor underlying the changes in the relative price of the dollar) explains more than 80 per cent of the total variance of the sample (Table A2).

Table A2
Principal Component Analysis Of The Log-Changes
Of The Bilateral Dollar Exchange Rate

First principal component	Second principal Component	Third principal component	Rest
84.2%	8.6%	2.8%	4.6%

Given the two measures for dollar shocks, we investigate their separate influence on the position of the lira within the ERM band through regression analysis. To this aim, we control for other economic variables which might be relevant in affecting the lira's position: Italian and German short-term (spot/next) interest rates (i(lira) and i(DM), respectively) and foreign exchange interventions (frxint). In Tables A3-4 we present 2 set of regressions estimated over the period January 1990-May 1992, whose dependent variable is the position of the lira within the ERM band (weekly average). The regressions shown in Table A3 have as independent variables, besides interest rates and forex interventions, the log "financial" effective exchange rate of the dollar and its changes; the regressions in Table A4 use the first principal component of the log-changes in the bilateral dollar exchange rate to identify dollar shocks.

Table A3
Factors Affecting The Lira's Position Within The ERM Band [1]

Regressors	General model (OLS) (1)	Preferred model (OLS) (2)	Instrumental variable estimation (3)
(1) i(lira)[-1]	0.0261 (3.440)	0.0253 (5.077)	0.0261 (3.998)
(2) i(DM)[-1]	-0.0388 (-2.303)	-0.0253 (-5.073)	-0.0261 (-3.998)
(3) Δi(lira)	0.0395 (3.790)	0.0379 (4.297)	0.0379 (4.289)
(4) Δi(DM)	-0.0357 (-1.692)	-0.0379 (-4.297)	-0.0379 (-4.288)
(5) log($)[-1]	0.208 (0.705)	-	-
(6) Δlog($)	2.579 (3.547)	2.470 (3.583)	2.405 (2.775)
(7) frxint	0.536 (6.370)	0.522 (7.050)	0.538 (2.938)
(8) d.v.[-1]	0.880 (24.407)	0.908 (55.104)	0.906 (40.024)
(9) cost.	0.124 (0.942)	-	-
stdreg	0.0845	0.0836	0.0837
mean dep.var	0.533	0.533	0.533
n.obs	124	124	124

[1] Dollar shocks are identified by the "financial" effective rate (weights are in column 1 of Table A.1). Estimation period: January 1990-May 1992. Data: weekly averages of daily observations. A [-1] indicates that the corresponding variable is lagged once. The variable dv refers to the lagged dependent variable.

Table A4
Factors Affecting The Lira's Position Within The ERM Band [1]

Regressors	General model (OLS) (4)	Preferred model (OLS) (5)	Instrumental variable estimation (6)
(1) i(lira)[-1]	0.0282 (3.769)	0.0255 (5.082)	0.0243 (4.122)
(2) i(DM)[-1]	-0.0389 (-2.356)	-0.0255 (5.082)	-0.0244 (-4.122)
(3) Δi(lira)	0.0412 (3.952)	0.0375 (4.234)	0.0374 (4.208)
(4) Δi(DM)	-0.0346 (-1.644)	-0.0375 (-4.234)	-0.0374 (-4.208)
(6) first pr.com.	0.314 (3.384)	0.314 (3.436)	0.3365 (3.196)
(7) frxint	0.521 (6.128)	0.524 (7.028)	0.466 (3.246)
(8) d.v.[-1]	0.902 (41.416)	0.906 (54.983)	0.912 (45.613)
(9) cost.	0.868 (0.710)	-	-
stdreg	0.0846	0.0839	0.0843
mean dep.var	0.533	0.533	0.533
n.obs	124	124	124

[1] Dollar shocks identified by the first principal component of dollar log-changes. See note to Table A3.

The results show that there is indeed a statistically significant effect of the dollar shocks on the position of the lira within the band (see rows 6 in the both tables). As expected, the sign of the coefficients indicates that when the dollar appreciates (a positive shocks), the lira tends to be stronger within the band and vice-versa.[35] Concerning regressions in Table A3, it should be noted that the results would not change significantly should the second set of weights in Table A1 be used in calculating the effective dollar rate.

Concerning the economic factors which underlay the observed asymmetry, they are presumably linked to international portfolio choices, which determine a positive covariation between shocks to the demand for dollars and shocks to the demand for lira (relative to the demand for Deutsche mark). Indeed, Giavazzi and Giovannini, op. cit., use different types of portfolio models to identify those underlying economic factors which are able to reproduce, in a theoretical framework, that regularity. They conclude that transaction costs affecting differently the various currencies might be at the origin of the asymmetry.[36]

APPENDIX 2

IMPLICIT FORWARD EXCHANGE RATES AND PROBABILITIES OF A LIRA DEVALUATION

One question that was raised in the aftermath of the 1992 crisis was whether the events of the summer (the result of the Danish referendum against the Treaty, in particular) caused the reversal of otherwise favorable expectations or whether they strengthened expectations of a devaluation already rooted in market participants' behavior.

An answer to this question, even only tentative, requires the quantification of expectations. The latter can be measured directly through market surveys or indirectly, by means of observed asset prices and through assumptions concerning the formation of expectations. In this appendix, we follow the indirect method: we estimate lira/Deutsche mark forward exchange rates and, assuming that forward rates equal expected rates (absence of risk premia), we derive probabilities of a lira devaluation (conditional on a measure of the expected change in the exchange rate).[37] The implicit forward lira/Deutsche mark exchange rates can be estimated from the 'closed' interest rate parity condition:

(A.1) $[1+i(t,T)]/[1+i^*(t,T+1)]=F(t,T)/S(t)$

where $i(t,T)$ is the spot interest rate on a lira-denominated asset at time t with maturity T, $i^*(t,T)$ is the interest rate on a perfectly equivalent instrument unless the currency of denomination (assumed to be the Deutsche mark), $S(t)$ is the lira/Deutsche mark spot exchange rate and $F(t,T)$ is the implicit forward rates at expiration date T. If it is assumed that the implicit forward exchange rate equals the future expected rate, relation (A.1) takes the form of the "open" condition which implies, in addition to perfect asset substitutability, the absence of risk premia (for example, the risk related to the uncertainty surrounding the expectation itself). In Figure A3 we report, together with the upper and lower fluctuation limits of the lira vis-à-vis the Deutsche mark, the estimated implicit forward rates for expirations dates 3, 6 and 12 months (forw3m, forw6m and forw12m, respectively) at the end of each week over the period January 1991-mid September 1992. The Figure shows that since mid-November 1991 the 12 month forward exchange rate stood above the 765.4 upper limit. At the beginning of June 1992, after the Danish referendum, also the 6 months forward rate passed that limit; it was followed one month later by the 3 month forward rate.

Figure A3
The Lira/Deutsche mark Implicit Forward Exchange Rates

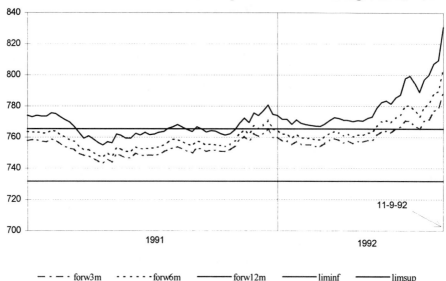

— · — · forw3m   · · · · · · forw6m   ———— forw12m   ———— liminf   ———— limsup

(1) The interest rates from which the implicit forward exchange rates are obtained are rates on lira and Deutsche mark eurodeposits of 3,6,12-month maturity. The fluctuations limits of the lira vis-á-vis the Deutsche mark (variables liminf and limsup) are 731.57 and 765.4 lira.

Conditional on the open parity, it is possible to derive for the 3,6, and 12 month horizons the probability of a devaluation of the lira as a function of the expected change in the exchange rate s. It can be shown, in particular, that the probability of a devaluation at time t within T is given by:[38]

(A.2) $p(t,T) = [F(t,T)/S(t)-1]/s.$

Figure A4 shows the probabilities computed applying (A.2) and assuming an expected depreciation of the lira of 7 per cent, while Figure A5 presents the same probabilities when assuming an expected depreciation of 11 per cent.[39] Even though the probabilities are sensitive to the hypothesis concerning the expected change in the exchange rate, we think that a reasonable assessment of the evidence would quantify the probability over the 12 month horizon (prob12m) in the 20-30 per cent range; over shorter time horizons the probability range appears lower (0-10 per cent for the 3 month horizon; 10-20 per cent over the 6 month horizon - prob3m and prob6m, respectively). In addition, the estimates indicate that starting from the beginning of June 1992 the probabilities on all time horizons significantly rose; the increase was higher for the 6 month horizon in the period from June 1992 to the beginning of August. In the first two weeks of September the increase was particularly steep for the 3 month horizon.

Figure A4
Estimated Probabilities Of A Devaluation Of The Lira
(expected depreciation=7 per cent)

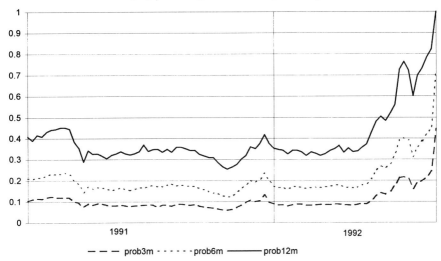

Figure A5
Estimated Probabilities Of A Devaluation Of The Lira
(expected depreciation=11 per cent)

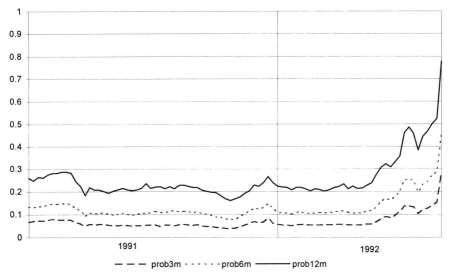

These results seem to indicate that expectations of a lira devaluation were relatively important before the events of the summer 1992, while a relatively high degree of uncertainty was surrounding the timing of the devaluation. The events of the summer 1992 acted mainly as catalyst factors of expectations around possible dates of a parity revision.

NOTES

[1] On the EMS crisis of 1992, see The Committee of Governors of the EEC Central Banks (1993); Temperton (1993); Steinherr (1994).

[2] The issue whether the events of the summer 1992 reversed favourable expectations on the parity grid or rather strengthened expectations of a devaluation already imbedded in market's behaviour is dealt with in Appendix 2.

[3] The weakening of the dollar caused by the expansionary US monetary policy placed added pressure on the grid of central rates of the EMS Exchange Rate Mechanism. The dollar lost ground most markedly against the Deutsche mark, which therefore tended to strengthen against the other ERM currencies. For an analysis of this asymmetry in the exchange rates of the leading currencies, which recurred also in more recent period of fluctuations of the lira, see Appendix 1.

[4] T. Padoa-Schioppa (1994) has defined the four elements of free trade in goods, complete freedom of capital movements, fixed exchange rates and autonomous monetary policies as an "inconsistent quartet." They can only be rendered consistent "by transforming the last element into monetary union or by eroding the first three in varying degrees." On the question of monetary coordination as part of European integration, see also Monticelli and Papi (1996).

[5] See Masera (1987); Giavazzi, Micossi and Miller (1988).

[6] Paolo Baffi, Governor of the Bank of Italy at the time of the negotiations over Italy's membership in the EMS, described the decision a decade later: "The concern [to avoid a systematic real appreciation of the lira to the detriment of exports] was what underlay the insistence on a broader band that would attenuate the dilemma between accepting recurrent periods in which the lira would be overvalued in real terms and requesting frequent adjustments of the central rate, each of which might cause friction and spur waves of speculation." Ministero Affari Esteri, IMI (1988).

[7] On the changes in the conduct of monetary policy in the eighties and nineties, see Passacantando (1996); Angeloni and Passacantando (1991).

[8] The contribution of the exchange rate to Italian disinflation in the eighties is studied in Gressani, Guiso and Visco (1988). For a more recent examination of the inflationary process in Italy and of the role of monetary policy in containing inflation, see Visco (1995).

[9] For example, such steps as the ratification of the Single European Act in 1986, opening the way to the single market and monetary union, the application to the lira of the narrow 2.25 per cent EMS fluctuation band and the complete liberalization of capital movements in 1990.

[10] See Visco, op. cit., for the most significant passages.

[11] "Report to the Senate Economic Planning and Budget Committee by Carlo Azeglio Ciampi, Governor of the Bank of Italy, on the consequences of recent events on the money and financial markets," Rome, 24 September 1992. See Banca d'Italia, Bollettino Economico, No. 19, October 1992.

[12] For an analysis of the macroeconomic function of constraints on capital movements, see Papadia and Rossi (1989).

[13] The increasing rigidity of the foreign exchange rules has been cited by some analysts as a decisive factor in precipitating the crisis of the EMS. De Grauwe (1994) argues that the broad fluctuation band enabled higher-inflation countries to offset a large part of the loss of competitiveness without having to adjust parities; and when central rate realignments proved unavoidable, at least they were limited in extent, permitting partial overlap between the old and new bands. This reduced the probability of discrete "jumps" in market prices. For another critique of the growing rigidity of the exchange system from 1987 onwards, see Masera (1994).

[14] The Basle-Nyborg agreements are described in Gavazzi, Micossi and Miller (1988).

[15] This was the last discount rate increase enacted by decree of the Treasury Minister. In February 1992 Parliament passed a law assigning to the Bank of Italy full powers to set official rates.

[16] The complex economic and political events of 1992-1994 were described in detail by the then Minister of the Treasury, Piero Barucci (1995).

[17] The Government's Forecasting and Planning Report for 1992 had indicated a target of just under 130 trillion lira for the annual borrowing requirement. The Treasury Minister's report to Parliament in March revised the forecast upwards to 150-160 trillion lira, in view of the downward revision of the forecast rate of GDP growth and a sizable upwards revision of estimates for interest rate payments. In mid-year the borrowing requirement was again revised upwards to around 180 trillion lira. The measures outlined by the Government were designed to bring the 1992 budget deficit back within the limit of 150 trillion lira.

[18] In the early nineties short-term and indexed government securities (Treasury Bills and credit certificates) still accounted for about 70 per cent of the total, compared with a maximum of almost 90 per cent in the mid-eighties. The reduction of inflation, the development of capital markets and new types of bonds and issue procedures made it possible to increase recourse to fixed-rate paper. Currently 50 per cent of outstanding government securities consists of bills and indexed certificates.

[19] Treasury Minister Barucci (op.cit.) recalls that on 26 August an unofficial meeting was held in Paris between the finance ministers and central bank governors of the four European Community G7 countries. The minutes of the meeting reveal the pressures on Germany to ease monetary policy in an unfavourable moment of the European cycle. The German representatives were nonetheless loath to yield, maintaining that the weakness of the dollar was chiefly the result of the United States' expansionary monetary policy and that German growth would in any case provide support for aggregate demand in the other European countries. Germany's priority was to curb inflationary pressures, which were fueled partly by high wage demands. The Italian delegation, consisting of Barucci and Governor Ciampi, argued for a concerted reply to the crisis in the System in terms of both exchange rates and interest rates. Ciampi put forward the argument, which he later took up officially, that the crisis was not only the fruit of the lira's difficulties, but directly involved the entire ERM. Ciampi affirmed: "Let nobody be deceived that he can save himself by acting alone; if we act in isolation, all today's weak currencies will end up like the Curiatii."

[20] Buiter, Corsetti and Pesenti (1996) use a theoretical model based on a "policy game" between one "central" country and several "peripheral" countries. They find that the solution originally suggested by Italy and Germany (moderate devaluation by a large number of countries) approximates the optimal solution of the model within a cooperative framework. Failing cooperation and policy coordination, however, the outcome is likely to be severe depreciation of a few currencies. The authors do, however, concede the possibility that "there existed no common realignment scheme that would have compensated for the common loss of anti-inflationary credibility."

[21] Freed of the intermediate target represented by the exchange rate, monetary policy focused on the monetary target in the broad definition of M2: "The aim of monetary policy will be to provide a stable frame of reference that will shape expectations and conduct so as to limit the direct impact of the devaluation on prices and prevent the rise in the cost of imports from triggering a wage/price spiral. With the exchange rate weakened as a means of exerting a direct restrictive effect, the money supply growth target takes on greater importance for liquidity management and interest rate policy in the short term." *Economic Bulletin*, October 1992.

[22] The increased dispersion of bid rates and the difficulties of financing the borrowing requirement led the Treasury to increase the spread used to determine the so-called stop-out yield from 1 to 1.5 percentage points. The stop-out yield allows for exclusion of bids placed for yields that are too high for market conditions; it is calculated by applying the spread to the average yield on the total distribution of bids at auction. Earlier, at the beginning of August, the floor price at auctions of medium and long-term securities had been abolished: since then all Treasury auctions have been conducted without any ceilings on yields.

[23] In a country whose public debt exceeded 100 per cent of GDP and whose average maturity was around 3 years, it was crucial to deter any manifestations of investor disaffection for Treasury paper. In other words, there was a need to ensure that the market operated properly and that the orderly formation of prices kept demand and supply in equilibrium.

[24] The "flight" from deposits to ready cash was at least partly a reaction to the provision of July 1992 that, as part of the corrective budget measures, had sanctioned an extraordinary tax of 0.6 per cent on bank and Post Office deposits.

[25] *Economic Bulletin*, No. 20, February 1995.

[26] See Ando, Guiso and Visco (1994); Bianco and Massaro (1996).

[27] See O'Brien (1992).

[28] See Group of Ten (1993) and BIS (Annual Reports, in particular since 1993).

[29] See EMI (1994).

[30] On international monetary cooperation and its prospects, see James (1996).

[31] The annual reports of the IMF and the EMI permit the interested reader to trace the evolution of the philosophy underlying the means and ends of international economic cooperation.

[32] Another issue is related to the possibility of reverse causation, i.e. whether shocks to the demand for lira can affect the dollar/Deutsche mark rate.

[33] See Turner and Van 't' dack (1993) for the methodology used in computing the effective rates of the dollar plotted in the figure. The Bank of Italy methodology is illustrated in *Economic Bulletin*, October 1992.

[34] Giavazzi and Giovannini, op. cit., use weights based on nominal GDP's as proxies.

[35] The Lagrange multiplier test indicates that at lag 1 the hypothesis of abscence of autocorrelation cannot be rejected (the autocorrelation coefficient at lag 1, equal to 0.25, is however small); at longer lags there is no evidence of autocorrelation. We estimated regressions characterized by a more complex dynamic structure showing no autocorrelation of residuals. Since the new regressions do not significantly differ from those reported in the tables, the inferences draw n in the text still hold.

[36] Among transaction costs, they explicitly consider those due to capital movements restrictions, which were relevant during the period covered by their analysis.

[37] The methodology employed in this appendix has been developed by the literature on the credibility of fluctuation bands (see, among others, Svensson (1991), Drudi, Majnoni (1992) and De Grauwe, op. cit.). The inferences that can be drawn from this methodology depends crucially on the assumption of absence of risk premia, which is a very restrictive and controversial assumption.

[38] The open parity implies $E[t,S(T)]=F(t,T)$, where $E[t,S(T)]$ is the time t expected exchange rate at expiration date T. $E[t,S(T)]$ can be written as $E[t,S(T)]=p*SD+(1-p)*S(t)$, where SD is the new level of the exchange rate if a devaluation takes place and p is the probability of a devaluation. By dividing the latter expression by $S(t)$, given SD and by assuming the open parity, A2 obtains.

[39] The measure of 7 per cent, which corresponds to the original proposal of the Italian and German authorities, roughly corresponds to the real appreciation of the lira in terms of producer prices since the end of 1986, immediately before the last realignment. The measure of 11 per cent corresponds to the real appreciation in terms of unit labor costs.

REFERENCES

Angeloni, I. and F. Passacantando, "Monetary Policy in Italy: Institutional and Economic Aspects," Bank for International Settlements, The Orientation of Monetary Policy and the Monetary Policy Decision-Making Process, Basle, 1991, pp. 87-111.

Ando, A., L. Guiso and I. Visco, eds. Saving and the Accumulation of Wealth, Cambridge University Press, Cambridge, England, 1994.

Banca d'Italia, Ordinary General Meeting of Shareholders, Abridged Report for the year 1979, 1980.

Banca d'Italia, Ordinary General Meeting of Shareholders, Abridged Report for the year 1991, 1992.

Banca d'Italia, Bollettino Economico, No. 19, October, 1992.

Banca d'Italia, Economic Bulletin, No. 15, October, 1992.

Banca d'Italia, Ordinary General Meeting of Shareholders, Abridged Report for the year 1992, 1993.

Banca d'Italia, Economic Bulletin, No. 17, October, 1993.

Banca d'Italia, Economic Bulletin, No. 20, February, 1995.

Bank for International Settlements, Annual Reports, Basle.

Barucci, P, "L'Isola Italiana del Tesoro - Ricordi di un Naufragio Evitato 1992-1994," Rizzoli, Milan, 1995.

Bianco, M. and R. Massaro, "La Struttura Finanziaria di Sei Paesi: un confronto sulla base dei Conti Finanziari," Banca d'Italia, mimeo, 1996.

Buiter, W. H., G. M. Corsetti and P. A. Pesenti, "Interpreting the ERM Crisis: Country-Specific and Systemic Issues," mimeo, 1996.

Ciampi, C. A., Audizione per l'esame delle conseguenze dei recenti avvenimenti sui mercati monetari e finanziari; Senato della Repubblica - 5-a Commissione permanente Programmazione economica, bilancio, Rome, 1992.

Committee of Governors of the Central Banks of the Member States of the EEC, Annual Report 1992, 1993.

De Grauwe, P. The Economics of Monetary Integration, Oxford University Press, Oxford, 1994.

Drudi, F. and G. Majnoni. "The determinants of yield differentials in favour of the lira: a quantitative analysis" in V. Conti, R. Hamaui and H. M. Scobie eds., Bond Markets, Treasury and Debt Management, Chapman and Hall, London, 1992, pp. 31-52.

European Monetary Institute, Annual Reports, Frankfurt.

Fazio, A., "Le Banche e i Mercati Finanziari," Bancaria, Volume 50, No. 6, pp. 92-96, 1994.

Giavazzi, F. and A. Giovannini. "The Dollar-Deutsche Mark Polarization," in A. Giovannini, ed., Limiting Foreign Exchange Flexibility, MIT Press, Cambridge, U.S., 1989, pp. 131-159.

Giavazzi, F., S. Micossi and M. Miller, eds. The European Monetary System, Cambridge University Press, Cambridge, England, 1988.

Gressani, D., L. Guiso and I. Visco, "Disinflation in Italy: An Analysis with the Econometric Model of the Bank of Italy," Journal of Policy Modeling, Vol. 10. No. 2, 1988, pp. 163-203.

Group of Ten, "International Capital Movements and Foreign Exchange Markets," Report of the Deputies to the Ministers and Governors, Banca d'Italia, Economic Bulletin, No. 17, 1993, pp. 89-108.

James, H., "International Monetary Cooperation since Bretton Woods," IMF and Oxford University Press, Washington D.C., New York, Oxford, 1996.

Masera, R. S, "L'Unificazione Monetaria e lo SME. L'esperienza dei primi otto anni," Il Mulino, Bologna, 1987.

Masera, R. S., "Single Market, Exchange Rates and Monetary Unification," The World Economy, Vol. 17, No. 3, 1994, pp. 249-279.

Ministero degli Affari Esteri, Istituto Mobiliare Italiano, Atti del Convegno su: Il Sistema Monetario Europeo a Dieci anni dal suo Atto Costitutivo: Risultati e Prospettive, 1988.

Monticelli, C. and L. Papi. European Integration, Monetary Co-ordination, and the Demand for Money, Clarendon Press, Oxford, 1996.

O'Brien, R, "Global Financial Integration: The End of Geography," The Royal Institute of International Affairs, Pinter Publishers, London, 1992.

Padoa-Schioppa, T. The Road to Monetary Union in Europe - The Emperor, The Kings, and the Genies, Clarendon Press, Oxford, 1994.

Passacantando, F., "Building an Institutional Framework for Monetary Stability: The Case of Italy (1979-1994)," BNL Quarterly Review, No. 196, pp. 83-132, 1996.

Santini, C. "An Italian Perspective," in P. Temperton, ed., The European Currency Crisis, Probus Publishing Company, Cambridge, England, 1993.

Steinherr, A., 30 Years of European Monetary Integration from the Werner Plan to EMU, Longman, London and New York, 1994.

Temperton, P., ed., The European Currency Crisis, Probus Publishing Company, Cambridge, England, 1993.

Turner, P. and J. Van 't' dack, "Measuring International Price and Cost Competitiveness," BIS Economic Papers, No. 39, Bank for International Settlements, Basle, 1993.

Visco, I. "Inflation, Inflation Targeting and Monetary Policy. Notes for discussion on the Italian experience," in L. Leiderman and L. Svensson, eds., Inflation Targets, Centre for Economic Policy Research, London, 1995.

5

The Single European Currency As A Stabilizing Factor In International Relations: A French View

ANDRÉ DE LATTRE
Former Deputy Governor, Bank of France

The successive French governments have supported the concept of a European single currency for complex reasons. The single currency can be seen as a necessary tool for the completion of the common market, and a strong factor of unification of minds. Some supporters, but by no means all, would understand it as a step towards more federalism at the decision-making level. Many Frenchmen see it as the irrevocable move which would once for all close the door on the everlasting inclination to solve the French problems through a devaluation of the currency.

For these various reasons, since the war, or at least since the Deutsche mark became the dominant currency in Europe, the French governments have constantly, if not always successfully, tried to establish a stable and credible link between the franc and the Deutsche mark, particularly, since 1978, through the European Monetary System.

This long quest for stability may at last be rewarded. The move to a single currency, scheduled for January 1, 1999, should be, at long last, the efficient mechanism which could bring about stability in intra-European relations and make a substantial contribution to stabilizing monetary relations in the world at large.

It is worthwhile recalling briefly the main steps along the road towards European monetary unity, to ask what has gone wrong and why, so as to assess the main objectives to be assigned to the new currency, inside and outside Europe.

EFFORTS, SUCCESS AND FAILURE IN THE MOVE TOWARDS EUROPEAN MONETARY UNITY

Why France Has Been Looking For A Stable FFR/DM Relationship?

As early as the late fifties, it became obvious that France would be, along with Germany, at the center of whatever monetary system would be built in Europe, and this was true not only because France and Germany have close trade and payment relations and are each other's first client and supplier. The Deutsche mark very soon became the strongest currency in Europe, and already in 1961 was subject to a revaluation (a move which, at the time, caused much surprise in a world only accustomed to devaluations). The countries close to Germany, notably the Netherlands and Belgium, Switzerland and later Austria, began to constitute the embryo of a prosperous DM zone. The U.K. had no intention to give up its sovereignty in exchange matters. Italy and the other Mediterranean countries had a somewhat lesser weight than today. Greece, Spain and Portugal were not yet members of the EEC There was no hope of making any progress towards an orderly monetary system in Europe as long as a viable and lasting relationship between the franc and the DM was not established. For instance in 1972, it was only after the meeting between President Pompidou and Chancellor Brandt to determine the magnitude of the Deutsche mark's revaluation vis-à-vis the franc that it became possible to decide, at the Azores conference, the size and format of the devaluation of the dollar.

The search for such a good and stable link had begun early in the sixties, amidst the turbulences of the international monetary system, the crises of the sterling in 1961 and 1963, and the mounting deficits of the US balance of payments. While the Treaty of Rome says nothing about exchange rates and there were no commitments or calendar of any kind in monetary matters, the condition for a more stable exchange relationship were laid down by the spectacular improvement in the French external position after the return to power of General de Gaulle and the success of the December 1958 devaluation.

In spite of the reappearance of inflationary tensions following the return of French population of Algeria to France, the French franc in 1967 was still worth nearly one Deutsche mark. Progress was being made in fiscal matters with the introduction in Germany of a Value Added Tax at an 11% and 12% rate, while the French VAT rate was 16%. An harmonization around 13% or 14%, making easier the taxation at the point of production and the suppression of fiscal frontiers, was in sight, and with it, may be, the move to a single currency.

The crisis of May 1968 put an abrupt end to these hopes. After the massive wage increases which were part of the global settlement of this month of turmoil, (+ 15% in most cases and + 35% for the minimum wage), a devaluation was inevitable. It would not have been possible, to decide it during the summer of 1968, to cancel immediately the wage increases just granted to the workers. And in November, General de Gaulle decided against a devaluation which was not accompanied by an efficient stabilization programme. It is only after his resignation in April 1969 that the devaluation took place, in an orderly manner, in August 1969.

After the closing of the gold window and the end of the convertibility of the dollar in 1972, international monetary events would for a time put the accent more on the relationship with the dollar and less on the franc/DM exchange rate. The long negotiation for a comprehensive reform of the international monetary system ended abruptly in Nairobi on October 6, 1973 when a new war in the Middle East led to the two oil shocks. At least for a few years, the dollar was no longer considered as a problem currency; people did not think about getting rid of the dollars any more, and the "substitution account" to be created at the IMF would never see the light.

With the dollar being once again at the center of the system, the French started looking once more for a more organized system in Europe.

With the benefit of the lessons of the Werner report of 1970, progress was first expected from the narrowing of the margins. It was the "snake in the tunnel ;" then, after the dollar fluctuated freely, "the snake without the tunnel."

However, as there was a clear lack of balance in the treatment reserved to the weak and the strong currencies - the whole burden of adjustment falling on the deficit country - the system was due to fail. First the U.K. then France on two occasions in 1974 and 1976 had to leave the "snake."

Created in 1978 by MM. Schmidt and Giscard d'Estaing, the European Monetary System took account of the shortcomings of the "snake." It introduced a currency band of par-values and instituted the obligation of corrective actions by both the debtor and the creditor. There was hope that, under normal circumstances, the system could enjoy relatively long periods of stability between the inevitable readjustments of par-values which were defined as "stable but adjustable."

Indeed the system worked, although the socialist experience of 1981-1983 in France added a new dimension to the gap between the franc and the DM which had to be settled by a series of devaluations between 1983 and 1986.

Then began, for the next five years, a period of uneasy stability. After the "Acte unique" of 1985 and the settlement of the major budgetary disputes, the Delors committee of governors laid the ground for the single currency in the Maastricht Treaty finally signed in December 1991.

As the accent was put on the need for economic convergence, there could be a reasonable hope that the precarious stability then enjoyed would smoothly evolve into a single currency without having to take the intermediate steps of narrowing the +/- 2.25% margins, but simply by the irrevocable fixing of parities at the chosen date of January 1, 1999.

As an ultimate precaution, the remaining inflation imbalances (U.K., Italy, etc...) would have to be corrected by a final adjustment, to take place at least two years before the irrevocable fixing of parities. It was likely that countries like the U.K.; Italy, Spain and a few other countries, where a backlog of price increases had been building up for some time, would avail themselves of this disposition. While there was hope that France might avoid it, with its currency having been substantially depreciated in the devaluations from 1983 to 1986 and its inflation rate being among the lowest.

In the event, the scenario was much less rosy. Violent crises erupted, in September 1992, January 1993 and July-August 1993, forcing the U.K. and Italy to leave the European Monetary System, and Spain and Portugal to devalue their currencies. Only the French franc, though heavily under attack, managed to keep its central rate unchanged, without even making use of the widening of the margin from +/-2.25% to +/-15% decided in August 1993.

But there is a great difference between the crises of September 1992 and January-July 1993.

The first one was primarily about Sterling, i.e. whether that currency, which had joined the EMS belatedly, with great reluctance, and a rate generally seen as too high, would be able to stay in the system. Indeed, many in the U.K. did see the outcome of the September 16th "black Wednesday" as a positive move. As Mrs. Thatcher said in Washington on Saturday 19th, "this is a great week where we have regained our freedom of maneuver." In effect, it was only a widening of the gap between the U.K. and a Maastricht Treaty that the U.K. had never liked very much.

1993 was another story. As early as in January, and again in July of that year, the French franc was under strong pressure, as the markets wanted to test the determination of the French authorities to keep intact a link with the Deutsche mark that none of the "fundamentals" in the French economy (a positive balance of payments, etc.) called for modify. Indeed, it was the future of the Treaty which was at stake.

And it is highly significant that the Banque de France was able to weather the storm, having in the process twice lost all its exchange reserves (and much more) and regaining calmness only with the decision to widen the margin to +/-15% in early August, 1993.

This did not prevent many commentators to announce that the EMS was dead and that the Maastricht Treaty would never be applied.

However, three years later in 1996, it appears that the move to the single currency is likely to take place after all at the normal date of January 1999. The French franc, in line with the hopes of the French authorities, and in spite of some recurring tensions, has reintegrated its +/-2.25% margin vis-à-vis the Deutsche mark around the central rate of 3.35 FFR which has been unchanged for ten years.

Maybe, after so many years of complacency towards exchange rates adjustments considered to be a minor evil or even as a welcome "kick" (said to be M. Pompidou's view), France will at last become a "credible" country. Indeed, if France had been consistently credible in the past, its currency would have counted, along with the Dutch guilder, the Austrian schilling, the Swiss franc, and to a lesser degree the Belgian franc and the Danish krone, among the currencies whose exchange rate with the Deutsche mark is never in doubt, and the need for a single currency would have been less obvious.

But now, with the single currency just ahead of us, it is worth asking why things went wrong in 1991-1993 and why they seem to go right now, in order to assess the chances of success of the new currency as a factor of stability.

What Went Wrong In 1991-1993?

One could be tempted to blame bad luck and political mistakes. Although it is vain to rewrite history, one could imagine a scenario whereby things would have gone smoothly as envisaged at the end of 1991.

Had the Danish referendum taken place at the end, and not at the very beginning of the process of ratification and after a series of positive parliamentary votes by the larger countries (France, Germany, U.K.), or even after a favorable vote by referendum by the Irish people, the Danish vote might have been positive, and, if negative, its impact much more limited. President Mitterrand might not have chosen the route of approval by a referendum, of which he probably thought impossible to deprive the French people after the Danish and the Irish had enjoyed it. Maybe the exchange rates readjustments for the pound, the lira and the peseta would have taken place in an orderly manner after the treaty had been quickly ratified by the French and other Parliaments.

The real explanation of the failure goes well beyond these circumstantial factors.

It lies in the illusion that, in the absence of a real convergence of economic policies, fixed par values with narrow margins can withhold the pressure of the markets. As the crises of 1992 and 1993 have demonstrated, no raise of short term interest rates (even to 500% or to 1000% as briefly tempted by Sweden) is able to match the possible gains of the operators in this "win/no-lose" game where the only issue is not whether the operators might have their fingers burnt by a possible reversal of the market, but whether the one way devaluation will take place now or later. This explains why it has not even been necessary for the central banks to activate the +/-15% margins, whose mere existence has immediately restored calm on the markets.

The demonstration was then made that, in the absence of sufficient economic convergence, "narrow margins" could not lead to "no margins," i.e. to fixed parities. Conversely, the situation since 1993, where major countries seem to be sincere in their efforts to achieve convergence, has raised serious hopes that the jump to fixed parities in January 1999 might take place without further attacks on the existing currency band of par-values.

THE SINGLE CURRENCY AS A STABILIZING FACTOR

The disappearance of exchange rate adjustments as a means of correcting imbalances among a substantial number of countries in Europe will have far reaching consequences both inside and outside these countries.

The Stability Of The EMU After The Move To The Single Currency

The debate on the merits and disadvantages of monetary integration is a respectable one. Since the beginning of 1995, the British authorities, particularly the governor of the Bank of England, Mr. Eddie George, have repeatedly stressed that while the British authorities intended to respect all the criteria of the Maastricht Treaty and were not ready to be refused access to the single currency for reason of insufficient performance on the criteria, they kept all their misgivings about relinquishing the possibility of exchange rate adjustments. In their view, among other reasons, the adjustments through mobility of labor would prove much more painful in Europe than, for instance, in the U.S. While the argument is indeed valid, one cannot but be impressed by the speed at which, inside the existing European nations, the least developed areas (Southern Portugal, Mezzogiorno, Brittany, Languedoc, Lorraine, Eastern Bavaria, etc.) have reached a level of wealth quite comparable to the rest of the nations, though the gap was, at the start, certainly wider than the one existing between the European countries now candidates to the single currency.

As the EU Ministers have acknowledged in Dublin in September 1996, the real issue is not whether those countries will show a sufficient degree of convergence in their economic policies to "pass the exam" of January 1999 (or rather of January 1998, when the respective performances will be judged), but whether they can durably respect a "pact of stability" i.e. demonstrate their genuine intention to achieve, after the move to the single currency and for ever after, a coherent and virtuous economic policy giving credibility to the "Euro" just as yesterday's German economic policy gave credibility to the Deutsche mark.

There lies probably the most efficient incentive to achieve stability with the single currency. To be able to borrow on the best terms and not be penalized by a negative "spread," each member country - including, and that is a major problem, its local collectivities - will have to watch very carefully the level of its Public Service Borrowing Requirements (P.S.B.R.).

It has been said that this constraint will inevitably lead to a federal government.

First, there is the need for some sort of "accountability" of the European Central Bank. While the parallel with National Central banks is not fully valid, it must be recalled that even those who are formally "independent" have some sort of link of subordination towards their elected Parliament and Government. And nobody is really willing to entrust this responsibility to a European Parliament whose composition and legislative record do not match, to say the least, those of the national Parliaments.

Second, so the argument goes, monetary policy and the management of interest rates are only one of the tools of a comprehensive economic policy. Just as governors of national Central Banks today make suggestions or recommendations to their respective governments in the field of budget and tax policies, some sort of federal government will emerge, maybe through a reinforcement of the present European Council of heads of state and government, which will receive these recommendations from the European Central Bank and transform them in directives to the national governments.

Though quite possible in the long-run, such an evolution is not inevitable. One could argue that member countries will spontaneously adopt such restrictive policies, just as today the countries whose currencies are linked to the Deutsche mark are careful not to undermine the credibility of their monetary policy by a laxist budgetary policy.

Member countries' willingness to "behave" durably will be reinforced by the mechanism of severe sanctions that punish those countries which would deviate from the agreed criteria, particularly regarding budgetary deficits.

It is encouraging to note that, in full knowledge of these future constraints, so many European countries (Italy, Spain, etc.) have proclaimed their firm intention to make every effort to join at the proposed date of January 1, 1999 and that Finland has decided to join the ERM in October 1996.

The Single Currency As A Stabilizing Factor Outside The EMU

The first and most obvious question to be addressed by the participants in the single currency is the establishment of a stable relationship between the EMU and those countries of the European Union which will not, at least temporarily, join the monetary union. But the EMU should also exert a stabilizing influence in the international monetary system at large.

A Renewed EMS

Long before the introduction of the single currency, indeed as early as the end of 1995, the European countries have addressed the issue of the relation between the "ins" and the "outs." This was made necessary, in the first instance, by the terms of the Maastricht Treaty itself which require that, before joining the EMU, countries must have abstain from any readjustment of central rates for a period of two years. The question was particularly complex in the case of the U.K., which on the one hand wishes to preserve its right to join the EMU if and when it chooses to do so, and which on the other hand seems quite reluctant to enter again any kind of European Monetary System.

But it is also due to the bitterness of the dispute raised by the so-called "competitive devaluations" (of the pound, the lira and the peseta) which have taken place in the wake of the 1992 and 1993 crisis.

The question of how to apply the exchange rate criterium to the U.K. will have to be solved, one way or another, some time in the second half of 1998. Unlike Spain and Portugal who have chosen in 1993 to devalue their currency rather than to leave the EMS, the U.K. has already missed the deadline of the Spring 1996 where it should have rejoined the EMS if it were to have enjoyed a two year period of exchange rate stability when the list of eligible countries (supposing the U.K. wishes to be one of them) will be fixed in the Spring of 1998. Conscious of that situation, the European Union Ministers have agreed to leave the question open until the middle of 1998. In case the U.K. wants to join, it might then be considered that a two year stability of the pound "outside the EMS" was in practice, equivalent to the two year stability "inside the EMS" required by the Treaty.

Mechanisms are being designed to avoid the repeat of the disturbances linked with the so-called "competitive devaluations" of 1992-1993. In this respect, it is very significant that the European Central Bank will be given a right of initiative to suggest appropriate corrective action or an orderly readjustment by the "out" country whose economy is getting out of step.

The approval of the readjustments within the renewed EMS would then take account of the evidence of progress towards convergence in the economic policy of the country.

Just as in the case of some of the convergence criteria set up in the Maastricht Treaty, such as public deficits and the level of public debt or, to take another comparison, in the progressive application of the capital ratios, ("tier one" and "tier two") of the Basle agreement (Cooke Committee), the important point would be that the country could demonstrate that it is moving closer towards the objective and not backward.

The renewed EMS would then be conceived in the perspective of the single currency. It would not only be seen as a protection against disorderly moves such as those registered in 1992 and 1993, but clearly as an anteroom to an adhesion which only the circumstances have prevented from taking place in 1999.

EMU and the International Monetary System

While the conduct of the exchange policy of the EMU vis-à-vis the other leading international currencies will be the first major consequence of the single currency, the EMU itself will be a factor of stability in the world monetary relations.

a) The Exchange Policy Of The EMU

One of the most important issues which the newborn European Central Bank will have to address will be the determination of the exchange policy vis-à-vis the dollar (and the yen), a responsibility which it will share with member countries' governments.

Both will be under the pressure of those who hope that their first concern will be to correct what they claim is an undervaluation of the dollar. Many in Europe (including some in the German industry) would welcome a weakening of the "Euro," which some voices in France have been asking for without great chances of success. Moreover, one should remember that the largest share of what are to-day European exports will go to countries within Europe and, that most of Europe's trade will take place in Euro - with less relevance to the external value of the Euro.

It is by no means assured that the spontaneous movements of the Euro will be downwards. Large capital movements may be attracted to Europe by the creation of a single monetary market, which will soon become quite comparable, in "breadth, depth and resiliency" to the New York market, and would push the "Euro" upwards.

And one does not really see the European Central Bank giving an artificial support to the exchange rate by massive purchases of dollars.

b) A "Reform" Of The International Monetary System

The "Euro" may prove, over time, to be the missing piece in the puzzle of the much talked about, and up to now never achieved, reform of the international monetary system.

In the last ten years, many authorized voices, such as Paul Volcker, John Williamson or the successive French finance ministers in their proposals (M. Balladur 1986, etc.) have tried to give flesh to the idea of a comprehensive reform or more modestly to the introduction of "target zones."

They have not been successful, and for good reasons.

First, a comprehensive reform with the introduction of an international currency might have been possible in 1964, before the development of the Euro dollar, and in a world of limited capital movements. But this time has passed. With the two oil shocks of 1973 and 1978, the world has discovered that there was no such thing as an "overhang" of dollars and no need for a "Substitution account."

Second, as Paul Volcker has stressed in a recent speech (November 29, 1995) "target zones" and the central banks' interventions to defend them can only work if and when the respective governments are able to convince the markets of the credibility of their intentions, which brings us back to the coherence of their economic and monetary policies.

The question is whether the single currency in Europe will bring about more stable international monetary relations than today's rather inbalanced situation.

Today the dollar is the only true world currency. It is a major reserve currency; it took nearly fifty years for the Deutsche mark to climb from 5% to 20% of world reserves, and the two other "strong" currencies, the Swiss franc and the yen, have carefully avoided playing that role. It is also the dominant "vehicular" currency, which many economies in transition have adopted as a second domestic currency (Russia and the Eastern European countries, Israel, Latin America, Vietnam, etc.).

Tomorrow, things could be quite different. With a large capital and monetary market, the currency of a European Union whose population, GNP and role in the international trade is larger than the United States, is likely to attract a much wider share of international reserves than the Deutsche mark in its heydays, even after its role has increased as a transaction currency in Eastern Europe and Russia. And it is quite possible that much of these holdings will remain attracted by a diversity of placements with plenty of good signatures (those of member states, regions, major European enterprises) and be less influenced by the variations in short term interest rates which have created, for instance, the bond "debacle" of 1994 when a reversal of the Fed policy prompted a watershed of sales in the New York and then in the European bond markets.

Indeed one cannot expect the economies of the U.S., the EU and Japan to move completely in step. Their phases of stagnation and recovery in the business cycle will continue to differ, as we have seen with the prolonged deflationary situation of the Japanese economy in 1993-95. Structural problems, such as the rigidity of the labor market or the acceptable level of social protection, will no doubt continue to be addressed quite differently in the U.S., Europe and Japan.

But, overtime, a constructive dialogue is likely to take place between the Federal Reserve, the European Central Bank and the Bank of Japan, which would have become partners of comparable weight on an appropriate pattern of monetary policies.

For more than thirty years, Working Party n° 3 of the OECD Economic Policy Committee and Central Bank governors in their Basle monthly meetings have searched that "Pierre philosophale," the coordination of the "policy mixes" of the countries of the developed world.

Maybe, with two pillars of comparable strength on each side of the Atlantic such coordination will be easier to attain. It would then be less necessary to think of an organized international monetary system, including "target zones" or similar exchange rate arrangements. Maybe without the consecration of an institutional framework, the present "non-system" would prove sufficiently stable and gain its legitimacy.

6

EMU And The Swiss Franc

KASPAR VILLIGER
Minister of Finance, Switzerland

INTRODUCTION

Even if Switzerland is not in a position to join the upcoming EMU at the outset, we are observing the convergence process with great interest. Given the importance of our relations with many European countries, the economic consequences of the introduction of EMU certainly cannot be neglected. The timing of the introduction of EMU and the stability of the future single currency will have a highly significant impact on economic developments in Europe as well as in Switzerland. Also, many uncertainties remain such as final decisions concerning a stability pact, the introduction of an EMS II, the setting of the exchange rate parities, as well as the development of economic growth in Europe and the expectations of the financial markets. In order to try to discern the precise effects which the future development of EMU will have on the Swiss capital and labor markets, we distinguish the following four scenarios:

SCENARIOS OF THE POSSIBLE DEVELOPMENT OF THE EMU PROJECT

Small Hard-Core EMU

Under this scenario, EMU is initiated on January 1, 1999 with strict application of the convergence criteria. Under these circumstances, only some of the EU countries are able to join the monetary union at the outset. Others will follow later. The European Central Bank (ECB) conducts a monetary policy oriented towards price stability, reduced public debt and restrained budget deficits. There are, however, uncertainties regarding the behavior of money demand in the new currency area: the introduction of an interlinking payment system (TARGET) increases the efficiency of cross-border payments and consequently reduces the demand for money. In the long run, the ECB will adapt its policy to this new demand. Inflation should reach a level corresponding to the present average level in Germany, and the ECB will acquire a reputation for being a stability-oriented central bank. In the short run, however, the aforementioned uncertainties could lead to large fluctuations in exchange rates.

Large EMU And Liberal Interpretation Of Convergence Criteria

Under this scenario, due to political reasons, the EU decides to start EMU on January 1, 1999 with practically all its member states. Efficiency gains and the resulting benefits for economic growth rise with the number of participants. However, a liberal interpretation of the convergence criteria is necessary. Fiscal consolidation no longer constitutes a prior policy goal, at least in the short run, particularly since some countries may be tempted to rely on a later bail-out by the hard-currency members. Also, monetary policy cannot be adapted to the specific needs of the different countries and therefore leads to regional disparities and demands for financial transfer payments. As investors do not have confidence in the stability of the Euro from the beginning, a large inflow of capital into hard currencies such as dollar, yen and Swiss franc can be expected. In the countries of the present DM-area, long-term interest rates are expected to rise and to reach at least the level of the present average interest rate of all EU countries. There is a high risk that such a monetary union will not be stable.

Postponement Of The Start Of EMU To A Fixed New Date

Under this scenario, the beginning of EMU is postponed in order to allow more countries to meet the convergence criteria which will be applied in a strict sense. The process of monetary integration continues. The postponement even allows for a better preparation of the common monetary policy, which increases the confidence of the markets in the Euro. Under these circumstances, the attractiveness of the currencies of the future EMU member states is enhanced, and they appreciate against the dollar, yen and Swiss franc. What follows is similar to Scenario 1.

Postponement And Gradual Abandonment Of The Emu Project

Under this scenario, political differences, especially in relation to fiscal policy, cannot be settled, and the postponement of EMU gradually results in abandonment of monetary union. The financial markets start to speculate against the European soft currencies, resulting in a depreciation of the same. On the other hand, confidence in the Deutsche mark is restored. The Deutsche mark appreciates against the Swiss franc and Germany's long-term interest rates decrease. As the pressure for fiscal consolidation is lower, a more expansive fiscal policy should promote economic growth.

All of these scenarios give an extremely simplified picture of possible developments. Consequently, the probability that any single scenario takes place is small. It is more likely that a combination of the different scenarios can be expected.

CONSEQUENCES FOR SWITZERLAND

Up until now, the consequences of EMU for Switzerland have mainly consisted in exchange rate movements. As has been shown in the past, upward pressure on the Swiss franc depends to a great extent on the expectations of the financial markets and can only partly be offset by a decrease in interest rates.

Further confidence crises and corresponding reactions of the markets must already be expected prior to the introduction of the EMU. Under Scenarios 1 and 3, the upward pressure on the Swiss franc would be temporary. Under Scenario 2, however, a larger and longer-lasting appreciation of the franc would have to be expected as investors would not have confidence in the Euro. The outcome would be a large inflow of capital into Switzerland.

The exchange rate of the Swiss franc might, however, behave differently in relation to the DM as opposed to the other EU currencies: while under Scenario 4, for instance, an appreciation of the DM is likely, the French franc as well as the soft currencies might depreciate against the Swiss franc, which would offset the positive effects for Switzerland's economy resulting from the appreciation of the DM. A gradual abandoning of the EMU project would thus not automatically lead to an improvement of Switzerland's price competitiveness.

SCOPE OF ACTION FOR SWITZERLAND

The main challenge for Switzerland before and during EMU will be to prevent the Swiss franc from an intolerable appreciation. Monetary policy can help to do this in various ways:

Fixing The Exchange Rate Of The Swiss Franc

Fixing the Swiss franc, for example in relation to the Euro, would prevent an appreciation and thus protect the Swiss export industry. However, speculation would have to be expected. In order to defend the fixed rate against speculation, the supply of money would have to be expanded, which would result in a rise in inflation. Moreover, a unilaterally fixed exchange rate would restrict the scope of action of Switzerland's monetary policy without providing for an appropriate right of co-determination.

If the exchange rate for the Swiss franc were to be fixed on a long-term basis, then the ECB would determine the development of prices in Switzerland. The short-term interest rates would fully adjust to the EU-level while the long-term rates might still show a slight difference which would decrease as confidence in the stability of the Euro grew.

If the exchange rate for the Swiss franc were to be fixed on a temporary basis, there would be no reason for interest rates to adjust since in the long run monetary policy would be oriented towards national price stability. However, later on, authorities might be obliged to allow short-term interest rates to rise if an expansive, inflationary monetary policy had been necessary in order to defend the fixed exchange rate against speculative pressures.

Maintaining Of Independent Monetary Policy Oriented Towards Price Stability

The present monetary policy of targeting a monetary aggregate in the medium-run could be maintained. In this case, the Swiss National Bank would be relying entirely on the effectiveness of automatic stabilizers. A slowdown in economic activity - caused by the appreciation of the Swiss franc - would lead to a decrease in the demand for money. If money supply continued to expand at the same rate as before, a decrease in interest rates would follow. Low interest rates would stimulate the economy and would reduce the attractiveness of the Swiss franc for foreign investors. These automatic stabilizers, however, only react with a time lag. Therefore, temporary costs in the form of losses in economic growth would have to be borne.

Easing Monetary Policy With A View To Preventing Exchange Rate Appreciation

If the automatic stabilizers were not sufficient to prevent a substantial appreciation of the Swiss franc, there would be the option of a discretionary ease in monetary policy. A strong appreciation of the franc would tend to depress economic activity. A more expansive monetary policy would not lead to an increase in inflation as long as the acceleration in money growth merely offsets the deflationary tendencies resulting from the appreciation. In practice it would, however, be difficult to estimate to what extent monetary policy could be eased without endangering price stability. In addition, in the short run, even a discretionary ease in monetary policy cannot prevent a slow-down of economic growth, given the well-known time lag of the effects of monetary policy.

Options aiming at influencing the value of the Swiss franc such as capital inflow controls or negative interest rates would not appear to be enforceable in view of the high degree of globalization of world-wide capital markets.

OPTIONS OF MONETARY POLICY UNDER THE DIFFERENT SCENARIOS

Under Scenarios 1 and 3 (hard-core EMU or postponement), in the short-run, larger capital inflows would take place, leading to a further appreciation of the Swiss franc until the ECB acquired the confidence of the financial markets. In the medium-run, however, no major impact on the Swiss franc would be expected. The temporary appreciation of the Swiss franc should be corrected as soon as investors gained confidence in the European Central Bank's ability to conduct a monetary policy oriented towards price stability. The hard core of the EMU would be similar to a somewhat larger DM area. A stable Euro could even enter into competition with the Swiss franc to assume its function of an international reserve currency. This would lead to a depreciation of the Swiss franc. Under these circumstances the costs of a rise in interest rates due to fixing the exchange rate of the Swiss franc would be deemed higher than the costs of a temporary slow-down of the economy due to exchange rate fluctuations. Under these scenarios the Swiss National Bank (SNB) should maintain an autonomous monetary policy and relying on the effectiveness of automatic stabilizers.

Should an intolerable appreciation of the Swiss franc in the transitional phase coincide with an economic slowdown and fiscal consolidation, the SNB would have to adopt temporarily a more expansive discretionary monetary policy to counter the negative effects this appreciation would have on our economy.

Under Scenario 2 (large EMU and liberal interpretation of convergence criteria), much larger exchange rate fluctuations would have to be expected. A considerable appreciation of the Swiss franc could have a drastic effect on the competitiveness of the Swiss economy. An expansive monetary policy response would most probably lead to inflation as experience shows that it is extremely difficult to take back the monetary base in time. Fixing the Swiss franc vis-à-vis the Euro, however, would import the negative effects of the unstable currency. The SNB would have to face the danger of future inflation and to accept an adjustment of the Swiss interest rates to the European level. This would turn out to be as disadvantageous as a strong appreciation of the franc would be. Under such circumstances, it would be practically impossible for Switzerland to protect its economy from the negative impact of an unstable European Monetary Union.

Finally, under Scenario 4 (gradual abandonment of EMU), there would be a risk of large exchange rate fluctuations, in the short-run, which would have to be countered by easing monetary policy in order to avoid deflationary tendencies. In the medium run, investors would regain confidence in the European hard currencies, especially in the DM, and this would work against the upward tendency of the Swiss franc.

All of the scenarios, however, are highly simplified representations of reality and only serve the purpose of analysis. In reality, it is more likely that a combination of the scenarios will take place. The optimal response of monetary policy will ultimately depend upon the specific circumstances which we will be confronted with, and will have to be flexible enough to adapt to rapidly changing conditions.

OTHER POLICY OPTIONS

In addition to the options of monetary policy discussed above, other economic policy measures have to be taken into consideration. The scope of action of fiscal policy is limited, however, in view of the current level of public debt. As regards the labor market, salaries must become more flexible and the supply of labor more mobile. In view of the increasing world-wide globalization, foreign economic policy should be oriented towards fostering the development of our comparative advantages in the international markets. In general, structural measures are necessary to improve Switzerland's ability to react to external shocks in a timely way.

CONCLUSIONS

Switzerland, as a small, open, and export-oriented economy, cannot shield its economy from the political and economic developments in the rest of Europe.

While we would benefit from a stable European Monetary Union, an unstable single currency would have inevitable negative consequences for our economy. Switzerland is therefore following the progress towards monetary union with great interest. We are convinced that a stable monetary union would provide a favorable framework for steady economic growth throughout Europe.

7

Exchange Rate And Economic Policy In Three Regional Blocks: The EU, The GCC And The CFA

FRANCO MODIGLIANI
Institute Professor Emeritus, The Massachusetts Institute of Technology
HOSSEIN ASKARI
Global Management Research Professor and Director of the Institute of Global Management Research, The George Washington University

INTRODUCTION

The central lesson from the Bretton Woods system of fixed parities was that there is a unique relation of the domestic price level (wage rate and interest rate) to the price level (wage rate and interest rate) in the rest of the world that is consistent with balance of payments equilibrium and full employment. Simply said, countries can simultaneously enjoy full employment and balance of payments equilibrium if they adjust parities to reflect divergences in economic policies or if they coordinate economic policies (a unique <u>real</u> exchange rate) while maintaining fixed nominal parities.[1]

Beginning in the mid 1960's, however, the Bretton Woods system was characterized by divergent policies, resulting in speculative capital flows, financial crises and the transmission of U.S. economic and financial policies to the rest of the world. In the post Bretton Woods era, countries have adopted a variety of exchange rate arrangements -- cooperative arrangements with limited flexibility in terms of a group of currencies or a single currency, currencies pegged to a single currency, and to the SDR or to customized baskets, currencies adjusted according to a set of indicators, and managed float and independent float.[2] Some of these arrangements have, either formally or informally, resulted in a system of fixed parities between groups of countries.

In this paper, we take a historic look at the financial and economic performance of three groups of countries with fixed parity systems. The three cases are the European Monetary System (EMS), the Gulf Corporation Council (GCC), and the CFA Franc zone (CFA), representing a range of relations from formal to informal, and differing arrangements from pegging to one currency to pegging to several currencies. In the case of the EMS, there is a formal arrangement with pegging to a basket; the GCC represents an informal pegging arrangement to the US dollar; and the CFA zone represents formal pegging to the French franc. Economic and financial crisis have adversely affected two of these arrangements and in the case of the third the required degree of adjustment has been delayed with a future crisis being inevitable. Countries in the EMS have exhibited slow growth (lower than their potential) resulting in high rates of unemployment and speculation against the weaker currencies. The countries of the GCC have been unable to develop a competitive non-oil sector and have delayed adjustment by running down their foreign assets and by recourse to deficit financing. Countries in the CFA experienced slow or negative growth, loss of international competitiveness and rapid accumulation of external debt, resulting in a massive devaluation of their currencies. The three cases suffer from the same symptoms and their problems, though different, have similar solutions.

LESSONS FROM THE BRETTON WOODS SYSTEM

Under any exchange rate system, changes in the real exchange rate are needed to transfer resources from a country that has excess full-employment savings (national) to a country that has an inadequate level of savings (at a common interest rate) -- the resource gap. With a flexible exchange rate system, an expansionary monetary policy will result in a reduction of domestic interest rates and a depreciation of the real exchange rate. As a result, the resource gap is satisfied by an increase in domestic investment (due to lower domestic interest rates) and by the transfer of the rest resulting from higher net exports (due to the depreciation of the real exchange rate). With a system of fixed parities, depreciation of the real exchange rate can be only achieved through changes in relative prices. If prices (wage rates) are not flexible, then a country with excess full employment savings will experience insufficient aggregate demand, slow growth and thus a high level of unemployment. Price flexibility, in turn, is closely related to wage flexibility; because of the close relationship between the behavior of wages and prices, flexibility of prices is intimately related to that of wages.

The experience with the Bretton Woods system was a confirmation of the above reasoning. In time, fixed parities drifted away from equilibrium because price levels did not automatically and quickly adjust to balance of payments disequilibrium, and countries were reluctant to reduce relative prices by raising unemployment (or increase relative prices, in turn fostering inflation).[3] Moreover, the drift of parities away from equilibrium was accentuated during the 1960's by the increasing mobility of capital. Eventually changes in parities were forced on countries in a manner that was made financially disruptive as they were delayed until they became a one way bet for speculators.

In a fixed parity arrangement, a country's ability to stimulate domestic economic activity through an expansionary monetary policy is limited. A fall in interest rates results in an outflow of capital, reducing the spot value of the country's currency. Given that the monetary authority has the obligation of preventing the market exchange rate from falling outside of some agreed band, the authority eventually has to intervene in the foreign exchange market, resulting in an outflow of reserves. This outflow, in turn, reduces the domestic money supply, moderating the country's expansionary policy, while increasing the money supply of some member countries and thus reducing their interest rates (provided reserve movements are not sterilized). While this helps the first country, by reducing the interest differential, it interferes with the monetary policy of some other member countries. The first country's ability to pursue an independent monetary policy is dependent on several factors, including the size of the permissible band of fluctuations of the exchange rate, the responsiveness of the balance of payments to changes in market exchange rate, the responsiveness of capital movements to covered interest differential, and the risk premium required by speculators to provide formal cover.[4]

During the earlier years of the Bretton Woods system, the responsiveness of capital mobility to the covered interest differential was low because of numerous impediments to capital movements and the lack of familiarity with foreign capital markets, thus affording monetary authorities substantial freedom in determining domestic monetary policy. By the latter part of the 1960's, capital responsiveness to interest rate differentials had increased, resulting in massive speculative capital flows as parities became unrealistic; the most dramatic example of unrealistic parities was the undervaluation of the mark in 1969. This severely limited the pursuit of independent monetary policy. These problems could have been somewhat ameliorated through wider bands around parity, restriction on capital flows and, most effectively, by a commitment to policy coordination. After a crisis, centering on French efforts to devalue the parity of the dollar in terms of gold by encouraging all holders of dollars to exchange their dollars for gold, the U.S. suspended convertibility and the dollar was allowed to float in August, 1971. The abandonment of fixed parities gave way to a system of mixed parities. Small groups of countries, amongst whom trade was significant or who had the long-term goal of economic integration and a single currency, returned to some sort of a fixed parity system between themselves.

How have three groups of such countries with differing exchange arrangements handled the potential financial and economic crises that were predictable for a system of fixed parities?

THE EUROPEAN MONETARY SYSTEM

First, a brief historical perspective may be useful. The EMS was established in 1979 with Belgium, Denmark, France, Germany, Ireland, Italy, Luxembourg, and the Netherlands as members; Portugal and Spain joined in 1986; the U.K. joined the system in 1991; Greece has never joined; in 1992 the U.K. and Italy dropped out under a powerful speculative attack as their currencies were considered as overvalued, and Ireland, Portugal and Spain re-imposed capital controls; and in 1993 in the midst of another crisis centering on the French franc, the band was widened from 2.25 to 15 per cent (de facto abandonment of the EMS), although by early 1994 many currencies were within the 2.25 per cent band. The basket currency has been the ECU, with each member selecting a central parity and maintaining a limited deviation between the actual value of their currency to the ECU and the central parity [(actual value - central parity) divided by central parity]. The general obligation was that actual cross rates could not deviate by more than 2.25 per cent from the central cross rate (the band was set at 6 per cent for U.K., Italy, Spain and for Portugal). In the event that divergence exceeds 75 per cent of the maximum allowable divergence, government authorities are obliged to adopt policy measures to affect market exchange rates, invariably a change in interest rates to make their currency relatively more attractive as an asset.

Given the lessons of Bretton Woods, what measures did the EMS incorporate to safeguard against speculation, financial disruptions and high unemployment (or high inflation)? The band was made wider, the system was made symmetric (intervention was to be done by both central banks as opposed to Bretton Woods system where the U.S. did not have to intervene, and intervention was to be in all EMS currencies as opposed to just the dollar under Bretton Woods), the role of policy coordination was recognized (the divergence indicator could trigger policy adjustment when a country's policies diverged from the EMS average), and regular meetings of central banks were envisaged to coordinate monetary policies - interest rate and price behavior. Were these safeguards sufficient? A priori, there were reasons to question whether these measures, by themselves, would have been sufficient. The slightly wider band was insufficient to reflect realistic divergences in monetary policy, and thus in price behavior and in real interest rates. The greater availability of resources for intervention, afforded by a symmetric system, was again realistically insufficient in a world of ever increasing capital mobility to absorb speculative and non-speculative capital flows. The "recognized" importance of policy coordination, in the absence of a solid commitment, was again likely to be insufficient given the economic and financial irrationalities of governments whether it is to save face, due to excessive pride, or whether it is simply due to the perception that a depreciation is a sign of weakness or even failure. While any single one of these three adjustments to the Bretton Woods system may have been insufficient, it was clearly "hoped" that the combination would be enough to achieve exchange rate stability, balance of payments equilibrium, sufficient real economic growth, moderate inflation, and full employment.

At the outset, the obvious should be stated. Western Europe's economic performance has not lived up to expectation. In comparison to US economic performance, Europe has achieved more rapid productivity growth, but has had output growth and labor force growth commensurate to that of the US.[5] At the same time, Europe has had much faster growth in real wages and therefore lower employment, with increasingly larger unemployment, especially in the 90's. Simultaneously, parities have come under pressure, resulting in speculative capital flows and financial disruptions. We argue that this adverse development on the European landscape is due to the system of fixed parities, the march towards Maastricht (with suffocating convergence criteria), and the tight monetary policy of the German Bundesbank. It is worth re-iterating the obvious that while the EMS is akin to a symmetrical Bretton Woods system, the imposition of the Maastricht Treaty has added a straight jacket that has made the EMS even more unrealistic. Namely, for all intents and purposes, the major European countries, especially France and Germany, have in effect announced to the world that their parities are not adjustable (the so called Franc Fort policy), necessitating even more policy coordination.

Tables 1 - 9 (shown at the end of this chapter) contain the essential facts for all EU countries and the US for four time periods 1961-70, 1971-80, 1981-90, and annually for 1991-1995:

- Table 1: Price deflator (GDP at market prices)
- Table 2: Gross domestic product
- Table 3: Real compensation per employee (total economy by GDP deflator)
- Table 4a: Nominal unit labor costs; total economy
- Table 4b: Real unit labor costs; total economy
- Table 5: Real long-term interest rates
- Table 6: Occupied population
- Table 7: Unemployment rate
- Table 8: Productivity Growth
- Table 9: Adjusted wage share

Based on the same set of facts for the EU as a whole, Modigliani concluded that[6]:

> "--- much if not all of the huge unemployment, at least during the second half of the 1980s, can be accounted for by an insufficient aggregate demand, due to a combination of a mercilessly tight German monetary policy and the endeavor of the members of the

EMS to maintain a stable exchange rate with the mark, while fostering freedom of capital movement. This combination forced them to adopt tight German policy."

Our goal in this section is to re-examine this conclusion; in different sub-periods since 1960 to determine whether the longer period has masked opposite economic developments in two periods; at the individual country level to look at the performance of individual EU countries (not just the aggregate) to assess individual country performance which may have off-set those of other countries to give wrong conclusions; and to assess any significant difference for countries that did not join the EMS, that left the EMS or that had a wider band from the central cross rate. Additionally, we will briefly examine the financial crisis of the summer of 1993.

From Table 7, it is clear that while the unemployment rate was much lower in the EU than in the US in the 1960's (2.2% versus 5.2%) and in the 1970's (4.2% versus 6.4%), it was significantly higher in the EU during the 1980's (9.6% versus 7.1%) and especially in the 1990's (10.0% versus 6.6%).[7] Some (e.g. Drèze, 1995) summarizing a line of reasoning popular in Europe, attribute this development to supply side factors (union power and rapid rise in real compensation in Europe) with the rise in real wages resulting in a slower increase in employment because of substitution of capital for labor, reduced international competitiveness and lower investment due to lower profitability. Others (e.g. Modigliani, 1996) have argued that the culprit has been insufficient aggregate demand, due to very tight German monetary policy, coupled with the fixed parity system (with the strict criteria for Maastricht), and exacerbated by high responsiveness of capital flows to real interest rate differentials.

The major thrust of the supply side argument is focused on the rapid increase in EU's real compensation per employee since 1960 (see Table 3).[8] While the increase in European real wages since 1960 has been much higher than that of the US, it is not as pronounced in every sub-period: 1970's -- 2.9% per year in the EU versus 0.6% in the US; 1980's -- 0.9% per year in the EU versus 0.7% in the U.S.; and 1990's -- 0.9% in the EU versus 1.2% in the US.[9] Thus while there has been a significantly higher real wage growth in the EU since 1960, it has not been markedly different since 1980. It is, therefore, difficult to conclude that the higher unemployment rate in the EU (than in the US) had been due to more rapid growth in real wages during the 1980's and 1990's. In fact the opposite is true. Namely, during the 1970's when the EU enjoyed a lower unemployment rate than the US, the EU had faster growth in real wages; while during the 1980's and 1990's, the EU experienced much higher unemployment than the US, yet real wage growth rates were commensurate!

By examining sub-periods, the simplistic conclusion that high unemployment and rapid growth in real wage rates go hand-in-hand cannot be supported by the facts; in fact, this examination by sub-periods gives further support to the assertion that growth in real wages do <u>not</u> go hand in hand with increasing unemployment.

Even if rapid growth in real wages could be the cause of the high unemployment rate in Europe, rapid productivity increase in Europe could in fact have more than offset this negative effect on employment. As Modigliani points out, there is an often forgotten identity which explains the change in the real wage rate[10]:

Δ Real wage rate = Δproductivity + Δlabor share of income

For the EU aggregate, the share of wages in output (see Table 9) was largely stable over the 1960's, indicating commensurate real wage and productivity growth; during the decade of the 1970's, the share of wages increased by 1.3% over the entire period indicating that real wage grew faster than productivity; decreasing by 2.4% in the 1980's, and another 2.1% from 1991 to 1995, indicating that real wage grew systematically less than productivity; and this phenomenon has been even more pronounced in the 1990's. On the basis of these facts, it is difficult to support the conclusion that rapid real wage growth has been the cause of Europe's high unemployment rate. If rapid real wage growth has been the cause of the high unemployment rate, unemployment should have been high in the 1960's and 1970's, not in the 1980's and especially not in the 1990's!![11]

At the disaggregated (country) level there are four cases that do not conform to the overall EU pattern -- Greece, Luxembourg, Portugal and the U.K.. In the case of Greece, the share of wages decreased substantially in the 1960's (with unemployment showing no particular trend), declined substantially in the 1970's (with significant decline in unemployment), increased during the 1980's (with a substantial increase in unemployment) and declined dramatically in the 1990's (with a significant rise in the unemployment rate but a rate that was generally well below the EU average); in the case of Luxembourg, the share of wages has increased steadily overtime, the highest amongst the EU during the 1980's and 1990's (with rising unemployment but one that is the lowest, 3.2% in 1995, in the EU); Portugal has had a steadily declining wage share (with unemployment rising in the 1980's but declining to 6% in 1995 and remaining generally the second lowest in Europe); and for the U.K. the share of wages has been stagnant (while unemployment has bounced around but has been below the EU average for 1993-95 and stood at 2% below the EU average in 1995).

These same observations are supported by real unit labor cost figures (see Table 4 b.) Since 1980, real unit labor cost has declined from 100 to 86.4 in the EU, whereas in the US the decline was to 99.2. A high level of real labor compensation does not go hand in hand with a high unemployment rate. Moreover, the country with the highest increase (as opposed to the large decrease for the EU as a whole) in unit labor cost in the EU, Luxembourg, had the lowest unemployment rate in the EU; and the U.K., which had the second worst record in unit labor cost, had the third lowest unemployment rate.

In sum, the facts when broken down by time periods and disaggregated by country, give even less support to the hypothesis that rapidly rising wages have been the cause of high EU unemployment. In Europe one thing is clear: output has not grown fast enough to absorb the growing labor force. Simply stated:

$$\Delta\text{Potential output} = \Delta\text{productivity} + \Delta\text{labor force}.$$

The crisis of high unemployment in the EU is due to the slow growth of output, at a rate far below its potential growth. The slow growth in output can be explained by insufficient aggregate demand. The low level of aggregate demand, in turn, is due to tight monetary policy, resulting from Germany's tight policy and the commitment to maintain fixed parity to the DM by some EU countries, especially France with its "Franc Fort Policy."[12] Tight monetary policy has resulted in high real interest rates which in turn has discouraged investment.

The price that Europe has paid for this policy stand is high unemployment and the resulting loss of potential output. But the crisis is by no means over. In the period up to January 1, 1999, when irrevocably fixed exchange rates will be adopted and the responsibility for monetary policy will be transferred to the European System of Central Banks (ESCB), economic and financial conditions could deteriorate further. Although the current band of +/-15% affords countries policy flexibility, the wide band is inconsistent with German interpretation of normal fluctuations and with the French "Franc Fort Policy." As such, the de facto size of the band of permissible fluctuations is considerably narrower than the stated 15%.

Given prevailing economic conditions in Europe, high unemployment (especially in France) and planned reductions in government expenditures to satisfy another Maastricht criterion, the time may be ripe for speculation. Substantial sales of the French franc by speculators would create an untenable situation for the French government. With unemployment approaching 13% and plans to reduce government expenditures, the French options are few - - increase short-term interest rates (exacerbating the unemployment conditions) or abandon the "Franc Fort policy." However, Germany could pre-empt any such speculation and ameliorate EU economic conditions by unilaterally reducing its real interest rates substantially now. Alternatively, the EU could agree to a one time realignment of parities, a revaluation of the mark (and the guilder) now before speculation raises its head. If the EU is indeed committed to meaningful policy coordination, it is curious that one or the other of these choices is not adopted now to ameliorate economic conditions.

The financial crisis of the summer of 1993 occurred at a time when French unemployment rates were lower than today and when there was more room for fiscal maneuver. In 1993, speculation was a one way bet and as today the authorities had two policies to counteract it. The preferable policy, then as now, was for the

Bundesbank to reduce interest rates. But coordination and commitment was not forthcoming. The other available policy was for countries facing exchange rate pressures to raise short-term interest rates, a tough choice in the face of high unemployment rates. The failure of the EMS has been that the participating countries want fixed parities and favorable economic landscape but are not committed to the sacrifices of meaningful policy coordination. Speculators are not blind and they take action when a currency reaches the limits of the band while the country has little political ability to raise interest rates. Thus speculation became a one-way bet in 1993.

If the EU does not adopt appropriate policies now, Maastricht may not survive. The French cannot tolerate a significant increase in unemployment. The only viable options are either German cooperation to reduce interest rates or an EU agreement to realign parities. While the benefits of single currency may be substantial for the EU, the long period leading up to 1999, characterized by essentially fixed parities and little or no coordination of monetary policies to achieve acceptable levels of employment, is proving to be an economic and social disaster. Coordination of monetary policy is in the end translated into the pursuit of similar price and wage policies; similar price policies are akin to similar wage policies given the close relationship between wage rate and prices. The lessons of Bretton Woods have gone by the wayside and the predictable policy inconsistencies have been exacerbated by the increasing mobility of capital.

The economic and financial basis underlying the Maastricht Treaty and the drive towards a single currency is that the projected benefits exceed the projected costs. The projected benefits have been broadly stated as increased economic efficiency and growth (through the elimination of currency transaction costs and because of reduced exchange risk that is built into real interest rates), and greater price stability (resulting in improved resource allocation) and lower exchange rate volatility of the single currency (due to a deeper market). While the projected costs -- loss of nominal exchange rates as a monetary policy tool and loss of sovereignty over monetary policy -- were seen as small, especially in comparison to the size of that projected benefits. While these predictions may have been justified in theory, in reality the long transitional period towards 1999 with no effective policy coordination may have already made this prediction obsolete. The several years of high unemployment in Europe with its associated loss in potential output were not incorporated into the calculation. These costs may already exceed projected benefits for a number of years after 1999, especially when these costs could continue to accrue for another two years with the possibility that a single currency may not be even adopted if European economic conditions deteriorate further.

THE GULF COOPERATION COUNCIL (GCC)

The GCC, incorporating Bahrain, Kuwait, Oman, Qatar, Saudi Arabia, and the United Arab Emirates, was formed in 1981. In the same year, the GCC ratified the "Unified Economic Agreement" to serve as the basis for establishing a comprehensive economic union in the future.[13] Officially, Bahrain, Qatar, Saudi Arabia and the United Arab Emirates peg their currencies to the SDR with a +/-7.25% band; Kuwait pegs to a trade weighted basket; and Oman pegs to the dollar. In practice, all of the countries (with the exception of Kuwait) maintain stable exchange rates with the dollar resulting in fixed cross parities (see Table 9). The benefits of exchange rate stability, whether in the Bretton Woods system or in the EMS, increase with intra-block trade and increasing capital flows. In the case of the GCC, parity to the dollar has been fixed, while imports from the U.S. represent 8.33% (in 1994) of total imports; and oil exports are not affected by exchange rate developments. In the case of the EU, intra-EU trade dwarfs trade with the rest of the world, but this is not the same for the GCC. Each GCC country is a net exporter of oil/gas, and oil/gas is by far the major component of exports, representing roughly 85%-90% of GCC exports. As a result, intra-GCC trade is quite small, representing roughly 5% (re-exports included) of their total imports. Thus one of the major benefits of fixed parties, namely reduced risk and transaction cost associated with international trade, is currently insignificant for the GCC. But at the same time, the GCC because of the similar economic structures of members, may avoid one of the costs of fixed rates, namely the differential impact (on member countries) of external shocks.

While the benefits of (informal) fixed parties may be small for the GCC, the cost of essentially losing control over nominal exchange rates as a policy tool could be quite high. To assess the potential economic loss, a brief examination of the nature of these economies is in order.

The economic and financial basis of countries that rely heavily on depletable resources for their net national product (NNP) is fundamentally different than that of other countries.[14] In depletable resource-based economies the conventional measure of net national product is not theoretically correct -- essentially conventionally measured NNP does not correspond to the maximum sustainable level of consumption (the Golden Rule). That is a large portion of current net national product must be saved to compensate for the depletion of the exhaustible resource. Thus such economies must transform a large part of oil wealth into non-oil sources of income if they are to maintain their level of NNP as oil is depleted. This central economic policy also implies that over time these countries will have to replace oil exports with non-oil exports or capital movements. One of the important policy instruments for developing non-oil sources of output and thus non-oil exports is an appropriate real exchange rate policy. While the GCC countries have correctly argued that exchange rate policy has no effect on oil exports (beside minor budgetary implications), they have unfortunately concluded that exchange rate policy is by default unimportant because non-oil exports are insignificant.

In the GCC countries, oil (as well as other minerals) belong to the society as a whole. This prescription is in fact derived from Islam. Moreover, Islamic teachings go further in indicating that minerals belong to present and future generations; with the implication that oil wealth should not be squandered by the current generation at the expense of future generations. Thus in a society that is managed on Islamic principles, there is the presumption that the depletion of minerals (in this case oil) should provide benefits to future generations as well as to the present generation. To the extent that oil is depleted by the present generation, it is incumbent on them to provide other sources of production for future generations that are commensurate with the benefits of oil depletion for current generation to-day. For the GCC, because oil revenues accrue to the government, intergenerational equity considerations become a government responsibility.

While exchange rate policy is an important instrument of monetary policy and economic adjustment, in developing countries it is also a major instrument for developing non-traditional exports, especially those of manufacturing. In this context, exchange rate policy is important for the GCC to develop non-oil sources of output and exports. In the GCC, whenever oil revenues increase it results in a commensurate increase in government revenues. To the extent that the increase in oil export revenues is offset by a commensurate capital outflow, domestic prices and the real exchange rate are not affected. But if higher oil revenues are in part translated into higher domestic government expenditures (which has invariably been the case in all GCC countries, with the possible exception of Kuwait and the United Arab Emirates), then domestic prices increase, resulting in an appreciation of the real exchange rate (as nominal exchange rates are fixed). The appreciation of the real exchange rate, in turn, has an adverse effect on non-oil exports, resulting in decline of employment and in aggregate demand. To counteract this negative effect on non-oil exports, the government can invest abroad instead of increasing domestic expenditures, or it can give export subsides. While two GCC countries, Kuwait and the United Arab Emirates have accumulated substantial foreign assets, in the case of the others higher oil revenues have been largely translated into higher domestic expenditures. In these latter countries, instead of giving selected export subsidies to encourage non-oil exports, the governments have given indiscriminate input subsidies for all sectors, whether exports or non-tradable. More recently, because of budgetary pressures, the level of these subsidies have been reduced. And as to exchange rate policy, the governments have fixed nominal rates to the dollar and thus have neglected real exchange rates as an instrument to develop their competitive advantage in non-oil exports. While real exchange rates may have a marginal effect for developing non-oil exports in the short-run, for the long-run export industries have to be profitable, either through an appropriate real exchange rate policy or through export subsidies; and such policies have to be maintained for some time for non-oil exports to develop.

The net result of the absence of an appropriate exchange rate policy is reflected in developments in real exchange rates and in GDP growth rates. Taking

1987 as the base year for real effective exchange rates, for Saudi Arabia the average value of the index was 187.79 for 1981-1985, 112.46 for 1986-1990 and 95.08 for 1991-1994; for Bahrain the corresponding numbers were 162.11, 113.87 and 92.72.[15] The large variability in real exchange rates are to be expected given the dramatic appreciation of the dollar from 1980 to early 1985, followed by roughly a commensurate depreciation between 1985 to 1990. The negative impact of real exchange rate appreciation in the early 1980's (see Table 10) and its variability is in turn reflected in real growth rates (see Table 11). During the first half of the 1980's (while the dollar appreciated) growth was negative, positive for the second half of the 1980's and was marginal for the period as a whole. The dismal growth performance of the early 1980's is largely due to the downturn in the oil market (that is due to deteriorating terms of trade). More significantly, oil and related products still dominate the export sector of these economies. For example in the case of Saudi Arabia, oil (mineral fuels, lubricants and related materials, such as chemicals) represented 99.16% of exports in 1989 while in 1990, oil and chemicals represented 94.13%; and in 1990 the export of manufactured goods (including re-exports) contributed 1.85%.[16]

Exchange rate policies have had an adverse effect on GCC growth and on their ability to develop their non-oil sector and in turn non-oil exports. Although unemployment figures are unavailable for these countries, it would appear that unemployment among nationals has become a serious issue. Expatriate labor force was roughly 75% of the total labor force in 1990, but the skills of citizens combined with their high job expectations (salary and benefits) have made the employment of local labor unprofitable. Unemployment of citizens is expected to become an even more serious issue due to rapid population growth during the 1970's and 1980's -- the average annual population growth rate in the GCC for 1971 - 1990 was 4.89% -- and due to slow economic growth of the non-oil sector. Employment opportunities will require economic growth, and especially growth of the non-oil sector.

Fixed parities to the dollar and in turn the implied fixed cross parities were tested in the aftermath of the Iraqi-invasion of Kuwait. Immediately, there was a run on the banks in the other five GCC countries. Demand for cash and in turn for foreign exchange increased dramatically. The authorities decided to maintain parity to the dollar and not to impose capital controls, accommodating the demand for dollars for transfer abroad. This was accomplished through central banks' holding of dollars and it appears through swap arrangements within the GCC and especially with the U.S. Federal Reserve. The crisis was smoothly managed with little or no financial disruption. This incident served as a confirmation of GCC commitment to maintain a fixed parity to the dollar, stable cross rates and the free flow of capital. Still the purpose of this policy is unclear. Even if fixed parities amongst the GCC were desirable, the policy of fixing to the dollar to achieve this end is still questionable. Such a policy, as opposed to fixing to the Saudi Riyal (asymmetric system), or to a basket of GCC currencies (symmetric system), would be less distortionary.

The policy of maintaining fixed parities to the dollar and in turn fixed GCC cross rates has not served a useful purpose. Trade with the U.S. in 1994 represented 8.33% of total GCC imports; while intra-GCC trade is only 4.8% of GCC imports. Thus the trade benefit of fixed parities are not large. Moreover, in the case of the GCC, there is no uniform tariff vis-a-vis the outside world, there are divergent subsidy structures and fiscal policies, while there is no serious commitment at monetary union. Under such circumstances it is difficult to understand why these countries attach such importance to fixed cross-rates and a fixed rate to the dollar. While they have pursued this policy, they have neglected the important role of real exchange rates in their economies -- to encourage non-oil NNP and non-oil exports. In such a context, a real exchange rate policy that would encourage the development of non-oil exports, with pegging to a trade weighted basket, would be a more appropriate exchange rate policy.

In the case of the GCC countries, the necessary structural adjustments and changes in policy have been delayed because of the luxury afforded by oil. The combination of current account surpluses of the past (1970's up to 1981), on-going oil revenues, the ability to at least marginally reduce very generous subsidies and public sector borrowing have enabled the GCC to postpone economic adjustments. For instance, in the case of Saudi Arabia, over the last fifteen years foreign assets have declined from around US$150 billion to less than US$20 billion, while government debt has gone from zero to over US$100 billion. At the same time, government subsidies on everything from housing, health education, electricity, water, and more have been only marginally reduced. Still the Saudi Arabian economy (non-oil) is not growing sufficiently to absorb its growing labor force, while current account deficits persist. While oil has been in one sense a blessing to their economies, it has also been a curse. Oil has enabled them to postpone necessary economic adjustments and crises. But economic pressures are continuing to build and the inevitable requirement for a massive devaluation accompanied by a change in exchange rate policy cannot be postponed indefinitely.

THE CFA FRANC ZONE

The CFA (Communauté Financière Africaine and Coopèration Financière en Afrique Centrale) franc zone was established in 1945 and today consists of the seven countries of the West African Economic and Monetary Union (WAEMU) -- Benin, Burkina Faso, Côte d'Ivoire, Mali, Niger, Senegal and Togo, the six countries of the Central African Economic and Monetary Community (CAEMC)-- Cameroon, the Central African Republic, Zaire, Equatorial Guinea and Gabon; and the Comoros which is a member of the franc zone but not of the monetary union. Each of the regions have their own central bank. The value of intra-zone trade (as a percentage of total trade) in 1994 was varied (see Table 12); while France has been the major trade partner of almost every member country.

We begin with a brief review of exchange rate arrangements and developments in the CFA zone, followed by an assessment of the impact of the exchange rate arrangement on economic performance in the fourteen countries.

The Central Bank of the West African states and the Bank of the Central African states issue their own respective CFA franc; thus within each region there is a common currency. The central bank of each region pools the external reserves of its member countries. In turn, each central bank maintains a fixed exchange rate to the French franc and promotes currency convertibility into the French franc with little or no restrictions on international transfer and payments on current transactions.

These efforts are supported with overdraft facilities at the French Treasury. Convertibility of the CFA franc is achieved by convertibility into Ff through the operations account with the French Treasury, whereby, the two regional central banks and the central bank of the Comoros deposit 65% of their foreign exchange holdings with the French Treasury; and the central banks are required to maintain a 20% foreign exchange cover of their sight liabilities. As a result, individual countries cannot affect the nominal exchange rate while external imbalances are financed by the French Treasury. From 1948 to January 1994 the exchange rate of the CFA franc was fixed as CFAf 1= Ff 0.02; in 1994 the rate was changed to CFAf 1= Ff 0.01, or a 50% devaluation (in the case of Comoros the Comorian franc was changed to Ff 0.013). More recently and within this context, the thirteen countries have agreed to coordinate policies towards achieving economic and monetary integration.

The economic characteristics of these countries are typical of poorer developing countries. Essentially, they exhibit low per capita incomes (about US$630 in 1992) with heavy dependence on agriculture (roughly 30% of GDP) and minerals. Still, the historic record of the CFA franc countries up to the mid-1980's had been significantly superior to the rest of sub-Saharan African - - from 1975-1985, the CFA franc countries had average annual real GDP growth rates of 4.6% as compared to about 1.4% for sub-Saharan Africa and inflation of 11.8% per year as compared to 17.8% for the other countries (see Table 13). However, in the period 1986-1993 average real growth was negative, while there was positive real growth rate of 2.8% in non-CFA countries; but inflation was a modest 1% per year as compared to 53.5% in the non - CFA countries. At the same time, external debt as a percentage of GDP increased from 38.2% during 1975-1985 to 82.3% during 1986-1993, while in the non-CFA countries the increase was from 25.2% to 53.9%.

The basis for cooperation between these countries has been the perceived gains from membership in the zone. The hypothesized gains include lower reserve requirements because intra-block transactions do not require foreign exchange and also partial reserve pooling, and superior macroeconomic performance as compared to similar countries. The gain from pooling of reserves is derived from the observation that individually countries would require a higher level of reserves than in the aggregate; that is, economic shocks between countries are less than perfectly correlated, thus reducing aggregate reserve requirements. Additionally, it can be hypothesized that because of the arrangement there are economies of scale associated with reserve management. Finally, to the extent that intra-regional trade is significant, intra-regional imbalances do not require reserve coverage because the countries have a common currency issued by the regional central bank, again reducing the level of required aggregate reserves. Finally, some authors have argued that the CFA arrangement has increased the central banks' ability to pursue a more independent credit policy and reduce the monetary financing of fiscal deficits, resulting in superior macro-economic performance.[17]

Allechi and Niamkey have estimated the net gains from the CFA arrangement.[18] They basically estimated the gains from pooling and the losses associated with the opportunity cost of maintaining an operation account with the French Treasury. Their conclusion was that on balance most CFA countries were net losers; and clearly the biggest losers being those that had positive balances in the operations account.

The essential performance characteristic of CFA countries is superior economic performance (faster growth and lower inflation) than sub-Saharan Africa up to roughly 1985 and less than satisfactory performance from 1985 to 1993. Most authors have attributed the reasons for their period of inferior performance to structural distortions in the period following 1985 and to their ability to avoid adjustment to macro-economic shocks (declining terms of trade) due to falling international commodity prices.[19] Their ability to delay appropriate adjustment was made possible by the arrangement with France.

Memberships in the CFA may have had benefits such as lower reserve requirements and increased monetary discipline for each member country, but at the same time the need for appropriate macro-economic adjustment could not be postponed indefinitely. The arrangement with the French Treasury could ameliorate cyclical and short-run adjustments but could also exacerbate required long-term adjustments through postponement. During the period 1979-1985, while the French franc depreciated, the economic performance of the CFA countries was superior to those of comparable countries in sub-Saharan Africa. But in the post 1985 period, two simultaneous but opposite developments -- the appreciation of the French franc, due to the Franc Fort Policy, and substantially lower prices for commodities (deterioration of the terms of trade) -- resulted in serious structural distortions in the CFA countries.

During the period 1986-1989, the real effective exchange rate of the entire group of CFA countries appreciated 5.9% while the terms of trade declined by 29%.[20] At the same time there were large and significant divergences in each of these indicators among the countries (see Table 14). For the terms of trade, Benin experienced a 57% adverse movement while Burkina Faso saw no measurable change. For real effective exchange rates, Cameroon experienced a 33% appreciation, while Niger had a 25% depreciation. The overall external deterioration required overall structural adjustments and at the same time divergences between the members required intra-block-adjustments. These divergences were in large part due to the fact that the goods exported and imported by each country are different (affecting the terms of trade), the share of trade with France and with other countries are dissimilar, and inflation rates are different amongst the countries (affecting real effective exchange rates). In retrospect, it is clear that countries were not committed to policy coordination given the size of divergences in real effective exchange rates.

In the face of these difficulties, the CFA countries postponed the required macro-economic adjustments. Their overall conditions stabilized somewhat in the period of 1990-1993. Terms of trade declined by only 1.5% and real effective exchange rates depreciated by 3.1% (1991-1993).[21] Structural adjustment were avoided because of the special relationship with the French Treasury resulting in a rapid increase in external debt (see Table 13). However, this dismal economic growth performance and the expectation for much of the same forced them to a nominal devaluation of 50% vis-a-vis the French franc, accompanied by macro-economic and structural changes, while increasing their commitment towards comprehensive economic integration.

The costs and benefits of complete economic integration among these countries, while a critical issue, is a different subject. But the lessons of the recent crisis (a crisis many years in the making) should not be forgotten, especially given that the members may be even more determined to maintain parity to the French franc and thus their commitment to fixed cross rates. The countries have to coordinate macro-economic policies to avoid significant divergences in economic performance. This coordination, while incorporating French policies (the impact of the "Franc Fort Policy") should also note the economic importance (in terms of GDP as a percentage of CFA zone's aggregate GDP) of Côte d'Ivoire (20% of zone's GDP) and Cameroon (23%). Although the CFA is a group of thirteen countries, adverse policies in the Côte d'Ivoire and in Cameroon could further exacerbate overall CFA economic performance. This could be further aggravated by the uncertainties surrounding the establishment of the Euro in 1999 and the ability of the French Treasury to maintain its commitment to the CFA franc zone.

In the end, the CFA should re-assess its on-going exchange arrangement -- are the benefits worth the costs? Assuming that complete economic integration is desirable in itself, several questions remain:

- Is fixing the nominal rate to the French franc more desirable than fixing to a trade-weighted basket?
- Is a nominal parity fix more desirable than a real parity fix?
- Is there a true commitment to policy coordination among the CFA countries?
- Can monetary discipline be maintained in the absence of the existing agreement

with the French Treasury?
- How will the common monetary policy be determined and enforced?
- Are the presumed benefits of the existing arrangement (reduction in reserve requirement, reduced risk in trade and in currency transactions, and enhanced monetary discipline) greater than its costs (delayed macro-economic adjustments, foregone national output and more rapid accumulation of external debt)?

None of these questions have simple answers. They will require a great deal of study and soul searching on the way to designing a best or at least a bearable solution.

As to be expected, the devaluation of 1994 has on the whole had the expected results.[22] There has been a significant increase in competitiveness -- the real effective exchange -- real growth has picked up, while short-run inflation went up (see Table 15). But in the medium-run and long-run, significant structural changes are still required and the CFA should re-examine the benefit and costs of the existing arrangement if it is to avoid re-occurring crises.

CONCLUSION

Because of ever increasing capital mobility, the lessons of Bretton Woods are even more applicable today than during the Bretton Woods era. Under a system of fixed exchange rates with narrow bands there is only one domestic price level (and interest rate structure) that is consistent with the price levels (and interest rate structures) of the rest of the world that results in balance of payments equilibrium and full employment. In today's world when groups of countries adopt fixed parities amongst themselves, there is still no escape from the implications and requirements of a fixed parity systems for balance of payments equilibrium and full employment and, in turn, for interest rate and monetary policy.

In the case of the EMS, fixed parities to the ECU and the float of the ECU relative to the rest of the world combined with the over tight policy direction of the Bundesbank, the de facto central bank of the system, have resulted in high interest rates, overvalued real exchange rates and thus in slow economic growth and historically high levels of unemployment. The key countries of the EMS should undertake expansionary monetary policies, reducing real internal rates, and exchange rates, increasing investment and exports (but not net exports) to enhance growth and employment. However, the inability to adopt such a coordinated (coordinated as required of a system of fixed parities) policy has brought on the current dismal economic conditions. At the same time, while it is noted that fixed parities (and in the longer run a single currency) do have their benefits in the form of reduced cost (risk) of trade and reduced transaction cost of foreign exchange, these benefits can be easily outweighed by the costs arising from residual policy divergences; costs which will increase with increasing policy divergences.

In the case of the GCC, with four out of six members fixing (formally or informally) their currency to the dollar, the results, while similar to the EU, are still somewhat different. On-going policies in the GCC have resulted in slow overall growth, in slow development of the non-oil sector and non-oil exports and in a number of glaring economic distortions. The neglect and the behavior of real exchange rates is the most glaring policy defect.

While structural and macro-economic adjustments have been avoided by running down historically accumulated reserves and by recourse to borrowing, oil has been the crutch for postponing necessary policy changes. But even for these "seemingly rich" countries the time for changes in policy cannot be postponed forever. Looming unemployment in the future will be the catalyst. The precise form of GCC exchange arrangements is questionable. Why fix to the dollar and not to a GCC trade-weighted basket? Moreover, if it is fixed to a trade weighted basket, then is it the real rate that should be maintained at an appropriate level? But if the latter system is chosen, then policy divergences will become problematic because Saudi Arabia, by far the dominant economy in the system, will have an enormous impact on the trade weights used and on overall policy of the group. Is in fact a fixed rate desirable between these countries, countries that have little trade amongst themselves?

In the case of the CFA, countries fixing to the franc and their special arrangement with the French Treasury afforded them savings in the form of external reserve requirement and forced monetary discipline. But when they were confronted with two external developments -- substantial appreciation of the French franc and a major deterioration in the terms of trade, they were unable to adopt necessary policies which would have further increased unemployment. The loss of international competitiveness and divergent policies amongst the CFA countries resulted in distortions. Structural and macro-economic adjustment were postponed for a time with substantial costs in foregone output but eventually adjustments had to be accepted in 1994. As in the case of the GCC, although the fixing of the CFA franc to a single currency may be questioned, in the case of the CFA zone a significance part of their trade is with France (and even more with the EU).

In conclusion, although fixed parities between groups of countries have their benefits, the potential costs must be also kept in mind. The arrangements must prevent the occurrence of the "Bundesbank syndrome" which has turned the march towards Maastricht into an unqualified disaster. The strongest and the most conservative central bank has turned into the unofficial central bank of the system, but without concern or responsibility for the other member countries. This has meant heavy costs, in the form of delayed structural and macro-economic adjustments, resulting in foregone output and in unemployment, costs which may greatly exceed potential benefits. And in the event that potential financial crisis are not addressed before they happen, financial disruptions could further exacerbate economic conditions.

Table 1
Price Deflator Gross Domestic Product at Market Prices
(National currency, annual percentage change)

	1961-	1971-	1981-	1991	1992	1993	1994	1995
Belgium	3.4	7.1	4.4	2.7	3.4	4.4	1.8	2.6
Denmark	6.4	9.7	5.8	2.5	1.9	1.7	1.6	2.1
West Germany	3.8	5.2	2.8	3.9	4.4	3.2	2.4	1.9
Germany	-	-	-	-	5.5	3.9	2.8	2.2
Greece	3.1	13.7	18.4	18.4	14.2	13.6	10.7	9.8
Spain	6.4	15.2	9.4	7.0	6.5	4.6	3.5	4.2
France	4.4	9.8	6.3	3.1	2.3	2.3	1.6	2.1
Ireland	5.5	13.8	6.8	1.1	1.3	3.6	2.9	2.5
Italy	4.5	14.8	10.5	7.7	4.5	4.4	3.4	3.3
Luxembourg	4.1	6.5	4.8	3.0	4.5	2.1	2.8	2.4
Netherlands	5.2	7.6	2.1	2.7	2.6	1.6	1.8	2.1
Portugal	2.9	16.1	17.9	14.1	13.4	7.4	5.1	4.9
United Kingdom	4.2	14.0	6.2	6.5	4.3	3.4	2.1	2.7
EUR 12-	4.4	10.9	6.7	5.4	4.3	3.6	2.6	2.8
EUR 12+	-	-	-	-	4.6	3.8	2.7	2.8
USA	3.0	7.5	4.5	3.9	2.9	2.0	2.2	2.9
Japan	5.4	7.7	1.7	2.0	1.6	1.4	1.4	0.4

Aggregates: Purchasing Power Standard (PPS) weighted; EUR 12-: including WD (West Germany); EUR 12+ : including D (Germany).
Source: Commission of the European Communities, Annual Report for 1995.

Table 2
Gross Domestic Product at 1985 Market Prices
(Annual percentage change)

	1961-	1971-	1981-	1991	1992	1993	1994	1995
Belgium	4.9	3.2	1.9	2.3	1.9	-1.7	2.2	2.7
Denmark	4.5	2.2	2.0	1.0	1.3	1.4	4.8	3.2
West Germany	4.4	2.7	2.2	5.0	1.8	-1.7	2.0	2.5
Germany	-	-	-		2.2	-1.1	2.5	3.0
Greece	7.6	4.7	1.5	3.2	0.8	-0.5	0.4	1.1
Spain	7.3	3.5	2.9	2.2	0.8	-1.1	2.2	2.8
France	5.6	3.3	2.4	0.8	1.2	-1.0	2.2	3.2
Ireland	4.2	4.7	3.8	2.9	5.0	4.0	6.0	5.6
Italy	5.7	3.8	2.2	1.2	0.7	-0.7	2.4	3.0
Luxembourg	3.5	2.6	3.6	3.1	1.9	0.6	2.3	3.0
Netherlands	5.1	2.9	2.0	2.3	1.3	0.3	2.3	3.2
Portugal	6.4	4.7	2.7	2.1	1.1	-1.2	1.1	3.0
United Kingdom	2.9	1.9	2.7	-2.0	-0.5	2.0	3.8	2.7
EUR 12-	4.8	3.0	2.4	1.7	1.0	-0.5	2.5	2.8
EUR 12+	-	-	-		1.1	-0.4	2.6	2.9
USA	3.8	2.7	2.7	-1.1	2.6	3.0	3.9	2.7
Japan	10.5	4.5	4.1	4.3	1.1	0.1	0.7	2.2

Aggregates: Purchasing Power Standard (PPS) weighted; EUR 12-: including WD (West Germany) ; EUR 12+ : including D (Germany.
Source: Commission of the European Communities, Annual Report for 1995.

Table 3
Real Compensation per Employee; Total Economy; Deflator GDP
(Annual percentage change)

	1961 -70	1971 -80	1981 -90	1991	1992	1993	1994	1995
Belgium	4.2	4.7	0.6	5.2	2.4	-0.2	1.4	0.2
Denmark	3.9	1.6	0.7	2.2	0.8	0.2	1.0	0.6
West Germany	4.6	2.9	0.8	1.9	1.3	0.1	0.1	0.7
Germany	-	-	-		4.6	0.6	0.4	0.8
Greece	6.1	4.0	1.1	-4.2	-3.7	-4.4	1.6	0.3
Spain	7.3	4.5	0.6	1.1	1.9	2.4	0.5	-0.3
France	4.9	3.5	1.0	1.3	2.0	0.2	0.8	0.6
Ireland	4.1	4.2	2.4	3.3	5.0	2.2	0.6	0.5
Italy	6.0	3.1	1.3	0.8	1.2	-0.7	0.4	1.0
Luxembourg	2.5	3.9	1.1	1.0	1.4	2.7	1.3	1.7
Netherlands	5.1	3.0	0.1	1.7	2.2	1.6	0.2	-0.3
Portugal	6.6	5.6	1.1	2.7	2.2	0.0	0.2	1.0
United Kingdom	2.8	1.8	2.2	2.0	1.2	1.4	1.9	1.9
EUR 12-	4.5	2.9	0.9	1.5	1.4	0.3	0.6	0.7
EUR 12+	-	-	-		2.3	0.5	0.7	0.8
USA	2.1	0.6	0.7	0.6	2.2	1.0	1.4	0.6
Japan	7.7	5.0	2.2	2.6	0.2	-2.2	-0.8	0.6

Aggregates: Purchasing Power Standard (PPS) weighted; EUR 12-: including WD (West Germany); EUR 12+ : including D (Germany).
Source: Commission of the European Communities, Annual Report for 1995.

Table 4a
Nominal Unit Labor costs; Total Economy[1]
Performance relative to 19 industrial countries; double export weights

	1961-70	1971-80	1981-90	1991	1992	1993	1994	1995
Belgium	84.6	98.1	82.2	85.0	86.9	89.5	91.4	92.3
Denmark	88.9	104.8	93.1	95.0	95.9	95.4	93.2	94.0
West Germany	86.2	102.6	89.9	88.6	93.1	96.8	95.7	96.1
Greece	146.0	105.6	99.7	92.1	90.8	88.6	91.7	93.9
Spain	76.0	88.8	85.9	100.7	101.6	89.7	84.1	84.8
France	103.1	94.0	85.9	80.8	82.4	84.0	84.1	83.8
Ireland	98.2	95.7	96.5	87.3	88.3	83.3	83.4	83.1
Italy	111.6	100.4	111.3	131.4	128.2	105.6	100.0	97.0
Netherlands	79.4	98.9	85.8	79.7	82.3	85.0	84.8	84.7
Portugal	112.0	119.7	94.8	112.9	128.9	124.0	122.4	125.5
United Kingdom	94.5	80.8	89.9	99.1	96.1	86.5	86.4	87.5
EUR 12-[2]	81.8	88.2	78.3	83.8	87.3	80.3	77.5	77.5
USA	153.8	114.3	120.7	101.2	98.8	103.5	104.1	104.4
Japan	72.5	100.7	117.4	124.4	129.1	151.9	162.5	162.6

Aggregates: EUR 12-: including WD (West Germany).
[1] compensation of employees adjusted for the share of self-employed in occupied population per unit of GDP at constant prices.
[2] EUR 12- relative to nine industrial non-member countries.
Source: Commission of the European Communities, Annual Report for 1995.

Table 4b
Real Unit Labor costs; Total Economy[1]

	1961-70	1971-80	1981-90	1991	1992	1993	1994	1995
Belgium	87.2	95.3	94.6	92.5	92.6	92.7	91.7	90.1
Denmark	98.3	99.7	94.2	91.5	91.0	89.3	86.2	85.4
West Germany	94.6	99.0	95.8	91.1	91.5	91.7	89.0	87.7
Greece	108.3	96.6	106.4	96.1	93.2	90.4	91.2	90.6
Spain	95.7	100.0	91.5	86.0	85.9	85.2	83.2	81.9
France	93.9	96.9	95.0	89.8	89.8	89.8	88.3	86.8
Ireland	96.2	95.9	89.9	85.9	86.3	85.4	83.2	81.5
Italy	97.1	101.5	98.8	97.1	96.5	93.8	90.5	89.4
Luxembourg	84.0	93.6	93.4	95.8	97.1	100.8	101.5	102.2
Netherlands	93.9	99.9	91.2	87.7	89.3	90.3	88.5	86.6
Portugal	86.6	103.5	90.5	83.4	83.8	83.1	82.1	80.6
United Kingdom	98.5	101.1	97.3	102.1	101.6	99.4	97.6	97.6
EUR 12-	97.8	100.5	94.4	90.7	90.6	89.7	87.5	86.4
USA	97.0	98.7	98.7	99.6	99.4	98.9	99.3	99.2
Japan	92.8	99.5	95.6	93.4	93.5	91.6	90.6	90.2

Aggregates: Purchasing Power Standard (PPS) weighted; EUR 12-: including WD (West Germany).
[1] Nominal unit labor costs deflated by the GDP price deflator.
Source: Commission of the European Communities, Annual Report for 1995.

Table 5
Real Long-term Interest Rates[1]

	1961-70	1971-80	1981-90	1991	1992	1993	1994
Belgium	2.8	1.5	5.7	6.4	5.0	2.7	5.9
Denmark	1.8	4.5	7.2	7.4	8.0	7.0	6.8
West Germany	2.9	2.7	4.7	4.5	3.4	3.0	4.2
Spain	-	-	4.5	5.0	5.4	5.4	6.0
France	2.0	0.5	4.8	5.7	6.2	4.4	5.8
Ireland	-5.2	-0.9	5.4	8.0	7.7	4.0	5.1
Italy	2.1	-2.8	4.1	4.9	8.8	6.6	7.0
Luxembourg	-	-	3.9	5.0	3.3	4.7	3.5
Netherlands	0.4	1.0	6.1	5.8	5.4	5.0	5.3
Portugal	-	-	-	3.7	1.8	4.7	5.5
United Kingdom	2.7	-1.3	4.4	3.2	4.6	4.3	6.0
EUR 12-	2.2	-0.5	4.3	4.6	5.4	4.3	5.5
USA	1.7	-0.2	5.5	4.0	4.7	4.5	5.1
Japan	-	-	4.8	4.6	3.6	2.6	2.8

Aggregates: Purchasing Power Standard (PPS) weighted; EUR 12-: including WD (West Germany).
[1] Nominal interest rates deflated by the GDP price deflator
Source: Commission of the European Communities, Annual Report for 1995.

Table 6
Occupied Population; Total Economy (SNA)
(% percentage change)

	1961 -70	1971 -80	1981 -90	1991	1992	1993	1994	1995
Belgium	0.6	0.2	0.2	0.1	-0.4	-1.4	-0.4	0.7
Denmark	1.1	0.7	0.5	-1.8	-0.1	-0.6	0.1	1.7
West Germany	0.2	0.2	0.5	2.5	0.9	-1.6	-1.2	0.4
Germany	-	-	-	-	-1.6	-1.8	-0.9	0.5
Greece	-0.8	0.7	1.0	-2.3	1.4	1.0	-0.3	0.2
Spain	0.6	-0.6	0.8	0.5	-1.2	-4.3	-0.6	1.6
France	0.6	0.5	0.2	0.1	-0.8	-1.1	-0.2	0.7
Ireland	0.0	0.9	-0.2	0.0	0.5	0.7	2.6	2.9
Italy	-0.5	1.0	0.6	0.8	-1.0	-2.8	-1.5	0.7
Luxembourg	0.6	1.2	1.8	4.1	1.8	1.7	1.7	1.9
Netherlands	1.2	0.2	0.5	1.3	0.9	-0.1	0.0	1.3
Portugal	0.2	0.1	-0.4	0.9	+0.6	-2.0	-0.4	0.1
United Kingdom	0.2	0.2	0.6	-3.1	-2.1	-1.6	0.0	0.7
EUR 12-	0.2	0.3	0.5	0.1	-0.6	-1.8	-0.6	0.8
EUR 12+	-	-	-	-	-1.2	-1.9	-0.6	0.8
USA	1.9	2.0	1.9	-1.1	0.2	1.4	2.9	1.9
Japan	1.4	0.7	1.1	2.1	1.1	0.2	0.4	1.0

Aggregates: EUR 12-: including WD (West Germany); EUR 12+ : including D (Germany).
Source: Commission of the European Communities, Annual Report for 1995.

Table 7
Unemployment Rate; Total Member Countries: Eurostat definition
(percentage)

	1961 -70	1971 -80	1981 -90	1991	1992	1993	1994	1995
Belgium	2.1	4.6	10.7	7.5	8.2	9.4	10.0	9.8
Denmark	1.1	3.7	7.6	8.9	9.5	10.3	10.2	9.0
West Germany	0.8	2.2	6.0	4.2	4.5	5.6	6.3	6.2
Greece	5.0	2.2	7.1	7.7	8.7	9.7	10.2	10.6
Spain	2.7	5.4	18.4	16.4	18.2	21.8	22.4	21.9
France	1.6	4.1	9.2	9.5	10.0	10.8	11.3	11.0
Ireland	5.6	7.7	15.7	16.2	17.8	18.4	17.7	16.8
Italy	5.8	6.1	9.7	10.1	10.3	11.1	11.8	11.1
Luxembourg	0.0	0.6	2.5	1.6	1.9	2.6	3.3	3.2
Netherlands	0.9	4.4	10.1	7.1	7.2	8.8	10.0	9.8
Portugal	2.5	5.1	7.0	4.0	3.9	5.1	6.1	6.0
United Kingdom	1.9	3.8	9.7	8.9	10.2	10.4	9.4	8.5
EUR 9-[1]	2.3	4.0	8.8	8.0	8.6	9.4	9.6	9.1
EUR 12-	2.2	4.2	9.6	8.7	9.4	10.5	10.9	10.4
USA[2]	5.2	6.4	7.1	6.7	7.4	6.8	6.2	5.9
Japan[3]	1.3	1.8	2.5	2.1	2.2	2.6	3.0	2.9

[1] Aggregates: EUR 9- and EUR 12- : including WD (West Germany).
[2] EUR 12 - excluding Greece, Spain and Portugal.
[3] OECD.
Source: Commission of the European Communities, Annual Report for 1995.

Table 8
Productivity Growth
(percentage)

	1977-86	1987	1988	1989	1990	1991	1992	1993	1994	1995	1996
Germany*	2.9	1.9	4.2	3.4	3.6	2.8	4.4	4.7	9.8	6.1	3.4
France	4.0	5.0	7.3	5.1	1.5	1.3	5.0	0.1	8.8	1.8	1.6
Italy	3.6	5.3	5.7	2.9	1.6	1.8	4.3	1.9	6.8	2.0	1.8
United Kingdom	2.9	4.9	5.1	4.4	2.2	2.2	4.4	4.5	4.6	3.8	4.3
EU	3.7	3.6	5.1	3.6	1.9	2.0	4.0	3.2	7.3	3.5	2.6
USA	1.7	6.4	2.4	0.6	1.7	2.5	1.9	3.7	4.6	2.3	2.2
Japan	3.3	4.1	7.4	4.5	2.8	1.5	-3.7	-1.6	3.5	4.5	1.4

* Data through 1990 applies to West Germany only
Source: IMF, World Economic Outlook, October 1995.

Table 9
Adjusted Wage Share; Total Economy
(percentage)

	1961 -70	1971 -80	1981 -90	1991	1992	1993	1994	1995
Belgium	70.0	74.9	74.4	73.0	73.4	73.7	73.1	71.8
Denmark	75.4	77.9	74.4	71.4	70.5	69.2	67.4	67.0
West Germany	71.6	73.7	70.9	67.8	68.4	68.8	66.9	66.0
Germany	-	-	-	69.1	69.9	70.1	68.0	66.9
Greece	78.5	69.5	76.1	70.9	69.5	66.6	67.7	67.8
Spain	74.6	77.0	71.6	68.0	68.4	67.0	65.7	64.9
France	72.8	73.8	72.5	68.5	68.3	68.1	67.2	66.0
Ireland	84.3	82.1	77.1	73.1	74.1	72.4	71.1	69.5
Italy	72.8	73.8	72.0	72.6	72.3	70.8	68.2	67.3
Luxembourg	67.8	76.9	79.6	83.5	85.5	89.6	90.1	90.6
Netherlands	69.5	74.4	67.7	65.3	66.8	67.9	66.8	66.0
Portugal	68.9	82.6	74.9	70.0	70.3	68.8	68.9	67.6
United Kingdom	72.7	73.8	73.3	76.5	76.0	74.1	73.0	73.5
EUR 12-	74.1	75.4	73.0	70.9	71.0	70.8	69.5	68.8
EUR 12+	-	-	-	71.1	71.3	71.1	69.7	68.9
USA	71.1	72.1	71.7	72.6	72.4	72.0	72.1	71.9
Japan	73.5	78.0	75.7	74.1	74.2	72.9	72.1	71.7

Aggregates: Purchasing Power Standard (PPS) weighted; EUR 12-: including WD (West Germany); EUR 12+ : including D (Germany).
Source: Commission of the European Communities, Annual Report for 1995.

Table 10
G.C.C. Currencies Per U.S. Dollar
(Period Average)

Year	Saudi Riyal	Kuwaiti Dinar	Bahraini Dinar	Omani Riyal	Qatar Riyal	U.A.E. Dirham
1977	3.5251	0.2866	0.3956	0.3454	3.9590	3.9032
1978	3.3996	0.7250	0.3875	0.3454	3.8767	3.8712
1979	3.3608	0.2762	0.3816	0.3454	3.7727	3.8157
1980	3.3267	0.2703	0.3770	0.3454	3.6568	3.7074
1981	3.3825	0.2787	0.3760	0.3454	3.6399	3.6710
1982	3.4282	0.2879	0.3760	0.3454	3.6399	3.6710
1983	3.4548	0.2915	0.3760	0.3454	3.6399	3.6710
1984	3.5238	0.2960	0.3760	0.3454	3.6399	3.6710
1985	3.6221	0.3007	0.3760	0.3454	3.6399	3.6710
1986	3.7033	0.2919	0.3760	0.3820	3.6399	3.6710
1987	3.7450	0.2775	0.3760	0.3845	3.6399	3.6709
1988	3.7450	0.2790	0.3760	0.3845	3.6400	3.6709
1989	3.7450	0.2937	0.3760	0.3845	3.6400	3.6709
1990	3.7450	0.2920	0.3760	0.3845	3.6400	3.6709
1991	3.7450	0.2843	0.3760	0.3845	3.6400	3.6710
1992	3.7450	0.3027	0.3760	0.3845	3.6400	3.6710
1993	3.7450	0.2984	0.3760	0.3845	3.6400	3.6710
1994	3.7450	0.3001	0.3760	0.3845	3.6400	3.6710

Table 11
GCC Real GDP Growth Rates
(Percentage, Period Totals)

	1980 - 1985	1985 - 1990	1980 - 1992
Bahrain	- 0.02	10.80	15.79
Kuwait	- 30.29	17.75	- 17.91
Oman	100.00	5.00	142.00
Qatar	- 13.56	27.45	13.56
Saudi Arabia	- 21.18	20.18	6.04
UAE	- 52.24	5.53	2.09
GCC Average	- 16.76	10.06	5.62

Table 12
Intra-CFA Zone Trade (in Percentage of Total Trade) and Principal Trading Partner

	Percentage share of Intra-CFA Trade in Total Trade.[1]				Principal Trading Partner in (1989).[2]	
	Exports		Imports		Export	Import
	1990-93	1994	1990-93	1994		
Benin	8.0	2.8	5.5	3.6	USA (20.1%)	France (21%)
Burkina Faso	8.5	14.9	24.5	31.2	France (34.4%)	France (31%)
Côte d'Ivoire	17.6	17.6	1.7	1.7	Holland (16.9%)	France (30.6%)
Mali	3.6	2.4	26.7	22.9	--	--
Niger	3.3	9.2	10.3	12.9	France (80%)	France (32.3%)
Senegal	14.0	19.4	9.8	9.7	France (28.5%)	France (36.4%)
Togo	6.9	6.4	8.8	11.7	France (12.2%)	France (24.8%)
Cameroon	9.5	16.3	3.5	8.2	France (28.2%)	France (40.0%)
Central African Republic	0.3	0.6	6.5	4.7	France (42.3%)	France (52.4%)
Chad	0.5	0.4	13.2	29.0	France (25%)	--
Congo	--	0.1	4.7	5.6	USA (42%)	France (47%)
Equatorial Guinea	--	--	36.9	37.6	--	--
Gabon	1.2	1.0	11.7	19.9	France (36%)	France (45%)

[1] **Source:** Clément et al. (IMF, Direction of Trade Statistics Yearbook).
[2] **Source:** Allechi and NiamKey.

Table 13
CFA Economic Indicators

	Average	
	1975	1986-93
	(Annual percentage changes)	
Real GDP growth		
CFA	4.6	-0.2
Non-CFA	1.7	2.8
Real per capita GDP growth		
CFA	1.7	-3.1
Non-CFA	-1.3	-0.1
Inflation[1]		
CFA	11.8	1.0
Non-CFA	17.8	53.5
	(in per cent of GDP)	
Overall fiscal balance		
CFA	-5.0	-7.2
Non-CFA	-6.1	-5.1
External current account balance (including grants)		
CFA	-6.5	-5.0
Non-CFA	-1.9	-0.9
External debt		
CFA	38.2	82.3
Non-CFA	25.2	53.9

[1] Based on consumer price index.
Note: Data provided by the authorities; and Fund staff estimates.
Note: Sub-Saharan Africa is defined here to include Nigeria and South Africa and to exclude Djibouti, Liberia, Mauritania, Somalia, and Sudan.
Source: Jean A. P. Clément, Johannes Mueller, Stephanie Cossé and Jean Le Dem, Aftermath of the CFA France Devaluation, Occasional paper #138, IMF, May 1996.

Table 14
CFA Terms of Trade and Real Effective Exchange Rates

	Terms of Trade 1986-1989 (% change)	Real Effective Exchange Rates 1986-1989 (% change)
WAEMU		
Benin	-56	1
Burkina Faso	---	-10
Côte d'Ivoire	-35	29
Mali	- 8	-19
Niger	- 7	-25
Senegal	- 5	-13
Togo	-15	- 6
CAEMC		
Cameroon	-52	33
Central African Republic	-10	- 3
Chad	-13	-20
Congo	-55	---
Equatorial Guinea	-26	-17
Gabon	-47	- 5
Weighted Average (by 1994 GDP)	-29	6

Source: Derived from IMF Sources.

Table 15
Recent Performance of the CFA

			CFA Zone[1]				
	1990-93 Average	1993	1994 Original program	Provisional	Deviation	1995	1996
			(Annual percentage changes)				
Real sector							
Real rate of growth	-0.4	-1.6	1.0	1.3	0.3	5.0	5.6
GDP deflator	-0.2	-0.4	34.7	36.5	1.8	8.3	3.2
Inflation (CPI)	0.1	-0.5	32.5	33.0	0.5	9.9	3.5
Nominal GDP	-0.7	-2.2	36.4	38.3	1.9	13.7	8.9

Note: Percentage change is real effective exchange rate in 1994 was -29.7.
[1] Source: Clément et al

NOTES

[1] For the sake of clarity, it may be appropriate up-front to define exchange rates as used in this paper. The real exchange rate is nominal exchange rate adjusted for relative movements in prices between countries. The real effective exchange rate is an index (weighted by trade) of real exchange rates between a country and its major trading partners. At the same time, it should be noted that the terms of trade is the price of exports divided by the price of imports (in a common currency).

[2] For details see "International Monetary Fund currency Arrangements," International Financial Statistics, IMF, 1993, p.6.

[3] For example see Franco Modigliani and Hossein Askari, The Reform of The International Payments System, Essays in International Finance, Princeton University, No. 89, September 1971.

[4] See Modigliani and Askari, 1975, p. 11-12.

[5] This section relies heavily on Franco Modigliani, "The shameful rate of unemployment in the EMS: causes and cures," De Economist, 144, No. 3, 1996.

[6] See Modigliani, 1996.

[7] In fact, the unemployment rate in the EU has been consistently higher than that in the US in every year since 1983, it is noteworthy that from 1979-1985, the US dollar appreciated by roughly 100% against the major European currencies.

[8] While this is the major argument for the supply driven position, others are: (i) generous welfare provisions for the unemployed and high taxes to cover social programs, resulting in a narrowing spread between take-home pay and unemployment benefits and thus a reduction in the incentive to work; (ii) the role of the long-term unemployed; (iii) mismatch of available jobs and skills; (iv) loss of jobs to developing countries; (v) effect of minimum wage; and more. Modigliani (1996) has refuted all of these with the exception of the minimum wage which would be unlikely to account for such a significant difference between EU and US unemployment rates.

[9] Thus while there has been a significantly higher real wage growth in the EU since 1960, it has not been markedly different since 1980.

[10] See Modigliani, 1996.

[11] The assertion that fast real wage growth would result in the substitution of capital for labor (higher investment) and in lower investment (due to lower profitability) would therefore be in doubt due to the effect of productivity growth. While the real effect on investment is in doubt, the negative impact of high real interest rates on investment is clear. Although in the EU the share of fixed capital formation in GDP declined from 23.1% in the 1960's to 19.9% in the 1980's, it has been consistently higher than that of the US (18.3% in the 1960's and 18.6% in the 1980's. As to the impact of real wages on international competitiveness, the overall changes in competitiveness is reflected in real exchange rates, with no uniform appreciation (+) since 1987. As of September 1995, the change in real exchange rate from 1987 (deflated by unit labor cost) are Belgium (+4.71%), Denmark (+9.9%), Germany (+16.2%), France (-2.8%), Netherlands (-0.2%), Austria (-3.3%), Greece (+21.3%), Portugal (nil), Italy (-20.9%), Sweden (-21.4%), Ireland (-24.5%), Finland (-27%), Spain (-5%), U.K. (-5.7%), source: Progress Towards convergence, EMI, November 1995.

[12] While supply factors, especially the minimum wage, could have contributed to this result, more likely demand (monetary and fiscal) is the prime candidate (see Modigliani, 1996).

[13] For a detailed discussion of the GCC, see Muhammad Al-Aitani, An Empirical Investigation into the Appropriate Exchange Rate Arrangement for the Gulf Cooperation Council States, Ph.D. Thesis, George Washington University, Washington D.C., December 1995.

[14] See H. Askari, Saudi Arabia's Economy: oil and the search for Economic Development, forward by Robert Solow and Appendix by Martin Weitzeman, JAI Press: Greenwich, Connecticut 1990, and H. Askari, V. Nowshirvani, and M. Jabber, Regional Economic Development in the GCC, unpublished manuscript 1996.

[15] Figures are available only for these countries and are taken from the IFS data base (IMF).

[16] International Trade Statistics Year Book, IMF, 1991.

[17] Clément et al., 1996.

[18] M'Bet Allechi and Madeleine NiamKey, "Evaluating the Net Gains from the CFA Franc Zone Membership: A Different Perspective," World Development, vol. 22, No. 8, 1994.

[19] S. Devarajan and J. DeMelo, "Membership in the CFA Zone: Odyssean Journey or Trojan Horse," Paper presented at the Conference on African Economic Issues, Nairobi, 1990.

[20] These are weighted (by GDP) average figures and were derived from IMF sources.

[21] Clément et al.
[22] For detail see Clément et al.

REFERENCES

Al-Aitani, Muhammad, "An Empirical Investigation into the Appropriate Exchange Rate Arrangement for the Gulf Cooperation Council States," Ph.D. Thesis, George Washington University, Washington D.C., December 1995.

Allechi, M'Bet and NiamKey, Madeleine, "Evaluating the Net Gains from the CFA Franc Zone Membership: A Different Perspective," World Development, vol. 22, No. 8, 1994.

Askari, H.. Saudi Arabia's Economy: oil and the search for Economic Development, forward by Robert Solow and Appendix by Martin Weitzeman, JAI Press: Greenwich, Connecticut 1990, and H. Askari, V. Nowshirvani, and M. Jabber, Regional Economic Development in the GCC, unpublished manuscript 1996.

Clément, Jean A. P., Johannes Mueller, Stephanie Cossé and Jean Le Dem, "Aftermath of the CFA France Devaluation," Occasional paper #138, IMF, May 1996.

Commission of the European Communities, Annual Report for 1995.

Devarajan, S. and DeMelo, J., "Membership in the CFA Zone: Odyssean Journey or Trojan Horse," Paper presented at the Conference on African Economic Issues, Nairobi, 1990.

IMF, World Economic Outlook, October 1995.

"International Monetary Fund currency Arrangements," International Financial Statistics, IMF, 1993, p.6.

International Trade Statistics Year Book, IMF, 1991.

Modigliani, Franco and Askari, Hossein, "The Reform of The International Payments System," Essays in International Finance, Princeton University, No. 89, September 1971.

Modigliani, Franco, "The shameful rate of unemployment in the EMS: causes and cures," De Economist, 144, No. 3, 1996.

Progress Towards Convergence, EMI, November 1995.

PART III

THE MEXICAN CRISES AND THE TEQUILA EFFECT

8

The Mexican Financial Crisis Of 1994-95: An Asymmetric Information Analysis

FREDERIC S. MISHKIN
Former Executive Vice-President and Director of Research, The Federal Reserve Bank of New York and currently A. Barton Hepburn Professor of Economics, Columbia University and Research Associate, National Bureau of Economic Research

INTRODUCTION

One of the major economic events in the 1990s has been the Mexican financial crisis in 1994-95. An important puzzle is how a country like Mexico, which had seemed to be pursuing reasonable policies, can shift dramatically from a path of reasonable growth before a financial crisis to a sharp decline in economic activity after a crisis occurs that is very damaging to both the economy and social fabric of the country.

This paper attempts to explain this puzzle by outlining an asymmetric information framework for analyzing financial crises in emerging market countries and then applies it to the Mexican experience in 1994-95. The paper concludes by drawing lessons from the Mexican experience to policymaking in emerging market countries. An important theme is that an appropriate institutional structure is critical to preventing financial crises in emerging market countries and to reducing their undesirable effects if they should occur.

AN ASYMMETRIC INFORMATION THEORY OF FINANCIAL CRISES

The financial system has an extremely important function in the economy because it enables funds to move from economic agents who lack productive investment opportunities to those who have such opportunities. Unless the financial system can do this job effectively, the economy will not function efficiently and economic growth will be severely hampered.

A crucial impediment to the efficient functioning of the financial system is asymmetric information, a situation in which one party to a financial contract has much less accurate information than the other party. For example, a borrower who takes out a loan usually has much better information about the potential returns and risk associated with the investment projects he plans to undertake than the lender does. Asymmetric information leads to two basic problems in the financial system: adverse selection and moral hazard.

Adverse Selection

Adverse selection is an asymmetric information problem that occurs before the transaction occurs when potential bad credit risks are the ones who most actively seek out a loan. Thus the parties who are the most likely to produce an undesirable *(adverse)* outcome are most likely to be *selected.* For example, those who want to take on big risks are likely to be the most eager to take out a loan because they know that they are unlikely to pay it back. Since adverse selection makes it more likely that loans might be made to bad credit risks, lenders may decide not to make any loans even though there are good credit risks in the marketplace. This outcome is a feature of the classic "lemons problem" analysis first described by Akerlof (1970). As pointed out by Myers and Majluf (1984) and Greenwald, Stiglitz and Weiss (1984), a lemons problem occurs in the debt and equity markets when lenders have trouble determining whether a borrower is a good risk (he has good investment opportunities with low risk) or, alternatively, is a bad risk (he has poorer investment projects with high risk). In this situation, a lender will only be willing to pay a price for a security that reflects the average quality of firms issuing the securities -- a price below fair market value (the net present value of the expected income streams) for high-quality firms, but above fair market value for low-quality firms. The owners or managers of a high-quality firm that know their quality then also know that their securities are undervalued and will not want to sell them in the market. On the other hand, the firms willing to sell their securities will be low-quality firms because they know that the price of their securities is greater than their value. Since asymmetric information prevents investors from determining whether some firms are high quality, these high quality firms will issue few securities and credit markets will not work as well since many projects with a positive net present value will not be undertaken.

Moral Hazard

Moral hazard occurs after the transaction occurs because the lender is subjected to the *hazard* that the borrower has incentives to engage in activities that are undesirable *(immoral)* from the lender's point of view: i.e., activities that make it less likely that the loan will be paid back. Moral hazard occurs because the borrower has incentives to invest in projects with high risk in which the borrower does well if the project succeeds but the lender bears most of the loss if the project fails. Also the borrower has incentives to misallocate funds for his own personal use, to shirk and just not work very hard, or to undertake investment in unprofitable projects that increase his power or stature. The conflict of interest between the borrower and lender stemming from moral hazard (the agency problem) implies that many lenders will decide that they would rather not make loans, so that lending and investment will be at suboptimal levels.[1]

Defining a Financial Crisis

In recent years, asymmetric information theory has been applied to understanding the nature of financial crises.[2] This theory provides the following definition of what a financial crisis is.

> **A financial crisis is a nonlinear disruption to financial markets in which adverse selection and moral hazard problems become much worse, so that financial markets are unable to efficiently channel funds to those who have the most productive investment opportunities.**

A financial crisis thus results in the inability of financial markets to function efficiently, which leads to a sharp contraction in economic activity.

Factors Leading to Financial Crises

In order to understand why financial crises occur and more specifically how they lead to contractions in economic activity, we need to outline what factors lead to financial crises. There are four categories of factors that promote financial crises: increases in interest rates, increases in uncertainty, asset market effects on balance sheets, and bank panics.

Increases in Interest Rates

As demonstrated by Stiglitz and Weiss (1981), asymmetric information and the resulting adverse selection problem can lead to credit rationing in which some borrowers are denied loans even when they are willing to pay a higher interest rate. This occurs because individuals and firms with the riskiest investment projects are exactly those who are willing to pay the highest interest rates since if the high-risk investment succeeds, they will be the main beneficiaries. Thus a higher interest rate leads to even greater adverse selection; that is, it increases the likelihood that the lender is lending to a bad credit risk. If the lender cannot discriminate among the borrowers with the riskier investment projects, it may want to cut down the number of loans it makes, which causes the supply of loans to decrease with the higher interest rate rather than increase. Thus, even if there is an excess demand for loans, a higher interest rate will not be able to equilibrate the market because additional increases in the interest rate will only decrease the supply of loans and make the excess demand for loans increase even further.[3]

The theory behind credit rationing can be used to show that increases in interest rates can be one factor that help precipitate a financial crisis. If market interest rates are driven up sufficiently, there is a higher probability that lenders will lend to bad credit risks, those with the riskiest investment projects, because good credit risks are less likely to want to borrow while bad credit risks are still willing to borrow. Because of the resulting increase in adverse selection, lenders will want to make fewer loans, possibly leading to a steep decline in lending which will lead to a substantial decline in investment and aggregate economic activity. Indeed, as Mankiw (1986) has demonstrated, a small rise in the riskless interest rate can sometimes lead to a very large decrease in lending and even a possible collapse in the loan market.

Increases In Uncertainty

A dramatic increase in uncertainty in financial markets, due perhaps to the failure of a prominent financial or non-financial institution, a recession, political instability or a stock market, crash make it harder for lenders to screen out good from bad credit risks. The increase in uncertainty therefore makes information in the financial markets even more asymmetric and makes the adverse selection problem worse. The resulting inability of lenders to solve the adverse selection problem renders them less willing to lend, leading to a decline in lending, investment, and aggregate activity.

Asset Market Effects on Balance Sheets

The state of the balance sheet of both nonfinancial firms and banks has important implications for the severity of asymmetric information problems in the financial system. Deterioration of balance sheets worsens both adverse selection and moral hazard problems in financial markets and if this deterioration is dramatic enough, it is a major factor leading to financial crises.

An important way that financial markets can solve asymmetric information problems is with the use of collateral. Collateral reduces the consequences of adverse selection or moral hazard because it reduces the lender's losses in the case of a default. If a borrower defaults on a loan, the lender can take title to the collateral and sell it to make up for the losses on the loan. Thus, if the collateral is of good enough quality, the fact that there is asymmetric information between borrower and lender is no longer as important since the loss incurred by the lender if the loan defaults is substantially reduced.

Net worth performs a similar role to collateral. If a firm has high net worth, even if it defaults on its debt payments as a result of poor investments, the lender can take title to the firm's net worth, sell it off and use the proceeds to recoup some of the losses from the loan. (Note that in a multi-period context, Gertler (1988b) shows that the concept of a borrower's net worth can be broadened to include the discounted value of future profits which is reflected in the market value of the borrowing firm.) In addition, the more net worth a firm has in the first place, the less likely it is to default because the firm has a cushion of assets that it can use to pay off its loans. High net worth also directly decreases the incentives for borrowers to commit moral hazard because they now have more at stake, and thus more to lose, if they default on their loans. Hence, when firms seeking credit have high net worth, the consequences of adverse selection and moral hazard are less important and lenders will be more willing to make loans.

Stock market crashes have an important role to play in promoting financial crises through the net worth effects on adverse selection and moral hazard problems described above. As emphasized by Greenwald and Stiglitz (1988), Bernanke and Gertler (1989), and Calomiris and Hubbard (1990), a sharp decline in the stock market, as in a stock market crash, can increase adverse selection and moral hazard problems in financial markets because it leads to a large decline in the market value of firms' net worth. (Note that this decline in asset values could occur either because of expectations of lower future income streams from these assets or because of a rise in market interest rates which lowers the present discounted value of future income streams.) The decline in net worth as a result of a stock market decline makes lenders less willing to lend because, as we have seen, the net worth of firms has a similar role to collateral, and when the value of collateral declines, it provides less protection to lenders so that losses from loans are likely to be more severe. In addition, the decline in corporate net worth as a result of a stock market decline increases moral hazard incentives for borrowing firms to make risky investments because these firms now have less to lose if their investments go sour. Because borrowers have increased incentives to engage in moral hazard and because lenders are now less protected against the consequences of adverse selection, the stock market decline leads to decreased lending and a decline in economic activity.

Although we have seen that increases in interest rates have a direct effect on increasing adverse selection problems, debt markets also play a role in promoting a financial crisis through both firms' and households' balance sheets. As pointed out in Bernanke and Gertler's (1995) excellent survey of the credit view, an important transmission mechanism of monetary policy, a rise in interest rates and therefore in households' and firms' interest payments decreases firms' cash flow, which causes a deterioration in their balance sheets.[4] As a result, adverse selection and moral hazard problems become more severe for potential lenders to these firms and households, leading to a decline in lending and economic activity. There is thus an additional reason why sharp increases in interest rates can be an important factor leading to financial crises.

In economies in which inflation has been moderate, which characterizes most industrialized countries, many debt contracts are typically of fairly long duration. In this institutional environment, an unanticipated decline in inflation leads to a decrease in the net worth of firms. Debt contracts with long duration have interest payments fixed in nominal terms for a substantial period of time, with the fixed interest rate allowing for expected inflation. When inflation turns out to be less than anticipated, which can occur either because of an unanticipated disinflation as occurred in the United States in the early 1980s or by an outright deflation as frequently occurred before World War II in the U.S., the value of firms' liabilities in real terms rises so that there is an increased burden of the debt, but there is no corresponding rise in the real value of firms' assets. The result is that net worth in real terms declines. A sharp unanticipated disinflation or deflation, therefore causes a substantial decline in real net worth and an increase in adverse selection and moral hazard problems facing lenders. The resulting increase in adverse selection and moral hazard problems (of the same type that were discussed in assessing the effect of net worth declines earlier) will thus also work to cause a decline in investment and economic activity.

In contrast to the industrialized countries, many emerging market countries have experienced very high and variable inflation rates, with the result that debt contracts are of very short duration. For example, in Mexico, almost all bank lending is with variable rate contracts which are usually adjusted on a monthly basis. With this institutional framework, a decline in unanticipated inflation does not have the unfavorable direct effect on firms' balance sheets that it has in industrialized countries, because the short duration of the debt contracts means that there is almost no change in the burden of the debt when inflation falls because the terms of the debt contract are continually changed to reflect expectations of inflation. Thus one mechanism that has played a role in low inflation countries to promote financial crises has no role in emerging market countries that have experienced high and variable inflation.[5]

On the other hand, there is another factor which affects balance sheets that can be extremely important in precipitating a financial crisis in emerging market countries that is not operational in most industrialized countries: unanticipated exchange rate depreciation or devaluation. Because of uncertainty about the future value of the domestic currency, many nonfinancial firms, banks and governments in emerging market countries find it much easier to issue debt if it is denominated in foreign currencies.[6]   This was a prominent feature of the institutional structure in Chilean financial markets before the financial crisis in 1982 and in Mexico in 1994. This leads to a factor that can lead to a financial crisis in emerging market countries which operates in a similar fashion to an unanticipated decline in inflation in industrialized countries. With debt contracts denominated in foreign currency, when there is an unanticipated depreciation or devaluation of the domestic currency, the debt burden of domestic firms increases. Since assets are typically denominated in domestic currency, there is a resulting deterioration in firms' balance sheets and the decline in net worth, which then increases adverse selection and moral hazard problems along the lines described above. The increase in asymmetric information problems leads to a decline in investment and economic activity.

Bank Panics

As we have seen, banks have a very important role in financial markets since they are well suited to engage in information-producing activities that facilitate productive investment for the economy. Thus the simultaneous failure of many banks reduces the amount of financial intermediation undertaken by banks, and will thus lead to a decline in investment and aggregate economic activity. Indeed, even if the banks do not fail, but instead just suffer a substantial contraction in their capital, bank lending will decline, thereby leading to a contraction in economic activity. Research in the United States suggests that this mechanism was operational during the early 1990s in the United States, and that the capital crunch led to the headwinds mentioned by Alan Greenspan that hindered growth in the U.S. economy at that time.[7]

As mentioned earlier, the source of a bank panic is again asymmetric information. In a panic, depositors, fearing the safety of their deposits and not knowing the quality of the banks' loan portfolios, withdraw them from the banking system, causing a contraction in loans and a multiple contraction in deposits, which then causes banks to fail. Asymmetric information is critical to this process because depositors rush to make withdrawals from solvent as well as insolvent banks since they cannot distinguish between them.

This process of runs on banks and bank panics is clearly more likely to occur when banks' balance sheets are in a weakened state, making it more likely that banks are insolvent. Weak bank balance sheets can occur because the supervisory/regulatory structure has not worked well enough to restrain excessive risk-taking on the part of banks. In addition, banks can be buffeted by shocks that cause a rapid deterioration in their balance sheets.

Negative shocks to banks' balance sheets can take several forms. We have already seen how increases in interest rates, stock market crashes, an unanticipated decline in inflation (for industrialized countries), or an unanticipated depreciation or devaluation (for emerging market countries with debt denominated in foreign currencies), can cause a deterioration in nonfinancial firms' balance sheets that makes it less likely that they can pay their loans back. Thus these factors can help precipitate sharp increases in loan losses which increase the probability of bank insolvency.

Increases in interest rates can also have a direct negative effect on bank balance sheets if the banks have a maturity mismatch because they are engaging in the traditional banking activity of borrowing short and lending long. The increase in interest rates will then lead to a larger drop in the value of the banks' longer-term loan assets than the decline in the value of the shorter-term liabilities, causing banks' net worth to fall. Similarly, an increase in interest rates can also cause losses in banks' trading accounts if, as is sometimes common, banks finance purchases of long-term government securities by borrowing in the short-term money markets.

Banks in emerging market countries face additional potential shocks that can make a banking crisis more likely. First is that emerging market countries which are often primary goods producers are often subject to large terms of trade shocks that can devastate banks' balance sheets whose assets are composed primarily of loans to domestic firms. The lack of diversification outside their country can thus be a severe problem for banks in emerging market countries that is not present for many banking institutions in industrialized countries which do have the ability to diversify across countries.[8]

Also banks in many emerging market countries raise funds with liabilities that are denominated in foreign currencies. A depreciation or devaluation of the domestic currency can thus lead to increased indebtedness, while the value of the banks' assets do not rise. The resulting deterioration in banks' equity capital then increase the possibility of bank failures and bank panics. Even if the exchange rate depreciation does not lead to bank failures directly, it can lead to substantial declines in bank lending because the resulting drop in bank capital results in a failure of banks to meet capital standards, such as the Basle requirements. The decline in bank capital then requires banks to shrink their lending until they can raise new capital to meet the capital standards.

APPLYING THE THEORY OF FINANCIAL CRISES TO MEXICO, 1994-95

Now that we have outlined an asymmetric information theory of financial crises, we can apply it to explain the sequence and impact of events in the Mexican financial crisis of 1994-95. Figure 1 provides a diagrammatic exposition of the sequence of events that occurred in Mexico in the 1994-95 period.

Figure 1
The Sequence of Events in the Mexican Financial Crises of 1994-1995

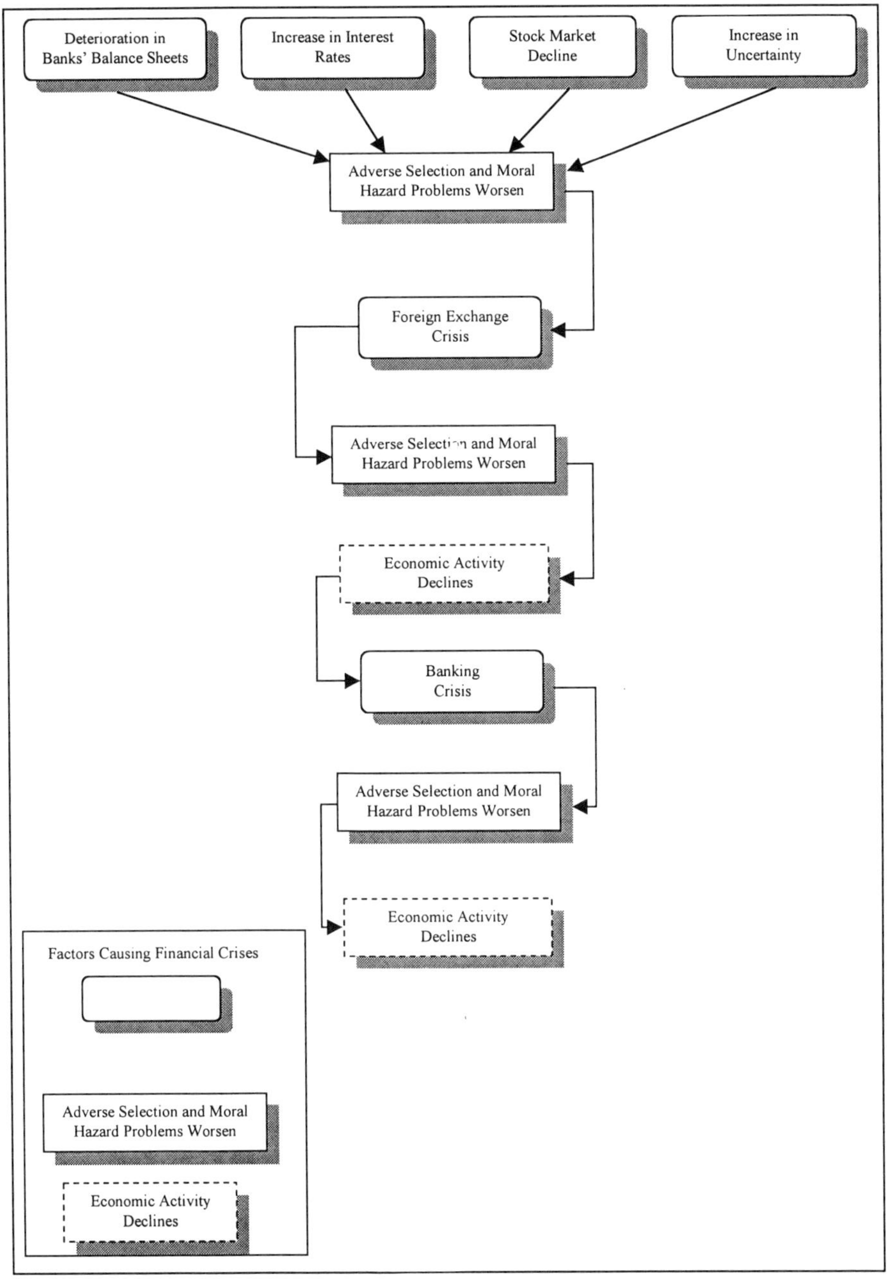

```
┌──────────────────┐  ┌──────────────────┐  ┌──────────────────┐  ┌──────────────────┐
│ Deterioration in │  │ Increase in      │  │ Stock Market     │  │ Increase in      │
│ Banks' Balance   │  │ Interest         │  │ Decline          │  │ Uncertainty      │
│ Sheets           │  │ Rates            │  │                  │  │                  │
└──────────────────┘  └──────────────────┘  └──────────────────┘  └──────────────────┘
```

Adverse Selection and Moral
Hazard Problems Worsen

Foreign Exchange
Crisis

Adverse Selection and Moral
Hazard Problems Worsen

Economic Activity
Declines

Banking
Crisis

Adverse Selection and Moral
Hazard Problems Worsen

Economic Activity
Declines

Factors Causing Financial Crises

Adverse Selection and Moral
Hazard Problems Worsen

Economic Activity
Declines

An important factor leading up to the Mexican financial crisis was the deterioration in banks' balance sheets because of increasing loan losses. As has been true in many countries in the world, deregulation of a financial system and rapid credit growth can be disastrous if banking institutions and their regulators do not have sufficient expertise to keep risk taking in check. A similar situation occurred in Mexico. In September 1982, Mexican banks were nationalized and not surprisingly, these nationalized banks directed a large percentage of their lending business to the government -- on the order of 50 per cent. When these banks were privatized in the early 1990s, their expertise in making loans to private firms and individuals was somewhat limited. For example, Mexican banks did not have formal credit bureaus for household and small business lending which would monitor loans to make sure that borrowers were not taking on excessive risk. In addition, as Figure 2 indicates, bank credit to the private nonfinancial business sector as a fraction of GDP accelerated dramatically, going from 10% of GDP in 1988 to over 40% of GDP in 1994. This lending boom, which stressed the screening and monitoring facilities of the banks, occurred both as a result of increased savings which flowed into the banking sector and an increasing share of banks' total lending going to private firms.

Figure 2
Bank Credit To Private Enterprises (Per cent of GDP)

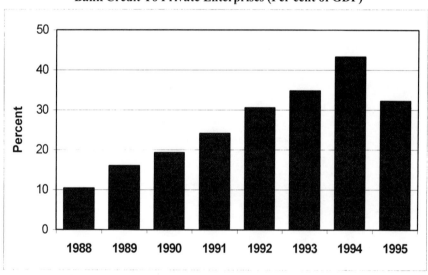

Source: Bank of Mexico

Furthermore, the primary regulator of banks in Mexico, the National Banking Commission (Comision Nacional Bancaria), also did not have the capability to monitor banks' loan portfolios and management practices to prevent inordinate risk taking. This lack of capabilities was exacerbated not only by the bank lending boom, but also by the tremendous expansion in lending by other financial institutions, such as credit unions, thrifts, and factoring and leasing companies. Not surprisingly, given what we have seen in situations like this in the United States and also in the Nordic countries, when Mexican banks and nonbank financial institutions expanded their loan activities, they did indeed take on excessive risk and many bad loans were the result. Figure 3 shows the increase in bank loan losses in the 1990s as reported by National Banking Commission. However, these numbers understate the extent of the growing problem because they would be substantially higher using U.S. generally accepted accounting principles.

Figure 3
Non-Performing Bank Loans/Total Bank Loans

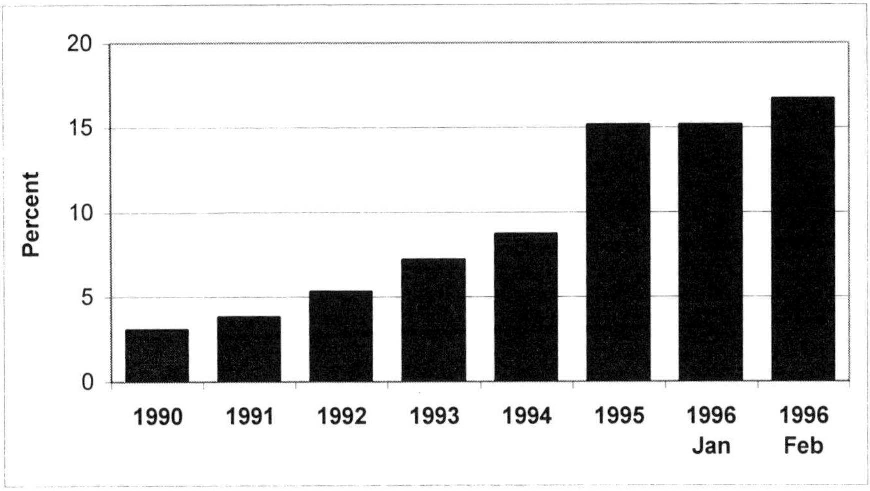

Source: Bank of Mexico

Another precipitating factor to the Mexican financial crisis was a rise in interest rates abroad. Beginning in February 1994, the Federal Reserve began to raise the interbank federal funds rate in order to proactively prevent incipient inflationary pressures from taking hold. Although this policy has been quite successful in keeping inflation in check in the U.S., as Figure 4 indicates, it did put upward pressure on Mexican interest rates, increasing asymmetric information problems in the Mexican financial system.[9] Another factor leading to the rise in Mexican interest rates was central bank actions to protect the value of the peso in the foreign exchange market when the peso came under attack. The rise in interest rates directly added to increased adverse selection in Mexican financial markets because, as discussed earlier, it made it more likely that those willing to take on the most risk would seek loans.

The rise in interest rates also led to the further deterioration of bank balance sheets. Many Mexican banks were purchasing long-term government bonds and financing these purchases by borrowing in the repo market, using the long-term bonds as collateral. When interest rates rose, the value of the long-term bonds declined, causing substantial losses in banks' trading accounts.

Figure 4
Interest Rates

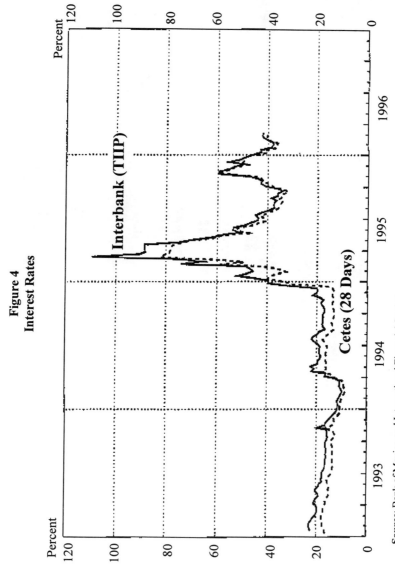

Source: Bank of Mexico and International Financial Statistics

Even more importantly, increased interest payments caused reductions in households' and firms' cash flow, which led to a deterioration in their balance sheets. Recall that debt contracts in Mexican financial markets have very short durations. Thus, the rise in Mexican short-term interest rates, which occurred partially as a result of rising short-term rates in the United States, meant that the effect on cash flow and hence on balance sheets would be substantial. We see this in Figure 5 which shows the net creditor or debtor position of both households and firms over the period 1987 through September 1995. The deterioration in households' balance sheets was quite sharp after the rise in Mexican interest rates in early 1994, while that for firms shows a less dramatic but steady deterioration. As asymmetric information theory suggests, this deterioration in households' and firms' balance sheets increased adverse selection and moral hazard problems in Mexican financial markets which made it less desirable for lenders to lend.

Increases in uncertainty in Mexican financial markets and a stock market decline precipitated the full blown financial crisis. The Mexican economy was hit by political shocks in 1994, specifically the assassination of Luis Donaldo Colosio, the ruling party's presidential candidate, and the uprising in Chiapas, which increased general uncertainty in Mexican financial markets. In addition, as shown in Figure 6, stock prices on the Bolsa fell nearly 20% from the peak in September 1994 to the middle of December 1994. As we have seen, an increase in uncertainty and the decline in net worth as a result of the stock market decline increase asymmetric information problems because it is harder to screen out good from bad borrowers and the decline in net worth decreases the value of firms' collateral and increases their incentives to make risky investments since there is less equity to lose if the investments are unsuccessful. The increase in uncertainty and the stock market decline, along with increases in interest rates and the deterioration in banks' balance sheets, were initial conditions that worsened adverse selection and moral hazard problems (shown in the top of the diagram in Figure 1) and made the Mexican economy ripe for a serious financial crisis when a full blown crisis developed in the foreign exchange market.

With the Colosio assassination and other political developments such as the uprising in Chiapas, the Mexican peso began to come under attack. Given the commitment to a pegged exchange rate, the Banco de Mexico intervened in the foreign exchange market to purchase pesos, with the result that there was a substantial loss of international reserves (see Figure 7). In addition, because of the uncertainty in the foreign exchange market, the government found it harder to finance its debt with peso denominated (cetes) bonds and so dramatically increased its issue of dollar denominated (tesobono) bonds, depicted in Figure 8. Even though the Mexican central bank raised interest rates sharply, the hemorrhaging of international reserves forced the Mexican authorities to devalue the peso on December 20, 1994.

Figure 5
Net Creditor (+) Or Debtor (-) Position Of Households With the Domestic
Financial System
(Stocks As Percentage Of GDP)

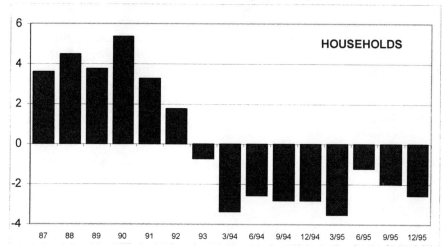

Net Creditor (+) Or Debtor (-) Position Of Enterprises With the Domestic
Financial System
(Stocks As Percentage Of GDP)

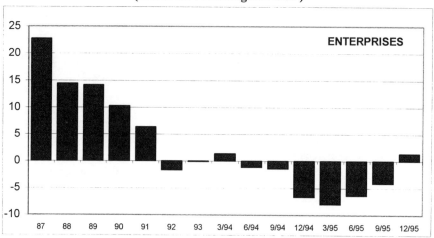

Source: Bank of Mexico

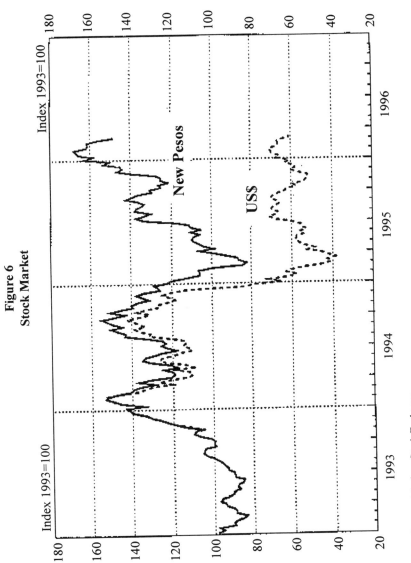

Figure 6
Stock Market

Index 1993=100

New Pesos

US$

Source: Mexican Stock Exchange

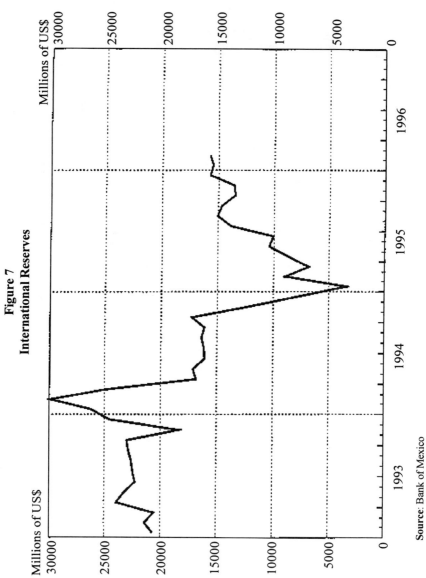

Figure 7
International Reserves

Source: Bank of Mexico

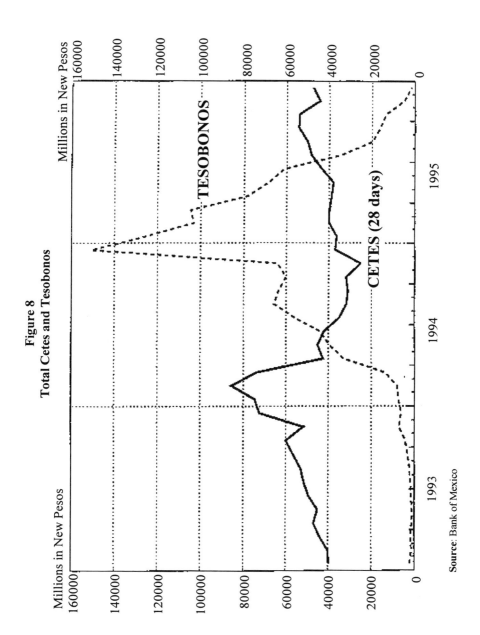

Figure 8
Total Cetes and Tesobonos

Source: Bank of Mexico

An important factor precipitating the Mexican foreign exchange crisis that is often not emphasized enough in the literature was the deterioration of bank balance sheets before the crisis.[10] With a weakened banking sector, the Banco de Mexico was faced with a difficult dilemma when speculative attacks on the peso occurred. In order to fight off a speculative attack, a central bank must be prepared to defend its currency by sharply raising interest rates. On the other hand, if interest rates are raised, this will cause a further deterioration in bank balance sheets. There will be a direct negative effect on bank balance sheets because banks typically have assets with longer durations than their liabilities, a consequence of their traditional financial intermediation activity of borrowing short and lending long, and so the value of the assets will fall more in value than the liabilities, leading to a deterioration in net worth. Furthermore, higher interest rates will hurt bank borrowers, making it harder for them to pay back their loans, leading to increases in loan losses for the banks, adding to the deterioration in bank balance sheets. Thus when the Banco de Mexico confronted the speculative attacks on the peso they were in between the proverbial rock and a hard place, making the defense of the currency using sharp hikes in interest rates highly problematic. Once speculators understood that it might be harder for the Mexican central bank to defend the peso with interest rate increases, a vicious circle was created in which a speculative attack was more likely to succeed, thus making a speculative attack more likely. Hence, the problems in Mexico's banking system were an important factor leading to the foreign exchange crisis in late 1994.

Once the foreign exchange crisis occurred, the institutional structure of debt markets in Mexico now interacted with the peso devaluation to propel the economy into a full fledged financial crisis. Devaluations are a highly nonlinear event because they result in a sharp change in the exchange rate. When the peso halved in value by March 1995 (see Figure 9), this led to a dramatic rise in both actual (Figure 10) and expected inflation. This combined with the desire of the Banco de Mexico and the Mexican government to limit the peso depreciation meant that interest rates on debt denominated in pesos went to sky high levels, exceeding 100% at an annual rate and the Mexican stock market crashed, falling another 30% in peso terms and by over 60% in dollar terms. Given the resulting huge increase in interest payments because of the short duration of the Mexican debt, households' and firms' cash flow dropped dramatically, leading to a deterioration in their balance sheets. In addition, because many firms had debts denominated in dollars, the depreciation of the peso resulted in an immediate sharp increase in their indebtedness in pesos, while the value of their assets remained unchanged. As we see in Figure 5, the depreciation of the dollar starting in December 1994 led to an especially sharp negative shock to the net worth of private firms, causing a dramatic increase in adverse selection and moral hazard problems. These asymmetric information problems were severe for domestic and foreign lenders. Foreign lenders would thus also be eager to pull their funds out of Mexico and this is exactly what they did. As Figure 11 shows, foreign portfolio investment inflows to Mexico which were on the order $20 billion (at an annual rate) in 1993 and early 1994, reversed course and the

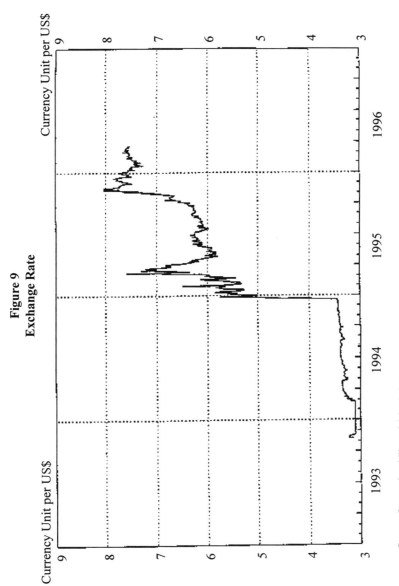

Figure 9
Exchange Rate

Source: International Financial Statistics

Figure 10
Inflation

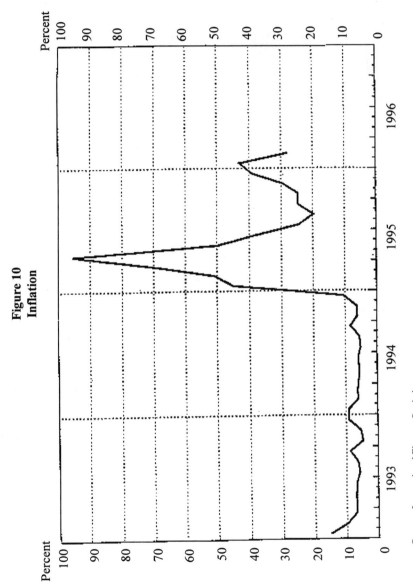

Source: International Finance Statistics

Figure 11
Foreign Portfolio Investment In Mexico (Quarterly Flows At An Annual Rate)

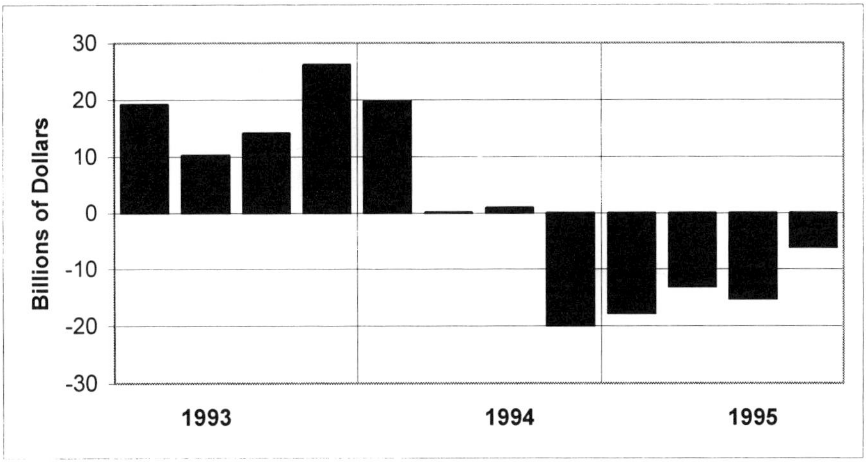

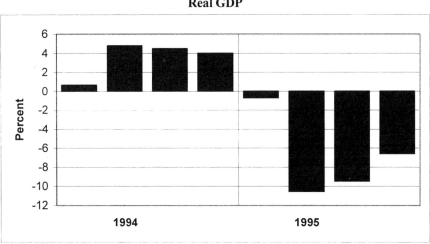

Source: Bank of Mexico
Note: Balance of Payments Data, Portfolio Investment = Portfolio Equity and Money Market Investment

outflows exceeded $10 billion at an annual rate beginning in the fourth quarter of 1994. Consistent with the theory of financial crises outlined in this paper, the sharp decline in lending helped lead to a collapse of economic activity, with real GDP growth falling from around a 4% to 4.5% annual rate in the last half of 1994 to negative growth rates in the -10% vicinity in the second and third quarters of 1995. (See Figure 12.)

Figure 12
Real GDP

Source: Bank of Mexico
Note: Real GDP in 1980 prices, growth from 4 quarters earlier.

As shown in the diagram in Figure 1, further deterioration to the economy now occurred because the collapse in economic activity and the deterioration in the cash flow and balance sheets of both firms and households led to a worsening banking crisis. The problems of firms and households meant that many were no longer able to pay off their debts, resulting in substantial loan losses for the banks. In addition, the depreciation of the peso had a direct negative impact on banks' balance sheets. As Table 1 shows, the foreign-currency denominated liabilities of Mexican banks jumped from 116.4 billion pesos at the end of December 1993 to 213.9 billion pesos at the end of December 1994, primarily as a result of the decline in the peso from 3.1 to the dollar to 5.3 to the dollar. Although, as Table 1 shows, Mexican banks did have offsetting foreign-currency denominated assets, their likelihood of being paid off in full was substantially lowered because of the worsening business conditions and the negative effect that these increases in the peso value of these foreign-currency denominated loans had on the balance sheet of the borrowing firms. An important point is that even if banks have a matched portfolio of foreign-currency denominated assets and liabilities and so appear to avoid foreign-exchange market risk, a devaluation can nonetheless cause substantial harm to bank balance sheets; when there is a devaluation, the mismatch between foreign-currency denominated assets and liabilities on borrowers balance sheets can lead to defaults on their loans, thereby converting a market risk for borrowers to a credit risk for the banks that have made the foreign-currency denominated loans.

Even more problematic for the Mexican banks was that many of their foreign-currency denominated liabilities were very short-term, so that the sharp increase in the value of these liabilities led to liquidity problems for the banks because they had to be paid back quickly. An additional serious problem for Mexican banks was that the depreciation of the peso interacted with capital requirements to cause a capital crunch. Even if a depreciation of the peso would not have resulted in a loss in bank capital because a bank had a perfectly matched portfolio of dollar-denominated assets and liabilities, a depreciation of the peso would lead to a decline in the so-called leverage ratio, the ratio of capital to the bank's assets. To see this, just recognize that in this case, a peso depreciation leads to an increased value of the dollar-denominated assets in terms of pesos and a corresponding increase in the value of the liabilities, with the result that bank capital in terms of pesos remained unchanged. However, because the total amount of assets in peso terms has now increased, the ratio of bank capital to assets would fall. Thus besides its other harmful effects on bank balance sheets, the peso depreciation also caused a capital shortage for the Mexican banks, reminiscent of the capital crunch that occurred in the United States in the early 1990s when capital requirements were raised. The resulting capital shortfall meant that banks either had to raise new capital or restrict their asset growth by cutting back on lending. Because of the weak economy, raising new capital was extremely difficult for banks, so they naturally chose the latter course. The result was that the capital crunch led to a credit crunch in which banks restricted their lending.

Table 1
Foreign Currency Exposure of Mexican Banks
(Pesos, in Billions)

	Dec-91	Dec-92	Dec-93	Dec-94	Mar-95	Jun-95	Sep-95	Dec-95
Aggregate Banking System								
Foreign Denominated Assets								
Tesobonos	0	0	0.4	3.6	1.4	0.8	0.4	0
Securities	0.3	0.4	1.5	6.3	6.4	9.1	11.5	22.5
Loans	18.2	33.9	54.0	99.2	130.5	126.7	124.4	146.3
Assets of Branches & Agencies	64.7	59.4	67.3	116.8	132.7	123.7	121.9	142.4
Total	83.2	93.7	123.2	225.9	271	260.3	258.2	311.2
Foreign Denominated Liabilities								
In Mexico	21.9	36.0	49.1	97.1	136.2	121.2	119.9	154.9
In Branches & Agencies	64.7	59.4	67.3	116.8	132.7	123.7	121.9	142.4
Total	86.6	95.4	116.4	213.9	268.9	244.9	241.8	297.3
Exposure								
Foreign Assets Minus Foreign Liabilities	-3.4	-1.7	6.8	12	2.1	15.4	16.4	13.9
Foreign Assets/Total Assets	10.5%	11.9%	15.6%	28.6%	29.7%	27.7%	27.3%	29.9%
Foreign Liabilities/Total Liabilities	11.0%	12.1%	14.7%	27.0%	29.5%	26.0%	25.6%	28.6%
Exchange Rate	3.071	3.1154	3.1059	5.325	6.8175	6.3092	6.4195	7.6425

Given the problems of the banking system, the collapse of the banking system would have been the inevitable result in the absence of a government safety net, but instead the Mexican government provided the funds to protect depositors, thereby avoiding a bank panic.[11] However, given the banks' loss of capital, the need for more capital in order to meet capital requirements and the need for the government to intervene to prop up the banks, the banks' ability and willingness to lend were sharply curtailed. As we have seen, a banking crisis of this type which hinders the ability of banks to lend also makes adverse selection and moral hazard problems worse in financial markets because banks are no longer as capable of playing their traditional financial intermediation role.

The theory of financial crises outlined in this paper provides a cohesive story behind the sequence of events that developed in the Mexican crisis of 1994-95. In addition, it explains the puzzle mentioned in the introduction to this paper: it shows how a emerging market economy can shift dramatically from a path of reasonable growth before a financial crisis, as was the case in Mexico in 1994, to a sharp decline in economic activity after a crisis occurs. The answer is that the financial crisis leads to such a substantial worsening of adverse selection and moral hazard problems in financial markets that there is a collapse of lending and hence in economic activity.[12]

POLICY IMPLICATIONS FOR EMERGING MARKET COUNTRIES

Experience with past financial crises in emerging market countries has led many analysts to suggest policy measures for emerging market countries that can reduce the likelihood of financial crises, but also reduce the negative impact on the economy if they occur. One advantage of the asymmetric information analysis of the Mexican financial crisis in this paper is that it provides a coherent rationale for many of these suggested policy measures. Thus, although the lessons for policy from the asymmetric information analysis in this paper are not entirely new, the analysis here can help us decide which policy measures are effective in preserving the health of an emerging market country's economy.

Policy Measures To Recover From Financial Crises

Given the disastrous consequences of financial crises, it is extremely important to examine what policies are appropriate to recover from financial crises and minimize the effects on the economy. Given our earlier discussion, it is not surprising that the institutional structure of the financial system plays an important role in what measures can be used by the authorities to stimulate recovery from a financial crisis. Institutional features of the financial systems in emerging market countries imply that it may be far more difficult for the central bank to promote recovery from a financial crisis. As mentioned before, many emerging market countries have much of their debt denominated in foreign currency. Furthermore, their past record of high and variable inflation has resulted in debt contracts of very short duration and expansionary monetary policy is likely to cause expected inflation to rise dramatically.

In industrialized countries, expansionary monetary policy is often used to stimulate a weak economy and promote recovery. In contrast, as a result of the institutional features of emerging market countries, expansionary monetary policy in these countries is unlikely to promote recovery from a financial crisis. Suppose that the policy prescription of expansionary monetary policy were followed in an emerging market country with the above institutional structure. In this case the expansionary monetary policy is likely to cause expected inflation to rise dramatically and the domestic currency to depreciate sharply. As we have seen before, the depreciation of the domestic currency leads to a deterioration in firms' and banks' balance sheets because much of their debt is denominated in foreign currency, thus raising the burden of indebtedness and lowering banks' and firms' net worth. In addition, the upward jump on expected inflation is likely to cause interest rates to rise because lenders need to be protected from the loss of purchasing power when they lend. As we have also seen, the resulting rise in interest rates causes interest payments to soar and the cash flow of households and firms to decline. Again the result is a deterioration in households' and firms' balance sheets, and potentially greater loan losses to banking institutions. Also because debt contracts are of very short duration, the rise in the price level from expansionary monetary policy does not affect the value of households' and firms' debts appreciably, so there is little benefit to their balance sheets from this mechanism as occurs in industrialized countries.

The net result of an expansionary monetary policy in the emerging market country with the above institutional structure is that it hurts the balance sheets of households, firms, and banks. Thus, expansionary monetary policy is likely to be counterproductive: it causes a deterioration in balance sheets and therefore amplifies adverse selection and moral hazard problems in financial markets caused by a financial crisis, thereby harming the economy rather than promoting recovery.

For similar reasons, lender-of-last-resort activities by a central bank in an emerging market country, may not be as successful as in a industrialized country. When the Federal Reserve pursued a lender-of-last-resort role during the 1987 stock market crash, there was almost no sentiment in the markets that this would lead to substantially higher inflation. However, this is much less likely to be the case for a emerging market country. Given the past record on inflation, central bank lending to the financial system in the wake of a financial crisis which expands domestic credit might arouse fears of inflation spiraling out of control. We have already seen that if inflation expectations rise, leading to higher interest rates and exchange rate depreciation, cash flow and balance sheets will deteriorate making recovery from the financial crisis less likely. The lender-of-last-resort role of a central bank must be used far more cautiously in an emerging market country with the institutional structure outlined here because central bank lending is now a two-edged sword.

The above arguments suggest that recovery from a financial crisis in many emerging market countries is difficult to achieve. Expansionary monetary policy is not an option for stimulating recovery from a financial crisis in most emerging market countries, in contrast to industrialized countries. Monetary policy must be restricted to promoting low inflation and restoring confidence in the domestic currency and therefore cannot be used to meet an additional objective of stimulating recovery from a financial crisis. Indeed, a speedy recovery from a financial crisis in an emerging market country may require foreign assistance because liquidity provided from foreign sources does not lead to any of the undesirable consequences that result from the provision of liquidity by domestic authorities. There clearly are other policy measures to stimulate recovery from a financial crisis if expansionary monetary policy is not an option, but discussion of them is well beyond the scope of this paper. Instead, the analysis in this paper makes the important point that certain institutional structures make a emerging market country's economy more prone to financial crises and make it more difficult to extricate the country from a financial crisis if it occurs. Thus it is especially important for emerging market countries to take active prophylactic measures to prevent financial crises from occurring in the future.

Policy Measures To Prevent Financial Crises

Because banks play a particularly important role in emerging market countries' financial systems, crises in the banking sector are a particularly important element in emerging market countries' financial crises. Our asymmetric information framework suggests that there is an important need for a government safety net for the banking system -- the key feature of which is not deposit insurance -- in order to prevent bank panics. Although a safety net is important, it nonetheless increases the moral hazard incentives for excessive risk taking on the part of the banks. In emerging market countries this moral hazard problem for banks may be even more acute because it is more difficult to acquire information in emerging market countries than in industrialized countries. Emerging market countries therefore need to pay particular attention to creating and sustaining a strong bank regulatory/supervisory system to reduce excessive risk taking in their financial systems.

A Strong Bank Supervisory System

Encouraging a strong bank regulatory/supervisory system takes on several forms. First, bank regulatory/supervisory agencies in emerging market countries need to be provided with adequate resources to do their job effectively. Without these resources, as we have seen in the examples of the S&L supervisors in the United States and the National Banking Commission in Mexico, the bank supervisory agency will not be able to monitor banks sufficiently in order to keep them from engaging in inappropriately risky activities, to have the appropriate management expertise and controls to manage risk or to have sufficient capital so that moral hazard incentives to take on excessive risk are kept in check. Second, accounting and disclosure requirements for financial institutions, which are often particularly lacking in emerging market countries, need to be beefed up considerably. Without the appropriate information, both markets and bank supervisors will not be able to adequately monitor the banks to deter excessive risk taking.[13] Proper accounting standards and disclosure requirements are therefore crucial to a healthy banking system.

Third, prompt corrective action by bank supervisors will stop undesirable bank activities and, even more importantly, close down institutions which do not have sufficient net worth and make sure that stockholders and managers of insolvent institutions are appropriately punished. Our asymmetric information framework indicates that prompt corrective action is particularly important, not only because it immediately prevents banks from "betting the bank" in order to restore the value of the institution, but also because it creates incentives for banks to not take on too much risk in the first place because they know that if they do they are more likely to be punished. Fourth, because prompt corrective action is so important, the bank regulatory/supervisory agency needs sufficient independence from the political process so that it is not encouraged to sweep problems under the rug and engage in regulatory forbearance. One way of doing this is to give the bank supervisory role to a politically independent central bank. This has desirable elements as pointed out in Mishkin (1991), but some central banks might not want to have the supervisory task thrust upon them because they worry that it might increase the likelihood that the central bank would be politicized, thereby impinging on the independence of the central bank. Alternatively, bank supervisory activities could be housed in a bank regulatory authority that is independent of the government.

Another measure to improve incentives for bank supervisors to do their job properly is to make them accountable if they engage in regulatory forbearance. For example, an important, but very often overlooked part of the 1991 FDICIA legislation in the United States which has helped make this legislation effective is that there is a mandatory report that the supervisory agencies must produce if the bank failure imposes costs on the Federal Deposit Insurance Corporation (FDIC). The resulting report is made available to any member of Congress and to the general public, upon request, and the General Accounting Office must do an annual review of these reports. Opening up the actions of bank supervisors to public scrutiny makes regulatory forbearance less attractive to them, thereby reducing the principal-agent problem. In addition, it reduces the incentives of politicians to lean on supervisors to relax their supervision of banks.

Liberalization of the Financial System

Deregulation and liberalization of the financial system in emerging market countries have become the rage in recent years. Although deregulation and liberalization are highly desirable objectives, the asymmetric information framework in this paper indicates that if this process is not managed properly, it can be disastrous. If the proper bank regulatory/supervisory structure is not in place when liberalization comes, the appropriate constraints on risk taking behavior will be nonexistent, with the result that bad loans are likely with potentially disastrous consequences for bank balance sheets at some point in the future. In addition, before liberalization occurs, banks may not have the expertise to make loans wisely, and so opening them up to new lending opportunities may also lead to poor quality of the loan portfolio. We have also seen that financial deregulation and liberalization also often lead to a lending boom, both because of increased opportunities for bank lending and also because of financial deepening in which more funds flow into the banking system. Although financial deepening is a positive development for the economy in the long-run, in the short-run the lending boom may outstrip the available information resources in the financial system, helping to promote a financial collapse in the future.

The dangers in financial deregulation and liberalization do not mean that emerging market countries should not pursue a liberalization strategy. To the contrary, financial liberalization is critical to the efficient functioning of financial markets so that they can channel funds to those with the most productive investment opportunities. Getting funds to those with the most productive investment opportunities is particularly critical to emerging market countries because these investments can have especially high returns in these countries, thereby stimulating rapid economic growth. Financial deregulation and liberalization thus needs to be actively pursued in emerging market countries, but has to be managed carefully. It is important that emerging market countries put in the proper bank regulatory/supervisory institutional structure before liberalizing their financial system. This means following the precepts outlined above of providing sufficient resources to bank supervisors, providing adequate accounting and disclosure requirements, encouraging bank supervisors to take prompt corrective action, and insulating bank supervision from the political process. Furthermore, emerging market countries may need to take the financial liberalization process slowly in order to keep a lending boom from getting out of hand which stresses the capabilities of both bank management and bank supervisors. Even though eating is essential to human health, eating too fast can lead to an upset stomach. A similar lesson applies to the process of financial deregulation and liberalization.

The asymmetric information framework for analyzing financial crises also illustrates that institutional features of the financial system besides bank regulation can be critical to how prone a emerging market economy is to a financial crisis and to the severity of the effects on the economy if a financial crisis comes.

Legal and Judicial Systems

The legal and judicial systems are very important for promoting the efficient functioning of the financial system, and the inadequacies of legal systems in many emerging market countries are a serious problem for financial markets. If property rights are unclear or hard to enforce, the process of financial intermediation can be severely hampered. For example, we have seen that collateral can be an effective mechanism to reduce adverse selection and moral hazard problems in credit markets because it reduces the lender's losses in the case of a default. However, in many emerging market countries, the legal system makes attaching collateral a costly and time-consuming process, thereby reducing the effectiveness of collateral to solve asymmetric information problems. Similarly, bankruptcy procedures in emerging market countries are frequently very cumbersome, resulting in lengthy delays in resolving conflicting claims. Resolution of bankruptcies, in which the books of insolvent firms are opened up and assets are redistributed can be viewed as a process to decrease asymmetric information in the marketplace, is an important part of the recovery process from a financial crisis. Slow resolution of bankruptcies can therefore delay recovery from a financial crisis because only when bankruptcies have been resolved is there enough information in the financial system to restore it to a healthy operation.

Currency Of Denomination Of Debt Contracts

Another institutional feature of emerging market countries is that many debt contracts are denominated in foreign currencies. The experience in countries such as Mexico illustrates how dangerous denominating a large amount of debt in foreign currencies can be. Denominating debts in foreign currencies is very tempting for firms, banks and governments in emerging market countries because instability in the value of the domestic currency makes it harder to attract capital, particularly foreign capital, if the debt is denominated in the domestic currency. However, it is extremely important that this temptation be resisted. Not only does denominating debt in foreign currencies make a emerging market country's financial system more prone to a financial crisis, but, in addition, it makes the negative consequences of a financial crisis much more severe. Furthermore, as we have seen, if a financial crisis does occur, an emerging market country with a lot of its debt denominated in foreign currencies has very limited policy options to extricate itself from the crisis. The dangers of denominating debt in foreign currencies is one of the most important lessons that we learn from the asymmetric information theory of financial crises in emerging market countries.

Exchange Rate Regime

The asymmetric information analysis in this paper also illustrates how dangerous a pegged exchange rate regime can be for an emerging market country if it has a fragile banking system, short duration debt contracts and substantial amounts of debt denominated in foreign currencies. With a pegged exchange rate regime, depreciation of the domestic currency when it occurs is a highly nonlinear event because it involves a devaluation. The resulting dramatic increase in interest rates and rise in indebtedness which results in a sharp deterioration in firms' and banks' balance sheets then tips the emerging market country into a full scale financial crisis, with devastating effects on the economy. Thus, a pegged exchange rate regime with the institutional features outlined above is like putting the economy on a knife edge. One slip and the economy comes crashing down, and as with Humpty Dumpty, it is very hard to quickly put the economy back together again. The reason that some emerging market countries have chosen to peg their currency to a stable currency like the dollar is because they are seeking a nominal anchor that will promote price stability. However, if they have an institutional structure of a fragile banking system, short duration debt contracts and substantial debt denominated in foreign currencies, this is a very dangerous strategy indeed.[14]

A flexible exchange rate regime has the advantage that movements in the exchange rate are much less nonlinear than in a pegged exchange rate regime. Indeed, the daily fluctuations in the exchange rate in a flexible exchange rate regime have the advantage of making clear to private firms, banks and governments that there is substantial risk involved in issuing liabilities denominated in foreign currencies. Furthermore, a depreciation of the exchange rate may provide an early warning signal to policymakers that their policies may have to be adjusted in order to limit the potential for a financial crisis.

Duration Of Debt Contracts

An additional important institutional feature of financial systems in many emerging market countries is the short duration of debt contracts, both domestic and those issued to foreigners. This leads to increased cash flow and liquidity problems for nonfinancial firms and banks when interest rates rise or when the domestic currency depreciates. Having an institutional structure in which debt duration is short thus increases the fragility of the financial system and makes emerging market countries more prone to financial crises. In order to promote financial stability, emerging market countries need to encourage the development of longer-term debt markets. One way they might do this is by trying to issue longer-term government debt to increase liquidity in markets for long-term debt.[15] However, one impediment to such a strategy is that financial institutions in emerging market countries might only be able to finance purchases of these securities in the money market with very short-term liabilities. The resulting maturity mismatch for these institutions can be highly problematic if there are substantial fluctuations in interest rates, a particular problem in emerging market countries. The resulting market (interest-rate) risk can be substantial and a sharp rise in interest rates which decreases the value of the long-term securities banks hold as assets while having little effect on the value of their short-term liabilities can cause a sharp deterioration in bank net worth and lead to insolvencies. Indeed this problem suggests that regulatory requirements or bank supervisory procedures to limit market risk may be especially important in emerging market countries. The problem of limiting interest-rate risk and encouraging longer duration debt contracts also suggests that it is important for emerging market countries to pursue the goal of price stability because without price stability there will be substantial fluctuations in interest rates, leading to high interest-rate risk and making it harder to induce private markets to issue long-term debt.

Price Stability

Price stability is especially important in emerging market countries because it makes it far easier for policymakers to take actions which extricate their economy from a financial crisis if it occurs. Countries with highly variable inflation have a credibility problem which limits what policymakers can do to promote recovery from a financial crisis. Without credibility, a central bank in a emerging market country that tries to use expansionary monetary policy to enhance the recovery from a financial crisis may do more harm than good. Instead of shoring up weakened balance sheets, the expansionary policy is likely to lead to rapid rises in expected inflation and hence in interest rates as well as an exchange rate depreciation, all of which causes balance sheets to deteriorate further, thus making the financial crisis worse. Similarly engaging in a lender-of-last-resort rescue might backfire because it leads to worries about the commitment to low inflation. With a credible commitment to price stability, this vicious cycle will not occur. Expansionary monetary policy and the lender-of-last-resort role can be effectively used to shore up balance sheets and either nip a financial crisis in the bud or promote rapid recovery when a financial crisis occurs. The asymmetric information analysis of financial crises in emerging market countries thus leaves us with the following conclusion: Having an independent central bank with a clear cut mandate for price stability is possibly even more important for emerging market countries than it is for industrialized countries.

However, just as with the worthy goal of financial liberalization, single-minded pursuit of price stability can be dangerous. A rapid disinflation process which leads to high real interest rates has adverse cash flow consequences for financial institutions such as banks. If the financial system is very fragile with already weakened balance sheets, the disinflation could result in a major financial crisis, with the resulting depressing effects on the economy. Thus, before engaging in an anti-inflation stabilization program, emerging market countries need to pay particular attention to the health of their financial system, making sure that the regulatory/supervisory process has been effective in promoting strong balance sheets for financial institutions. Otherwise, financial institutions may not be able to safely weather the stresses from an anti-inflation stabilization program. Successful monetary policy in emerging market countries, therefore, requires successful regulation and prudential supervision of the financial system.

NOTES

[1]Note that asymmetric information is not the only source of the moral hazard problem. Moral hazard can also occur because high enforcement costs might make it too costly for the lender to prevent moral hazard even when the lender is fully informed about the borrower's activities.

[2]See, for example, Bernanke (1983), Calomiris and Gorton (1991) and Mishkin (1991,1994).

[3]Jaffee and Russell (1976) have demonstrated a second type of credit rationing in which lenders make loans but limit their size to less than the borrower may want. This occurs because the larger the loan, the greater are moral hazard incentives for the borrower to engage in activities that make it less likely that the loan will be repaid.

[4]Additional recent surveys which discuss this monetary transmission channel are Hubbard (1995), Cecchetti (1995) and Mishkin (1996).

[5]However, a decline in unanticipated inflation during periods when an anti-inflation program is in progress in emerging market countries has often been associated with very high real interest rates. Thus an unanticipated decline in inflation can negatively affect firms' balance sheets in emerging market countries through the cash flow mechanism discussed above.

[6]Note that in some industrialized countries, a substantial amount of debt is denominated in foreign currency. This was the case for the Nordic countries and helped exacerbate their banking crises in the late 1980s and early 1990s. As this example makes clear, the distinction between industrialized and emerging market countries in terms of the institutional structure of their financial system is not clear cut. Some industrialized countries have attributes of their financial structure that are typical of emerging market countries and vice versa.

[7]For example, see Bernanke and Lown (1991), Berger and Udell (1994), Hancock, Laing and Wilcox (1995) and Peek and Rosengren (1995) and the symposium published in the Federal Reserve Bank of New York Quarterly Review in the Spring of 1993, Federal Reserve Bank of New York (1993).

[8]However, even in industrialized countries, the institutional structure of the banking system may prevent diversification, resulting in banks which are subject to terms of trade shocks. For example, because banks in Texas in the early 1980s did not diversify outside their region, they were devastated by the sharp decline in oil prices that occurred in 1986. Indeed, this terms of trade shock to the Texas economy which was very concentrated in the energy sector resulted in the failure of the largest banking institutions in that state.

[9]Bank of Mexico officials believe that the interbank interest rate (TIIP, tasa interbancaria promedio) is a better measure of money market interest rates than that on cetes, the peso denominated Treasury bills. Cetes rates might have been artificially low because cetes were required to be held in certain domestic investment funds and foreigners were discouraged from purchasing other money market instruments besides cetes by regulations in their own countries, making cetes the instrument generally used for repurchase operations.

[10]However, Gavin and Hausman (1995) and Kaminsky and Reinhart (1996) do emphasize the importance of the linkage from banking crises to foreign exchange crises.

[11]The National Banking Commission has estimated that the present value of the cost of this assistance was 8% of GDP.

[12]Of course, other traditional transmission mechanisms operating through higher interest rates and fiscal policy responses to the crisis also helped to worsen the economic downturn.

[13]The importance of disclosure is illustrated in a recent paper, Garber and Lall (1996), which suggests that off balance-sheet and off-shore derivatives contracts played an important role in the Mexican crisis.

[14]See Obstfeld and Rogoff (1995) for additional arguments why pegged exchange rate regimes may be undesirable.

[15]However, there is one advantage from governments issuing short-term debt: it reduces the incentive for the government to pursue inflationary policies to reduce the real value of their liabilities. Similarly, an advantage to denominating government debt in foreign currency is that there is no longer an incentive to lower the value of the debt by inflation and depreciation of the domestic currency. It is not clear how important these advantages are in practice.

REFERENCES

Akerlof, G., "The Market for Lemons: Quality Uncertainty and the Market Mechanism," Quarterly Journal of Economics, Vol. 84, 1970, pp. 488-500.

Berger, A.N. and G.F. Udell, "Did Risk-Based Capital Allocate Bank Credit and Cause a "Credit Crunch" in the United States?" Journal of Money Credit and Banking, 26, 3, August, 1994, pp. 585-628.

Bernanke, B.S., "Non-Monetary Effects of the Financial Crisis in the Propagation of the Great Depression," American Economic Review, Vol. 73, 1983, pp. 257-76.

Bernanke, B.S, Gertler M., "Agency Costs, Collateral, and Business Fluctuations," American Economic Review, Vol. 79, 1989, pp. 14-31.

Bernanke, B.S., and Gertler M., "Inside the Black Box: The Credit Channel of Monetary Policy Transmission," Journal of Economic Perspectives, Fall 1995, 9, pp. 27-48.

Bernanke, B.S. and C. Lown, "The Credit Crunch," Brookings Papers on Economic Activity, 2, 1991, pp. 205-39.

Calomiris, C.W. and Gorton, G. "The Origins of Banking Panics: Models, Facts and Bank Regulation" in Hubbard, R.G. (ed.), Financial Markets and Financial Crises, University of Chicago Press, Chicago, 1991, pp. 109-173.

Calomiris, C.W., Hubbard, R.G., "Firm Heterogeneity, Internal Finance, and `Credit Rationing'," Economic Journal, 100, 1990, pp. 90-104.

Cecchetti, S.G., "Distinguishing Theories of the Monetary Transmission Mechanism," Federal Reserve Bank of St. Louis Review, May/June 1995, 77, pp. 83-97.

Federal Reserve Bank of New York, "The Role of the Credit Slowdown in the Recent Recession," Federal Reserve Bank of New York Quarterly Review, Spring, 18, #1, 1993, pp. 1-114.

Garber, Peter M. and Subir Lall., "The Role and Operation of Derivative Markets in Foreign Exchange Market Crises," mimeo. February, Brown University, 1996.

Gertler, M., "Financial Capacity, Reliquification, and Production in an Economy with Long-Term Financial Arrangements," University of Wisconsin, mimeo, 1988.

Greenwald, B., Stiglitz, J.E., "Information, Finance Constraints, and Business Fluctuations," in Kahn, M., and Tsiang, S.C., eds., Finance Constraints, Expectations and Macroeconomics, Oxford University Press, Oxford, 1988, pp. 108-140.

Greenwald, B., Stiglitz, J.E., and Weiss, A., "Information Imperfections in the Capital Market and Macroeconomic Fluctuations," American Economic Review, Vol. 74,, 1984, pp. 194-99.

Jaffee, D. and Russell, T., "Imperfect Information, Uncertainty, and Credit Rationing," Quarterly Journal of Economics, Vol. 90, 1976, pp. 651-66.

Hancock, D., Laing, A.J. and J.A. Wilcox, "Bank Capital Shocks: Dynamic Effects on Securities, Loans and Capital," Journal of Banking and Finance 19, 3-4, 1995, pp. 661-77.

Hausman, R. and M. Gavin, "The Roots of Banking Crises: The Macroeconomic Context," Inter-American Development Bank mimeo, October, 1995.

Hubbard, R.G., "Is There a "Credit Channel" for Monetary Policy?," Federal Reserve Bank of St. Louis Review, May/June 1995, 77, pp. 63-74.

Kaminsky, G.L. and C.M. Reinhart, "The Twin Crises: The Causes of Banking and Balance of Payments Problems," Board of Governors of the Federal Reserve System, mimeo. February, 1996.

Mankiw, N.G., "The Allocation of Credit and Financial Collapse.," Quarterly Journal of Economics, Vol. 101, 1986, pp. 455-70.

Mishkin, F.S. "Asymmetric Information and Financial Crises: A Historical Perspective," in Hubbard, R.G., ed., Financial Markets and Financial Crises, University of Chicago Press, Chicago., 1991, pp. 69-108.

Mishkin, F.S., "Preventing Financial Crises: An International Perspective," Manchester School, 62, 1994, pp. 1-40.

Mishkin, F.S., "The Channels of Monetary Transmission: Lessons for Policy," Banque de France Bulletin: Digest 27, March, 1996, pp.: 33-44.

Myers, S.C., and Majluf, N.S., "Corporate Financing and Investment Decisions When Firms Have Information that Investors Do Not Have," Journal of Financial Economics, Vol. 13, 1984, pp. 187-221.

Obstfeld, M. and K. Rogoff, "The Mirage of Fixed Exchange Rates," Journal of Economic Perspectives, Fall, 9, #4, 1995, pp. 73-96.

Peek, J. and E.S. Rosengren, "Bank Regulation and the Credit Crunch," Journal of Banking and Finance, 19, 2-4, 1995, pp. 679:92.

Stiglitz, J.E., and Weiss, A., "Credit Rationing in Markets with Imperfect Information," American Economic Review, Vol. 71, 1981, pp.393-410.

9

The Argentine Banking Panic After The "Tequila" Shock : Did "Convertibility" Help Or Hurt?

ROQUE B. FERNANDEZ
Minister of Finance, Argentina
LILIANA SCHUMACHER
Assistant Professor of International Finance and Banking, The George Washington University

INTRODUCTION

In April 1991, after forty years of high inflation and two years of hyperinflation, Argentina adopted a monetary regime based on a fixed exchange rate with full convertibility of the domestic currency into American dollars and bimonetarism. Under such a regime the money supply is endogenous and any attempt to issue currency above this endogenous amount will end up in a loss of reserves and a subsequent threat to the convertibility of the domestic currency. This iron corsage was seen at the time as the only type of legal framework that could discipline the social forces that traditionally had put heavy pressures on the government, leading to high fiscal or quasi fiscal deficits and then to inflation.

One of those forces was represented by the banking sector. As of December 1989, the total loss incurred by the Central Bank for deposit insurance and different forms of bank bail-outs was US$14.6 billion (Fernandez 1990), roughly equivalent to the size of all private banks assets as of 1991. Thus, one of the goals that the economic authorities had in mind in 1991, was to set limitations to the ability of the Central Bank to bear the consequences of the excessive risk undertaken by the Argentine financial institutions. In particular, with a fixed exchange regime and convertibility, banks should expect that in case of trouble, they would not be bailed out by the Central Bank with money creation. An additional non-desired consequence of Convertibility was that the Central Bank could not have a very active role in creating liquidity and behaving as a lender of last resort.

This general framework required specific regulations that could make the basic philosophy and its consequences believable for all economic agents and would force the banks to internalize the risk of undertaking financial intermediation. Thus, the foundations of the Argentine banking regime at the time were given by: (i) removal of deposit insurance and new rules to address the issue of bank liquidation; (ii) liquidity regulations that required the banks to keep and pay for their own liquidity sources in the form of high reserve requirements; (iii) capital regulations that required riskier banks to have larger capital in order to be able to face the eventual losses. Removal of deposit insurance and the no bail-out policy was expected to make depositors and other bank debt holders to exercise enough market discipline on banks and thus minimize moral hazard. Specific rules about liquidity and capital -prudential regulation- would make sure that even if the market discipline created was not enough, banks would have an incentive to put limitations to the risk undertaken and/or would have the resources to face the consequences of it.

The system developed without visible problems for four years but the Mexican devaluation of December 1994 started a confidence crisis of major consequences with an outflow of capital away from all Argentine financial markets. In particular, between December 20, 1994 and May 1995, US$8.4 billion left the banking system (about 18.4% of total deposits); as of September 1996, out of a total of 129 private banks, nine banks failed and over thirty institutions were acquired or merged. The rest of the institutions were also affected by a drop in their deposits but they survived the shock. The GNP that had grown 7.1% in 1994 fell 4.4% in 1995 and total credit that grew 23.6% in 1994 suffered a reduction of 0.8% in 1995.

Since the size and dynamics of the panic is well known[1], this paper will explore some of the links between the monetary and banking regime and the consequences of the crisis. Section 1 will describe the main features of the Convertibility regime and the legal framework of the banking sector as of November 1994 and examine their role in reducing or augmenting the macroconsequences of the shock. Section 2 will address the microconsequences; it will discuss some developments that took place in 1994 in order to establish whether and up to what extent the problems, that ended up in failures and mergers, began sometime before the Mexican devaluation and were the result of some sort of discipline exercised by the market and enhanced by the banking regime. In particular we will examine: (i) the increase in the international interest rates; (ii) the impact of capital and provisioning regulations; and (iii) the characteristics of failing and merging banks. Section 3 presents the conclusions. The evidence seems to suggest that:

1. The rules in place as of November 1994 were crucial in setting limitations to the macro consequences of the crisis. In particular, the liquidity needs were faced with resources that had been allocated to the bad (panic) state beforehand, limiting in this way the creation of new liquidity by the Central Bank, that never exceeded the amount that was allowed within the Convertibility rules. Total credit reduction was small and although there was an impressive fall in the GNP in 1995[2], it could be argued that the drop could have been larger and more extended in the absence of a mechanism -high reserve requirements- that had smoothed the natural credit expansion under heavy and persistent capital inflows before 1994 and without a disciplinary framework that had put limitations to banks risk before the panic and prevented a generalized bail-out once the crisis started. Thus, the Convertibility regime was quite successful in playing the difficult trade-off between internal and external equilibria.

2. The legal banking framework required by the Convertibility Plan seems to have been able to create a substantial amount of market discipline in the system. The failures and mergers that are sometimes viewed as a direct microconsequence of the panic appear to be rooted in the specific features of bank portfolios as of November 1994 and their inability to react to some events that took place before then. Thus, although the confidence crisis started by the Mexican devaluation was a major shock for Argentine banks assets values, its role was to exacerbate some trends that could clearly be identified by November 1994.

SECTION 1: CONVERTIBILITY AND THE BANKING REGIME

As mentioned in the introduction, in order to make the implications of the Convertibility Plan believable by the economic agents and to make banks internalize the costs of their actions, a set of regulations was put in place, basically these include: (i) removal of deposit insurance and a new regime for banks liquidation, (ii) liquidity regulations, (iii) capital regulations, and (iv) some other rules that completed the legal picture. These regulations were contained in a set of amendments introduced by the Argentine Congress to the Central Bank Charter Act (CBCA) and the Financial Institutions Act (FIA) and in several regulations issued by the Central Bank.

Removal Of Deposit Insurance And Banks Liquidation Rules

Deposit insurance funded with fiscal resources was eliminated gradually. In 1991, the Central Bank limited coverage of the existing insurance to US$1,000. One year later a set of amendments were introduced to the CBCA; a crucial one was the prohibition for the Central Bank to insure explicitly or implicitly any bank liabilities, which implied total removal of deposit insurance funded with fiscal resources. Finally, in April 1995, in the midst of the crisis, the Argentine Congress created a new deposit insurance designed to preserve market discipline; it was totally funded by the banks with limited coverage based on the amount of the deposit, maturity, and the interest rate paid; given these characteristics, this insurance had almost no effect on depositors behavior at the time.

The procedure for closure and liquidation of institutions in trouble was also in line with the limitations mentioned above and was established in 1992 in another amendment to the Financial Institutions Act (FIA). The Central Bank could suspend the bank in trouble for thirty days and request a Capitalization Proposal. After the proposal was presented, the Central Bank could only do one of these two things: (i) reopen the bank; or (ii) remove its charter if the proposal was considered unsatisfactory. If the charter was removed, the bank became subject to the laws ruling corporations in general and it was a court's problem to deal with bankruptcy, to liquidate assets and to pay depositors and other claimants. The 1992 amendment was the response of the Convertibility Plan to the question of how to address the failure of banks without committing fiscal resources. In the years before, there had been a combination of deposit insurance and Central Bank intervention that in practice made all banks liabilities insured. This strategy was funded with money creation and as mentioned in the introduction, made a significant contribution to the hyperinflationary process of the late eighties.

When the Central Bank authorities faced for the first time the consequences of the 1992 amendment, after the Mexican devaluation, they realized that such a court's early intervention would probably not minimize the costs involved in the liquidation of the institutions, in particular depositors losses. Thus, in February 1995 Congress passed another amendment to the FIA that extended the period during which an institution could be suspended up to 90 days and gave powers to the Central Bank to have a large involvement in the liquidation of an institution *without committing fiscal resources*. The Central Bank could then arrange the sale of the bank in trouble or, if the bank could not be sold as such, the Central Bank could split the banks' assets before a court's intervention and sell at best price the good assets in order to apply the proceeds to pay deposits and other senior debt (Central Bank loans). The remaining assets and liabilities followed the usual bankruptcy procedure. The Central Bank of Argentina made use of this power during the panic in five cases.

Liquidity Regulations

Several reasons provided justification for a policy of high reserve requirements, in particular: (i) the provision of a mass of liquidity that could be released in case of a run; (ii) to smooth the growth of credit in the presence of intense capital inflows; and (iii) the creation of incentives for banks to hold high capital asset ratios.

Under the Convertibility rule, 100% of the monetary base had to be backed by international reserves. 20% of those international reserves could be Argentine public bonds denominated in foreign currency[3]; this provided some flexibility to the Central Bank but to a large extent the money supply in Argentina was endogenously determined and any attempt to issue currency above this endogenous amount could end up in a loss of reserves and a subsequent threat to the convertibility of the domestic currency. Thus, it was clear at the time, that banks should be made to keep and pay for their own liquidity reserve.

An additional justification for high reserve requirements was to smooth capital inflows that were at the time very intense given the low and decreasing international interest rates. Independently of the policy stance taken by different countries, the problem of capital flows reflects the closed economy conventional wisdom of the money multiplier and banking multiplier. A fractional reserve requirement banking system would never have enough liquid reserves to attend massive capital outflows (or bank runs). And a fixed exchange rate or convertibility - by limiting the lender of last resort capability of the Central Bank - would certainly convert a balance of payment's problem into a banking problem.

Powerful and simple, the money and banking multiplier is perhaps the most widely used instrument for monetary targeting and financial programming given the assumption that the Central Bank controls the monetary base. In an open economy simple multiplier effects must be carefully inspected to understand the role of capital flows. In what follows, we will work out a backward determination of the money multiplier from monetary aggregates to monetary base to deal with the exogeneity of foreign investors' mood i.e. confidence in to emerging economies.

From the definitions of money "M" and monetary base "B" in terms of currency "C," deposits "D," and reserve requirements "R," we obtain a linear system with five unknowns in two equations: $M = C+D$ and $B = C+R$. The closed economy "multiplier" results from solving the system under the assumption that B is exogenous and adding the equations $C=cD$ and $R=rD$ where "c" is a constant and "r" is a binding legal reserve requirement. The solution is represented by $M=mB$, where $m=[(1+c)/(c+r)]$. A "Tequila" effect for an emerging open economy producing capital outflows implies that M is exogenously determined by foreign investor confidence and the multiplier determines the endogenous value of the monetary base B. To illustrate the financial vulnerability from a "Tequila" effect, subtract the second equation from the first to obtain $M-B=D-R=L$, where L represents the loanable capacity generated by deposits. As $m>1$, a change in foreign investors' mood producing capital outflows and reducing M implies a credit contraction. That is, the comparative static of the system gives $dL/dM=(m-1)/m>0$. As loans cannot be immediately recalled the capital outflows by reducing M produce a banking crisis. Thus, "high reserve requirements" are good to reduce financial vulnerability because as $r \to 1$, $m \to 1$ and $dL/dM \to 0$.

Finally, high reserve requirements were also seen as a way to indirectly enforce a given desired capital to asset ratio in the banking system. This follows from the fact that, by altering the cost of funding loans with capital relative to deposits, the reserve requirement affects the bank's financial structure choice (Fernandez and Guidotti 1995).

Since reserves requirements were a tax on the financial system, the optimal structure was to levy a higher rate on the most inelastic deposits and hence the rates were set at 43% for checking accounts and 3% for term deposits.

Capital Regulations

In June 1993, the Central Bank replaced the old minimum capital regulations based on activity and location and established a required capital to asset ratio where the rate was based on an increasing schedule that would reach 11.5% in January 1995. Assets were adjusted by risk following, in general the suggestions of the Basle Committee for Banks Regulation for credit risk with one important difference: an additional adjustment to loans was introduced based on the interest rate charged by the bank.

Since the Central Bank was aware that capital regulations were useless in the absence of rules that guaranteed an accurate loan pricing, new provisioning rules came out in June 1994 and were scheduled to be gradually introduced between then and September 1995. These new provisioning rules called for a new classification of loans based on the client's capacity to repay the loan and not solely on its actual performance in repaying.

High capital requirements were set to make banks internalize the cost of risk undertaken and also as an additional mechanism to smooth credit growth. As emphasized in Fernandez and Guidotti (1995), reserve requirements and capital requirements jointly determine the structure of the financial system and under some conditions, explicitly considered in standard prudential banking regulation, capital flows could be largely irrelevant to the stability of the banking system. Capital requirements establish a minimum amount of capital as a proportion "k" of risky assets "A" (this is a Basle constraint of the form, $K \geq kA$). The balance sheet of the consolidated commercial banking system is: $A + R = D + K$. Taking K as a predetermined variable on the basis that commercial banks are not free to change it at will without the previous consent of the Central Bank, assuming zero legal reserve requirements -that is, banks are free to determine the technical level for R- and assuming that the Basle constraint holds as strict equality, then $D - R = K[(1-k)/k]$. This means that the loanable capacity out of deposits is independent of M (that is $dL/dM = 0$), implying that capital outflows cannot produce a banking crisis if the Basle constraint (and not legal reserve requirements) dominates the expansion and contraction dynamics of banks. This ability to smooth the impact of capital flows comes from the fact that excess supply of international short-run capital cannot be immediately converted into deposits because the commercial bank capital will first have to increase. This takes time, thus, insulating the domestic system from externally generated financial volatility.

Additional Regulations

Argentine banks were free to engage in both classic banking activities and securities activities but, as an additional device to prevent moral hazard, they had limitations to hold equity shares in non financial corporations (up to 15% of bank capital and cannot be funded with deposits) and there were also restrictions on (i) lending to affiliates (up to 5% of bank capital to each affiliate with a maximum of 20% for the whole group of affiliates); and (ii) clients diversification (lending limits up to 15% of bank capital without collateral and 25% with collateral per client).

The rejection of deposit insurance and bank bail-outs with fiscal resources did not mean that Argentine laws did not protect the small-uninformed depositor. The 1992 amendment to FIA made deposits the most senior of all banks liabilities up to an amount of US$3,000 and the 1995 amendment to FIA raised that limit up to US$5,000 and created a deposit insurance fully funded by the banks that covered deposits up to US$10,000 or US$20,000 depending on maturity.

Finally, and since market discipline required availability of information about banks portfolios, in June 1993 the Central Bank began the monthly publication of balance sheets, profits and losses and quality of loans data about each financial institution (banks and thrifts) in the system.

In summary, given the general policy goals and constraints imposed by the Convertibility regime, how did Argentina address the main issues about banking regulations, in particular panic prevention, moral hazard and the protection of the small depositor?

With respect to *panic prevention,* the main response was given by: high capital, reserve requirements and a system of monthly release of information about bank portfolios that aimed at minimizing the problem of asymmetry of information that usually arises in a panic.

With respect to *moral hazard,* it was expected that the lack of deposit insurance and highly believable limitations to bank bail-outs would create incentives for depositors to monitor banks, set a price to bank portfolios risk in normal times and punish institutions selectively in case of a panic, and there were also some limitations in lending to related companies. Finally, very high capital requirements would have an ex-ante role since losses would first affect shareholders' wealth.

The *protection of the small-uninformed depositor* was achieved by a system of seniorities that was then reinforced with a deposit insurance fully funded by the banks that covered deposits up to US$10,000 or US$20,000 depending on maturity.

Given the set of regulations in place as of November 1994, when the confidence crisis started, it was fought with resources that had been allocated beforehand to the bad (panic) state. As of November 1994, Argentine banks had:

- an average nominal capital asset ratio for the system of 13.4% (18.2%) when assets are adjusted by risk), that served as a buffer against the losses suffered by banks.

- a system of incentives designed to create enough depositor discipline.

- US$9.4 billion liquid resources, that is to say about 20% of total deposits were invested in deposits at the Central Bank. This mass of liquidity was helpful in two ways:

(i) in the first place, it allowed to control the rate of credit growth over the pre-panic period when, given the high and persistent capital inflows, deposits grew 450% between April 1991 and December 1994.

(ii) it was used as much as possible to compensate for the fall in total deposits during the panic and thus to minimize the total fall in credit and bank losses.

Table 1 shows the interaction between the policy response and the shock between December 21 and July 31, 1995. The total loss in deposits as of mid-May 1995 was US$8 billion, that is to say about 18% of total deposits. Out of this total, US$3.4 billion was compensated by releasing reserve requirements, US$2.3 billion with repurchased agreements and Central Bank loans to the banks and US$1 billion was credit reduction. That is to say 42% of the total fall in deposits was compensated by releasing reserve requirements and only 12% with a credit cut. This credit cut represented 2.3% of total credit outstanding as of December 21, 1994.

As shown in Figure 1, the liquidity created during the panic was never above the amount of liquidity that was allowed within the Convertibility rules.

An additional tool to fight the panic, was the contribution of multilateral organizations that helped to renew the confidence in the sustainability of the foreign exchange regime and the convertibility of the domestic currency.

Table 1
Interaction Between The Policy Response and The Shock
December 1994-July 1995

	Total Deposits	Credit to Private Sector*	CB Creation of New Liquidity			CB New Liquidity /Dep. Fall	Credit /Dep. Fall
			Repos	Loans for Banks	Reserve Require-ments		
			millions of pesos				
Stock-Dec.21	45,367	48,221	0	58	9416**	93.31%	
Dec 21-Feb 28	-3,242	304	369	256	2400	93.31%	-9.38%
Mar 1-Mar 31	-4170	-1,424	436	842	1000	54.63%	34.15%
Apr 1-May 14	-948	9	15	439	0	47.89%	-0.95%
May 15-Jul 31	3,357	110	-431	16	-200	-18.32%	-3.28%
Until May 14	-8,360	-1,111	820	1537	3400	68.86%	13.29%
Until Jul 31	-5,003	-1,001	389	1553	3200	102.78%	20.01%

* The figures for credit are an unofficial estimation using banks' balance sheet data and a daily survey conducted by the Central Bank.
** Reserves in Central Bank accounts + Reserves for dollar deposits + Cash in vault as of December 21th.
Note: New liquidity created by CB + fall in credit to the private sector do not add up to 100% due other sources of liquidity, e.g. external credit lines.
Source: BCRA (1995), "Managing a Liquidity Shock."

Figure 1
Foreign Reserves and Monetary Liabilities

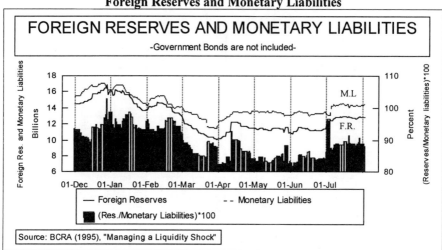

SECTION 2: 1994: PRELUDE TO THE CRISIS

The following section will review some new developments that took place in 1994 and their impact on bank portfolios together with the inability of some banks to react to the new financial environment.

The Evolution of International Interest Rates

Until the end of 1993, the Convertibility Plan developed in an international context that was characterized by decreasing interest rates. This together with a substantial improvement in the country's legal security, price stability, deregulation and privatization provided incentives to Argentine and foreign investors to make investments in Argentina and in particular to make deposits in Argentine banks. The total supply of deposits to Argentine banks grew 350% between April 1991 and December 1993.

At the beginning of 1994, the Federal Reserve interrupted five years of decreasing interest rates and in an effort to assure stable growth for the American economy, decided to increase the Federal Funds rate with an impact on all other American rates. The immediate consequence for the Argentine economy -and for many "emerging markets" - was a reduction in the flow of funds to financial markets with a consequent drop in the rate of growth of bank deposits and an extra drop in the price of bonds issued by Argentine residents. Figures 2, 3 and 4 show the evolution of international interest rates for the period February 1991/December 1995, their impact on the rate of growth of banks deposits and on the price of Argentine Brady Bonds.

Figure 2

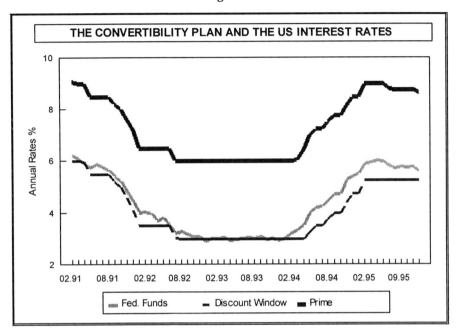

Figure 3

Figure 4

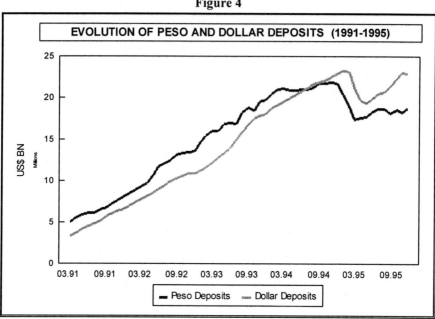

This "flight to quality" by investors impacted Argentine banks in different ways. Wholesale banks for whom a larger fraction of their activities was represented by holdings of bonds and active trading in capital markets were mainly affected by the fall in bond prices. Retail banks (especially retail domestic banks) that depended heavily on the domestic market were more affected by the reduction in deposit growth and the increase in competition. On the whole, return on assets and return on equity fell down for both types of banks.

Tables 2 through 5 show the evolution of balance sheets and returns for private wholesale and retail Argentine banks between January 1991 and December 1995. It can be seen that while in 1994 net interest margins (NIM), measured as the difference of Interest Revenues from loans minus Interest Expenses on Deposits to total assets ratio, went up, reflecting higher interest rate risk, financial margins, as NIM + Capital Gains, came down as a consequence of lower (or negative) capital gains and this showed in lower ROA's and ROE's for all private Argentine banks. It can also be seen that this effect had a larger impact on wholesale banks for whom the main component of returns came from trading. Thus, for these banks at an aggregate level, rates of return were negative during 1994.

Table 2
Balance Sheet For Wholesale Banks (1991-1995)

		I 91	II 91	I 92	II 92	I 93	II 93	I 94	II 94	I 95	II 95
Number of Institutions		31	30	33	33	35	35	36	35	37	33
1. Assets		100.0	100.0	100.0	100.0	100.0	100.0	100.0	100.0	100.0	100.0
1.1.	Cash	7.6	9.5	12.5	7.8	8.1	6.6	5.7	7.3	4.4	4.2
1.2.	Bonds	13.8	12.2	11.5	10.7	10.6	11.2	8.2	6.8	11.9	11.7
1.3.	Financing less Reserves	54.4	53.6	51.6	61.0	58.3	50.3	50.6	58.9	46.4	40.6
1.3.1.	Normal	48.4	46.8	48.1	56.0	54.2	46.8	45.8	54.3	41.4	36.8
1.3.2.	Irregular	6.0	6.8	3.4	5.0	4.1	3.5	4.8	4.5	5.0	3.9
1.3.3.	Reserves	-2.2	-3.0	-1.8	-2.0	-1.4	-1.6	-1.4	-2.0	-2.5	-1.7
1.3.a.	Loans	50.8	50.6	48.1	59.6	55.0	42.9	40.8	49.8	42.7	33.8
1.3.b.	Other Financing	5.8	6.0	5.2	3.4	4.8	9.0	11.1	11.0	6.1	8.6
1.4.	Futures	3.8	2.0	4.5	1.3	5.3	9.9	11.5	6.7	7.7	8.8
1.5.	Shares in other Companies	0.3	2.5	3.2	3.3	2.6	2.6	2.4	2.4	2.5	2.5
1.6.	Fixed Assets	12.9	13.5	9.2	10.6	6.7	4.7	3.9	4.8	5.9	4.3
1.7.	Other Assets	7.3	6.7	7.5	5.3	8.3	14.6	17.7	13.1	21.2	27.9
2. Liabilities		73.4	67.4	78.7	73.6	82.1	84.6	87.3	83.4	81.0	85.6
2.1.	Deposits	28.4	32.1	26.7	35.8	30.6	26.3	25.0	32.8	20.4	16.6
2.2.	Other Liabilities	43.3	33.3	50.6	36.0	49.7	56.8	61.4	49.4	59.5	67.9
2.2.a.	Interbank Loans	11.4	5.5	15.6	9.1	15.7	12.3	11.4	5.7	8.6	6.0
2.2.b.	BCRA	0.4	0.4	0.2	0.2	0.1	0.0	0.0	0.1	1.6	1.6
2.2.c.	Bonds	0.0	0.0	0.4	0.7	0.9	2.2	1.6	2.5	3.1	2.8
2.2.d.	Loans from Abroad	11.8	11.7	11.4	14.1	13.0	6.4	8.6	9.9	11.7	11.0
2.2.e.	Repos	4.6	3.6	3.5	2.1	6.4	10.9	12.3	10.0	4.7	10.9
2.3.	Other Liabilities	1.7	2.0	1.4	1.8	1.8	1.5	0.9	1.2	1.1	1.1
3. Net Wealth		26.6	32.6	21.3	26.4	17.9	15.4	12.7	16.6	19.0	14.4
Assets (US$Million)		2327	1925	3404	2890	4894	6542	7709	6533	6493	8581

Table 3
Balance Sheet For Retail Banks (1991-1995)

		I 91	II 91	I 92	II 92	I 93	II 93	I 94	II 94	I 95	II 95
Number of Institutions		100	98	98	96	96	95	95	94	77	63
1. Assets		100.0	100.0	100.0	100.0	100.0	100.0	100.0	100.0	100.0	100.0
1.1.	Cash	14.5	14.3	14.1	15.1	13.7	15.0	13.1	11.6	10.3	7.6
1.2.	Bonds	10.3	5.9	5.8	4.1	5.0	5.5	3.8	3.3	3.7	8.4
1.3.	Financing less Reserves	53.8	61.9	65.9	68.7	69.4	67.4	70.1	73.9	69.6	66.1
1.3.1.	Normal	49.2	57.0	61.1	63.1	63.4	61.2	62.8	65.0	58.2	54.6
1.3.2.	Irregular	4.6	4.9	4.8	5.6	6.0	6.2	7.3	9.0	11.5	11.5
1.3.3.	Reserves	-2.3	-2.1	-1.9	-2.0	-2.4	-2.8	-2.8	-3.3	-4.1	-3.8
1.3.a.	Loans	53.0	59.2	63.2	69.1	69.8	67.4	69.1	74.0	70.6	65.9
1.3.b.	Other Financing	3.1	4.8	4.6	1.5	2.0	2.8	3.7	3.2	3.2	4.1
1.4.	Futures	0.6	1.7	0.6	0.5	1.2	1.3	1.4	0.5	0.5	2.5
1.5.	Shares in other Companies	0.9	1.0	1.4	1.1	1.5	1.5	1.6	1.7	2.0	1.9
1.6.	Fixed Assets	14.0	11.1	8.6	7.4	6.3	5.5	5.2	5.5	5.9	5.4
1.7.	Other Assets	5.9	4.2	3.5	3.2	2.9	3.8	4.8	3.4	8.1	8.1
2. Liabilities		75.9	80.1	83.5	84.8	85.8	86.6	87.4	87.0	86.2	87.5
2.1.	Deposits	47.2	53.6	56.7	60.4	61.4	61.6	60.7	63.2	55.3	55.3
2.2.	Other Liabilities	25.5	23.8	24.4	21.5	21.8	22.7	25.0	22.0	29.1	30.5
2.2.a.	Interbank Loans	4.2	2.9	4.3	3.2	3.8	2.6	3.4	2.8	2.5	2.2
2.2.b.	BCRA	2.3	2.0	1.4	1.2	1.0	0.7	0.7	0.7	3.5	1.9
2.2.c.	Bonds	0.0	0.5	1.4	3.1	3.1	5.2	4.8	5.6	5.4	5.1
2.2.d.	Loans from Abroad	7.7	6.5	7.0	7.2	6.9	5.7	6.5	6.2	8.2	7.8
2.2.e.	Repos	1.5	1.6	0.7	0.3	1.4	1.4	1.9	1.1	1.1	5.6
2.3.	Other Liabilities	3.1	2.8	2.4	2.8	2.5	2.2	1.6	1.7	1.8	1.8
3. Net Wealth		24.1	19.9	16.5	15.2	14.2	13.4	12.6	13.0	13.8	12.5
Assets (US$ Million)		12238	15251	20253	23471	29048	34915.89	39791	41433	41600	46558

Table 4
Profits and Losses For Wholesale Banks (1991-1995)

RETURNS AS OF		I 91	II 91	I 92	II 92	I 93	II 93	I 94	II 94	I 95	II 95
1.	Interest Income from Loans and Repos	35.0	9.7	4.5	7.6	5.3	3.9	4.2	6.3	6.9	4.3
2.	Interest Expense on Deposits and Repos	-4.9	-3.9	-1.3	-2.4	-1.5	-1.3	-1.4	-2.1	-1.6	-1.2
NET INTEREST MARGIN		30.1	5.8	3.1	5.2	3.8	2.7	2.8	4.2	5.3	3.1
3.	Other Interest Income	0.4	0.3	0.2	0.2	0.1	0.0	0.1	0.0	0.0	0.1
4.	Other Interest Expense	-17.2	-4.0	-1.7	-2.7	-1.5	-1.2	-1.4	-1.9	-3.1	-2.3
4.1.	BCRA	-0.2	-0.2	0.0	0.0	0.0	0.0	0.0	0.0	-0.1	-0.2
4.2.	Other financial institutions.	-8.3	-0.4	-0.5	-1.0	-0.3	-0.3	-0.3	-0.4	-0.6	-0.4
4.3.	Other	-8.7	-3.4	-1.1	-1.7	-1.1	-0.9	-1.1	-1.6	-2.4	-1.7
TOTAL NET INTEREST MARGIN		13.4	2.0	1.6	2.7	2.4	1.5	1.5	2.3	2.2	0.9
5.	Loans Provisions	-4.2	-1.0	-0.6	-0.5	-0.7	-0.9	-0.4	-0.9	-1.4	-0.7
TOTAL NET INTEREST MARGIN – LOANS PROV.		9.2	1.1	1.1	2.1	1.6	0.6	1.0	1.4	0.8	0.2
6.	Income from Services	4.5	5.3	3.1	5.1	2.7	1.9	1.5	1.8	1.6	1.3
7.	Expense on Services	-0.6	-0.7	-0.2	-0.4	-0.3	-0.3	-0.2	-0.2	-0.4	-0.2
FINANCIAL MARGIN WITHOUT CAPITAL GAINS		13.1	5.7	3.9	6.9	4.1	2.1	2.3	3.0	2.0	1.3
8.	Cap. Gains on Securities other than Bonds	0.3	1.7	0.5	-0.2	0.3	1.6	0.1	0.7	-0.7	-0.1
9.	Cap. Gains on Bonds	11.2	6.3	2.8	1.7	2.8	3.4	-1.2	0.6	2.2	1.6
FINANCIAL MARGIN		24.6	13.6	7.2	8.4	7.2	7.1	1.2	4.3	3.5	2.7
10.	Other income/expense	-10.0	4.1	0.2	2.1	0.4	1.0	0.6	-0.3	-0.6	1.4
TOTAL FINANCIAL MARGIN		14.7	17.7	7.4	10.5	7.6	8.1	1.8	4.0	2.9	4.1
11.	EXPENSES	10.9	12.4	5.0	6.5	3.9	3.5	3.0	4.0	4.7	3.6
10.1.	Salaries	4.6	4.7	3.2	4.2	2.5	2.4	2.1	2.8	2.2	1.7
10.2.	Maintenance	6.3	7.7	1.8	2.3	1.3	1.1	0.9	1.2	2.4	1.9
RETURNS BEFORE TAXES		3.7	5.3	2.3	4.0	3.8	4.6	-1.2	0.0	-1.8	0.5
12.	Taxes	1.3	0.5	2.0	2.3	1.7	1.6	1.0	1.2	0.6	0.5
12.1.	Income Tax	0.3	0.0	0.2	0.4	0.3	0.6	0.1	0.2	0.3	0.3
12.2.	Other Taxes	1.0	0.5	1.8	2.0	1.4	1.0	0.9	1.1	0.3	0.2
ROA		2.4	4.8	0.4	1.6	2.0	3.0	-2.2	-1.3	-2.3	0.0
ROE		8.9	14.6	1.8	6.2	11.3	19.3	-17.1	-7.7	-12.3	0.1
ASSETS (US$ million)		2327	1925	3404	2890	4894	6542	7709	6533	6493	8581

Table 5
Profits and Losses For Retail Banks (1991-1995)

RETURNS AS OF		I 91	II 91	I 92	II 92	I 93	II 93	I 94	II 94	I 95	II 95
1.	Interest Income from Loans and Repos	34.3	11.6	12.3	13.9	13.2	11.5	11.5	12.4	15.2	11.4
2.	Interest Expense on Deposits and Repos	-13.3	-3.0	-4.0	-4.7	-4.5	-3.7	-3.5	-3.9	-4.8	-3.7
NET INTEREST MARGIN		**21.0**	**8.6**	**8.3**	**9.2**	**8.7**	**7.9**	**8.0**	**8.5**	**10.5**	**7.7**
3.	Other Interest Income	0.3	0.0	0.0	0.0	0.0	0.0	0.0	0.0	0.1	0.1
4.	Other Interest Expense	-7.9	-1.9	-1.1	-1.2	-1.1	-1.0	-1.1	-1.3	-2.3	-1.8
4.1.	BCRA	-1.3	-0.2	-0.1	-0.1	-0.1	0.0	0.0	0.0	-0.4	-0.4
4.2.	Other financial institutions.	-2.2	-0.5	-0.3	-0.3	-0.2	-0.1	-0.1	-0.1	-0.2	-0.1
4.3.	Other	-4.4	-1.1	-0.7	-0.8	-0.9	-0.8	-1.0	-1.2	-1.8	-1.3
TOTAL NET INTEREST MARGIN		**13.4**	**6.7**	**7.2**	**8.1**	**7.6**	**6.9**	**6.9**	**7.2**	**8.2**	**6.0**
5.	Loans Provisions	-2.7	-1.2	-1.1	-1.6	-2.0	-2.2	-1.6	-2.4	-3.5	-2.4
TOTAL NET INTEREST MARGIN- LOANS PROV.		**10.6**	**5.5**	**6.1**	**6.4**	**5.6**	**4.7**	**5.3**	**4.7**	**4.7**	**3.5**
6.	Income from Services	9.1	7.9	8.0	7.4	6.9	6.2	5.8	5.8	5.9	4.5
7.	Expense on Services	-0.9	-0.8	-0.4	-0.4	-0.4	-0.4	-0.3	-0.3	-0.7	-0.5
FINANCIAL MARGIN WITHOUT CAPITAL GAINS		**18.8**	**12.6**	**13.7**	**13.4**	**12.1**	**10.6**	**10.8**	**10.2**	**9.9**	**7.5**
8.	Cap. Gains on Securities other than Bonds	0.2	0.2	-0.1	-0.3	0.1	0.3	0.0	0.0	-0.1	0.0
9.	Cap. Gains on Bonds	9.8	2.9	1.3	0.4	1.5	1.3	-0.7	0.3	0.6	0.9
FINANCIAL MARGIN		**28.8**	**15.7**	**14.9**	**13.6**	**13.6**	**12.2**	**10.1**	**10.5**	**10.4**	**8.4**
10.	Other income/expense	-7.1	0.3	1.2	1.8	0.9	1.5	0.8	0.8	0.3	0.8
TOTAL FINANCIAL MARGIN		**21.7**	**16.1**	**16.2**	**15.3**	**14.5**	**13.7**	**10.9**	**11.3**	**10.7**	**9.2**
11.	EXPENSES	19.2	14.0	10.5	9.6	9.1	8.1	7.8	8.0	9.5	7.6
10.1.	Salaries	7.4	5.4	6.7	6.3	6.1	5.4	5.3	5.4	4.2	3.5
10.2.	Maintenance	11.8	8.6	3.8	3.4	3.0	2.8	2.6	2.6	5.2	4.2
RETURNS BEFORE TAXES		**2.5**	**2.0**	**5.6**	**5.7**	**5.5**	**5.5**	**3.1**	**3.3**	**1.2**	**1.5**
12.	Taxes	1.5	0.7	3.8	3.3	3.4	3.0	2.4	2.4	1.1	1.0
12.1.	Income Tax	0.1	0.0	0.3	0.3	0.4	0.4	0.1	0.3	0.4	0.5
12.2.	Other Taxes	1.4	0.7	3.5	3.0	2.9	2.6	2.3	2.2	0.7	0.6
ROA		**1.0**	**1.3**	**1.8**	**2.4**	**2.1**	**2.5**	**0.7**	**0.9**	**0.1**	**0.5**
ROE		**4.3**	**6.7**	**11.2**	**15.8**	**14.7**	**18.9**	**5.7**	**6.5**	**0.6**	**4.2**
ASSETS (US$ million)		12238	15251	20253.37	23471.24	29048.39	34915.89	39790.77	41432.67	41600	46558

Table 6 and 7 present the second consequence of the "flight to quality" with a comparison of annual dollar and peso interest rates with annualized monthly rates of growth of dollar and pesos deposits.

Table 6
Peso Deposit Growth (annualized) and Interest Rates

	Total Peso Deposits Growth	Peso Term Deposits and Peso Savings Accounts Growth	Weighted Average of Int. rates on 30-59 Day Peso Dep. And on Peso Savings Accounts
Dec. 1991/April 1991	76.13	27.56	17.80
Dec. 1992/Dec. 1991	69.45	77.40	13.54
Dec. 1993/Dec. 1992	44.68	54.83	6.40
Feb. 1994/Dec. 1993	40.48	44.65	5.96
June 1994/Feb. 1994	*0.65*	*-7.66*	*6.09*
Nov. 1994/June 1994	9.03	19.36	6.65
Nov. 1994/Feb. 1994	*5.31*	*7.07*	*6.40*

Source: Informe Economico, Ministerio de Economia de Argentina. Several issues.

Table 7
Dollar Deposit Growth (annualized) and Interest Rates

	Total Dollar Deposits Growth	Dollar Term Deposits and Dollar Savings Accounts Growth	Weighted Average of Int. rates on 30-59 Day Dollar Dep. And on Dollar Savings Accounts
Dec. 1991/April 1991	124.82	90.72	NA
Dec. 1992/Dec. 1991	66.70	71.40	NA
Dec. 1993/Dec. 1992	65.53	75.79	5.32
Feb. 1994/Dec. 1993	36.07	37.04	4.96
June 1994/Feb. 1994	26.38	26.30	5.10
Nov. 1994/June 1994	20.17	21.13	5.15
Nov. 1994/Feb. 1994	23.90	24.46	5.13

Source: Informe Economico, Ministerio de Economia de Argentina. Several issues.

These tables show the high rate of growth of deposits until the end of 1993 and the deceleration that took place in 1994. The tables also show that while before 1994 monthly deposit growth rates were on average always above the monthly interest rates paid on each type of deposits, between June and February 1994 rates of monthly peso deposit growth were well below the interest rates paid on peso deposits. And although between July 1994 and November 1994 there is a recovery, the rate of growth of peso deposits is just slightly over the interest rate when the complete period data between February and November 1994 is considered. Besides it should be taken into account that the published interest rates used in Tables 6 and 7, are based on a sample of thirty first-rate selected public, domestic private and foreign banks, and consequently, for most banks out of the sample, interest rates paid on deposits were considerably higher. For the same period, dollar deposits grew well above the dollar interest rates.

Thus, the reduction in the rate of deposit growth during 1994 had a higher impact on peso deposits, - an effect that will be seen again during the first phase of the future panic - and translated into an increase in competition for those banks that were more active in the peso deposit market. Additionally, rates on peso deposits became positive in real terms for the first time in 1994. Figures 5 and 6 show the interaction between monthly interest rates and monthly rates of deposit growth for both currencies. Figure 7 shows the inflation rates and peso interest rates

It is interesting to recall that at that time Argentine economic newspapers viewed this increase in international interest rates as "a external shock, an exam that the Convertibility Plan had not taken in the previous years"[4].

Minimum Capital Regulations and New Provisioning Rules

As mentioned in Section 1, in June 1993, the Central Bank issued new capital regulations. Tables 3 and 4 show that as of June 1991 the nominal capital to asset ratios was 26.6% for wholesale banks and 24.1% for retail banks. Due to the preceding hyperinflation, bank deposits represented less than 50% of bank assets and most probably bank assets shrank over the period before the Convertibility Plan. The practical consequence of this was that capital-to-asset ratio regulations were not binding for a long time. Figure 8 presents the evolution of nominal capital to asset ratios for private wholesale and retail banks between 1991 and 1995. The fact that capital to asset ratios were not binding is suggested by the fact that these nominal ratios decreased over time. But this process seemed to have reached an end in 1994 where nominal capital asset ratios actually rose. Thus, during 1994, capital regulations became binding for some institutions.

Figure 5

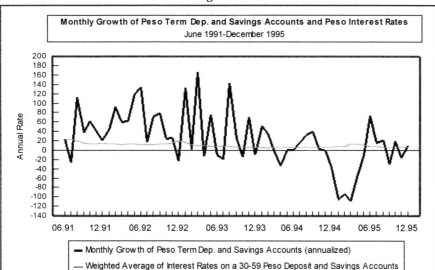

Figure 6

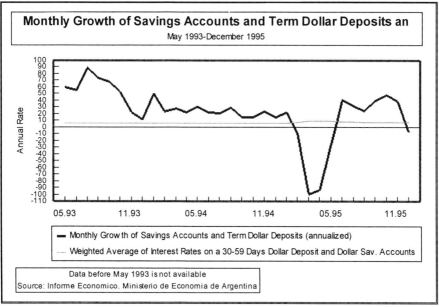

Figure 7

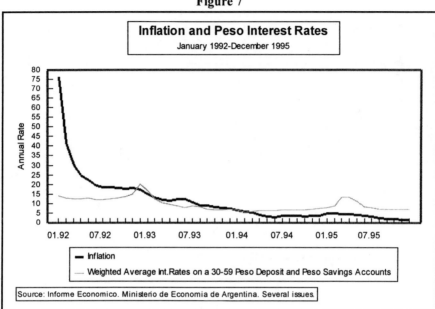

Figure 8
Nominal Capital Asset Ratios for Argentine Private Banks

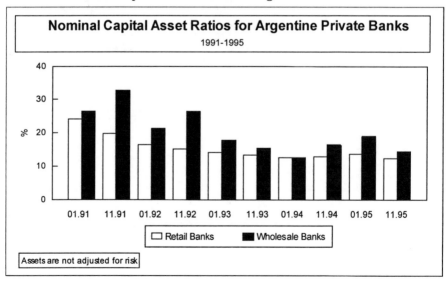

An additional circumstance that contributed to increase capital requirements was the new provisioning rules that came out in June 1994 and were scheduled to come into effect gradually between then and September 1995. These new provisioning rules called for a new classification of loans based on the client's capacity to repay the loan and not solely on its actual performance in repaying. In general, the new criteria implied higher provisioning, and consequently, this had an impact on the calculation of actual capital that made some banks situation still more difficult.

Characteristics of Failing and Merging Banks

The increase in competition affected more those banks that were more active in the peso market deposits, making it more difficult for them to meet the higher capital to asset ratios. Thus many small retail banks with possible unexploited economies of scale and scope, began to consider merging strategies during 1994, that only took place after the panic. Additionally, the new financial environment could have forced some banks to undertake growth strategies in an effort to survive.

Table 8 presents the results of the Mann-Whitney- Wilcoxon non parametric test for differences in the distributions of some crucial variables representing risk and efficiency as of November 1994 for surviving banks vs. merging and failing banks. In Figure 9, the histograms for the actual distributions of the variables for both types of banks are included.

Table 8
Differences In Distributions Between Merging And
Failing vs. Surviving Banks
(Data As Of November 1994)

	Wilcoxon Statistics
Log Assets	-4.222
Non Interest Expense/ Assets	+4.596
Peso Deposits / Total Dep.	+4.527
Bonds / Assets	-4.395
Actual to Required Capital	-4.768
(Non Perf. Loans-Prov.)/Capital	+4.774
ROA 94	-0.408
Net Interest Margins / Interest Earning Assets	+3.963
Assets Growth 1993/1994	+1.982
Big Deposits/Total Deposits	-3.923
Term Deposits / Total Dep.	+1.884

A negative sign for the statistics means that failing and merging banks were ranked among the lowest range of the variable being considered while a positive sign means that those banks were ranked among the highest range. Since the statistics are normally distributed, the usual criteria about significance apply.

The tests show substantial differences between both types of banks. In general, failing and merging banks were among the smallest banks and among those banks with the highest non-interest expense to assets ratios; they were also among the most active banks in the market for peso deposit, oriented to traditional activities with a lower bonds to asset ratios. On the whole, these four variables taken together provide some evidence that these banks were among the most poorly managed banks with possible unexploited economies of scale and scope and a higher exposure to the increase in competition that took place in 1994.

Additionally they had lower capital to asset ratios and higher non performing loans to capital ratios, which means that these banks were also riskier than surviving banks. Their higher rate of asset growth and the higher net interest margins also signaled that these banks may have undertaken higher risk than the rest of the banks in the system. Interestingly, merging and failing banks had higher net interest margins but lower ROA's. Taken together this result suggests that although they undertook higher risk and consequently charged a higher spread for their activities, their inefficiency did not allow them to obtain extra returns.

Figure 9

Distributions Of Variables Representing Risk And Inefficiencies In Failing And Merging Banks Vs. Surviving Banks

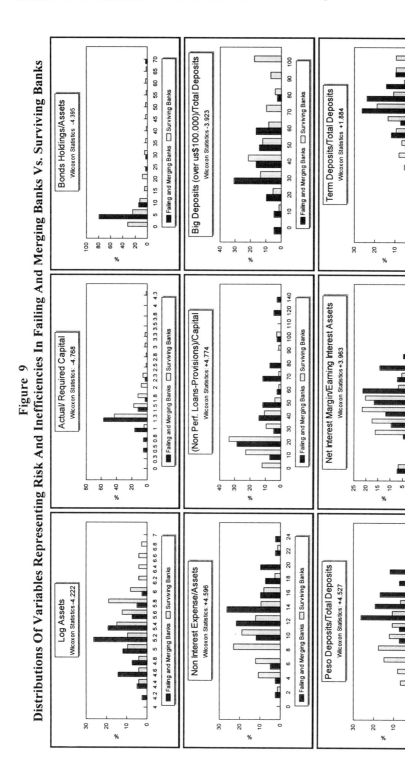

It is well known that the Argentine panic was mostly caused by the large depositor (over US$100,000). Between March 1995 and November 1994, 3,490 large depositors (on average 17.5 depositors per bank) were responsible for a drop of US$3 billion, that is to say 90% of the accumulated total fall in term deposits and 64% of the fall in total deposits. Interestingly, the test shows that as of November 1994, the large depositor had discriminated against the future failing and merging banks and so these banks had lower big deposits to total deposits ratio, that is to say they were not particularly affected by the dynamics of the panic.

Thus, the analysis of merging and failing retail bank portfolios as of November 1994 suggests that these banks were significantly different from surviving banks with respect to a set of variables representing risk and efficiency. There is also evidence that these differences were perceived by depositors, and consequently, merging and failing banks suffered statistically higher withdrawals than surviving banks during the panic and also paid higher interest rates during the pre-panic period (Schumacher 1996).

Finally, it should be observed that although wholesale banks suffered severe losses during 1994 and through the panic (Table 4), in general they did not fail[5], given their high capital to asset ratios (Table 2 and Figure 8).

SECTION 3: CONCLUSIONS

The Convertibility Plan adopted by Argentina in 1991, provided the rationality for a set of financial regulations that were crucial in setting limitations to the macroconsequences of the crisis. In particular, the liquidity needs were faced with resources that had been allocated to the bad (panic) state beforehand, limiting in this way the creation of new liquidity by the Central Bank, that never exceeded the amount that was allowed within the Convertibility rules. Total credit reduction was small and although, there was an impressive fall in the GNP in 1995, there is room to speculate that the drop could have been larger and more extended in the absence of a mechanism -reserve requirements- that had smoothed the natural credit expansion under the heavy and persistent capital inflows received before 1994 and without a disciplinary framework that had put limitations to bank risk before the panic and prevented a generalized bail-out once the crisis started. Thus, the Convertibility regime was successful in playing the difficult trade-off between internal and external equilibria.

The difficulties encountered by wholesale banks began with the fall in Argentine bonds prices during 1994, although they became more acute with the rise in country risk as a consequence of the Mexican devaluation. But, in general, these banks did not fail over the panic, since they had very high capital to asset ratios.

The strategy to merge was evaluated by some retail banks during 1994 as a way to face the increased competition and to improve returns that could help to meet capital asset ratios, but was probably delayed by "entrenched" managers that risked the loss of their positions, particularly if we consider that most merging banks were mutual banks. Thus, the dramatic fall in total deposits during the panic put a rush on a process that was already rooted in the pre-panic period.

Finally, very high and increasing non-performing loans, together with low capital to asset ratios, higher rates of asset growth and higher spreads, indicate that higher risk undertaken in 1994 could have played a large role in the difficulties encountered by some retail banks that ended up in failure.

On the whole, the analysis of the financial environment as of November 1994 and the characteristics of merging and failing bank portfolios as of the same date, suggest that the Argentine banking panic had extraordinary market discipline components, and put a rush on a process of mergers and failures that on the whole improved the safety and soundness of the financial system.

NOTES

[1] For a detailed description of the dynamics of the panic, see Banco Central de la Republica Argentina (1995) and Schumacher (1996) chapter 2.

[2] For an exploration into the causes of the output reduction see Calvo (1996)

[3] The Central Bank established that the proportion of Argentine bonds issued in foreign currency that could account for foreign reserves would increase to 30% after the first Central Bank board were renewed, or if Congress authorized the use of a higher proportion (not higher than 30%) before the new board took office. Given that the behavior of reserves allowed to meet the required reserves to monetary base ratio, it was not necessary to increase this ceiling over the panic.

[4] Santangelo and Melconian C. "La Argentina dolarizada, sufre de tasas menos que Mexico" Ambito Financiero 23.9.94, page 14.

[5] The exception is Extrader that failed in January 1995, that is to say immediately after the Mexican devaluation. This bank was suspected to have a hidden off-shore branch and the Argentine Superintendency had been following its activities since mid 1994.

REFERENCES

Calvo, Guillermo, "Why is 'The Market' so unforgiving? Reflection on the Tequilazo," University of Maryland, mimeo, 1996.

Fernandez Roque, "Comentarios Sobre el Proyecto Oficial de Reforma de la Carta Organica del Banco Central de la Republica Argentina," mimeo, 1990.

Fernandez Roque, Guidotti, Pablo, "Regulating the Banking Industry in Transition Economies," mimeo, 1995.

'Managing a Liquidity Shock: Regulating the Financial System in Argentina," Banco Central de la Republica Argentina, December 1994/Julio 1995, mimeo.

Schumacher, Liliana, "Bubble or Depositors Discipline. A Study of the Argentine Banking Panic, December 1994-May1995," Ph.D. Dissertation, University of Chicago, 1996.

PART IV

THE TRANSFORMING ECONOMIES

10

The Consolidation Of Russian Banking: The Big Picture

JACOB NELL
Former Assistant Editor, Central Banking journal (U.K.) and H.M. Treasury Official

Over the last ten years Russia has been utterly transformed. Gorbachev's programmes of political reform (glasnost or openness) and economic reform (perestroika or restructuring) led to the end of the Cold War and the abolition of the leading role of the party in the Soviet Union, but little changed in the economic picture. In 1990-1991, the economy drifted into crisis. The growing budget deficit, due to political disputes between the republics and the Center, and decreasing central control over financial transactions, depleted foreign exchange and gold reserves, created a large, unstructured, short-term debt burden, and brought about a growing "monetary overhang," as the deficit was financed by monetary growth in a situation of price controls. At the same time the economy slid into recession.

After the failure of the 1991 August putsch attempt to restore the old style Soviet Union, Yeltsin, the democratically elected leader of Russia, eclipsed General Secretary Gorbachev. Yeltsin banned the Communist Party of Soviet Union (CPSU), appointed a team of academics and economists to lead his first government under Yegor Gaidar, and, in a speech on October 24, 1991, outlined a comprehensive reform programme based on liberalization of prices and foreign trade, privatization of most state-owned assets and stabilization of inflation and output. On December 8, 1991 Yeltsin signed the Belveshkaya Accord from which date "the Soviet Union ceased its existence."

Despite hyperinflation, an armed uprising, the MMM Ponzi scheme, a secessionist war in Chechnya and major opposition, the government's reform programme was pushed through. Prices were liberalized on January 2, 1992; the mass privatization programme of 1992-94 put most state assets into private hands; the coordination of fiscal and monetary policy, following Gerashchenko's ouster from the Central Bank of Russia (CBR) in October 1994, combined with a substantial reduction in the deficit and the shift to financing through the T-bill market rather than by printing money reduced inflation from 18% in January 1995 to the stabilization target of 1% a month in the summer of 1996.

There is a major reef, however, which may yet wreck the Russian ship of state before it can reach calmer waters: the parlous state of the banking system. Inefficient banking, runs this line, is being exposed by stabilization. The excess profits initially available from access to cheap central bank money, trade credits and foreign exchange dealing, and latterly from high T-bill yields, are disappearing, at the same time as bad loans cease to be automatically eroded by inflation. This faces the CBR with an apparent choice between monetary stability (i.e. refusing to bail out banks as they go bust) and financial stability (i.e. intervening to prevent any systemic effects from a banking crisis).

More generally, the financial sector is of pivotal importance to the success of reforms in Russia. Investment is needed to return to growth, after the continuous decline in output since 1990. And investment requires financing by private domestic sources given Russia's huge investment needs and the limited resources available to the government struggling to contain its deficit. Also international financial institutions and the continuing caution shown by foreign investors need to be addressed. Fortunately there is plenty of scope for financing investment, since Russia has a vast pool of savings - currently calculated at over 30% of GDP. The bottleneck is the financial sector, whose task is to draw these savings from under beds and out of dollars and back to Russia, and channel them into productive uses in the Russian economy. Since the key players in the financial sector are the banks, the success of transition depends upon the success of the Russian banks in turning themselves into efficient financial intermediaries.

To date the banks have not performed this task of maturity transformation - borrowing short to lend long - since they have been making plenty of money by borrowing short to lend short. Loans to the economy only constitute a small percentage of GDP. This suggests that Russian banks are not performing their intermediation role efficiently yet; although it also reduces the vulnerability of the Russian economy to a banking crisis. However, as I explore in the remainder of this article, the CBR is making a major effort to establish its regulatory credibility and has developed a plausible strategy for the consolidation of the industry.

GOSBANK TO BANKING BOOM

After the revolution the Soviet government nationalized all banks by decree on December 14, 1917. Banking was declared a state monopoly. A new Russian State Bank was founded in October 1921 and in 1923 it was re-organized into the State Bank of the USSR, which was granted the monopoly right to issue banknotes and was assigned the task of conducting credit, settlement and cash operations.

The consolidation of the system of state planning in the economy of the USSR, whose proclaimed objective in those years was building socialism, required further centralization of control over financial resources and their distribution. In 1930-1932 the Soviet Union carried out a credit reform, which replaced commercial loans and bill discounting with direct financing from the State Bank. The State Bank of the USSR was a truly universal bank. All enterprises, organizations and institutions were required to keep their funds in the State Bank, which concurrently performed the functions of an issuing, commercial, deposit, investment, land, and savings bank. It was directly accountable to the Council of Ministers (Soviet Government) and all its activities were conducted strictly in accordance with the state plan.

In the middle of the 1980s the Soviet Union realized that its planned economy was beginning to falter and made a certain departure from the orthodox principle of centralism in managing the economy. That period, which came to be known as *perestroika*, saw the appearance of some market incentives and tendencies in the country's economy, but the foundations of central planning remained intact.

The partial decentralization of the economy was accompanied by an overhaul of the banking system. In 1987 new specialized banks were created to meet the specific needs of different sectors of the economy. The new banking system consisted of the State Bank and five specialized state banks: Foreign Trade Bank (Vneshekonombank), Industrial Construction Bank (Promstroibank), Agro-Industrial Bank (Agroprombank), Utility Services and Social Development Bank (Zhilsotsbank - for schools, hospitals and cultural centers) and Savings and Credit Bank (Sberbank). The specialized banks (spets banks) were created as universal banks to finance, credit and effect settlements on current activities and capital investments in particular spheres of the economy. The State Bank was responsible for central management of the credit system in accordance with the plan and remained the sole issuing and settlement center, as well as pursuing a exchange rate policy and coordinating and supervising the specialized banks.

However, the development of the small business sector at the time of *perestroika* led to the demand for a different range of banking services. Eventually the establishment of co-operative and commercial joint-stock banks was permitted.

Thus the second stage of the banking reform began late in 1988. The appearance of these new credit institutions and the growth in their number was a revolutionary change in the country's banking system.

As can be seen in Table 1, the Russian banking industry grew at a breakneck pace. There appeared to be a number of motives for founding a bank: access to cheap central bank credit; preserving deposits from seizure by the state; and to provide funding for an enterprise. As in other transition economies, the licensing requirements were at first extremely low, and so there was a rash of foundings and takeovers of the local branches of the spetsbanks. The most dramatic growth in the number of banks took place in the last quarter of 1990 when the number of registered banks increased from 250 to 1077 as a result of branches of spetsbanks being turned into independent banks on the basis of an August 1990 CBR order. One of the spetsbanks, Zhilsotsbank, utterly disappeared in Russia.

Table 1
Banking Boom: Russian Credit
Organizations 1989-1996

Date (January 1)	Number
1989	23
1990	131
1991	1077
1992	1297
1993	1736
1994	2011
1995	2517
July 1996	2582

THE CENTRAL BANK OF RUSSIA'S REGULATORY POWERS

This dramatic growth in banks required a system for licensing the new commercial banks and supervising them. In December 1990, the Russian Federation, which was still a part of the Soviet Union, passed new central bank and banking laws, which laid the foundations of a two-tier banking system in Russia, comprising the central bank and commercial banks, and drew a clear dividing line between their functions. The amended central bank law passed in April 1995 further clarified the role of the CBR. It laid down one of the Bank of Russia's three main objectives as being to develop and strengthen the banking system of the Russian Federation.

The Bank of Russia is the lender of last resort for the commercial banks and is responsible for the system of bank refinancing. The central bank registers credit institutions, issues and revokes the licenses of credit institutions and organizations that audit them, supervises the activities of credit institutions, defines the procedures for banking operations and accounting rules for the banking system, registers issues of bank securities and organizes and exercises foreign exchange control directly as well as through authorized banks. The CBR has 80 regional centers, known rather fearsomely as the "main territorial institutions of the Bank of Russia," whose basic function is supervision of and provision of services to commercial banks, including licensing banks, monitoring compliance with legislation, collection and analysis of reports. The CBR also regulates primary dealers, who are mainly banks, on the government securities market.

The CBR, besides issuing and revoking licenses, also regulates mergers and takeovers in the banking sphere, which gives it the power to shape the structure of Russian banking. The CBR must pursue a balance between consolidation, a process usually referred to as "the concentration of banking capital," which will lead to fewer and larger banks and be able to take advantages of economies of scale, and avoiding monopolistic structures and ensuring conditions for fair competition banking. Currently, the domestic banking system is represented mainly by a host of miniature banks: banks with a declared charter capital of under 5 bn roubles, i.e. US$1 mn, account for 73% of all banks. 152 banks have an authorized capital of 5 bn or more roubles, i.e. a sum approximately equivalent to 5 mn Ecus.

DEVELOPMENT OF BANKING REGULATION

The low barriers to entry in the early years of commercial banking in Russia clearly fuelled the banking boom. This liberal entry policy has had positive repercussions in that the Russian banking system has a low state share, with just two banks remaining majority state-owned, admittedly with 25% of total banking assets. It also means that the Russian banking industry is quite competitive, in the sense that no bank has a dominant market share in any field, except Sberbank in the market for deposits, and that many of the largest banks are new banks rather than former state-owned banks. But it also meant that Russia has had too many small, inefficient and underregulated banks, who were prepared to break all the rules to stay in business.

One interesting feature of the Russian banking industry, certainly when compared with other countries in transition such as Hungary, the Czech Republic and Poland, is the restricted role of foreign banks. In 1994, foreign banks, with the exception of a small group of foreign banks who had already been granted licenses, were denied access to the Russian market until 1996, on the grounds that Russian banking was an "infant industry" and needed protection for a limited period to allow it to compete with more experienced foreign banks. As a result, foreign banks play a small role in the Russian banking system and only account for 2.5% of banking system assets. (See Table 2)

Table 2
Foreign Banks in Russia

Type	Number
Over 50% foreign owned	17
(of which 100% foreign owned)	(13)
Branches	1
Representative offices	139

Memo: Foreign banks hold 2.5% of banking system assets

The first step towards a new regulatory regime was taken under Gerashchenko when licensing requirements were raised and priced in a more inflation-resistant numeraire than the rouble. Since March 1, 1994 the minimum charter capital for all banks has been equivalent to 1 mn Ecus, or 250,000 Ecus for credit institutions with a limited license. At the same time, the CBR committed itself to a capital adequacy target of 4% of assets. Under Gerashchenko, the CBR also began to revoke banking licenses.

In 1995 when Paramonova was acting governor, the CBR fought a bruising battle with the commercial banks to impose new accounting rules. The CBR wanted commercial banks to report average balances over the reporting period rather than the balance on the reporting date, and wanted each bank to prepare one set of accounts rather than allowing different branches of each bank to report separately. Reasonable requests but anathema to some Russian bankers, who would cook the figures by transfers between branches and accounts just before the reporting date to evade various regulatory requirements and reduce reserve requirements. The storm of protest when Paramonova pushed through the changes led commercial bankers to spend substantial sums lobbying the Duma to block her confirmation, ultimately successfully.

In the early reform years, banking legislation and regulation was quite low on the policy agenda, as the government struggled against political opposition, large deficits and hyperinflation to implement the "liberalization, privatization and stabilization" program. The key turning point in this struggle was, paradoxically enough, Black Tuesday on October 10, 1994, when the rouble lost a third of its value in one day. This sobering experience, caused as a result of loose monetary and fiscal policies leading excess liquidity to appear on the forex market as excess demand for dollars, created a broad consensus in favor of tight policies. It also lead Yeltsin to sack Gerashchenko, the governor of the central bank, who had pursued and advocated inflationary policies. In 1995, the Government pushed through two key changes. The deficit was lowered dramatically, and the government ceased to finance it in an inflationary fashion. The consequence was a dramatic growth in the T-bill market and a fall in the monthly inflation rate from 18% in January 1995 to -2% in summer 1996.

The shock that galvanized the authorities to develop plans for the banking sector, much as "Black Tuesday" galvanized the authorities into following a tight monetary and fiscal policy, was the situation which arose on the Moscow interbank market in August 1996. The interbank rate went skyhigh, over 1000%, and the CBR refused to lend, as the market seized up for three days. The problem was that with falling inflation the lack of a professional approach to the management of liabilities, and to the balancing of the structure of assets and liabilities was clearly exposed. The Bank of Russia did manage to control the situation successfully, by purchasing T-bills and extending short term credits. But the crisis claimed some prominent banks, including the Mytishshinski Bank, and gave the authorities a fright. Anatoli Chubais, then the deputy prime minister responsible for the economy and finance, described it as a grenade going off in a closed room, without having any idea of the casualties.

In the words of one critic, describing the causes of the liquidity crisis on the Moscow interbank market in August 1996, "the main cause of the unfavorable position of many Russian banks was their risky credit policy and their inadequate liquid assets as a result of the failure to observe the prudential ratios set for credit organizations, unqualified management, lack of strategic planning, absence of a rationally constructed credit portfolio, lack of credit risk management and growth of nonpayments to enterprises." Strong words for a central bank governor to use of his own banks (see extract from interview in Appendix.) Earlier in 1996, Dubinin admitted that: "There are serious violations in the work of more than 80% of the banks we inspected." Foreign concerns about the behavior of Russian banks are severe. The fear, made plausible by anecdote and the numerous contract killings of Russian bankers, is that they are sieves for laundering illegal money and capital flight. The Bank of England and the Fed have to date not granted permission for any new Russian bank to open a branch or subsidiary in London or New York.

THE ROLE OF THE INTERNATIONAL FINANCIAL INSTITUTIONS

The IMF has been the lead international financial institution (IFI) in Russia, since they have negotiated the annual programmes with the Government in 1993, 1994 and 1995, as well as the three year 1996 Extended Fund Facility, which the IMF loans have been disbursed to support. They have also played a prominent role in the provision of technical assistance, which has been of crucial importance in facilitating skills transfer, often through borrowing experts from the BIS or EU central banks. The IMF has advised on key laws, on payments system reform, on central bank organization, accounting, monetary policy implementation and research, as well as on banking supervision and regulation. In fact, the IMF has stationed a resident adviser in banking supervision in the CBR since 1992.

The IMF, of course, has no monopoly on expertise. In fact, the obvious center of excellence in banking supervision is the Bank for International Settlements, the central bankers' bank in Basle. The BIS runs a Service for Eastern European Countries and International Organizations, which keeps track of who is doing what, and stops the technical assistance providers from stepping on each other's toes. Further, Russia has now been represented on the Basle Committee of Banking Supervisors for several years, and contacts between Russian and other banking supervisors both formal and informal will further increase when the CBR becomes a member of the BIS. Following the invitation issued by the BIS to the CBR to become a member of the exclusive central bankers' club on September 9, 1996, membership formalities are expected to be completed by spring 1997. This may indicate that technical assistance on banking supervision will henceforth be largely channeled through Basle; although Camdessus' recent speech on the importance of banking supervision at the Washington meeting of the IMF may be a sign that the IMF wishes to remain involved in this area. The Joint Vienna Institute, a cooperative center set up in 1991 by the BIS, EBRD, IMF, IBRD and OECD to train key officials and executives from the countries in transition, offers another opportunity for the technical assistance providers to coordinate their work.

Despite the presence of the banking system adviser and a resident general adviser in the CBR, relations with the IMF have not always been smooth. One key controversy was over the elimination of interest rate floors at credit auctions in 1994. The issue may seem arcane, but the issue of principle was clear: the IMF wanted the market to determine the interest rate, while the CBR wanted to retain some administrative control over interest rates. Only after much tortuous argument and discussion did the CBR lift the interest rate floor.

In fact, there seems to be in many cases a lag between a policy commitment made in the joint statement issued by the Government and Central Bank, or reported in the IMF press release, and its actual fulfillment. For instance, in April 1995, the joint statement aimed to reduce inflation to 1% a year by the second half of 1995; and it was the second half of 1996 before this was achieved. Similarly in 1995, the joint statement talked of developing new instruments to manage liquidity and of strengthening regulatory and supervisory capacity, while in 1996 the IMF press release, after criticizing the restructuring of the banking sector for being "slow," made virtually identical commitments. Once again, however, what was promised for 1995 seems to have been delivered in 1996. (See "The 1996 Supervisory Plan" below)

On the commercial bank side, the EBRD and the IBRD have joined hands in the Financial Institutions Development Programme, launched in 1994. This programme involves selecting a core group of 30-40 prominent Russian banks, 32 having been selected to date, and providing them with loans to upgrade their systems and improve their business plans, and twinning programmes with international banks, at which point they will be eligible to draw on credits provided by the EBRD and

IBRD to a Project Implementation Unit in the Ministry of Finance for onlending to privatized enterprises. The EBRD in particular stresses financial institutional development as a key to success in reform, and works by channeling financing through Russian banks, as a way of hitting two targets - aiding business and banking development - with one blow. The Russia Small Business Fund, a joint initiative of the EBRD and G-7 plus Switzerland, for instance, makes small loans and provides micro-credits for small business through the Russian banking system.

THE 1996 SUPERVISORY PLAN

Banking regulation is becoming an increasingly international business, as banks increasingly operate across jurisdictions, and effective regulation requires regulators to develop common regulations and share information. The key common regulation that has been agreed, the famous Basle Accord on capital adequacy which sets a floor to capital of 8% of risk-weighted assets, has become a minimum standard. Banks that don't meet it won't get licensed abroad, and are unlikely to find it easy to raise money in international markets, while jurisdictions that eschew the CAD are liable to be penalized with higher interest rates, on the grounds that they are poorly regulated.

In order to meet international standards and to be seen as well-regulated, the Russian banking regulators are implementing radical changes. By mid-1996 the Central Bank had established a new system of banking regulation and supervision, which gives it better intelligence on market developments and the capacity to intervene if problems arise. The innovations include:

- An early warning system so that the CBR is not caught short by a sudden collapse. This is based on monthly reporting of key prudential ratios; banks who fail to report can be forced to close their correspondent accounts with other banks and make all settlements exclusively through the CBR.
- A ranking of banks into one of three groups depending upon risk of failure. In evaluating the asset quality of a bank portfolio, all assets are divided into six groups, depending on the risk level of investments and possible loss of a part of their value. At June 1, 1996, there were 50 banks in the highest risk group and 253 in the next highest, indicating a likelihood of closure without the infusion of new capital.
- A revised set of prudential standards, as laid out in (i) a revised Instruction No. 1 in January 1996, which is the cornerstone of banking regulation in Russia, and (ii) in the revised law "On Banks and Banking" in April 1996. The centerpiece of this raising of standards is an increase in capital adequacy standards, which will bring Russian banks to the Basle CAD standards of capital of 8% of risk-weighted assets by 1999. See Table 3 for details.

Table 3
The New CBR Regulations

Regulation	New rules
Capital adequacy	The capital adequacy ratio will be raised from currently 4% as of July 1996 to 8% as of February 1st 1999. Liquidity standards will be adapted accordingly in the same period.
Licensing requirement	The minimum capital for new banks with a general banking license will be raised from 2 million Ecu in April 1996 to 5 million Ecu by July 1st 1998 (January 1st 1999 for those banks already existing).
Loan loss provision	At present all bank loans are divided into five risk groups: standard, substandard, doubtful, dangerous and hopeless. Commercial banks must create a reserve for possible losses on loans in the third, fourth and fifth risk groups (30%, 65% and 100% respectively). As for the loans in the first and second risk groups, it is up to the bank to decide whether it should create a loan loss reserve or not (at 2% and 5% respectively). The requirement that banks should create reserves for possible losses on loans also applies to credits granted in foreign currency
Exposure to individual borrower	Maximum ceilings for exposure to one borrower (including affiliated companies) will be reduced from 60% in July 1996 to 25% of capital as of February 1st 1998. Total large loans i.e. loans exceeding 5% of the capital are to be reduced successively from 12 times capital in 1996 to 8 times by 1998.
Exposure to individual shareholder	Maximum credit given to one shareholder will be reduced from 60% of capital in July 1996 to 20% by the start of 1997. The sum of credits given to shareholders should not exceed 50% of total capital by the start of 1998. Lending to insiders, i.e. individuals personally related to the bank such as employees and management and their relatives, will be reduced from 10% of capital in July 1996 to 2% in July 1997.
Ceiling on depositor	The maximum deposit by one depositor, currently 60% of capital, is to be reduced to 25% by February 1998.
Deposits to capital ratio	Private household deposits as a whole should not exceed the bank's capital.
Ceiling on shareholdings	A bank's investment in the shares of other companies as a whole will have to be reduced from 45% of capital in July 1996 to 25% at the start of 1997. The share in one company is limited to 10% of capital.

- An electronic payment and settlements system in Moscow, set up in 1994, which settles across the CBR. This system permits the CBR to monitor the overall liquidity situation of the major Moscow banks at the core of the Russian banking system. With the extension of the RTGS system being tested in Ryazan oblast to the rest of the country by the end of 1997, the CBR's intelligence from the payment system should further improve.
- A stronger banking supervision function, with the number of staff devoted to supervision more than doubling from 1993 to 1996 (See Table 4).
- Creation of a special department (OPERU-2) to supervise the systemic banks. At the moment 10 of the largest Moscow banks are subject to OPERU supervision, although up to 50 will eventually be subject to OPERU supervision. OPERU-2

will eventually have a total staff of 300. The department has been given broad powers over local banking supervision units of the CBR.

Table 4
Measures Of Supervisory Activity

Date	Number of supervisors	Licenses revoked
1993	1,683	19
1994	2,574	65
1995	3,187	225

Memo: About 10% of supervisors are Moscow-based (285 in 1995).

- The CBR is supporting the development of a deposit insurance scheme. It argues that the potential liability, having to make a payout if a bank collapses, is minor, since the funds for the scheme will be provided by commercial banks and only the first $3000 or so of any deposit will be fully covered. However, the gains could be major, since it will increase public confidence in the banking system, and so lead to a flow of savings from dollars under mattresses into banks, as well as eliminating the unfair competitive advantage that Sberbank holds in the market for household deposits, where it is the only bank whose deposits have a state guarantee. A law on deposit insurance is expected to come before the Duma in autumn 1996. In the meantime, the CBR has taken some special regulatory measures to reduce the risk of irresponsible deposit-taking: new banks have been forbidden to attract personal deposits during their first year, and new subsidiaries of banks in which the sum total of the deposits exceeds their capital have been restricted from taking deposits.
- The CBR has developed a range of instruments to facilitate banks' liquidity management, including Lombard auctions, a Lombard window, a repo facility, and an emergency short-term credit facility.

There is still substantial scope for improvement. One particularly urgent issue, given the fact that the process of consolidation under way in the Russian banking system suggests bank collapses are inevitable, is to draft a number of laws to detail such banking procedures as bankruptcy, merger, takeover and liquidation of commercial banks.

Another outstanding issue is in the division of supervisory responsibilities. This is both a problem internally and externally. Within the CBR at the moment there are no less than six supervisory department in the central apparatus of the CBR: for licensing, for prudential supervision, for inspection, for sanitation (closing and restructuring banks), for banks' activities on the securities markets and for foreign exchange control. This means that knowledge and responsibility are in danger of being too fragmented. For instance five departments report to Deputy Governor Turbanov, who reports to First Deputy Governor Khandruev, while the department supervising banks' activities on the securities markets reports to Deputy Governor

Kozlov, who reports to First Deputy Governor Aleksashenko. It is also unclear what is achieved by separating licensing and sanitation, beyond providing another departmental post to distribute. Since Russian banks are universal banks and able to carry out any transaction with securities, effective supervision will require good communication across these departmental boundaries, as well as externally with the Federal Securities Commission. The lack of a formal procedure for coordination may be due to the changing status of the Federal Securities Commission this year, which has changed from being an independent ministry in spring 1996 to being demoted to a department reporting to the Ministry of Finance after Yeltsin's election to being reconfirmed as an independent ministry. However it is a serious potential weakness, particularly as bank's equity holdings are expected to increase rapidly with expected stock market growth.

These problems should be kept in perspective. Great improvements have been made, and the formal improvements have been matched by action. More banks have been shut since the beginning of 1996 than have been founded. Three of the largest banks have been subject to regulatory action, including the removal of a banking license from Tveruniversalbank and the installation of temporary administration at Inkombank. The CBR seems to have an achievable route to international regulatory standards and the credibility to get there.

The major outstanding concern is that the government and central bank are seen to be separate from the commercial banks. The problem is that the revolving door revolves too quickly. Dubinin was a director of the Imperial Bank between being Acting Minister of Finance and being confirmed as Central Bank Governor. The Deputy Prime Minister is in charge of the Economy, Vladimir Potanin, was head of Uneximbank before being appointed this summer. Unless the CBR can convince that it treats all banks equally, and that there are no favors for insiders, mutterings of the type audible in Tver this summer that their bank (Tveruniversalbank) was only shut because it lacked the right connections, will undermine the CBR's attempts to manage consolidation in the banking sector while fending off political pressure for bailouts.

APPENDIX: GOVERNOR SERGEI DUBININ ON RUSSIAN BANKING

AN EXTRACT FROM THE INTERVIEW WITH GOVERNOR SERGEI DUBININ IN <u>CENTRAL BANKING</u>, VOL. VII NO. 2, U.K., AUTUMN 1996

A lot has been said about the problems of the Russian banking sector, particularly in the wake of the liquidity crisis in August 1995. What are the principal problems at the moment?

The crisis in August 1995 was connected above all with the distorted development of the interbank market, which encouraged commercial banks to use "short" money on the interbank market as a basic source of investment funds and for the support of liquidity. It revealed the weak side of banking activity and showed that the main cause of the unfavorable position of many Russian banks was their risky credit policy and their inadequate liquid assets as a result of the failure to observe the prudential ratios set for credit organizations, unqualified management, lack of strategic planning, absence of a rationally constructed credit portfolio, lack of credit risk management and growth of nonpayments to enterprises. The situation was made more difficult still by the lag between the legal basis in place for the functioning of the banking system and its real needs. At the moment extremely important changes an additions are being made to the existing banking legislation including, above all, the preparation of a civilized procedure for bankruptcy and liquidation of banks and minimization of losses for their clients.

What plans does the CBR have for dealing with these problems?

The central problems at the moment are to increase the reliability of the banking system, and to improve the arrangements for the work of the Bank of Russia with commercial banks that are in difficulties.

The Bank of Russia has prepared a Conceptual Framework for the Stabilization and Improvement of the Reliability of the Banking System, determining a set of measures for improving the licensing and regulation of banks on the basis of prudential ratios, stabilization measures in relation to the banks in difficulty, who are losing capital and becoming illiquid, and also problems and procedures connected with the bankruptcy, reorganization and liquidation of banks.

Do you have any view on what sort of banking system is appropriate for Russia in the long-run? Should it be a system with many (hundreds or thousands) of competing banks or with a smaller number of large banks?

As of July 1st, 1996, the number of commercial banks in operation amounted to 2131. The registration of new credit organizations has continued, but this process now goes much more slowly then in the recent past. The extensive development of the Russian banking system, accompanied by a fast growth in the number of credit organizations, has finished. In fact, in 1996, for the first time the number of banking licenses revoked exceeded the number of new banks registered. The largest contraction is expected above all in small, weak banks with a charter capital of 1 billion roubles or less (about US$0.2 mn). The number of medium sized and large banks by Russian standards with a charter capital above 5 billion roubles (about $1 mn) has increased to 152. At the same time it should be emphasized that a reduction in the total number of credit organizations in Russia is not at the moment a task of the CBR. Russia is a huge country and the level of provision of banking services is still far from ideal, except in Moscow and St. Petersburg.

The Conceptual Framework for the Stabilization and for Improving the Reliability of the Russian Banking System worked out by the Bank of Russia envisages certain institutional changes. In particular, a certain restructuring of the banking system is envisaged as a result of closing weak banks and processes of merger and acquisition and, as a result, the concentration of banking capital.

Further development of the branch network of stable commercial banks can be expected. This will take place both through the creation of new branches of existing credit organizations and through the transformation of previously independent commercial banks into branches.

It is expected that in the future types of banks that are comparatively new for Russia will develop, serving particular goals and needs, such as investment and mortgage banks.

What sorts of arrangements for deposit insurance and banking supervision do you prefer?

The creation of a Corporation for the guarantee of deposits is planned to provide a guarantee on the return of individual depositors' funds and compensation for the loss of income on invested funds. The funds for this Corporation will be provided through contributions from insured banks. A bill on this subject is being considered in the State Duma at the moment. Anyway, in accordance with the Russian law "On banks and banking activity" commercial banks have the right to create deposit insurance funds to guarantee the return of deposits and the payment of income on them.

In order to improve banking supervision, the Bank of Russia considers it essential to strengthen the licensing requirements for credit organizations, the observance of prudential ratios on banking activity and the creation of reserves (provisions) against possible bad loans. The Bank of Russia has created a special supervisory department to oversee the largest commercial banks in Moscow and in other financial centers.

How do you see the role of the bank as a lender of last resort?

In accordance with the Law on the CBR, the CBR is responsible for carrying out the function of the lender of last resort. Consequently the CBR has recently made particular efforts to develop the system for refinancing commercial banks with the aim of supporting the liquidity of the banking system.

The system of providing credit resources on a market basis until 1996 was in practice limited to the conduct of credit auctions which provided two-month credits. From April of this year [1996] auctions of Lombard credits were introduced which provide credit for 7-14 days. At the moment the CBR is considering making the Lombard window a standing facility. This should broaden the options for the refinancing of commercial banks. The Bank of Russia is also considering using repo operations with GKOs and other government securities which will allow banks to meet temporary liquidity shortages. Bank of Russia credits will only be provided against reliable collateral. However, the Bank of Russia in particular cases may provide commercial banks, who display the first symptoms of problems, with emergency credits.

REFERENCES

Anderson, E. Bergloef and K. Mizsei, "Banking Sector Development in Central and Eastern Europe," Forum Report of the Economic Policy Initiative, no.1, London, 1996.

EBRD, Transition Report 1995, 1996, London.

IMF, various press releases, including 95/21 & 96/13.

Nell (ed.), "Special Issue on the Bank of Russia in Transition," Central Banking Vol. VII, No.2, Central Banking Publications, London 1996.

OECD, OECD Economic Surveys, The Russian Federation 1995, Paris 1995.

Routava (ed), "Russia's Financial Markets and the Banking Sector in Transition," Bank of Finland Studies, A:95, Helsinki, 1996.

11

Managing Financial Turbulence: Czech Experience

JOSEF TOŠOVSKÝ
Governor, Czech National Bank

Since the start of political and economic transition, the Czech Republic - and former Czechoslovakia - enjoyed a relatively smooth progress, with, in the long run, a remarkable degree of internal and external monetary stability. Yet one must admit that during the first four transformation years (1990-1993), the country twice had to face turbulence which brought it near the brink of a financial crisis. The first turbulent period came in 1990 amid preparations of the full transformation program - which was to include partial convertibility and liberalized external trade. The second turbulence was a by-product of the split-up of former Czechoslovakia into two independent states. In both cases, the break-up of a regional trading block also played some role, yet the decisive cause of turbulence was deeper and much more complex.

ON THE EVE OF PARTIAL CONVERTIBILITY: A LESSON ON THE ROLE OF EXPECTATIONS

After the Czechoslovak "Velvet Revolution" of November 1989, the program of political and economic transformation started to be formed, and widely discussed, in 1990. The final version of the transformation program, as started in January 1991, included five main pillars:

1. Liberalization of prices: after 40 years of central price fixing, the bulk of prices were to be freed.
2. Liberalization of external trade and introduction of partial convertibility (for resident firms' current account transactions). That required a devaluation, toward an exchange rate seen as viable from the point of view of the balance of payments.
3. Macroeconomic stabilizing restrictive fiscal and monetary policy to remove the monetary overhang and to reintroduce macroeconomic equilibrium.
4. Massive and rapid privatization, including the use of the voucher scheme.

The program aimed to re-establish the role of prices and markets for an efficient allocation of resources. For the start, rationalization of price relations implied a rise of the price level, owing to a monetary overhang, and to low downward price elasticity.

In a small open economy, it made no sense to free internal prices without opening the economy to external competition and to world price relations. And, there could be no meaningful liberalization of imports and exports without current account convertibility, introduced at least for resident firms.

The experience from elsewhere showed that free trade and partial convertibility should not be attempted without a preceding macroeconomic stabilization. The first year of transformation - 1990 - was practically devoted to the stabilization goal; further transformation steps taken in 1991 were accompanied by continuing stabilizing policy.

Measures seeking external stability were an indispensable part of the program. It was understood that the exchange rate would have to be undervalued in relation to purchasing power parity to sustain the liberalized trade and a partly convertible currency.

Compared to steps as freeing of prices, freeing of external trade, and introduction of partial convertibility, it was clear that privatization would be a gradual, more time-consuming process. In the meantime, steps would be taken to stop state subsidies to firms (as well as to prices), and to let the firms face a hard budget constraint; that included also a stricter credit policy.

The transformation program was a result of a full year of discussions among the Government, the Czechoslovak State Bank, the political parties, home and foreign economic experts, and the general public. During 1990, even discussions on devaluation got ample publicity in the media. Open discussions and gaining wide public support for all parts of the program were seen as absolutely vital. As a negative by-product of this political necessity, however, devaluation expectations were aroused which, in the second half of 1990, led to financial turbulence.

In 1990, the economy was still practically 100% state-owned. The system of central planning had been abandoned, the central control over the economy was breaking down, and the markets were not yet liberalized to play their proper role. Managers of state-owned firms followed the discussions about privatization, a stop to subsidies, an expected price increase, harder competition, liberalized external trade, convertibility, and devaluation, with a mixture of hope and fear. In the first half of the year, they still predominantly behaved i.ı the old "planned economy" logic; in the second half, gaining a safer starting position for the expected reforms became their dominant concern. Firms were aware that reforms would newly define their positions as winners or losers - at a time when subsidies to loss-makers were to be stopped.

Already in January 1990, the Czechoslovak Koruna (CSK) was devalued for trade purposes by 18.6% (to the level of 17 CSK/1 US$), with the main aim to increase the share of profitable exports (from about 45% to 60%). A further devaluation was discussed as being necessary on or before launching resident convertibility and free external trade. However, due to the implied uncertainty on further macroeconomic developments, exchange rate levels seen as sustainable for he balance of payments varied widely from CSK 17 to CSK 34.

The discussions reflected also some vested interests of the old bureaucracy. In February 1990, the State Planning Commission pleaded to continue the central rationing of foreign exchange (by trade licensing), asserting that a sustainable exchange rate for free trade could be as high as CSK 45/1 US$. In discussions, all kinds of selective administrative regimes were proposed: limits of convertibility for selected sectors, multiple exchange rates, differentiated import surcharges, advance CSK deposits for selected sorts of imports, differentiated taxes, a selective duty to surrender foreign currency to state-owned banks, etc.

In May 1990, the Czechoslovak Government agreed on a first version of the transformation program which was to start in 1991. For external relations, the program explicitly outlined a liberalized external trade without administrative barriers. It also confirmed a possibility of a further devaluation at the end of 1990, probably up to CSK 24% per US$. The new exchange rate was to be supported by a temporary over-all import surcharge. Equal access of firms to foreign exchange was to be accompanied by a general surrender duty.

The response of firms reflected the safe bet on an increase of domestic prices during 1991, and on devaluation of the currency at the end of 1990 (possibly a larger one than officially planned). Czech and Slovak export-import firms, and producers dependent on imports, rushed to replenish and increase their inventories; imports in convertible currencies soared. Moreover, speculation became widespread based on leads and lags in trade payments (advance payments for imports, delayed receipts for exports). The extent in which firms reacted took the Government and even the central bank by surprise; it was a lesson on the impact of expectations on firms' behavior.

The external balance was aggravated by the breakdown of trade within the C.M.E.A. trade block. Fall of mutual trade resulted both from increasing insolvency of Russian (and some other C.M.E.A. countries`) importers and from the opening of East- and Central-European markets to western goods (which, being new, attractive, and in a wide choice, were massively preferred by consumers). Czech and Slovak exports to C.M.E.A. plummeted; during 1990, trade in non-convertible currencies fell by 31.5%. It was clear that this trade would not be restorable in the old structure and quality. Instead, trade in convertible currencies grew by 23% - a favorable re-orientation, except that the import side showed a 36% increase. The Persian Gulf crisis, preventing Czechoslovak exports to Iraq, and stopping Iraq's repayments of old debts by oil had an additional serious adverse effect.

The combined effect (in spite of improving Terms of Trade) was a turn of the trade balance in convertible currencies into a deficit in 1990. As a result, the current account in convertible currencies also ended with a deficit of US$1.1 billion On the capital account, there were some inflows of foreign direct investment (mainly into hotel building). On the other hand, there were large outflows of short-term capital, reflecting both the behavior of domestic firms, and the repatriation of foreign banks` deposits due to lack of trust in economic stability of the country. The balance of payments in convertible currencies showed a total deficit of US$700 million; foreign currency reserves of the Czechoslovak State Bank fell by almost US$600 million, reserves of the banking system fell by US$1.1 billion during 1990.

The above outcome already incorporated the effect of steps taken, in view of the aggravating situation in the second half of the year, to prevent a financial crisis. In the conditions of advancing deregulation, the previous rigid forms of central control were losing their previous dominating role. Under the pressure of the deteriorating liquidity of domestic banks and continued depletion of reserves due to capital flight and dramatically increasing imports in the latter half of 1990, the devaluation planned for December had to be undertaken earlier. On October 15, 1990, the CSK was devalued by 55.4%.

Yet the devaluation was not sufficient to stop the speculative behavior, and to re-establish trust in the currency. Foreign exchange reserves kept decreasing. A stand-by credit from the IMF which was under negotiation was not to come before 1991 (Czechoslovakia's membership was renewed in September 1990, and in December 1990 the member quota was deposited). It was also difficult was also to obtain credits from the World Bank and other international institutions. Private bank credits were almost the only possibility for replenishing the reserves; the Czechoslovak State Bank also made gold swaps to relieve the pressure on reserves. Liberalization, for the public, of foreign exchange accounts with domestic banks, contributed somewhat by increasing the volume of foreign exchange deposits.

Thus, liquidity and solvency of the country in international payments was preserved. However, a third devaluation of the currency became inevitable, before the freeing of imports and introduction of partial convertibility could be undertaken. On December 28, 1990, the CSK was devalued by another 16% for trade purposes. A unified exchange rate for trade and tourist purposes was set at the level of CSK 28 per US$, and the CSK was pegged to a basket of five currencies. (Some experts suggest that a lower exchange rate level could have been sufficient, if it were not for the preceding speculation; on the other hand, the new exchange rate proved a longer-than-expected viability).

Trends in the official exchange rate to US$ during 1990-1991, compared to parallel market rates of CSK in foreign banks, are shown in Figure 1. The chart shows that after the last (December 1990) devaluation, official and parallel rates came close together and showed the same stability in 1991.

Figure 1
Official and Parallel Exchange Rates (CSK per US$)

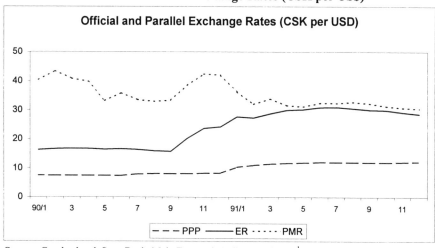

Source: Czechoslovak State Bank, Main Economic Indicators, OECD[1]

The freeing of external trade, and the introduction of partial convertibility, together with other transformation steps introduced on January 1, 1991, quickly calmed down the financial situation of the state. For 1991, help was already available from international financial institutions. Stand-by credits were granted by the IMF (the first tranche US$755 million was drawn in January 1991). Later, credits also were available from the World Bank, the European Union, and Group 24. At the start of reforms, the IMF credit especially had a significant stabilizing effect by increasing the foreign exchange reserves.

The internal strength of the economy soon proved sufficient to absorb the reforms. Both the current and capital accounts of the balance of payments in convertible currencies, turned into a surplus. As a result, during 1991, reserves of the banking system grew by US$2.1 billion, of which US$0.9 billion represented an increase of reserves of the Czechoslovak State Bank.

In spite of a transformation recession which inevitably characterized the first two years, the new exchange rate proved sustainable from the point of view of the balance of payments, both in the short-and medium-term. Since the end of 1990, the exchange rate remained stable and acted as a nominal anchor for liberalized prices.

SPLIT-UP OF A COUNTRY: CURRENCY SEPARATION

A second wave of financial turbulence was connected with the split-up of Czechoslovakia into two independent states - The Czech Republic and the Slovak Republic - as of January 1, 1993. After it became clear that the split-up was politically inevitable, it was time to think about economic consequences. Evidently, costs of disintegration of a single economy were to be high, especially in the short-run. The links between Czech and Slovak enterprises were characterized by a long-term and very close mutual cooperation in production. Coming in the midst of economic transformation, the separation meant an additional risk. Fortunately, both new states strived to reduce the costs in terms of lost production - to give the firms more time for adaptation, and to secure a bilateral payments system that would suit the exceptionally close economic ties between the new states.

In spite of expectations of the split-up, the Czechoslovak economy was in fairly good shape by the end of 1992. It had overcome the trough of recession tied with the first steps of transformation and showed a turn toward revival (in the last quarter of 1992, GDP increased - for the first time since 1989 - by 4%). Yearly inflation rate was 12%. Both accounts of the balance of payments showed a small surplus - with a moderate trade deficit more than covered by a surplus of services, and with the outflow of short-term capital covered by long-term inflows. Foreign direct investment in the first ten months of 1992 reached US$1 billion.

Before the split-up, the governments of the two Republics signed around thirty agreements defining future mutual relations. Most importantly, in the economic field, were agreements on a customs union and on the continuous use of the common currency. The latter reflected the priority given to maintaining monetary stability and confidence in the currency. None of the two parts wished to further exacerbate the split of Czechoslovakia by immediately effecting a currency separation. It was understood that a switch to payments in convertible currencies would speed up the breakdown of existing monetary relations and induce a shock which might result in a rapid decline in production.

It, however, remained a controversial issue whether, in the long-run, it was also desirable and realistic to consider a more integrated monetary arrangement - given the trend towards relaxing the deep interdependence of both economies. There was an obvious intention of Slovakia to create its own independent economic policy.

The two republics had a different starting position. An analysis of the Vienna Institute for Economic Comparisons in June 1992 showed that in 1991, labor productivity was 8% lower in the Slovak Republic, and GDP per head 24% lower compared to the Czech Republic (difference in wages being below 2%). There was a yearly budgetary transfer from the Czech Republic to the Slovak Republic, estimated in 1992 at CSK 25 billion, i.e. US$900 million. For the population, the most palpable difference was in unemployment rates: in 1992, unemployment was 4.9% in the whole of Czechoslovakia, 2.57% in the Czech Republic, but 10.6% in the Slovak Republic. Also, foreign direct investment was unevenly distributed within the federation with 93% going to the Czech Republic during 1992.

Slovakia was also relatively more dependent on imports, on trade with the former C.M.E.A. countries, and, being the smaller part of the federation, also on mutual trade with the Czech Republic. Mutual trade in 1992 was characterized by two trends: (i) decrease of exports from the Czech Republic to Slovakia - by almost 17% against 1991; and (ii) a quickly rising trade surplus of the Czech Republic in relation to Slovakia (the surplus doubled in 1992, from CSK 8.2 billion to 16.3 billion). These figures show that disintegration of the common economy actually started at the microeconomic level well before the official split-up.

In view of the overall political and macroeconomic climate, it was to be expected that after a certain transition period the succeeding states were likely to introduce separate currencies. The first result of negotiations, however, was a temporary use of common currency, as stipulated by the Monetary Agreement concluded in October 1992.

The agreement was a very important achievement, but it had one fundamental inconsistency -- it demanded a coordination of economic policies at a time when the development of both economies as well as differences in the political climate implied divergent tendencies. In reality, the Monetary Agreement tried to address just first phase of the gradual transition to independent currencies. It was not intended to establish a lasting monetary union since neither its title nor the long-term intentions of the parties indicated a need to do so. The preamble of the Monetary Agreement declared this arrangement temporary and predicted the later introduction of two separate currencies.

The Agreement established a Monetary Committee composed of representatives of the central banks of both Republics for the period of the temporary use of a single currency. The Monetary Committee was given executive powers to decide on common monetary policy.

The special provisions (the so called Articles of Termination) which were included in the Agreement specified circumstances for potential withdrawal from it. Either contracting party was allowed to withdraw from the Agreement under any of the following conditions:

• In the case of failure of the Monetary Committee to agree on basic monetary issues;
• In the case of failure to keep the budget deficit of one of the parties below 10 per cent (in terms of budget revenues);
• In the case of failure to keep the external reserves of one of the parties above the monthly volume of imports (measured in convertible currencies); and
• In the case of speculative capital flight from one country to another higher than 5 per cent of total bank deposits.

Both parties to the Monetary Agreement also agreed to coordinate their economic and monetary policies to prevent the occurrence of any of the above listed conditions until at least June 30, 1993. However, as early as at the beginning of February 1993, the agreement had to be terminated and the currency separation was effected on February 8, 1994.

Looking back at the period of a single currency, it is difficult to distinguish the influence of some of the underlying factors associated with long-term economic trends (especially changes due to the split of the Federal economy) from the merely speculative behavior of businesses, banks and the public in expectation of the currency separation. Each of the individual Articles of Termination contributed to the early termination of the Monetary Agreement; the immediate cause, however, was a dangerous fall of foreign currency reserves, observed on both parts.

The real problem was in lack of credibility of the Monetary Agreement. It was expected that Slovak economic situation would demand implementation of more expansive policies than was necessary for the Czech Republic. In Slovakia, the benefits of common federal economic policy were already being questioned in 1991 and 1992. A full lack of coordination of fiscal policies, together with expectations of devaluation of Slovak currency after a currency separation (based on lower export performance of the Slovak Republic), opened a one-way bet to speculators.

Data on further developments prove that it was a correct bet. Indeed, Slovak budget deficit during first quarter of 1993 highly exceeded the limits that would have been required within the monetary union (see Table 1). And, the Slovak currency was forced to devalue by more than 11% soon after the July 1993 currency separation, in spite of some administrative measures to curb imports.

Table 1
Balance Of The Czech And Slovak Government Budgets
January - December 1993

Czech Republic	1	1-3	1-6	1-9	1-12
Government budget revenues	21.8	86.4	175.2	258.6	358.0
Government budget balance	-2.8	10.4	5.6	4.3	1.1
Surplus (+) or deficit (-) as a percentage of revenues	-12.8	12.0	3.2	1.7	0.3
Slovak Republic	1	1-3	1-6	1-9	1-12
Government budget revenues	7.0	25.3	65.2	105.4	150.3
Government budget balance	-1.5	-11.0	-14.8	-15.9	-23.0
Surplus (+) or deficit (-) as a percentage of revenues	-21.4	-43.5	-22.7	-15.1	-15.3

Note: Revenues and balance in billions of CSK, CZK and SKK, figures cumulated at the end of the period
Source: Indicators of the Monetary and Economic Development, no. 5, 1994 and 7, 1994, Czech National Bank

Expectations of an early currency separation, which would be followed by a devaluation on the Slovak part, triggered speculation against foreign currency reserves of both countries. Within a month, an imminent threat of a financial crisis appeared. Originally, specialists (pointing to a low performance of Slovak exports vis-à-vis Czech ones) forecast that problems concerning foreign reserves would mostly affect Slovakia. In reality, foreign exchange reserves were decreasing sharply on both sides because the banking systems of the two new states were not fully separated.

Common reserves had decreased substantially under the influence of the upcoming break-up of the Federation. In November and December 1992, sales of foreign currency by the Czechoslovak State Bank became so heavy that on December 22, 1992, the Bank suspended trading for a period of time. While at the end of August 1992, the foreign exchange reserves of the Czech and Slovak banks totaled US$5.6 billion, by the end of December 1992 they fell to US$4.4 billion, out of which US$1.2 billion were the reserves of the central bank. In the period between September 1992 and the end of 1992, both the current and the capital accounts of the balance of payments deteriorated.

The Czech Republic therefore commenced its independent existence with a relatively low level of reserves; on January 1, 1993, the foreign exchange reserves of the Czech banking system were US$3.58 billion, of which US$842 million were reserves of the Czech National Bank. When trading on the interbank forex market was resumed on January 9, 1993 the volume of sales remained high.

In anticipation of the currency separation, Czech commercial banks had enough free reserves for the purchase of foreign exchange, since the volume of money in circulation decreased while deposits rose. The greater need of the Czech commercial banks for foreign exchange was also partly caused by Slovak businesses effecting their payments to and purchases from abroad through the Czech banking sector.

During January 1993, the official reserves of the Czech National Bank fell by US$297 billion. At the end of the month, total foreign exchange reserves of the Czech banking system were still US$3.5 billion, out of which, however, CNB reserves represented only US$545 million. By February 9, 1993, the CNB's foreign exchange reserves fell further, to US$462 million. The so called parallel exchange rate of the Czechoslovak currency abroad also fell as a consequence of a loss of credibility. Some foreign banks even terminated trades and ceased quoting bid-ask spreads.

The development of foreign exchange reserves in Slovakia was even more dramatic. After the split of the Federation, Slovakia's share of foreign exchange reserves was less than US$1 billion, US$350 million of which were reserves of the National Bank of Slovakia. While the turbulence over foreign exchange reserves in the Czech Republic mostly took the form of a transfer of foreign currency from the central bank to the commercial banks, Slovakia experienced a steady decrease of foreign exchange reserves due to an increased demand for foreign currency from the business sector, which financed higher purchases abroad, as well as from individuals. It is estimated that in January 1993 the National Bank of Slovakia lost 60 per cent of its foreign exchange reserves.

Further development of reserves of both Republics in 1993 is shown in Table 2. From the point of view of viability of the Monetary Agreement, it appears that the relation between reserves and imports (as stipulated in one of the Articles of termination) could have been kept in the Czech Republic, while in the Slovak Republic, it would have posed problems. It is, of course, hard to say what the situation would have been without the currency separation.

Table 2
Czech And Slovak Foreign Exchange Reserves And Monthly Imports

	12/92	1993			
Czech Republic		3	6	9	12
Foreign Exchange Reserves					
Banks total	3.60	4.00	4.90	5.90	6.20
NBS	0.80	1.20	2.30	3.20	3.80
Imports	0.43	1.15	1.19	1.14	1.42
Slovak Republic					
Foreign Exchange Reserves					
Banks total		0.80	0.87	1.32	1.42
NBS	0.40	0.19	0.25	0.57	0.48
Imports	0.26	0.53	0.60	0.52	0.74

Note: Foreign exchange reserves (in billion of US$) at the end of a month; imports (in billion of US$) without trade with the other Republic
Source: Indicators of the Monetary and Economic Development, no. 5, 1994 and 8, 1994, Czech National Bank; Bulletin of the Slovak Statistical Office

A contributing factor for the currency separation was fear of speculative flows between the two newly established states. Until the currency separation, the banking systems of the Czech and Slovak Republics were not truly separated; the existence of a single currency gave both businesses and the public the alternative to use either Czech or Slovak banks.

The actual extent of a transfer of deposits from Slovak to Czech banks is, however, difficult to prove, since in January 1993, deposits rose in both Republics, with those in Slovakia rising noticeably slower. In expectation of a currency separation, the public deposited currency which would normally have been in circulation, to avoid future time-consuming exchange of large amounts of cash. Thus, the fall of reserves was a much more clear indicator of the necessity of a currency separation than the flow of deposits.

To sum up, one month of the existence of the two separate Republics with a single currency arrangement was sufficient to prove the instability of a monetary arrangement which lacked credibility. Entrepreneurs and households as well as commercial banks, kept undermining the feasibility of the Monetary Agreement by their behavior. The clearly declared temporary nature of the monetary arrangement encouraged expectations of a currency separation in the near future.

The Czech National Bank anticipated the instability of the Monetary Agreement. Steps necessary to effect a currency separation were prepared in advance. In January 1993, the central banks of both Republics initialized the process of stamping the banknotes. At the end of January, the Czech and Slovak Prime Ministers concluded an agreement on currency separation; and on February 2nd currency separation legislation was passed by both Parliaments. On the same day, the Czech and Slovak governments announced the exact date of the currency separation for February 8, 1993. The monetary system, planned for at least six months, actually lasted only 38 days.

Despite its short duration, the Agreement played at least one important role by providing a time lag between the split of the Federation and separation of the currency. Such a time period was necessary for reassuring the public, ensuring the technical and logistical background of the currency separation, and preparing a framework of payments for transactions after the separation.

Thanks to a timely termination of the period of common currency, split-up of the federal Czechoslovakia did not result in a serious financial crisis. Trust in the Czech and Slovak currencies was re-established soon after the currency separation. Currency reserves started to grow in both new states, as shown above in Table 2. In the Czech Republic, the new currency (CZK) was introduced and kept on the initial CSK exchange rate set in January 1991.[2]

After the currency separation, payments between the Czech and Slovak Republics were based on a Clearing Agreement which functioned relatively well till its termination in October 1995 (on introduction of convertibility in the sense of IMF Article 8 for the Czech currency). Mutual trade relations between the Slovak and Czech Republics have, since the split-up, declined but still remain at a very important level for both countries. Mutual trade is supported by a customs union and by membership in the CEFTA trading block.

NOTES

[1] Data taken over from Hrnèío, M., 1993.
[2] The exchange rate has remained stable since the start of transition. In February 1996, a +7.5% fluctuation band was introduced - without a change in the central parity. The wider band is aimed to improve the control over the money supply, and to enable steps preventing the trade deficit from growing to dangerous levels. From a longer perspective, the wider band can be seen as a step toward verification of the exchange rate by market forces, to allow a credible future peg into the EU currency system.

REFERENCES

Czech National Bank, Annual Reports.
Czech National Bank, Indicators of the Monetary and Economic Development.
Czechoslovak State Bank, Report on the Balance of Payments, 1990, 1991.
Dìdek, O., et al., "The Break-up of Czechoslovakia: An In-depth Economic Analysis," Avebury 1996.
Hrnèío, M., "Exchange Rate Regime in the Transition Period," IASA International Workshop, 22-24 April 1993, Prague.
Janáèková S., Janáèek, K., "Après la partition de la Tchécoslovaquie: Les perspectives des nouveaux états," Revue du Marché commun et de l'Union européenne, No. 369, Juin 1993, p. 537 - 540.
Janáèková, S., "Parting with the common state and currency," Eastern European Economics, March-April 1994.
OECD, Main Economic Indicators.
Pehe, J., "Czechs and Slovaks Define Postdivorce Relations," RFE/RL Report, 13 November 1992.
Slovak Statistical Office, Bulletin.
The Czech Republic and its Integration with the European Union, Country Study, European Commission, Brussels 1995.
Williamson, J. (ed.). Currency Convertibility in Eastern Europe, Washington D.C., 1991.

12

Stabilization Without Recession: The Success Of A Long-Awaited Financial Adjustment In Hungary

LAJOS BOKROS
Former Minister of Finance, Hungary

TWENTY YEARS OF GOULASH COMMUNISM IN HUNGARY

Two hundred years after the French Revolution another great systemic change hook the European continent : the fall of communism. The destruction of the Berlin Wall is as important of a symbol of this clearly not less remarkable social tremor as the siege of the Bastille was at that time. The decline of state-party dictatorships had been accelerated by the disintegration of the underlying command economies which obviously failed to satisfy the growing needs of consumers in Central and Eastern Europe. Some countries tried to hold back the clock of history by reimposing a neoStalinist version of harsh grip on society and curbing international trade and human contacts, limiting domestic consumption, reducing or even eliminating foreign debt, etc. Czechoslovakia and Romania offer good examples for the application of this desperate strategy. Others, like Poland and Hungary were more fortunate: their party elite had learnt the lessons of bloody uprisings in the past and pursued a policy of gradual, albeit cautious liberalization of both economic and cultural life. Trade with Western countries was constantly growing, travel restrictions were eased step-by-step, and education was increasingly free-wheeling. Even capitalism was tolerated to a growing extent by having allowed the establishment of small family ventures. (People were given the incentive to undertake extra work in second and third jobs in order to provide a better living for themselves and at the same time not to be left with any spare time and inclination to be involved in any political activity.)

But here the similarity between the situation of Poland and Hungary ends. In Poland one cannot and perhaps should not forget the brutal suppression of the Solidarity movement and the imposition of martial law in December 1981. In Hungary there was no massive political discontent or any open confrontation between the political class and the society after 1956. Market oriented reforms were initiated as early as in the mid-1960s and a so-called New Economic Mechanism was introduced in 1968 which eliminated the direct command-type realization of the central plan at the level of the enterprises. The latter were expected to respond to financial incentives determined by indirect regulation which, in turn, was supposed to reflect the requirements of the macroeconomic plan. Agriculture, although formally collectivized, was based on the symbiosis of large state farms and cooperatives responding to financial regulation with small household plots which provided the bulk of all labor-intensive produce such as fruits, vegetables, milk, eggs, poultry ,etc. The peaceful coexistence and   close interdependence of these two forms of agricultural enterprise in Hungary contrasted very much to the sharp confrontation of the dominant private farming with hostile state regulation in Poland. This unique and pragmatic setting contributed considerably to the abundance of domestically produced food and was a source of constant surplus in agricultural foreign trade.

The relatively high Hungarian living standard was based on the achievements of this policy plus on an increasing reliance on foreign borrowing. This latter was not used for massive industrialization - like in Poland - but to build up a premature welfare state. When the fiscal and current account deficits reached unsustainable levels at the beginning of the 1980s, the government took a bold step by joining the IMF and the World Bank and at the same time allowing small scale private enterprise at home. So once again instead of confrontation, the Hungarian way of development was further liberalization coupled with some soft belt-tightening. Fortunately, the quickly emerging capitalist sector (supported by an even faster growing shadow economy) was able to lubricate the aging mechanisms of the state-owned industrial sector, thus alleviating the burden of repeated financial restrictions and making possible the maintenance of generous social transfers to large groups of society.

Thanks to this relatively efficient coexistence of the state-owned enterprises with the small private ventures - which were often operating within the state firms, using their premises and machinery for some nominal fee - the living standards of the most mobile and active groups in society was constantly rising even at the time of recession and when general austerity was hitting the rest of the people. However, this experimental capitalism was a double-edged sword. On the one hand, it helped to maintain the competitiveness of the Hungarian economy and resulted in much higher exports which made it possible for Hungary to maintain by far the highest per capita foreign debt in the region without running the risk of default and rescheduling. On the other hand, the increased efficiency of one part of the economy alleviated the pressure for introducing serious enterprise reforms and made also possible the maintenance of a generous welfare system which was clearly not justified by the efficient running of a well-established market economy.

As a result of Gorbachev's glasnost and perestroika in the Soviet Union, the small countries in Central and Eastern Europe were given more and more freedom in managing their own domestic affairs. Not all the countries took advantage of that, some very conservative dictators like Honecker of East Germany or Zhivkov of Bulgaria even became frightened and horrified by this perspective.

Hungary remained a front runner in making reforms in the second half of the 1980s. Many important steps were taken which paved the way for a smooth transition to a market economy. The major structural reforms were the following:

1. In 1987, a two-tier banking system was established by separating central and commercial banking functions. Three large state-owned financial institutions were carved out of the structure of the old National Bank of Hungary. New banks were allowed to start their operations, including some with foreign participation.
2. Corporate and municipal bonds were issued and traded in a fast growing secondary market. Even private individuals were encouraged to buy them. As a result of the competition for household savings, interest rates on deposits were also liberalized.
3. In 1988, the government introduced a Western style personal income and value added tax systems.
4. A new law opened the gates to and provided generous incentives for foreign direct investment.
5. In 1989, the new company act reintroduced the concept of limited liability and gave an impetus to the further growth of the private sector by allowing small family ventures, economic associations and partnerships to transform into limited and joint stock companies. Special legislation was enacted to provide a framework for the corporatization of state-owned enterprises.
6. Foreign trade was gradually liberalized further. In 1989, almost 90 % of imports were already deregulated. Export licenses were given out to hundreds of small and medium size ventures.
7. In February 1990, a privatization agency was already set up partially in order to bring under control the spontaneous privatization which quickly followed the corporatization of state-owned enterprises.
8. In April 1990, the last non-democratic parliament approved a new securities act which started to regulate the unofficial share trading which took place as a consequence of the transformation of small ventures, corporatization and spontaneous privatization of state-owned firms. The formal reopening of the Budapest Stock Exchange as early as in June 1990 constituted a high profile

symbol of the transition to capitalism just one month after the first democratically elected government had been formed.

SHOCK THERAPY NOT NEEDED, FINANCIAL ADJUSTMENT POSTPONED

Newly elected democratic governments were forced to apply a shock therapy treatment to the serious financial imbalances they inherited from the communist period when their respective economies had been:

- isolated from the world market by maintaining a state monopoly over foreign trade;
- seriously distorted by artificially determined and long ago fixed prices of many commodities which obviously did not reflect supply and demand or even the most rudimentarily calculated cost conditions;
- prices had been supported by large amounts of subsidies for many years which led to a growing dualization of the economy with huge shortages and blockouts transformed into long queues not only in front of the shops but also in production and distribution in the official sector of the economy;
- the availability of the same goods in parallel or black markets at multiple prices and/or only for hard currency resulted in an increasing dollarization of the whole economy which was reflected by multiple exchange rates of the domestic currency with huge difference between the official and the equilibrium rate offered in the parallel or black markets, and whereby a sizeable amount of forced household savings created a monetary overhang threatening with the outburst of a galloping inflation.

In Hungary, none of these factors were present in any meaningful way. As was already mentioned, imports had been increasingly liberalized well before the systemic change with almost 90% of imports deregulated by 1990. Prices were also largely free and reflected supply and demand. Subsidization of consumer goods were restricted to those items where prices had remained fixed and established below costs. Energy, housing rent, mass transport and some public utilities were the main areas of its application. No consumer goods and services, not even basic foodstaples, were supported in any substantial way. There were no shortages whatsoever except for housing, car and telephone. Consequently, the domestic currency had remained fairly strong and the country did not experience any dollarization of the economy. The black market rate of exchange was only 10-15% higher than the official one which reflected the limited availability of foreign exchange for Hungarian citizens at official prices. No forced savings existed except for cars. It was much more the low level of domestic household savings which constituted a problem rather than any monetary overhang. The relative overdemand for consumer goods inherent to all socialist economies as a consequence of their inefficient productive structure was neutralized by a constant foreign trade deficit financed largely by heavy foreign borrowing. It also helped to cool down inflationary pressures while the growing indebtedness seemed to be sustainable. Repeated attempts to lower trade deficits were always transforming into a temporarily higher rate of inflation. This clearly shows that there was a trade-off between debt financing and inflation which was a unique feature of the Hungarian economic setting. In most other countries where the above mentioned distorting elements dominated the economic landscape, the trade-off constituted itself between shortage and inflation. It was therefore obvious that a sudden liberalization of external trade, prices and foreign exchange would immediately bring in a brutal one-off adjustment in prices at exorbitant rates. Provisional hyperinflation is the price to be paid for the abrupt elimination of shortages and monetary overhang. Shock therapy is nothing else but a complete elimination of both shortage and overhang by a far-reaching one-step liberalization of prices of goods, services and foreign exchange coupled by a complete liberalization of foreign trade. In Hungary, it was neither necessary nor applicable.

The first democratically elected Hungarian government which took office in May 1990 seems to have understood this important distinguishing characteristic feature of our economic heritage. Nevertheless, it failed to realize the very precise nature of this difference. It was thought that the lack of those factors which enforced the adoption of a rather drastic, textbook case type of shock therapy in Poland, for example, meant that there was no need for any financial adjustment at all in Hungary. This myopic view was very much reinforced by some Western scholars who openly castigated Hungary for not having followed the Polish path. The financial disequilibrium was substantial even in Hungary which would have required the application of a more classic type of austerity, which may have resulted in a temporary increase of the inflation rate but not the outbreak of a hyperinflation. But the government wanted to remain popular at any rate. Instead of implementing a stabilization package by curbing budget expenditure and imports by some monetary and exchange rate adjustment, it placed the blame for all the hardships it may have caused to the people on the bad economic policies of the previous non-democratic governments. The political leaders of the new administration even started to deny the allegation that the country had been living well beyond its means. Characteristically, they put all the blame on the high debt service which they believed squeezed a substantial amount of national income out of the Hungarian economy. While this was obviously true, the moralistic rather than economic policy conclusions drawn from this sad situation proved to be not only misleading but clearly counter-productive. Some high ranking officials started openly to speculate about a possible debt forgiveness and rescheduling which immediately increased the financial costs of debt service. Finally, the government decided not to go for any renegotiation on the foreign debt, but at the same time, the opportunity for restoring financial equilibrium by the introduction of a comprehensive macroeconomic stabilization was lost.

RECESSION AND SUPPLY SIDE ADJUSTMENT IN THE FIRST HALF OF THE 1990s

In spite of the lack of any coherent stabilization and reform policy which could have been applied in a conscious way, the Hungarian economy did undergo a rather spontaneous adjustment. First of all, the sharp decline of intra-regional trade in Central and Eastern Europe as a consequence of the break up of the former Comecon and the disintegration of the Soviet Union resulted in a marked recession which paradoxically was leading to an improvement of the external balances by eliminating the most distorted and less efficient elements of the productive structure. Real GDP declined by 3.5%, 11.9% and 3.0% in the years 1990-92 respectively. At the same time, the current account of the balance of payments showed a small surplus in all these three years. (See Table 1)

Table 1

	1989	1990	1991	1992	1993	1994	1995	1996
Real GDP Growth in %	0.7	-3.5	-11.9	-3.0	-0.8	2.9	1.5	1-1.5
CPI Y avg. chg. In %	18.1	28.0	35.0	23.0	22.5	18.8	28.2	23-24
Unemployment	0.5	1.6	7.5	12.3	12.1	10.4	10.3	10.2
Real wage growth/ employee			-7.0	-1.4	-3.8	7.0	-12.2	-3- -4
Export volume growth in %	0.3	-4.1	-4.9	1.0	-13.1	16.6	8.1	8-10
Import volume growth in %	1.1	-5.2	5.5	-7.6	20.9	14.5	-4.0	4-5
Trade balance in US$ m	1044	528	364	-3	-3247	-3635	-2442	1800
CA balance in US$ m	-571	373	411	359	-3458	-3911	-2480	1800
CA in % of GDP			0.8	0.9	-9.0	-9.5	-5.7	
CG balance in % of GDP			-3.8	-5.9	-4.9	-6.2	-4.9	
GG balance in % of GDP			-3.2	-7.0	-5.5	-8.3	-6.5	
CG debt in % of GDP			74.2	78.5	89.0	86.6	89.4	
Net foreign debt in US$ bn	14.9		14.6	13.1	14.9	18.9	16.8	

Sources: MoF, NBH & CSO of Hungary.
1996: estimates

The second important factor contributing to the soft landing of the Hungarian economy was the sharp increase of household savings. While the savings ratio of the household sector as compared to disposable income was only a weak 5% in 1989, it almost reached the level of 18% in 1991. This positive change in behavior was clearly due to the sharp increase in unemployment from virtually zero to more than 12% in 1992 and shows the strengthening of the precautionary motive in financial decisions of the people. Moreover, this upshoot in domestic savings was enough to finance the once again growing fiscal deficit in 1990-92, which allowed to sustain a positive current account during the same period.

The rapid growth of domestic savings was also a response to the restrictive monetary policies of the National Bank of Hungary which resulted in a sharp increase of interest rates. It was not the first time in postwar Hungarian economic history that the task of trying to prevent a repeated deterioration of the external equilibrium was undertaken unilaterally by the central bank. Restrictive monetary regulation aiming at offsetting the negative impact of a continuously expansionary fiscal policy was experienced in the second half of the 1980s as well. The lack of determination on the part of any government before and after the political systemic change to consider any substantial reform in the public finance sector and undertake any meaningful streamlining of the premature welfare state led to high deficits again and again which were either financed by heavy foreign borrowing (when the central bank pursued an equally lax monetary policy) or were maintained at the detriment of growth when financed by domestic savings in cases of monetary restraint. Since financial policies were synchronized only if both monetary and fiscal management was accommodating and expansionary, the stop-go nature of central bank behavior resulted in a greater recessionary impact by systematically crowding out the enterprise sector from the use of longer term funding. Thus it is not surprising that the Hungarian economy was largely characterized by long term stagnation throughout the last two decades.

A very positive outcome of the systemic change was that - contrary to what was happening to the public finance sector - the enterprise sector ceased to be considered a sacred cow any longer. The new government was determined to carry out a comprehensive privatization program as quickly as possible. Moreover, privatization was not tailored according to any ideological blueprint but was managed in a rather pragmatic way. Apart from an aborted attempt of the first democratic government to draft a limited mass privatization scheme of a redistributional nature at the end of its tenure in 1993-94 in order to enhance its chances for reelection, all major transactions of privatization were undertaken in view of the need for capital and governance. Hungary was very fortunate to have an almost complete national consensus among the leading political forces who all regarded privatization as a powerful instrument for improving the efficiency of the corporate sector rather than an end in itself. In addition, this pragmatic approach was extended even to those transactions when the new owners were foreign investors.

Supply-side adjustment in Hungary was further accelerated by an enormous influx of foreign direct and portfolio investment. It is a well-known fact that between 1990 and 1995 Hungary was able to attract almost half of all foreign direct investment in Central and Eastern Europe. By the end of 1995, after the unprecedented privatization of a good part of the energy sector and a final divestiture of the state from telecommunication, the small country had already accumulated more than US$15 billion worth of FDI. It is also remarkable that more than half of all private capital formation during this period was financed by foreign investment.

In 1992, an exceptional and strange phenomenon hit the economic stage: an almost shock therapy type of enterprise restructuring. The starting point of this move was the strong desire of the government to try to wipe out the growing snowball of the unpaid intercorporate debt. The monetary authorities also supported the initiative because the widespread use of forced commercial credit threatened to paralyze the effective use of monetary regulation. The parliament, therefore, adopted an unusually harsh bankruptcy act together with a new Western-standard accounting law. In addition, new legislation was introduced to govern commercial banking for the first time with the great innovation of asset classification and adequate provisioning requirements. While in the previous years fiscal authorities tried to tax away even part of the imaginary profit calculated on the basis of unrealized interest income, after 1992 banks not only ceased to behave like cash cows but turned out to be very much in need of additional budgetary support due to the their fast deteriorating loan and investment portfolio positions which far outpaced their capacity to generate reserves.

The impact of the implementation of the new rules embodied in these three pieces of law went far beyond the original intentions and anyone's expectation. More than ten thousand old state owned and new private enterprises filed for bankruptcy and/or outright liquidation in less than two years. The authorities were horrified by the outcome of these changes and initiated a certain easing of the rules.

As a consequence of the concentration of explicit losses in the portfolio of the commercial banks a massive restructuring and recapitalization of the state-owned large financial institutions became inevitable. Although the need for a consolidation of the sector was above any question, the way how it was really carried out proved to be far from very efficient. There were three consecutive attempts of rehabilitation because of the lack of a well-articulated program at the outset. Banks benefited from the support of the government to the extent of their political importance rather than heritage and past proven efforts. Directors and management were not subject to well-defined, monitorable and strict performance criteria. The laxity and moral hazard created by this situation inflated enormously the final cost of restructuring which exceeded 10% of GDP and put an additional burden on the central budget.

REPEATING THE OLD MISTAKE: A JUMP ON THE PATH OF UNSUSTAINABLE GROWTH

By the end of 1992, the government became increasingly fed up with the recessionary environment created by the collapse of Comecon trade and the sweeping wave of bankruptcy and liquidation in the enterprise sector. Unemployment reached unprecedented levels: it had already exceeded the frightening double-digit threshold. Tax revenue was stagnating, while there were new claims for growing expenditure. Enterprises paid less and less taxes as a consequence of privatization, preferential treatment of foreign investors, bankruptcies and massive evasion. The deficit of the general government more than doubled in terms of GDP even without undertaking any major extension of the social programs.

However, political forces were very much misled by some of the characteristic features of the economic situation. As it was already mentioned, the current account of the balance of payments showed a small but remarkable surplus now three years in a row. The problem of external disequilibrium seemed to have been largely eliminated. No further questioning about the applicability of any debt rescheduling was heard. Inflation was successfully checked: it went down by twelve percentage points within a year. The strict adherence to any further belt tightening seemed to be less and less justifiable and reasonable. All political forces were pressing for government action to initiate economic growth.

Even the generally more conservative central bank felt the necessity to abandon the until then relatively restrictive monetary policy. In order to contribute to the reduction of the mounting interest burden of the central budget paid on the fast increasing public part of the domestic debt and at the same time to stimulate credit expansion towards the corporate sector, the National Bank decided to reduce sharply its interest rates. Unfortunately, this proved to be a typical overshooting which resulted in a quick drying up of domestic savings.

Public consumption was on the rise and domestic demand now got a further boost by the spending spree of the enterprise sector. Without any slack in effective capacity and hit by the sharp deterioration of their financial condition, domestic enterprises were hardly in a position to satisfy this growing demand even in consumer goods. Imports skyrocketed by a volume growth of more than 20% while exports declined by 13%. As corporate restructuring was far from completed, supply-side adjustment proved to be very weak. The trade balance showed more than US$3.4 billion deficit. The current account deteriorated so dramatically that the deficit immediately reached 9% of GDP. The first democratically elected government committed just the same mistake as many of its much less legitimate predecessors: pushed the economy onto the path of unsustainable growth fuelled by fiscal overspending, consumption and imports.

It is interesting to see, however, the operation of time lags in the Hungarian economy. The increase of the budget deficit in 1992 still did not result in an external disequilibrium, since it was easily financed by an adequate amount of domestic savings. It was a typical crowding out situation for the enterprise sector which was not able to compete for the funds released by the household sector. Now, the first step in 1993 to create an artificial boom was the further growth of public consumption coupled with a marked credit expansion which drove up imports already in the same year. But government overspending and renewed enterprise activity led to some real economic growth only in 1994. Nevertheless, this growth was not particularly strong even in terms of output volume expansion, and, since it was not based on exports and investments financed either by domestic savings or non-debt type foreign funds, it proved to be unsustainable. The artificial upswing in the business cycle was extremely short lived. As the current account deficit reached intolerable levels very quickly and there was a danger of immediate bankruptcy, growth was no longer a feasible alternative.

Restarting economic growth did not turn out to be an outright political success either. It did not help the first democratic government to retain political power in the second parliamentary elections held in May 1994. In spite of some additional desperate attempts to bribe the electorate such as to allow a 7% real wage increase in 1994 by giving generous handouts in almost all sectors of the economy, the Socialist Party, which was in opposition until then gained, a landslide victory with an absolute majority of the vote in the new Parliament. An even greater chance to put the house into order emerged when the Socialists decided to form a coalition government with the more liberal-minded Free Democratic Alliance, thus acquiring a 72% majority of parliamentary seats supporting it.

It is an equally sad story therefore that the new government also missed the historic opportunity to act very fast. Due to his personal distaste towards his first minister of finance, the new Socialist prime minister did not support any corrective measure aimed at restoring financial equilibrium. Apart from the introduction of a mild supplementary budget which tried to prevent an even larger deterioration of the fiscal equilibrium and some small corrective devaluations of the domestic currency by the central bank in order to give more impetus to exports and contain the growth of imports, no other action was taken. The new budget put together for 1995 proved to be completely unrealistic already by the time of its approval. Financial processes went out of hand. The Hungarian state once again was heading towards a financial collapse.

THE STABILIZATION PROGRAM OF MARCH 12, 1995 AND ITS IMPACT ON THE ECONOMY

The first quarter of 1995 showed an accelerating deterioration of the financial situation both externally and internally. Had it not been for the introduction of the rather shocking type of austerity measures the current account and general government deficits might have well exceeded 10-12% of GDP. The international financial markets increased their risk premiums enormously on Hungarian borrowing, thus increasing the cost of debt refinancing even further. One has to remember that all this happened at the aftermath of the Mexican crisis, and there was much speculation in the international financial community about who comes next.

The stabilization package which was announced after an exceptional government meeting held on Sunday, March 12th was deliberately tailored in such a way that it wanted to improve the financial equilibrium very quickly but, at the same time, to avoid pushing the economy once again into a deep recession. The intention was clearly to break the vicious circle of the past twenty or so years when Hungary used to have either a not too high economic growth with a quickly deteriorating financial position or a somewhat restrictive economic policy aimed at restoring primarily the external financial equilibrium but resulting immediately in a stagnation or even decline of output. As a consequence of these alternative stop-go policies, Hungary has not been able to enjoy both economic growth and financial equilibrium at the same time at least since 1974. In other words, the last twenty years can be characterized as a period of stagflation, and the political systemic changes did not seem to have modified this scenario either.

Therefore, the real challenge was how to initiate sustainable economic growth. The real question was whether it was possible to stimulate the factors of sustainable economic growth, namely exports and investments, to such an extent that the unavoidable short-term recessionary impact of belt-tightening could be more than outweighed by the expansion of the export sector and that of investments financed by non-debt type funding ?

The specific elements of the stabilization program were the following:

1. Exchange Rate Policy Modifications

a) There was an upfront 9% devaluation of the Hungarian currency aimed at an immediate restoration of a near equilibrium level of the exchange rate in order to give impetus for exports as its competitiveness was restored by the elimination of the effects of the unsustainable and unjustifiable domestic input price and wage increases which occurred in 1994.

b) The National Bank of Hungary introduced a preannounced crawling peg type evaluation mechanism with a 1.9% monthly rate for the second quarter of 1995 and a lower 1.3% rate for the second half of the year. As time went on and the first encouraging signs of improving financial equilibrium were detected during the summer, the government was able to preannounce the rate of the crawl for the whole year of 1996 as early as August 31, 1995. The point was not just having an even lower monthly rate of 1.2% throughout 1996, but it was for the first time in modern Hungarian economic history that exporters and importers were able to calculate rather precisely their foreign trade revenues and costs. The very essence of this exchange rate policy change was to achieve a turning point in regaining the confidence of the general public. This predictability and reliability of the exchange rate policy helped enormously to eliminate the negative speculative forces in the foreign exchange market which had been working very much against financial equilibrium in the past and led to consecutive devaluations as a self-fulfilling prophecy even at times of no real need for such an adjustment (or not an adjustment of that extent). The preannouncement itself plus the government's proven track record to adhere to it has even helped to generate speculation for the further strengthening of this equilibrium.

c) Although it was not an exchange rate policy measure, it is important to mention that the government authorized resident corporate entities to maintain foreign exchange accounts with domestic financial institutions. Until then it had been allowed only for private individuals to accumulate financial holdings in hard currency; enterprises were obliged to surrender all their forex revenue to the banking system which, in turn, was also held on short leash by the central bank regarding the management of its foreign exchange assets and liabilities. While the forced centralization of the foreign reserves of the country in the central bank had been perhaps justified by the need of an efficient foreign debt management in the past it became less and less effective and enforceable as liberalization swept away all other barriers of forex transactions. The intention was to stimulate the accumulation of the biggest possible part of reserves in the domestic banking system while at the same time give a further reassurance to the corporate sector about the availability of foreign exchange whenever it was needed for normal and smooth operation.

2. Fiscal Revenue Enhancing Measures

a) The introduction of a temporary import surcharge of 8% was aiming at generating additional revenue at the amount of 1-1.5% of GDP in order to bring down the central budget deficit immediately. Given the overextended nature of the fiscal sector in Hungary it would have been an obvious task to reduce not only the deficit but to achieve it in such a way that the size of the government also be cut back. Unfortunately this was not a realistic option in the short-run since most of the specific items of expenditure happened to be determined by separate pieces of legislation, therefore long parliamentary procedures were necessary to modify the provision of any social services in any meaningful way. Thus the rolling back of the frontiers of the welfare state proved to be a slow process. In order to bridge this marked discrepancy between the need to reduce the deficit very quickly and the impossibility of acting immediately on the expenditure side of the budget made it unavoidable that revenue boosting measures were also applied. But it is remarkable that the 8% import surcharge introduced as an integral part of the stabilization package was meant to be a provisional measure. It was publicly announced at the time of its introduction that it will be eliminated entirely no later than mid-1997. It was clearly assumed that the phasing out of the import surcharge will go very much in line with the eventual reduction of government expenditure as a consequence of the advancement of the time consuming public finance sector reform.

It was equally important that a smaller upfront devaluation of the Hungarian currency coupled with an import surcharge was more beneficial not only for the budget but also for exports. It was fascinating to see that leading exporters publicly warned the government to avoid a double-digit one-off sharp devaluation since they knew that, while exporting rather soft goods, importers would be able to reduce their hard currency prices if they were getting information about the windfall revenue of exporters in domestic currency terms. Due to this high price elasticity of Hungarian exports, an income redistribution as a consequence of a sharp devaluation would not necessarily have favored exporters but, to a growing extent, foreign importers. Therefore the best way to keep this increased revenue at home was to split it between the government and the domestic exporters by way of applying a smaller devaluation coupled with an import surcharge.

One could possibly argue against the introduction of any measure which would make imports unilaterally more expensive by saying that it would hurt exports as well. In a small and open economy where exports are not only very much import intensive but where many items of export are still new and carry a relatively low domestic value added due to the deep restructuring and a quick reorientation of foreign trade, an import surcharge almost equal to the rate of the devaluation recaptures most of the revenue which was originally intended to have been channeled to the export sector by increasing simultaneously the prices of imported inputs and thus neutralizing the export stimulating impact of devaluation. So instead of a structural change and an improvement in the trade balance, there is only a higher level of inflation.

While devaluation is a general device, an import surcharge can be applied in a selective way. This special characteristic feature made it possible that its impact on growth and inflation could also be taken into account. In order to minimize its adverse effect on export, investment and inflation, three major areas were exempted from its application. First of all it was not levied on the importation of primary energy. As there is no substantial domestic production of primary energy in Hungary, there was nothing to be protected from foreign competition. This was also a major step to avoid general inflationary pressure in the economy. Secondly, direct import components of exported goods and services were also exempted. Thus exporters were largely allowed to retain all of their competitive advantage ensured by devaluation. Finally, the import surcharge paid on the importation of investment goods could be reclaimed in order to avoid any further restriction imposed on corporate restructuring.

In summary, the specific mixture of these measures proved to be an exceptionally favorable combination from the viewpoint of improving external equilibrium with a maximum growth of exports. The foreign trade deficit came down by more than US$1 billion and the current account improved by almost US$1.5 billion. Exports remained strong, volume growth was more than 8%, while its value went up by more than 20% in US$-terms. Import volume declined by 4%, but in value it was also up by almost 10%. And all this within a three-quarter-of-a-year period of time as these measures were introduced only in late March, 1995.

b) Apart from the introduction of the import surcharge, some excises, especially on cars and gambling, were also raised. These were clearly seen as revenue boosting measures while at the same time they wanted to check imports further. The additional amount collected was negligible but the import of these non-essential items was significantly reduced.

3. The Initial Steps Of Welfare Reform With Some Social Cost-Cutting

a) Although the introduction of the import surcharge and other revenue generating measures were aiming at a quick reduction of the budget deficit -- even before a substantial cutback on government overspending could exercise a major positive impact on the fiscal equilibrium, the intention to start a welfare reform was publicly announced at the very beginning of the stabilization. After some heated and sometimes aggressive debate, the Hungarian parliament voted into law the following:

- a radical change of the family allowance payment system from one based previously on universal entitlement to another characterized by means testing that linked per capita family income to a degressive scale increments in allowance and had an absolute ceiling on it;
- a similar modification of the child care payment system supporting families with children under the age of three years;
- a substantial increase of the burden to be borne by employers and employees in case of illness and a marked reduction of the sick leave payment to be paid by the social security fund;
- a requirement to pay social security contributions on non-wage type personal income (such as fees honoraria, etc.) in order to eliminate the distortions in the wage system and bring all types of income under equal treatment as in the case of the personal income tax system;
- an introduction of partial payment on the part of the clients for dental services, non life-saving ambulance transportation, post-hospital treatment, sanatoria, etc.; and
- an application of a symbolic tuition fee for college and university education.

Although the last four measures can formally be considered as revenue enhancing ones in reality these were primarily aimed at containing the otherwise unlimited demand for the public goods and services in question and therefore contributing to the curtailment of the growth of fiscal spending in the respective areas. In all cases, the intention was to change the attitude of the people who took for granted the provision of social services on the basis of universal entitlement and the completely free access to a wide range of public goods and services. This proved to be an even greater shock than what had been caused by the political systemic changes in 1989. People started to realize that the Hungarian welfare system had really been built up prematurely and it was absolutely unsustainable for it had never been supported by an efficient market economy.

Nonetheless, these steps were considered just an integral part of the stabilization and not a substitute for a far-reaching, comprehensive public finance sector reform. The government realized that this latter cannot be carried out without a critical mass of public support and a minimum level of consensus among the leading political forces across the whole parliamentary spectrum. The above described measures were intended to create the necessary psychological atmosphere for the real reform to be prepared during the time bought by the successful stabilization. It was also hoped that the implementation of these initial measures would cut out some of the most obvious waste from the welfare system and thus contribute to the quick stabilization. (Unfortunately it did not because the Hungarian Constitutional Court postponed the introduction of most of these measures requiring a relatively long period of transition in order to give time to the citizens to adapt their life strategies to the new and more difficult circumstances).

Stabilization was in itself an indispensable prerequisite for public finance sector reform from strictly fiscal point of view. It was obvious that a comprehensive reform which would include the reconstruction of health care, pension system, social security, public education, science & research, culture financing, taxation, local government, treasury management, public administration, housing finance, etc. may not produce substantial upfront savings. On the contrary, substantive reforms in some of these areas would inevitably involve transitional arrangements which may even increase budgetary outlays at least temporarily. Of course one of the main objectives of the public finance reform is to change the behavior of the citizens in such a way that they would be willing to contribute more to the common pool of public goods and services and at the same time being interested in forcing budgetary institutions to operate more efficiently. This modification of attitude should result in a marked reduction of the further growth of fiscal expenditure and thus release much needed funds for sustained economic growth. In the long run therefore a successful public finance reform is the best guarantee to avoid any further need for introducing additional measures of belt-tightening. The reform itself can be the final anchor for sustaining financial stability.

b) Apart from the above mentioned steps some additional cost-cutting measures were taken in the areas of government administration, ministries, auxiliary activities, public media, etc. A 10-15% selective reduction of the number of civil servants was also carried out. Local governments were deprived the opportunity to raise excessive debt. Only a few institutions, like the police, tax and customs authorities were exempted from the general application of government austerity.

4. The Income Policy Element: A Double-Digit Reduction Of Real Wages

Although some leading politicians later declared that the more than 11% reduction in real wages was just an unintended and unpleasant byproduct of the otherwise necessary stabilization, it is important to emphasize that it was an absolutely integral part of the program. The Hungarian stabilization package was characterized by the IMF as being of a "heterodox nature" precisely because of its heavy reliance on income policy. There was a widespread fear amongst professionals that the program might be derailed because it seemed highly unlikely that employees would accept such a drastic reduction of real wages in a country which had already liberalized wage regulations many years ago and where labor costs were the highest among the Visegrád four. It is very remarkable, therefore, that society accepted this tough measure without any major strike or labor unrest. It is even more important that the sharp decline in real wages was not achieved exclusively by a seemingly uncontrollable upshoot of inflation but primarily through the enforcement of deliberate limitation of nominal wage increases. Moreover, the rise in nominal wages was not only checked in the public sector, but it was effectively curtailed in the competitive sector as well.

The successful moderation of relative labor costs was exceptionally beneficial from the viewpoint of restoring financial equilibrium, stimulating export-led growth and curbing inflation. Export oriented enterprises were able to enjoy the combined positive impact of devaluation and unit labor cost decline. Profit margins went up tremendously with renewed prospects for expansion through investments. The international competitiveness of Hungarian labor was largely restored.

Once again, one might argue that a fall in real wages is probably the best recipe for a deep recession. Of course, no one should or can deny the inevitable recessionary impact of this move, especially on domestic consumption. But the real question is not the very existence of this effect but whether there is any other policy mix that would have less detrimental influence on the factors of sustainable growth. From this viewpoint the application of fiscal austerity together with a real wage reduction seems to be quite justifiable. The curbing of domestic demand is unavoidable and the restriction of consumption, especially that of imported goods and services is very much desirable and it is not necessarily greater than in case of an unilateral and hence much more drastic cut in government overspending. Moreover, import led consumption is not a factor of sustainable growth anyway.

It is important to mention, however, that this policy mix had not only an obviously more positive impact on exports, investments and inflation but interestingly enough on unemployment as well. On the one hand, there was a gradual, preannounced, and carefully phased reduction of the number of civil servants which helped to mitigate not only the political effects but to ease the burden on the labor market as well. On the other hand, the expanding export sector and some of the government sponsored investment projects largely absorbed the redundant workforce released from the public sector. As a consequence of that, unemployment did not rise in 1995 and has even been reduced since then.

THE SHORT-TERM ACHIEVEMENTS OF STABILIZATION

As we have seen, the most important short term goal of the stabilization, namely, to save the country from an outright current account crisis and a collapse of the state budget was largely achieved. The deficit of the current account was reduced dramatically from more than US$3.9 billion in 1994 to less than US$2.5 billion in 1995. This trend seems to be well established because the deficit of the first seven months of 1996 was less than US$1 billion which is less than half of the figure for the corresponding period of the previous year. Even by very conservative estimates, it is highly likely that the overall current account deficit will remain below US$2 billion for the whole of 1996, which will be easily financed by the incoming foreign direct investment. (Hungary has been able to attract more than US$2 billion a year FDI on average since 1990)

The decisive factor behind this very favorable tendency is the unbroken and continuous growth of exports. Once again, until the end of July 1996 the volume of export grew by 9% while imports only by 2.5%. A 8-10% export volume growth compared to a 3-5% import volume growth are expected for the whole of 1996. If it happens then the deficit of the trade account will be around US$1.8 billion, much less than in 1995. Net receipts from tourism have skyrocketed. The surplus accumulated in the first seven month of 1996 was almost US$600 million; it was hardly more than 100 million in the same period of 1995. This result is even more remarkable if we take into consideration that as a final step of foreign exchange liberalization the government eliminated the rationing of hard currency for private individuals. From January 1, 1996, people are allowed to buy seemingly unlimited amounts of hard currency for current transactions.

The burden of foreign debt which is obviously one of the most negative heritage of the past was considerably eased. In July 1995, the gross foreign debt of the country was US$33.2 billion and the net debt US$21.6 billion. At the end of July 1996, the corresponding figures were US$28.5 billion and US$15.3 billion respectively. This marked reduction of both gross and net debt was due not only to the direct impact of the stabilization on the current account but to a windfall surplus in the capital account. In 1995, the amount of additional net FDI arriving at Hungary was almost US$4.5 billion as a consequence of the successful privatization of the second tranche of MATAV (the telecommunications corporation) and that of the gas and electricity distribution companies. In spite of the lack of any major new privatization transactions in the first half of 1996, the country received an additional US$1 billion worth of FDI until the end of July, which was just enough to cover the whole current account deficit of the first seven months, therefore the debt burden did not increase even in absolute terms. With a continuous growth of exports, it is now highly likely that Hungary might be able to grow out of the external debt problem in the coming three-four years.

Domestic financial equilibrium was also considerably improved. The deficit of the central budget was down from 6.2% of GDP in 1994 to 4.9% in 1995 and that of the general government from 8.3% to 6.5%, respectively. The target for the overall fiscal deficit was set at 4% of GDP for 1996. In the case of the central budget, the trends are very encouraging. The deficit for the first eight months was just HUF 121 billion which is precisely HUF 100 billion less than in the corresponding period of the previous year. The better than targeted results in the central budget are nevertheless very much necessary for the attainment of the target of the overall deficit because the two social security funds are likely to have a four times greater deficit than planned due to the lack of structural reforms in that area.

The importance of reducing further the fiscal deficit cannot be overestimated. Apart from having a large external debt raised primarily through the National Bank of Hungary the government has seen a rapid growth of the domestic component of the debt after 1989. The gross debt of the central budget was growing from 66% of GDP to almost 90% between 1990 and 1993, and the only achievement of the stabilization in this respect was that it did not grow further in 1995. Even though the relative size of the outstanding domestic debt went down in that year, the greater unrealized loss involved by a bigger devaluation plus the higher interest burden due to the upshoot of inflation and domestic interest rates more than outweighed its impact on the overall debt burden at least temporarily. In 1995, the interest payments from the central budget amounted to 475 HUF, almost 30% of all outlays and 9% of GDP. It is fair to say therefore that the most vulnerable element of the stabilization is the continuing very high level of domestic debt service.

Inflation has remained a problem. While the almost 10% point increase in CPI in 1995 was an unavoidable byproduct of the one-off restrictive measures (basically that of the initial devaluation and the introduction of the import surcharge), inflationary pressures have remained strong ever since. Hesitation and ineptitude on the part of the government to implement the long delayed and committed energy price hikes maintained inflationary expectations at high level without having the benefit of renewed investment activities in the sector as a result of guaranteed return. There were many slippages in the social security area as well. By the end of the last year, the prime minister decided to restore free ambulance transportation and the largely free access to dental services in a desperate move to regain popularity. The leaders of the autonomous health care fund were able to abuse their influence on both the government and the parliament to get an approval for a completely unrealistic budget for 1996 without any structural reform. Most of the measures intended to have been part of the stabilization in this area are still being discussed by the parliament. It is very fortunate, therefore, that the central budget has performed even better than expected and that Hungarian labor seems to have largely accepted another, although somewhat milder reduction of their real wages in 1996. As inflation for 1996 on a CPI basis will likely remain between 23-24%, it will imply a further 3-4 % real wage loss throughout the year. (This is clearly not something to be repeated in many years to come).

The first half of 1996 can be generally characterized as a period of overall stagnation on the surface with very strong adjustments in the structure of the real economy behind the scenes. Investment were down as compared to the first six months of the previous year but not in manufacturing and agriculture which constitute the most important export sectors. Hugh investment preparations are taking place in the energy supply and telecommunications sectors which were privatized quite recently. Construction already started to recover after a prolonged period of decline. Several large projects in physical infrastructure such as highway construction have been started or continued. Housing construction remained strong. There is no further reduction in consumption. Net domestic savings of the household sector have been constantly growing. It is not impossible that Hungary will be able to reach a positive 1-1.5% growth rate in 1996 as well.

In order to stimulate economic growth, the government already started to decrease the rate of the import surcharge. On July 1st and October 1st, one percentage point reductions were implemented showing a growing confidence of the authorities in their ability to preserve external equilibrium. Further gradual reduction of the prevailing rate is expected in the first half of 1997 with a complete elimination in July as planned.

THE TASKS FOR THE FUTURE

The real merits of the Hungarian stabilization of 1995 can be summarized as follows:

1. It very quickly improved both external and domestic financial equilibrium by reducing the current account deficit by almost 4% of GDP and the fiscal deficit by almost 2%;
2. The restoration of external equilibrium was basically achieved by an accelerated and continuous growth in exports, leaving some room for a modest import growth as well;
3. The combination of devaluation, crawling peg and import surcharge was successful in promoting export-led growth and structural adjustment while easing the recessionary impact on the economy;
4. Fiscal balance was improved by applying both revenue boosting and expenditure cutting measures;

5. Reforms of the welfare state were started head-on as part of cutbacks on government overspending;
6. Heavy reliance on a substantial real wage reduction helped to stimulate exports, maintain the level of employment, and an avoid an outbreak of an uncontrollable level of inflation; and
7. As a consequence of all these steps, factors of sustainable growth have been enormously strengthened.

This "heterodox" policy mix was put together in order to break the vicious circle of stagflation characterized by consecutive periods of stop-go policies which resulted in some years of artificial growth fuelled by consumption, imports, and government overspending followed repeatedly by another couple of years of recession brought about by "orthodox" austerity measures of devaluation, inflation, and fiscal belt-tightening. Now the real question is whether Hungary has been able to escape this twenty-year long tradition of stag-flation and put its economy firmly on the path of sustainable economic growth ?

It seems to be too early to give a final answer to this historic question although the first signs of adjustment are very encouraging. There are still some weak elements of the economic situation which need very careful attention and further action. Inflation is the number one enemy. It cannot be substantially decreased without additional cutbacks in government overspending. A 4% deficit of the fiscal sector is simply too big in a hardly growing economy. The overall deficit rate should be pushed below the rate of economic growth, if growing out of the domestic debt is to be achieved. This is the only way to bring down interest rates and ease the prevailing crowding out of the corporate sector from domestic financing. A marked fall of interest rates could also help the central budget to reduce the cost of servicing its public domestic debt. Moreover, opportunities for easy savings in expenditure have been largely exhausted. Further gains at least in a slower growth of government outlays could come only as a consequence of far-reaching and comprehensive public sector reforms. The remodeling of the whole welfare system with more emphasis on self-care and insurance and less reliance on nationwide solidarity should take place in the next couple of years if the remarkable, but still fragile results of stabilization are to be preserved and enhanced.

PART V

SPECIAL TOPICS: PUBLIC DEBT AND WAR

13

Self-Fulfilling Public Debt Crises

DANIEL GROS
Senior Research Fellow and Director, Economic Policy Programme, Centre for European Policy Studies (CEPS), Brussels and Professor, University of Frankfurt

INTRODUCTION

This paper shows that under certain conditions highly indebted countries could fall into a low credibility trap. This occurs when a government is judged not to be credible by financial markets. It then has to pay a risk premium in terms of higher interest rates. The higher debt service burden that results, if inflation is kept low, makes it even more likely that the authorities will abandon the attempt to stabilize and try to reduce the real value of the debt through a surprise inflation, hence this further increases the risk premium demanded by financial markets, possibly leading to a spiral of increasing interest rates until the government caves in.

However, the debt trap is not the only equilibrium. The same country could also end up with low interest rates if it can start a virtuous circle of high credibility and low interest rates. All that is needed to reach this equilibrium is that markets think a priori that the government will be tough on inflation. It will then pay lower interest rates and thus have, at the same inflation rate, a lower debt service burden to carry. This in turn could validate the initial assumption. Hence there could be two equilibria in financial markets and a mere shift in expectations leading to the bad equilibrium would have to be validated even by a hard nosed government.

The current crisis in Italy is a good illustration of the bad equilibrium. It is often argued that the Banca d'Italia cannot tighten monetary policy because increasing interest rates increases the fiscal deficit even further. However, it seems that the national bank of Belgium does not have a similar problem. Belgium and Italy can be compared because they have a similar public finance problem in that the debt/GDP ratio is somewhat higher in Belgium than in Italy (140 versus 125) whereas the Belgian deficit is somewhat lower. But Belgium seems to be in the good equilibrium in the sense that interest rates are close to German levels, whereas Italy seems to be stuck in the bad equilibrium in the sense that its government pays 5 to 6 percentage points more on it public debt although the inflation rate is only about 2 percentage points higher than in Belgium.

This paper differs from previous models of public debt crises because it emphasizes the feedback from the initial assumption prevailing in the market to the eventual choice of the government. In the framework of Giavazzi and Pagano (1980) the public does not know the preferences of the government in terms of the fraction of the deficit that should be monetized. In this paper the preferences of the government are known and the government can act in the (short term) interests of the country.

The problem is, this part is well known, that a government that cannot bind its hands, could end up in a bad equilibrium. The novelty of the paper is that it shows that there is also a good equilibrium that is locally stable. However, once financial markets are far away from the good equilibrium they make it very difficult for the government to stabilize.

THE MODEL

The starting point is a standard social loss function, L_t, given by:

(1) $L_t = [\alpha q_t^2 + p_t^2]$ $\alpha \geq 0$

where p_t stands for the inflation rate and q_t stands for tax revenues as a percentage of GDP, which is equivalent to the average tax rate. High taxes and high inflation create distortions and are thus socially costly. The parameter α indicates the relative weight of taxes in the social loss function. A high α could be interpreted to mean that the tax collection system is not efficient, i.e. that it causes high distortion costs for a given revenue, or it could be interpreted to mean that the politicians in power dislike high taxes (for example because their marginal rate is a households with high marginal tax rates).

The aim of the authorities, as usual no distinction is made between the central bank and the ministry of finance, is to minimize this loss subject to the budget constraint :

(2) $d(b_t) = g_t + b_t(i_t - p_t) - q_t - p_t\sigma$

where b_t is the public debt/GDP ratio and g_t represents (non-interest) expenditure relative to GDP. The last term in this budget constraint represents seigniorage revenues under the assumption of a constant velocity money demand function with velocity equal to σ. Real growth is, for simplicity, assumed to be zero. Government expenditure could be made endogenous, as in a number of other contributions on the optimal choice of taxes and inflation, but this is not done here as it would not affect the main results of the paper, which concentrates on the incentive to use inflation to reduce the value of the public debt.[1]

The crucial point about the budget constraint (2) is that ex-post real interest payments, given by $b_t(i_t - p_t)$, are a function of the difference between the nominal interest rate and inflation. This formulation implies that all government debt has the same maturity equal to the length of the period of this model. Another interpretation would be that b represents only the government debt that matures this period. Interest payments on other government debt would then be subsumed under general government expenditure. This is not a serious limitation of the model since countries like Italy have a relative short average duration of the debt (and some long-term debt is indexed on short-term interest rates).

The nominal interest rate, i_t, can be written as the sum of the real interest rate, r, and expected inflation, $E_{t-1}(p_t)$. The real interest rate demanded by financial markets is here assumed (as usual) to be constant. The budget constraint can then be re-written as:

(2)' $d(b_t) = g_t + b_t(\rho + E_{t-1}(p_t) - p_t) - q_t - p_t\sigma$

The authorities determine inflation after financial markets have formed this expectations and set the interest rate.

The F.O.C. for a minimum of the loss (1), subject to the constraint (2)' are :

(3) $\delta L_t/\delta q_t = O = 2 [\alpha q_t - \lambda_t]$

(4) $\delta L_t/\delta p_t = O = 2 [p_t - \lambda_t(b_t + \sigma)]$

Where λ_t is the shadow price associated with the budget constraint (2)'.

In order to simplify the notation, only the steady state will be considered with a constant debt/GDP ratio, denoted b.[2] Conditions (3) and (4) then yield a simple relationship between inflation and tax revenues (as a percentage of GDP):

(5) $p_t = (b + \sigma) \alpha q_t$

This can be substituted into the budget constraint (2)' to obtain an expression for the steady state 'tax rate'. If one assumes that the public anticipates inflation correctly (i.e.

that the public knows the incentives of the government and has rational expectations), the debt to GDP ratio remains constant only if :

(6) $O = g_t + b\rho - q_t - \sigma(b + \sigma)\alpha q_t$

If expenditure is constant at $\breve{g}$ the optimal tax ratio also becomes a constant given by :

(7) $q = [\breve{g} + b\rho] / [1 + \sigma(b + \sigma)\alpha]$

The loss under discretion L_d would then be given by :

(8) $L_d = \alpha\{[\breve{g} + b\rho] / [1 + \sigma(b + \sigma)\alpha]\}^2 +$
         $\{[\breve{g} + b\rho] [(b + \sigma)\alpha] / [1 + \sigma(b + \sigma)\alpha]\}^2$

In order to highlight the role played by the interest burden on public debt it will henceforth be assumed that $\sigma = 0$. This elimination of seigniorage from the model could also be justified with the fact that over the last years seigniorage has not played a significant role in EU public finances as shown by Gros and Vandille (1995). The tax basis for seigniorage is the monetary base which is in most countries below 10% of GDP. In contrast, the debt/GDP ratio is above 100% in a number of countries.

Suppressing seigniorage as a source of revenues has the advantage that it implies that the social optimum would be (for the government) to announce that it will set inflation to zero. If believed by the markets this would lead to a lower loss because it would imply the same tax ratio as under discretion. This model would thus yield the usual result of the literature that stresses the incentive for governments to engineer surprise inflation in order to increase employment or output. The problem, again as usual, is that the announcements of zero inflation are in reality not credible.

Inspection of equation (8) (and (2)) shows that the sum $\rho b + g$ is all that matters. Hence $\breve{g}$ can from now on just be interpreted as representing the sum of non-interest expenditure plus (ex ante) real interest payments on the public debt. The loss under discretion then collapses to :

(9) $L_d = \alpha\breve{g}^2 + (\breve{g}b\alpha)^2 = \alpha\breve{g}^2 (1 + b^2\alpha)$

It is clear that the loss under the social optimum, i.e. under a credible stabilization plan, is lower than this since the second term would then just fall away. This is a standard result.

What happens if the government does keep inflation stable, but this is not believed ex ante by financial markets? In this situation the ex post real interest rate will be higher. This means that the size of the social loss under a stabilization plan that is only partially credible ex ante, but actually implemented, is determined by the budget constraint which implies, in turn, that taxes have to be increased to pay for the higher <u>ex post</u> real interest rates :

(10) $q = \breve{g} + b\, E_{t-1}(p_t)$

Assuming risk neutrality in financial markets the expected inflation rate is given by the product of the probability that the stabilization fails and the inflation rate expected in case the government gives up. The subjective belief of the market concerning the probability that the government will give up the attempt to stabilize is denoted by π_s, and it will be determined in a model consistent manner in section titled "Multiple Equilibra." The next section determines first the inflation rate the government should create given the value of π_s that has been incorporated into the nominal interest rate.

GIVING UP

What would be the optimal inflation rate if the government were to give up the plan to stabilize? In designating this case with the subscript "$_{gu}$" one can start with the budget constraint which yields:

(11) $O = \breve{g} + b\,(\pi_s\, p_{gu} - p_{gu}) - q_{gu}$

where it was assumed that the rate that will be chosen in case the government gives up, p_{gu}, is equal to the one anticipated by the market.

The relationship between taxes and inflation calculated from the F.O.C. for loss minimization under given expectations of inflation, and equation (5) is still valid. It implies that $p = b\alpha q$. Using this relationship (5), in equation (11), yields a solution for the tax rate that becomes optimal when the government wants to abandon the attempt to stabilize and minimize the one period loss:

(12) $q_{gu} = \breve{g}[1 + (1-\pi_s)\, b^2\alpha]^{-1}$

Using equation (5), marginal incentives to use inflation or taxes also yields the solution for the optimal inflation rate to chose if the government gives up:

(13) $p_{gu} = \breve{g}b\alpha[1 + (1 - \pi_s)\, b^2\alpha]^{-1}$

It follows that the loss that results if the government gives up 'in an optimal manner' can be written as:

(14) $L_{gu} = \alpha[1 + (1 - \pi_s)\, b^2\alpha]^{-2} + (b\alpha)^2\, [1 + (1 - \pi_s)\, b^2\alpha]^{-2}$

$$= \breve{g}^2 \, [1 + (1 - \pi_s) \, b^2\alpha]^{-2} \, [a + (b\alpha)^2]$$
$$= \alpha\breve{g}^2 \, [1 + (1 - \pi_s) \, b^2\alpha]^{-2} \, [1 + b^2\alpha]$$

By abandoning the attempt to stabilize (in other words by fooling the markets) the government can achieve actually a lower social loss (at least for one period) as becomes apparent if one compares equation (14) to equation (9).

Giving up also yields a smaller loss than stabilizing. This is again a well known result in the context of the general time inconsistency approach. It can be shown to hold in this model as well. Under stabilization the need for taxes is determined by the budget constraint with actual inflation equal to zero (but expectations of inflation positive):

(15) $q_{stab} = \breve{g} + b\pi_s p_{gu} = \breve{g} + \alpha \, b^2 \, \pi_s \breve{g} \, [1 + (1 - \pi_s)b^2\alpha]^{-1}$

The loss under stabilization then becomes:

(16) $L_{stab} = \alpha\breve{g}^2[1 + \alpha b^2\pi_s / (1 + (1 - \pi_s) \, b^2\alpha)]^2$

which can be written as:[3]

(17) $L_{stab} = \alpha\breve{g}^2 \, [1 + (1 - \pi_s) \, b^2\alpha]^{-2} \, [1 + b^2\alpha]^2$

Is it always better to stabilize? The answer could be no if the stabilization plan is not fully credible ex ante. Comparing equation (17) to equation (14) shows that the loss under stabilization with only partial credibility is larger if $[1 + (1 - \pi_s) \, b^2\alpha]^{-2} \, [1 + b^2\alpha]$ exceeds one. This will be the case if π_s equals one. If the government has only a very low credibility with the markets it would do its country a favor if did not even try to stabilize. But a perfectly credible stabilization ($\pi_s = 0$) always leads to a lower loss. The borderline subjective probability that leads to the same welfare loss under discretion and under stabilization can be determined from the condition:

(18) $2 \, (1-\pi_s) + (1 - \pi_{s2}) \, b^2\alpha = 1$

A comparison of equations (17) and (14) also shows that as long as b and α are positive the loss under stabilization is larger than under 'giving up'. The difference in welfare under the two policies is:

(19) $L_{stab} - L_{gu} = \alpha\breve{g}^2[1 + (1 -\pi_s) \, b^2\alpha]^{-2} \, \{(1 + b^2\alpha)^2 - (1 + b^2\alpha)\}$
$$= \alpha\breve{g}^2[1 + (1 - \pi_s) \, b^2\alpha]^{-2} \, (1 + b^2\alpha) \, b^2\alpha$$

which is always positive, as argued above. Of course, the gain from fooling people cannot be reaped often. But the temptation certainly exists. A number of studies have concentrated on the game theory implications of the fact that giving up yields, at least for one period, a lower social loss. This paper does not go along this route. Instead it wants to show that more than one consistent equilibrium model might exist if the decision of the government is uncertain.

MULTIPLE EQUILIBRIA

It is useful at this point to take a step back and consider the alternatives for the government under two polar assumptions concerning the subjective probability beliefs held by the public: i) the credibility of the anti-inflationary stance is perfect ($\pi_s = 0$), and ii) the credibility is zero ($\pi_s = 1$). This is done in Table 1 below:

Table 1

Ex post: Ex ante:	Stabilize	Give up (inflate)	Temptation
credible	$\alpha\breve{g}^2$	$\alpha\breve{g}^2(1+b^2\alpha)^{-1}$	$\alpha\breve{g}^2b^2\alpha/(1+b^2\alpha)$
not credible	$\alpha\breve{g}^2(1+b^2\alpha)^2$	$\alpha\breve{g}^2(1+b^2\alpha)$	$\alpha\breve{g}^2b^2\alpha(1+b^2\alpha)$

This table shows the four possible combinations of ex post outcomes and ex ante expectations that are possible in this model. It is apparent that in each row (i.e. given the market expectations) the loss is always smaller (essentially from lower taxes) if the government does inflate. Whether or not it will do so depends on whether there are other effects that impinge on the perceived cost of inflating.

Assume now for simplicity that the cost of reneging on the commitment to price stability is equal to a constant Γ. The size of Γ is determined by confidence effects and possibly by the importance a member country of the EU attaches to its credibility with the rest of the Union. If Γ goes to infinity, the authorities will always keep price stability because the temptation (the one period lower loss from higher inflation) is more than offset by the loss of credibility. The markets will anticipate this and this policy will be credible. Vice versa, if Γ is very small, the government will always minimize the loss and hence, as the markets know this, the discretionary equilibrium is the only solution.

At first sight it appears that there must be a critical value for Γ that separates these two situations: if Γ is below this critical value, which is given by the incentive, the commitment to price stability is not credible and high inflation is the only possibility. The problem is that this critical level of Γ depends on the interest rate set by the market as can be seen in the last column of this table.

For values of Γ intermediate between the two 'temptations' two equilibria are possible: if the market initially believes that the government will stabilize the costs (or loss) in terms of higher taxes needed to do so will be low and the government will stabilize. Vice versa, if the market initially believes the government will not stabilize the cost of stabilizing will be high and the government will indeed not do so.

The region inside which two equilibria are possible is represented graphically below:

$$\alpha\breve{g}^2\,[b^2\alpha/(1+b^2\alpha)] \qquad \alpha\breve{g}^2\,(1+b^2\alpha)^2[b^2\alpha/(1+b^2\alpha)]$$

| price stab. credible | two equilibria | high inflation |

$$0 \xrightarrow{\hspace{9cm}} \Gamma$$

The size of the region for Γ with two equilibria is an increasing function of $\breve{g}^2$, b^2 and α as can be seen by taking the difference between the two temptations which is equal to:

$$\alpha\breve{g}^2\,[b^2\alpha/(1+b^2\alpha)]\,[(1+b^2\alpha)^2 - 1]$$
$= \alpha\breve{g}^2 b^2\alpha[(1+b^2\alpha) - (1+b^2\alpha)^{-1}]$. This implies that the more serious the potential inflationary problem, the more likely it becomes that two equilibria might exist.

In this section there is no uncertainty about the outcome once the public has decided what to believe. But there is nothing to guide the public in its expectations. Will this feature disappear if one acknowledges that in reality the decision of the government whether or not to inflate is not 100% certain because it will depend also on other, possibly non-economic, factors? This is discussed in the following section where it is assumed that the probability that the government will inflate will normally still be positive (but small) even if the gain through lower taxation is slightly below the cost of doing so.

UNCERTAINTY

The less than perfect credibility ex ante makes it costly for the government to stabilize because it has to pay a risk premium on its debt. But so far the lack of full credibility, i.e. a positive value of π_s has only been assumed. The crucial innovation proposed in this paper is to say that the probability that government does give up should be a function, at least inter alia, of the difference in the loss. This is an intuitively attractive assumption because the larger the welfare loss, even if only for one period, the more likely the government should come to override other considerations that would induce it to attempt stabilization against the odds.

A similar idea is contained in a series of papers by Ozkan and Sutherland who pursue a somewhat different approach. In their framework (e.g. Ozkan and Sutherland (1994)) there are external stochastic shocks that can drive the economy away from a politically acceptable equilibrium and the government abandons the attempt to stabilize with certainty once it pays to do so. The decision of the government is based on expectations of stochastic variables, but the rule is perfectly known by the public and the decision criterion is clear. This can also create self-fulfilling speculative attacks.

The probabilistic approach of this paper seems to be closer to reality in that financial markets can never be entirely certain about what course of action the government will eventually chose because many individuals and institutions concur in this decision. The preferences of different actors (prime minister, finance minister, central bank, etc) are never perfectly known, and the distribution of power among them fluctuates over time. Moreover, other considerations (e.g. pro-European sentiments or reputation effects) also play a role and their relative weight also fluctuate over time. The financial press reflects this uncertainty with its endless speculation about the likely future course of monetary policy. Hence it will now be assumed that the decision process of the government is such that the <u>probability</u> that it abandons the attempt to stabilize is an increasing function of the difference in the loss.

In order to obtain a simple solution it is assumed here that the 'objective' probability, π_o, that the government gives up depends on the square root of the difference in loss as in (a more general formulation is provided below):

(20) $$\pi_o = \gamma \, [L_{stab} - L_{gu}]^{0.5} + \Gamma$$

where γ and Γ are two arbitrary constants. Equation (20) is, of course, only defined over the range $0 < \pi_o < 1$. If the RHS of equation (20) is negative π_o must be set to zero, and if the RHS exceeds one π_o must be set equal to one. Assuming these restrictions are observed, this equation implies that the probability of not implementing zero inflation is equal to Γ when implementing zero inflation were to lead to the same social loss as the high inflation discretionary equilibrium. Γ thus represent other factors that influence the choice whether to stabilize or not, it could be zero or it could even be positive if the country is in political turmoil. A country that attaches great importance to achieving zero inflation (over and above the effect operating through the social loss function for the current period), for example, because it wants to participate in EMU at some point in the future, would have a Γ that is negative. In this case, the probability of abandoning the stabilization attempt might be zero even if the social loss is somewhat greater than under discretion (as usually the case here). Henceforth it will be assumed that Γ is negative.

The parameter γ indicates the impact of an increase in the net cost of stabilization on the probability of failure. The higher the value of γ the more important the cost/benefit analysis becomes in influencing the decision whether to stabilize against the odds set by the market.

The sequence of events in this set up could be described as follows: The economy starts in the discretionary equilibrium. The government makes a plan to stabilize and announces it. The public then forms its subjective probability, π_s, that the plan will actually succeed. The reaction of the public determines (via equation (12)) the level of expected inflation (i.e. interest rates) which then determine the gain (or loss), ex post the government would make (or have to bear) if it actually implemented the plan. This, in turn, determines the objective probability, π_o, that the government will actually implement the plan (equation (13)). The public knows this and hence a model consistent equilibrium can hold only if the belief about the probability of failure by the public is equal to the objective probability of failure ($\pi_s = \pi_o = \pi$). Equations (12) and (13) can thus be used to determine the probability of failure, and hence the expected inflation rate (equal here to the nominal interest rate). The implicit solution for the model consistent probability of failure is then (using equation (19) in equation (20)):

(21) $\quad \pi = \gamma \ [\ [1 + (1 - \pi) \ b^2\alpha]^{-2} \ \breve{g}^2 \ \alpha \ (1 + b^2\alpha) \ b^2\alpha]^{0.5} + \Gamma$
$\qquad = \gamma \breve{g} b \alpha \ [1 + (1 - \pi) \ b^2\alpha]^{-1} \ (1 + b^2\alpha)^{0.5} + \Gamma$

This implies a quadratic solution for π.[4] If one defines the composite term on the RHS as $\cap \equiv \gamma b \alpha \breve{g} (1 + b^2\alpha)^{0.5}$ this can be rewritten as:

(22) $\quad \pi^2 \ \alpha b^2 - \pi \ [1 + \alpha b^2(1 + \Gamma)] + \cap + \Gamma(1 + \alpha b^2) = 0$

The solutions to this quadratic expression are given by:

(23) $\quad \pi_{1,2} = 0.5 \ \{[1+\Gamma+(\alpha b^2)^{-1}] \pm [(1+\Gamma+(\alpha b^2)^{-1})^2 - 4(\alpha b^2)^{-1}(\cap+\Gamma(1+\alpha b^2))]^{0.5}\}$

It is apparent from equation (21) that if either b or α are equal to zero the only equilibrium is the one where the probability of giving up is zero. The reason is that if α is zero the government does not have an incentive to use surprise inflation, and the lower taxes it can impose are worth zero. If b is zero the government does not gain from surprise inflation.

The intuition behind the two solutions in equation (23) can be seen more clearly if one analyses equation (21) graphically with the help of a numerical example. The value of the RHS of equation (21) can be displayed on the vertical axis as a function of the probability of failure assumed by financial markets (π_s). The equilibrium is then determined by the intersection between this curve and the diagonal as in Figure 1. For Figure 1 and the subsequent figures, it was assumed that b, the debt/GDP ratio is equal to one and that the expenditure ratio ğ is equal to 0.5.

Figure 1
Two Cases: (i) One Internal Equilibrium and (ii) Two Internal Equilibria.

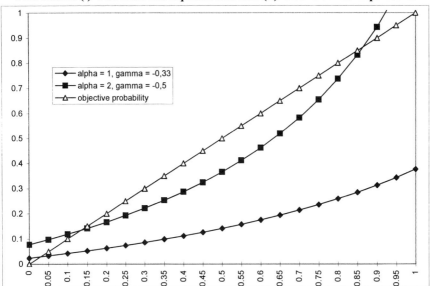

Figure 1 shows two cases: the first case is the line labeled "alpha = 1, gamma = -0.33" which shows the value of the right hand side when a equals 1 and $\Gamma = -0.33$. In this case there is only one equilibrium, namely at the point where the probability of failure assumed by financial markets is equal to the one that results from the incentives for the government. This equilibrium is stable in the sense that if the private sector were to start an initial guess of a lower value of π it would find that the incentives for the government imply a higher probability (and vice versa). For this parameter constellation a non negative value of Γ would imply that the only equilibrium is at zero.

To illustrate the potential for two internal equilibria, the second line in Figure 1 is based on the value $\alpha = 2$. For this value of α a low expected inflation equilibrium and a high expected inflation equilibrium can exist inside the interval (0,1), depending on the value of Γ. The curve shown in this figure intersects the diagonal twice because Γ was set equal to -0.5. A lower value Γ would shift the curve downwards (at a certain point $\pi=0$ zero becomes the only equilibrium) and vice versa for higher values of Γ (until $\pi=1$ becomes the only equilibrium).

The potential for two equilibria exists, however, also in a more general formulation of the link between the welfare gain from giving up and the probability that this happens actually. Instead of the square root assumed in equation (20) one could just postulate that the objective probability is a more general function of the gain from cheating:

(24) $\pi_o = \gamma \, [L_{stab} - L_{gu}]^{\varepsilon} + \Gamma$ with $\varepsilon > 0$

If one substitutes again for the expression of the welfare loss from equation (19) one obtains the generalized equivalent to equation (21):

(25) $\pi = \gamma \, [\, [1 + (1 - \pi) \, b^2\alpha]^{-2} \, \check{g}^2 \, \alpha \, (1 + b^2\alpha) \, b^2\alpha]^{\varepsilon} + \Gamma$

The right hand side of this equation is a convex function of π since the second derivative is always positive in the region $(0, 1)$.[5] Hence the potential for two solutions always exists when the RHS of equation (25) is positive at $\pi = 0$. Figures 2 and 3 show the numerical results for the same parameter constellations as before but with different values for ε. The only difference was that the values for Γ were in some cases adjusted to ensure that the curves were in the range between zero and one. Figure 2 shows the case of $\varepsilon = 1$ and Figure 3 shows the case of $\varepsilon = 2$. A comparison of these two figures with the first one shows that even these wide variations in ε do not affect the nature of the results. For low values of α (which are equivalent to low values of b) only one equilibrium is possible whereas the case $\alpha = 2$ always gives the potential for two equilibria. (The value of Γ determines the position of the curve and hence whether there are actually two equilibria in the interval $(0, 1)$.)

Figure 2
Linear Relationship Between Welfare Gain And Objective Probability

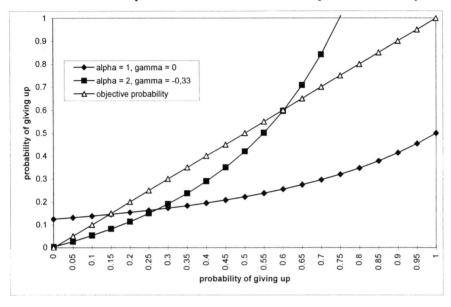

Figure 3
Quadratic Relationship Between Welfare Gain And Objective Probability

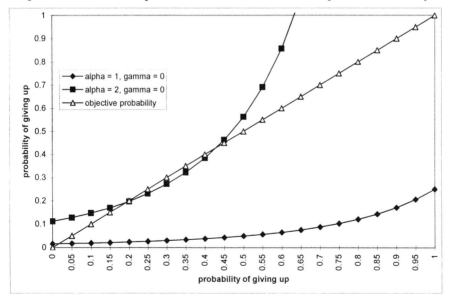

What could cause a shift from the good equilibrium to the bad one? Small perturbations should be corrected since the good equilibrium is locally stable. A small increase in the 'guess' of financial markets would increase the incentive by the government to give up only very little. To the right of point A (within a finite neighborhood) the objective probability would be below the subjective one as guessed by the market. One would normally assume that the market adjusts the initial guess downwards if it exceeded the objective probability. If this is the case, the good equilibrium is stable and a large shock is needed to drive the economy far away from the good equilibrium. Once the economy has reached the bad equilibrium (point B) the situation changes dramatically. In the neighborhood of this point the (ex post) real interest rate is very high, and the marginal cost of further tax increases necessary to finance the large primary surplus needed to stabilize the debt/GDP ratio is also very high. A one unit increase in the subjective probability of failure assumed by the market, at this point, leads to an increase in the objective probability of failure that is larger than one unit. Hence the bad equilibrium is not stable.[6] An economy that had reached the bad equilibrium could thus be driven to a corner solution in which the risk premiums demanded by financial markets are so high that the government gives in with probability one, and the economy effectively is stuck at the discretionary equilibrium.

An example of a shock that was not large enough to lead to the bad equilibrium could be the experience of Belgium after the 1993 ERM crisis. The central bank did not hesitate to increase short-term interest rates once the crisis had started with the result that after several months of uncertainty interest rates and the Belgian franc/DM exchange rate returned to their pre-crisis equilibrium.

However, a small discrete change in the parameters could also mean that the good equilibrium is no longer possible, for example, if a new government comes in that has different preferences. The Berlusconi government in Italy declared and made it clear in 1994 that it would not levy new taxes. This could be viewed as being equivalent to an increase in α. Moreover world wide real interest rates increased in 1994. As mentioned above this would be equivalent to an increase in expenditure $\breve{g}$.

Reducing the maturity structure of public debt would also be equivalent to increasing b as shown above. A government that wants to stabilize and wants to avoid the bad equilibrium should thus lengthen the maturity of public debt and/or issue indexed debt. If the closed economy model of this paper were changed, indexed debt would be equivalent to foreign currency debt as long as PPP holds continuously.

CONCLUDING REMARKS

The purpose of this paper is to show how a highly indebted country could fall into a debt trap in the sense that a high risk premium demanded by financial markets could force the government to abandon any attempt to have low inflation because low inflation would result, ex post, in very high real interest payments on public debt. The central theme of the paper is that, under certain conditions, a given economy could fall into either one of two equilibria: The bad equilibrium, which could be called a 'debt trap', and a virtuous equilibrium with good credibility and low interest rates. It is obviously more attractive to stabilize the economy under the good equilibrium. The debt trap with high ex post real interest rates, if the government does not inflate, could actually be worse than not even attempting to stabilize.

In a probabilistic framework there might also be a third intermediate equilibrium with a high (but less than 100%) probability that the government will give up. However, this equilibrium is not stable.

Once a country is in the debt trap small changes in policy instruments (e.g. increasing the discount rate a bit) might not have any effect. What is needed to get out of the debt trap would be a discrete change in any one of the parameters that is large enough to put the economy to the left of the debt trap or even eliminate the possibility of a debt trap. If the minimum threshold of action has been reached the rewards would be large in the sense that the economy should then go to the good equilibrium.

How important is the mechanism modeled in this paper? Table 2 below shows the debt level and yields on public debt of some highly indebted countries and Germany for comparison. The most striking fact in this table is that in early 1995 Italian government debt yielded almost 6 percentage points more than German public debt. There were still considerable amounts of lower interest rate debt outstanding, but this table calculates what would have happened if early 1995 yields were to persist and became incorporated in the entire stock of public debt. The fourth column of this table thus shows that given the high level of the (net) public debt in Italy, the Italian government could save almost 7 % of GDP in interest expenditure if it had German interest rates. Even if Italy were to reach 'only' Belgian interest rates the savings would still be in the order of 5 to 6 % of GDP. For Belgium, the interest rate differential with Germany is much lower, hence the gain from having German interest rate would also be limited. For the Netherlands, there seems to be absolutely no problem of credibility. Sweden and Spain also seem to have a credibility problem, but since their debt levels are so much lower than that of Italy, their debt trap is much less severe.

Table 2
Public Debt and Debt Service in Highly Indebted Countries

	Debt/GDP	Yield on public debt	Savings at German yield	inflation	Savings at German real yield
Germany	35.8	7.0		2.4	
Belgium	130.0	7.9	1.2	1.7	2.1
Netherlands	60.1	7.2	0.1	2.4	0.1
Italy	117.9	13.0	7.0	4.3	4.8
Spain	42.2	12.0	2.1	4.8	1.1
Sweden	20.2 (80.0)	11.0	0.8 (3.2)	2.6	0.8 (3.2)

Source : The Economist April 1-7, 1995 for yields on public debt, OECD Economic Outlook, 56, December 1994, for net financial obligations (net government debt). For Sweden the net debt is given at 20 % of GDP but gross debt is given at 80 %. This is the only country with such a large difference between net and gross debt.

Table 2 intends to give just an idea of the order of magnitude of the problem. A more detailed empirical analysis would have to take into account, first of all, the average maturity structure of public debt.

NOTES

[1] See for example Mankiw (1987).

[2] In a similar model Gros (1990) shows that this should not affect the conclusions.

[3] Equation (16) can be rewritten as $L_{stab} = \alpha \breve{g}^2 [1 + (1 - \pi) b^2 \alpha]^{-2} [1 + (1 - \pi) b^2 \alpha + \alpha b^2 \pi]^2$, the step to equation (17) is obvious.

[4] Equation (21) implies $\pi(1 + (1 - \pi) b^2 \alpha) = \gamma b \alpha \breve{g}(1 + b^2 \alpha)^{0.5} + \Gamma \pi(1 + (1 - \pi) b^2 \alpha)$.

[5] This can be proven by noting that the part of this expression that depends on π, namely $[1 + (1 - \pi) b^2 \alpha]^{-2\varepsilon}$ is convex. The first derivative (with respect to π) of this expression is equal to: $2\varepsilon(b^2 \alpha) [1 + (1-\pi) b^2 \alpha]^{-2\varepsilon-1}$ and the second derivative is equal to: $2\varepsilon(b^2 \alpha)^2(2\varepsilon + 1) [1 + (1-\pi) b^2 \alpha]^{-2\varepsilon-2}$. As long as π is between zero and one (and ε is positive) these expressions are always positive.

[6] A more sophisticated '*tatonnement*' process would lead to different conclusions regarding the stability of the two equilibria: one could also assume that when at two consecutive '*trials*', i.e. subjective probabilities (the absolute value of) the difference between the subjective and the objective probability increased the next guess should be lower (and vice versa if the (absolute value of the) difference had diminished). If the signs of the difference had changed the new guess should be in between. Under this tatonnement process both internal equilibria are stable. The dividing line would be the point of maximum distance between the diagonal and the line representing the objective probability.

REFERENCES

Davies, Gareth and David Vines, "Equilibrium Currency Crises: Are Multiple Equilibria Self-Fulfilling or History Dependent?," CEPR Discussion Paper, No. 1239, September, 1995.

De Grauwe, Paul, "The Economics of Convergence Towards Monetary Union in Europe," University of Leuven and CEPR, April, 1995.

Flood, Robert P., Garber Peter M. and Kramer Charles, "Collapsing Exchange Rate Regimes: Another Linear Example," NBER Working Paper Series, Working Paper No. 5318.

Giavazzi, Francesco and Pagano, Marco, "Confidence Crises and Public Debt Management," NBER Working Paper Series, Working Paper No. 2926, April 1989.

Gros, Daniel. "Seigniorage and EMS discipline," chapter 7 in Paul de Grauwe and Lucas Papademos, eds., The European Monetary System in the 1990s, Longman, London, 162-177, 1990.

Gros, Daniel and Guy Vandille, "Seigniorage and EMU: The Fiscal Implications of Price Stability and Financial Market Integration," Journal of Common Market Studies, Vol 33, No. 2, June, 1995, pp. 175-196.

Mankiw, G.N., "The Optimal Collection of Seigniorage, Theory and Evidence," Journal of Monetary Economies, Vol 20, 1897, pp. 327-341.

Obstfeld, Maurice, "Rational and Self-fulfilling Balance of Payments Crisis," Americal Economic Review, Nr. 76, pp. 72-81, 1986.

Obstfeld, Maurice, "Modles of Currency Crises with Self-Fulfilling Features," NBER Working Paper Series, Working Paper 5285.

Ozkan, Gulcin and Alan Sutherland, "A Model of the ERM crisis," CEPR Discussion Paper Nr. 879, 1994.

14

The Impact Of The Iraqi Invasion On The Kuwaiti Banking And Financial System: Lessons Learned From A Financial Crisis

SALEM ABDUL AZIZ AL-SABAH
Governor, Central Bank of Kuwait

In their reference to historical outlines of economic development, Robert Baldwin and Gerald Meier cited the British historian Lewis B. Namier: "Thus the past is on top of us and with us all the time; and there is only one way of mastering it even remotely in any one sector: by knowing how these things have come to be, which helps to understand their nature, character, and their correlation, or lack of correlation, to the present realities of life".[1] Baldwin and Meier found this true of the historical processes governing economic development. It is just as true for Kuwait's recent experience of invasion and liberation. For Kuwait, controlling the impact of the Iraqi occupation on the banking and financial sector required an accurate assessment of the repercussions of the invasion. The experience of meeting the crisis has affirmed the correlation between the development of Kuwait's banking and financial sector and the realities of Kuwait's economic circumstances, before and during the occupation. Thus, I can find in this statement an appropriate beginning for a historical and analytical demonstration of the lessons learned by the Kuwaiti banking and financial system from the financial crisis caused by the Iraqi invasion of Kuwait on August 2, 1990.

This article focuses on the crucial lessons learned from that financial crisis, with emphasis on the efforts exerted by the Central Bank of Kuwait (CBK) during the period of the Iraqi occupation, and the period following the liberation of Kuwait on February 26, 1991. The time has come to bring these lessons into focus through an in-depth analysis of the consequences and impact of this financial crisis on the Kuwaiti banking and financial system. Therefore, this article has been arranged to comprise four complementary parts. The first covers the background of the main economic and monetary conditions prevailing during the period prior to the invasion. The second and third parts deal with the CBK's efforts during the occupation and developments after the liberation. The final part draws the crucial lessons learned from the financial crisis. We hope these lessons will provoke further attention to how the State of Kuwait responded to the impact of this vicious crisis on the Kuwaiti banking and financial sector.

THE PERIOD PRIOR TO THE INVASION

A knowledge of the background of the main economic and monetary conditions during this period will be useful in understanding the impact of the Iraqi invasion on the performance of the banking and financial sector, and on the Kuwaiti economy's pre-invasion aspirations, which included enhancing the performance of the domestic economy and reactivating its momentum in the short-run, handling major issues pertaining to its course, formulating its strategic directions in both the medium and long runs, and preparing for an economic plan for the period 1990/91 - 1994/95. The Iraqi invasion curtailed thes . intensive efforts that were aimed at the achievement of these goals.

To elaborate on the performance of the Kuwaiti economy before the invasion, the following points may be helpful:

1. During the five years ending in 1989, the oil sector accounted for an average of 45% of overall GDP, 90% of export proceeds, and 88% of total government revenues. This distinct dominance of the oil sector over the economy explains the emphasis given to supporting and enhancing the non-oil sectors, especially the banking and financial sector.

2. The Kuwaiti economy has always depended heavily upon imports. As a result, domestic inflation has been subject to international price and exchange rate fluctuations. The consumer price index increased by only 1.5% and 3.3% in 1988 and 1989 respectively.

3. Since 1985, when the Five-Year Plan for the period 1985/86 - 1989/90 was launched, the Kuwaiti authorities have given priority to confronting Kuwait's structural problems, such as the population and labor force imbalances, and to

expanding the productive base of the non-oil sectors in order to diversify sources of the national income.

4. Starting from the fiscal year 1981/82, the State general budget began to record deficits ranging, before the Iraqi invasion, from a minimum of KD 106.1[2] million in fiscal 1981/82 and a maximum of KD 1,302.3 million in fiscal 1986/87. The invasion increased this deficit to KD 7,368.2 and KD 5,528.8 million in the two fiscal years 1990/91 and 1991/1992 respectively.

5. The performance of Kuwaiti banks and other financial institutions during the pre-invasion period was characterized by significant progress in eliminating the effects of the difficult debt problem, in order to focus on their normal role in the economy, i.e., receiving funds from depositors, rendering various banking services, financing different economic activities, playing an intermediary role in transactions with the outside world, and managing others' funds.

Due to the openness of the banking and financial units to the outside world, the CBK started long before the invasion to seek adjustments that would enable them to face vibrant competition resulting from the existing and expected international economic blocs occurring in different parts of the world. It is important to say here that the total volume of Kuwaiti bank assets exceeded KD 12 billion at the end of May, 1990 and that foreign assets constituted 25.5% of this total. The value of foreign assets had reached KD 3,061 million by the end of May, 1990, against KD 1,644.4 million for foreign liabilities.

THE PERIOD OF THE OCCUPATION

During this period the CBK played its role in exile and exerted massive efforts in more than one direction, with its attention given to three main areas of responsibility: (i) organization of Kuwaiti banks abroad, (ii) providing support to help them meet their financial obligations to foreign banks, and (iii) to prepare a comprehensive plan to revive the banking and financial sector after the liberation of Kuwait.

1. Reorganizing Kuwaiti Banks Abroad:

The CBK issued directives from its temporary operations base in exile for the management of Kuwaiti banks and the protection of their financial assets. As many bank officials as possible were kept in constant communication, and missing information and bank records were reassembled through cooperative contact with foreign banks. Authorized signatures of the pre-invasion period were restricted to certain chairmen and their deputies.

During the occupation, the vaults of the CBK had been looted of gold, coins and currency notes of the KD Third Issue; the CBK, after determining quickly the looted currency notes, abrogated them as legal tender through an Amiri decree. The CBK prepared the new KD Fourth Issue, which became ready in December 1990. This move to prevent the occupiers from benefiting from Kuwait's national currency was complemented by an earlier measure, a request that Kuwaiti assets abroad be frozen. This measure helped in protecting Kuwait's assets abroad.

2. Extending Support To Kuwaiti Banks:

The limitation on authorized signatures enabled certain Kuwaiti bank transactions to continue, with confidence in bank security. The reorganization of bank officials and the reconstruction of bank records further extended stability during the crisis. Other measures by which the CBK helped the Kuwaiti banks to honor their obligations included the drawing up of schedules for the settlement of transactions and for interest payments on bank liabilities. As Kuwaiti banks reassumed control over their affairs in given areas, the CBK asked the concerned monetary authorities to lift the freeze on Kuwaiti's assets.

It was important for the longer term to sustain confidence in Kuwait's banking system, anticipating the re-establishment of the banking and financial sector after liberation. GCC (Gulf Cooperation Council) monetary authorities extended their support by continuing to exchange Kuwaiti dinars, thus aiding Kuwaitis in exile.

3. Preparing A Plan For The Post-Liberation Period:

From the earliest days of the occupation, the CBK anticipated liberation and planned for the rapid re-establishment of the banking and financial sector and its vital components, namely restored confidence in the Kuwaiti currency, stable exchange rates, inflation control, and domestic and international confidence in the banking system. The CBK established short-and long-term plans for the maintenance of the banking and financial system during the occupation and its restoration immediately upon liberation.

The long-term plan for rebuilding the financial sector involved maintaining contact with bank officers in different countries, so as to be able to mobilize them upon liberation. The CBK maintained contact within Kuwait itself during the occupation; it drew up instructions and procedures to be implemented by banks immediately upon their return to Kuwait. These instructions involved the release of customers' accounts and the conversions of KD into foreign currency.

The banks were instructed to set their accounts at their August 1, 1990 levels, and to pay interest on savings and fixed deposit accounts for the entire period of the occupation.

The CBK prepared to assess economic conditions and determine the initial KD exchange rate, designate banking functions to be temporarily suspended, and limits to be set on others during the inevitable transition period immediately following liberation. In this respect, the phased settlement of international obligations already referred to, served as preparation for domestic operations after liberation.

The long-term plan also included the preparation of studies on several other important matters, such as the following:

a) Determining the number of branches that each bank will operate during the transitional post-liberation period.

b) Stopping the activities of the exchange companies during the transition period, and determining the conditions they would have to meet in order to be allowed to resume their activities, including the settlement of all outstanding transactions with their correspondents abroad. These transactions involved transfers to their customers that had not been completed due to the invasion.

c) Determining the procedures to be followed after liberation regarding the exchange of the new currency notes (Issue Four) for the old ones.

d) Drafting the regulations for cash withdrawals from customers' accounts at local banks, and for conversions of Kuwaiti dinars into foreign currency. These regulations were to be followed during a short-term period after liberation, for the purposes of limiting pressures on local banks and on the Kuwaiti dinar.

e) Following-up on Kuwaiti banks with respect to the liquidation of their foreign assets, in order to assist them with the liquidity pressures that they would face after the liberation.

f) Discussing different views on ways to treat the local banks' collection of debts from their customers whose financial positions were negatively affected by the invasion.

THE PERIOD SINCE THE LIBERATION

After the liberation of Kuwait came the immense task of rebuilding the war-shattered Kuwaiti economy, which had sustained damage to its infrastructure and the destruction of its production and development capacity. The oil sector, for example, was hindered by the fires in over 700 oil wells, and subsequently by the stoppage of oil-production and export, the main source of the country's income. Another example can be found in the banking and financial system, which underwent complete cessation of activities, yielding the threat of monetary instability, lost confidence in the national currency and a rise in the increasing rate of domestic inflation.

The CBK was responsible for reviving the activities and the role of the banking and financial sector. To get banking activities to normal levels again, the CBK exerted its efforts on many fronts, principally in the preparation of this sector to resume its normal activities, and in the search for the most effective way to handle the expected rush on customers' deposits at local banks.

Local banks were able, in record time, to quickly resume basic banking facilities, meeting the challenges imposed on them as a result of the Iraqi invasion. These challenges can be explained by the exceptional working conditions immediately after the liberation: a lack of technical manpower and of basic services such as electricity, the breakdown of computer systems and equipment, the lack of accounting records and systems and the deficiency in the domestic and international communications network. Nevertheless, local banks were ready to exchange the Third Issue currency notes for those of the new Fourth Issue as of March 24, 1991[3].

From the CBK's point of view, there were several issues that were critical to monetary management and the CBK's objectives, especially the following:

1. the smooth and effective resumption of withdrawals from customers' accounts at local banks, and ultimately of money conversions from the Kuwaiti dinar to foreign currency;

2. the confidence in the Kuwaiti dinar;

3. the reduction, followed by stability, in the general level of domestic prices; and

4. the difficult debt problem.

1. Withdrawals From Customers' Accounts:

The full extent of this problem cannot be seen without actual figures showing both the extent of the withdrawals and the immense challenge created for the CBK. Monthly data on withdrawals and deposits at local banks immediately after the liberation reveal the following astonishing facts:

a) Withdrawals increased sharply during the first three months after the liberation, to reach a peak in May 1991 (Table 1), with a value of KD 1,102.9 million (85% of which were in KD, and the rest in foreign currency). The CBK was able to reverse this increasing trend during the following two months (June and July 1991). The CBK emphasized on many occasions its support for the relative stability of the Kuwaiti dinar, and achieved this stability through the KD exchange rate system and the interest rate on KD deposits, which enjoyed favorable margins over corresponding deposit rates on major currencies, together with certain temporary controls on withdrawals and conversions due to technical and logistical considerations. These controls did not cover transfers needed for legitimate economic activity, and exceptions were made for humanitarian reasons.

Table 1
Monthly Withdrawals and Deposits at Local Banks Immediately After The Liberation [1]
(Million Dinars)

Description		1991[2]					
		March	April	May	June	July	Total
Withdrawals	In KD	48.7	194.9	934.9	206.0	131.7	1,516.2
	In FC[3]	4.1	75.6	168.0	66.5	41.7	355.9
	Total	52.8	270.5	1,102.9	272.6	173.4	1,872.2
Deposits	In KD	41.0	196.5	183.6	127.9	97.9	646.9
	In FC	0.1	2.5	16.7	24.4	8.7	52.4
	Total	41.1	199.0	200.3	152.3	106.6	699.3
Withdrawals (-) Deposits	In KD	-7.7	1.6	-751.4	-78.2	-33.8	-869.5
	In FC	-4.1	-73.1	-151.3	-42.1	-33.0	-303.6
	Total	-11.8	-71.5	-902.6	-120.3	-66.7	-1,172.9

[1] Including the Kuwait Finance House, and figures are rounded.
[2] One KD equals 3.4642, 3.4321, 3.4567, 3.4032 and 3.4238 U. S. dollars during these five months respectively.
[3] FC = foreign currency

The CBK was successful in reducing withdrawals substantially to a minimum of KD 173.4 million in July 1991, and thus controls were eased in that month by increasing the maximum limit on withdrawals and transfers allowed for each customer from his accounts in local banks from four thousand dinars to six thousand. Later, on August 3, 1991, these controls were lifted completely and necessary precautions were taken by the CBK to meet any possible large capital outflows. It is worth mentioning here that fewer deposit withdrawals from banks and transfers to foreign currencies occurred than had been anticipated according to various possible scenarios.

b) Deposits at local banks ranged between KD 41.1 million in March 1991 and KD 200.3 million (92% of which were in Kuwaiti dinars) in May 1991, reflecting confidence in the banking and financial system, and reducing the severity of withdrawals, as the difference between withdrawals and deposits was reduced from KD - 902.6 million in May 1991 to only KD -66.7 million in July 1991.

To further encourage deposits at local banks and promote the credibility of the banking system as a whole, the CBK instructed local banks after the liberation to reset the balances of all customers' accounts to what they had been on August 1

, 1990, before the invasion, and to pay interest on savings and fixed deposit accounts for the whole period of the Iraqi occupation of Kuwait.

2. Confidence In The Kuwaiti Dinar:

Monetary policy instruments differ in their effectiveness according to the different economic and monetary circumstances within which they work. The KD exchange rate system is suitable to Kuwait's economic and monetary stability, being practical and consistent with the principal features of the Kuwaiti economy. In the forefront of these features are the dependence on the production and export of oil, which is priced and paid for in U. S. dollars, the crucial role of imports in satisfying a substantial portion of domestic aggregate demand within Kuwait's free trade and payments system (that places no constraints on currency transfers), and lastly the openness of the Kuwaiti economy in areas of trading and investing abroad, which necessitates regulating the flow of capital to and from the domestic economy, in addition to limiting speculation on the Kuwaiti dinar.

The present KD exchange rate system has been in force since March 18, 1975. It involves a linkage with a special basket of currencies, and was quite effective in maintaining stability before the invasion, and played a vital role immediately after the liberation in restoring the confidence in and stability of the Kuwaiti economy in general, and the banking and the financial sector in particular. The need for confidence and stability stemmed from the anticipated rush on customers' accounts at local banks, and the expected money conversions from the Kuwaiti dinar to foreign currency.

Two important facts illustrate the favorable outcome of the KD exchange rate system in maintaining confidence and stability:

a) The average buying and selling rates of the U.S. dollar against the Kuwaiti dinar, according to the adopted basket of currencies and as declared by the CBK on March 24, 1991 (the first day of bank operations after the liberation), was

287.500 fils, against 287.490 fils on August 1, 1990, the day before the invasion. That an almost identical exchange rate existed between the U.S. dollar and the Kuwaiti dinar before and after the invasion was fundamental in giving the public a clear message of the intention to maintain confidence and stability by resuming the KD exchange rate system from where it had stood before the invasion.

b) The KD exchange rate system continued immediately after the liberation to give relative stability to the KD against major currencies. Specifically, available monthly statistics on two periods before and after the invasion (from January 1985 to July 1990, and from March 1991 to December 1996) reveal that fluctuations in the U.S. dollar exchange rate against the Kuwaiti dinar were at a very small rate if compared with its fluctuations against other major currencies, as the highest rise and lowest decline of the dollar against the dinar were 3.3% and -5.3% in the first period, against only 2.2% and -1.5% in the second period respectively. But fluctuations of the dollar against other major currencies were at much higher rates, as shown in Table 2.

Table 2
The U.S. Dollar Exchange Rate Against the KD and Major Currencies

(I) The First Period (January 1985 - July 1990)

	Highest Increase (%)	Lowest Decline (%)
Sterling pound	8.98	-11.58
Deutsche mark	8.63	-8.96
Swiss franc	9.31	-10.03
French franc	9.08	-7.82
Italian lira	10.63	-6.62
Japanese yen	8.05	-8.21
Kuwaiti dinar	3.31	-5.30

(II) The Second Period (March 1991 - December 1996)

	Highest Increase (%)	Lowest Decline (%)
Sterling pound	16.16	-5.32
Deutsche mark	6.03	-6.86
Swiss franc	6.79	-8.01
French franc	5.85	-6.75
Italian lira	15.22	-6.07
Japanese yen	9.93	-8.38
Kuwaiti dinar	2.17	-1.48

3. **Monetary Stability and Domestic Prices:**

Within the framework of macro-economic efforts to rebuild the productive capabilities of the Kuwaiti economy, stabilize the dinar (domestic currency) and rehabilitate the banking and financial sector, monetary policy was concerned with achieving and maintaining domestic price stability. This concern stemmed from the fact that domestic inflation during this post-invasion period was essentially a combination of shortages in available goods and services due to damaged ports and storage facilities on one side, and high levels of aggregate demand, nourished by excessive domestic liquidity, on the other.

Demand for cash in the post-liberation period was quite noticeable; bank clearings at the CBK indicated a drop in the number of transactions from 211.5 thousand (with a value of KD 366.9 million) in July 1990 to only 62.1 thousand (with a value of KD 229.1 million) in September 1991. It was the responsibility of the CBK to limit the predictable increases in the rate of inflation, which were seen as a reflection of the imbalance between monetary demand and the supply capacity of the economy, in view of the damage to the ports and transport system, and the supply network. Maintaining stability in this broad sense was an essential contribution of monetary policy during the exceptional post-liberation period.

According to the domestic price indicator prepared by the CBK during that period, prices rose in April 1991 by 85% over their level before the invasion (the base period of May 1990), compared with less that two per cent during 1989/90. Fortunately, in the two weeks ending on September 7, 1991, this price indicator showed an increase of only 12.8% over the pre-invasion base period, compared to 9% by the end of December 1991. Available annual data on the CPI (Consumer Price Index) show increases in domestic prices of -0.6%, 0.4%, 2.5% and 2.7% for the four years ending in 1995 respectively.

4. **The Difficult Debt Problem:**

This problem received considerable attention from the CBK during the post-liberation period, stemming from the CBK's conviction about the negative effects which this problem could be expected to have on the ability of the banking and financial sector to perform its role of strengthening the performance of the domestic economic sectors.

The difficult debt problem was initiated by the stock market crash in the early 1980's. The Central Bank of Kuwait began setting the criteria for provisions required against difficult bank debts in 1985, in order to assess the volume of the problem. Later, the CBK introduced the Difficult Credit Facilities Settlement Program, which was implemented starting from the end of 1986. By the end of the first half of 1990 almost 90% of the program was finished.

The difficult debt problem was exacerbated by the Iraqi occupation of Kuwait in 1990, as these debts increased to KD 6,262 million, representing 47% of the aggregate balance sheet of local banks, and covering 10,423 debtors, whose debts had been purchased and managed against Debt Purchase Government Bonds. Thus, post-liberation cleaning up of local banks' balance sheets from the severe and prolonged difficult debt problem has reflected positively on their performance, solvency and profitability, as well as their credit ratings according to international rating agencies.

THE LESSONS LEARNED FROM THE CRISIS

As background information on the effectiveness of these lessons, available statistics reveal that several banking indicators reflected positively the impact of Kuwait's post-liberation period monetary policy; these indicators included the following:

1. an increase in net profits of local banks to KD 129 million in 1995, representing a rise of 35.2% over the previous year, and showing the highest profits since 1984.

2. a rise in private deposits at local banks from KD 5,780.6 million immediately after the liberation (end of March 1991) to levels the minimum of which was KD 5,297.6 million at the end of August 1992, and the maximum of which was KD 7,089.2 million. More recently, private deposits at local banks at the end of October 1996 were KD 6,873.5 million, an increase of KD 1,092.9 million and 18.9% over their level of March 1991.

3. a high average capital adequacy ratio of local banks of 28% in 1995, against the minimum required ratio of 8% according to international standards.

4. relatively good credit ratings, which the State and local banks have received lately from international ratings agencies.

Although these banking indicators are examples of the rapid and outstanding recovery of the Kuwaiti banks from the financial crisis inflicted on them by the Iraqi invasion, they do not represent the ultimate goals and aspirations of monetary policy in Kuwait. The future outlook of the CBK's monetary policy includes ways to further improve the performance of the banking and financial system, and increase its effectiveness in serving the national economy. Specifically, the CBK is seeking to achieve in coming years, with the aid of mergers and foreign participation, banking and financial units that are capable of producing outstanding performance, of meeting international standards and of providing excellent services and free competition, locally and abroad.

On the level of lessons learned from the crisis of the Iraqi invasion, Kuwait has won international commendation for the expert financial management skills it demonstrated from the time of the Iraqi occupation in 1990/91. With its country under foreign occupation, its productive sectors shut down, its domestic institutions inoperative, the Kuwaiti authorities in exile nevertheless managed and controlled the country's extensive financial holdings worldwide, stabilizing its dispersed financial institutions, and putting in place a post-liberation restructuring scheme. The lessons of the Iraqi invasion cover a wide range, including the value of analytical skills, cooperative communication, experienced and dedicated personnel, clear lines of authority, well-understand procedures, and flexibility.

The first lesson learned from the Iraqi invasion was the value of having a strong, flexible, knowledgeably-run institutional infrastructure already firmly in place before the crisis occurred. Like buildings in an earthquake, those institutions survive the greatest stresses which have the strongest foundations. It would not be too much to say that the groundwork for Kuwait's successful financial management during the Iraqi occupation had been laid many years before. In a crisis, decisions must often be taken in a minimum of time and with a minimum of information, relying on the analytical wisdom of experienced authorities. Such analytical skills are acquired over time, within a well-organized system. Kuwait's monetary authorities operated in just such a milieu before the invasion; its soundness was proven in the crisis of 1990/91.

Specific characteristics of that effective system were shown to be of crucial value during the occupation. These involved the relationship between the CBK and the local banks. Clearly-defined principles, based on a legal and administrative framework, have always governed the interaction between the CBK and the banks. In the years before the invasion, various functions and supervisory rules of the CBK were specified, and the obligations of the banking system were laid out.

As a result, over the years the banking sector had become accustomed to the impartial authority of the central bank, and to the procedures for operating and reporting required of them. There was continual communication and information-sharing among them, recognizing that understanding between the CBK and the banks under its supervision could not be based solely on the figures on the balance sheet.

Furthermore, this lesson learned from the Iraqi invasion about the necessity of having strong and efficient financial institutions explains the CBK's efforts after the liberation to achieve the following:

a)   enhancing the professional performance of the Kuwaiti banks. These efforts required the CBK to adopt new supervisory systems, among which were the regulations on maximum credit concentration, the required conditions for members of banks' boards of directors to obtain credit facilities from their banks, and the required experience that ought to be expected of members of banks' boards of directors, and of top executives of these banks;

b) reforming the financial system base through the termination of financial companies which were not capable of continuing their activities by means of effective financial systems that were accepted locally and internationally. Also, the CBK requested able companies to strengthen their capital base, and to reform their internal control systems;

c) expanding the diversified base of the banking and financial system through the establishment of new investment companies that can perform their activities according to Islamic principles, and the preparation of a new legislation pertaining to Islamic banking, currently in progress.

An effective working relationship among the banks was the second lesson of the Iraqi invasion of Kuwait. A close, well-established working relationship between the CBK and its constituent banks was evident in the dispatch with which the CBK restructured the Kuwaiti banks in order to secure their operations and enable them to continue to honor or settle foreign transactions. Directives governing the replacement of bank officers and the reorganization of authorized signatures were issued, adopted and communicated to international authorities. The decision to abrogate currency notes of the KD Third Issue as legal tender was handled as smoothly. These actions point to an efficient monetary authority, accustomed to lines of authority and cooperative operations.

The crisis of the invasion taught us, as a third lesson, that we were right in adhering to the principle of honoring all our commitments and obligations, no matter how costly and troublesome they might be. To get around these commitments and obligations by not honoring them would have caused us many problems, one of which would have been lost confidence and respect in our banking system. This explains why the Kuwaiti banks were instructed to settle all their out-standing transactions with their counter-parties abroad, to set their customers' accounts at their August 1, 1990 levels, and to pay interest on savings and fixed deposit accounts for the entire period of the occupation.

Honoring our commitments and obligations without hesitation recalls a statement which I made in a speech in 1991: "As a central bank, God willing, we shall prove to all in Kuwait, as well as in the region and the world, that we are capable of overcoming all challenges put to us, and time shall testify to this."[4]

The need to be able to accurately assess a crisis situation was the fourth lesson garnered from the Iraqi invasion of Kuwait. In the sudden, precipitous crisis, Kuwait's monetary authorities were able to assess the danger accurately to take decisions and initiate effective action. They recognized the threat to the currency, to the credibility of the banking and financial sector, to national assets, and to the well-being of Kuwaitis in exile, and drew up plans for both the short- and long-run.

The fifth lesson the crisis taught us was to anticipate possible developments and events. Since time should be used most efficiently during any crisis, considered measures and timely actions are needed, the CBK was faced with this task. For example, the CBK expected that during the period immediately following liberation there would be massive withdrawals from customers' accounts at local banks, and conversions from KD into foreign currencies. The CBK developed practical views on possible criteria with which to counter that challenge with flexibility, resulting in the gradual application of controls during a specific period of time, after which they would be eliminated.

The importance of being in continual communication with other monetary and financial authorities was the sixth lesson. For example, the CBK consulted with the Ministry of Finance and the Kuwait Investment Authority, and with GCC (Gulf Cooperation Council) monetary authorities. It also communicated with the IMF, the World Bank and other international financial and monetary authorities. As the restructured Kuwaiti banks assumed control in various areas, the CBK communicated requests to the authorities in these areas to lift the freeze on Kuwaiti assets which had been implemented to prevent their looting by the Iraqi occupiers. Given the magnitude of these agreements, it is clear that a spirit of cooperation and trust existed between the Kuwaiti monetary authorities and those of the international community.

Recognizing the importance of plans and procedures for post-liberation restoration constitutes the seventh lesson. This planning would better enable the concerned authorities to direct the course of future events toward specific goals, and allow more control over unforeseen challenges. This task further demonstrated the analytical skill and institutional organization of the Kuwaiti monetary authorities, who recognized that phased limitations and phased operations must be built into their plans, to accommodate changed circumstances as reconstruction proceeded. Hence a "transition" period was designated, and the flexibility of the system was called upon to make the modifications in operations that would become necessary as time passed.

The eighth lesson, a substantial one, was to give priority and concern to the stabilization policies; these polices were altogether necessary in light of the war-shattered economy and the disordered banking and financial sector which remained in the wake of the occupation. They involved the CBK's tireless efforts to defend the stability of the Kuwaiti dinar after liberation.

We must admit that any noticeable decrease in the KD exchange rate, no matter how it could be justified on economic bases, would have created a general expectation that further decreases were possible and would be implemented soon. This lesson learned from the crisis would make us give priority to stabilization policies in general, and to those connected with the national currency in particular.

The way the CBK anticipated and reacted to the negative repercussions of the difficult debt problem on local banks' activities constitutes the ninth lesson of the crisis. The severity of these expected repercussions explains the reason why this problem received so much attention from the CBK during the post-liberation period. One might say that the greatest achievement in solving this problem, according to the CBK's views, was in handling it through two phases, the first of which was aimed at cleaning up local banks' balance sheets from this severe and prolonged difficult debt problem, and the second of which was concerned with views on how to treat the local banks' collection of debts from their customers whose financial positions had been negatively affected by the Iraqi invasion. Cleaning up the balance sheets, through Debt Purchase Government Bonds, was a necessary first step to allow these banks to properly perform their role in the national economy.

Apart from the negative impact of the crisis on the physical facilities of the banking and financial sector, that impact on monetary authority personnel and bank officers should also be assessed as the human element and is the tenth lesson learned from the crisis. The CBK maintained continuous contact with its officers in different countries, so as to be able to mobilize them upon liberation. It is proper during crises not to lose track of trained employees, since training new ones would be very costly time - and money - wise. As a matter of fact, some of these officers were working in exile for the CBK, which had a strong presence in exile. Needless to say, the monetary policy personnel, who were working for the CBK in exile, were put under severe pressure, and were on call for duty continuously. Here the crisis taught us the value of qualified persons, who can use their mettle to face problems and difficulties fast, and in an assured and confident manner. These dedicated and experienced persons, as they lived the crisis, turned its agony into challenges, and its fearful situation into assured confidence and optimism.

It is clear that Kuwait's ability to withstand the massive shock to its banking and financial system posed by the Iraqi occupation was made possible by the maturity and soundness of the CBK, as well as the banking and financial institutions, operating within an economy which has for years been characterized by openness and interaction with the outside world. This openness appears in the absence of controls on the transfer of capital funds abroad, and in the fact that exchange rates on the KD have for years been linked to a basket of currencies, giving the Kuwaiti currency its enviable stability. The entire system is stabilized by the clearly-delineated supervision of the nation's banking and financial institutions by the CBK.

In conclusion, there are no guarantees against crisis, and Goldman Sachs Chairman E. Gerald Corrigan has said: "… at the end of the day, it is that great intangible of the credibility of the central bank and its leaders that will be decisive".[5] Kuwait's monetary authorities have built and sustained such credibility through a massive crisis.

NOTES

[1] Meier, G. M., and Baldwin, R. E., Economic Development (New York: John Wiley, 1957), page 139.
[2] One KD equals 3.5235 U. S. dollars.
[3] The date when Kuwaiti banks resumed their normal activities.
[4] "Crucial Tasks of the Central Bank of Kuwait During the Iraqi Invasion and After the Liberation of Kuwait," delivered on November 30, 1991, in Manama, Bahrain, on the occasion of the 17th Inter-Arab Cambist Association.
[5] An address on: "Central Bank Management of Financial Crisis," delivered on October 25, 1995 in Shanghai, China.

PART VI

THE ROLE OF THE IMF

15

Financial Crisis Management And The Role Of The IMF: 1970-1995[1]

AGE F. P. BAKKER
Deputy Governor, Central Bank of The Netherlands
AREND J. KAPTEYN
Economist, Monetary and Economic Policy Department, Central Bank of The Netherlands

INTRODUCTION

From the IMF's point of view, the period covered by this book starts with the most disturbing crisis of all: the fall of the Bretton Woods system. For an institution whose primary responsibility had been to watch over a system of fixed parities, the floating of exchange rates posed a direct challenge to the Fund's legitimacy. As we shall argue, however, the Fund quickly regained its central position within the international monetary system due to its pivotal role in four major financial crises. The Fund's leadership in combating these crises is the focus of this paper.

We start out by describing the origins and workings of the IMF, particularly as the monetary character of the Fund makes it uniquely different from other international organizations. As such, it enables the Fund to react to financial crises with a remarkable degree of flexibility and decisiveness. We then proceed to discuss the Fund's role in four crises, notably the oil crisis, the debt crisis, the collapse of centrally planned economies, and the Mexico crisis. This will be followed by lessons drawn from the Fund's role in these events and some concluding remarks.

BACKGROUND OF THE IMF

Origins And Objectives

The role envisioned for the International Monetary Fund in the management of financial crises is inextricably bound to the unique historical circumstances in which the Fund was founded in Bretton Woods, New Hampshire, in 1944. As one author put it: "The last forty years had been dominated by two major wars, several minor wars, vast expenditures preparing for wars, and large expenditures to repair the damages of wars.[2]" From an economic viewpoint and particularly that of the international monetary system, competitive devaluations, the sharp contraction of world trade (60% between 1929-32), and memories of the Great Depression of the 1930s were fresh in the minds of those present at the conference.

History conveys that it is only after severe crises and widespread conflicts that fertile grounds are found for the gathering of international consensus on norms of behavior to avert their re-emergence[3]. The order which countries set out to establish in 1944 is a direct reflection of these painful memories. On the diplomatic front, this led to the creation of the United Nations, while economically, the International Monetary Fund (IMF), International Bank for Reconstruction and Development (IBRD) and the General Agreements for Tariffs and Trade (GATT) were established. The IMF principles in particular, contrasted the destructive beggar-thy-neighbor policies of the interwar period (see Box 1).

Box 1

The Articles of Agreement state that: "The purposes of the International Monetary Fund are:
i)   to promote international monetary cooperation through a permanent institution which provides the machinery for consultation and collaboration on international monetary problems;
ii) to facilitate the expansion and balanced growth of international trade, and to contribute thereby to the promotion and maintenance of high levels of employment and real income and to the development of the productive resources of all members as primary objectives of economic policy;
iii) to promote exchange stability, to maintain orderly exchange arrangements among members, and to avoid competitive exchange depreciation;
iv) to assist in the establishment of a multilateral system of payments in respects of current transactions between members and in the elimination of foreign exchange restrictions which hamper the growth of world trade;
v)   to give confidence to members by making the general resources of the Fund temporarily available to them under adequate safeguards, thus providing them with opportunity to correct maladjustments in their balance of payments without resorting to measures destructive of national or international prosperity; and
vi) in accordance with the above, to shorten the duration and lessen the degree of disequilibrium in the international balances of payments of members."

The central features of the international monetary system which emerged from these deliberations were a fixed but adjustable exchange rate system anchored to the US dollar whereby the dollar was in turn linked to gold, and a monetary framework in which current account transactions predominated and international capital flows were limited. The dominance of the current account over the capital account reflected the reality that trade and invisibles made up the bulk of the balance of payments at the time (even though it took some time before current account transactions were fully liberalized). In fact, due to the experience of the interwar period, countries explicitly did not wish to liberalize capital flows and most maintained an elaborate system of capital restrictions[4]. In this environment, US willingness to run sustained current account deficits provided ample liquidity for balanced growth of international trade. In combination with the "self-enforcing" nature of the par value system (the rules-based system rendered domestic policymaking, and with it international policy coordination, largely endogenous), this resulted in an extended period of remarkable stability.

Two major changes in the world economy added instability to the system. The first source of instability was of course the fall of the par value system in 1971 and the subsequent floating of exchange rates in March 1973.[5] This led to a "re-nationalization" of economic policy making as the international monetary system gradually shifted in emphasis from rules (the par value system) to discretion (a country's ability to determine its own exchange rate and, consequently, its own economic policies). As surveillance of the international monetary system became more informal, the Fund became reliant on bilateral consultations with its member states to monitor performance and peer pressure to encourage remedial measures judged necessary[6]. The second major development adding instability to the system was the tremendous increase in gross capital flows between countries, due to a combination of capital account liberalization, technological advances and financial innovations. These gross flows, consisting of portfolio investment, currency exchange transactions etc., were not only much larger in size than needed to finance current account imbalances but also much more volatile[7].

Surveillance Function Vs. Financial Function

To maintain its influence (and some semblance of control) over the international monetary system, the Fund reevaluated its two primary instruments in preventing and dealing with monetary disturbances: surveillance and credit facilities.

A key role of the IMF had always been to map out externalities of member states' financial policies. In the new setting where exchange arrangements were left to the choice of countries, policy assessments would need to rely on judgement to a greater extent. The surveillance principle seeks to draw a road map that lays down the constraints that apply to national discretion: "one of the tasks of Fund surveillance will be to identify exchange rate policies leading to inappropriate rates at an early stage, and thus to reduce the economic costs and international frictions associated with such rates"[8]. In this context, annual bilateral consultations were introduced (so called article IV-consultations) which were to increase the Fund's awareness of problems that might potentially disturb financial systems. Also, due to the greater interdependence and spill-over effects of countries' individual policies, studies were made of these effects in, for instance, the bi-annual World Economic Outlook exercise. In this context, orderly adjustment by countries making temporary use of the Fund's credit facilities was intended to remain a fall-back position only.

However, the floating rate system did not achieve what its proponents had envisaged: instead of the exchange rate behaving as an `automatic' adjustment mechanism correcting imbalances, exchange rate movements sometimes exacerbated domestic problems by engendering devaluation/inflation spirals. The 1970s were a decade of experiments by governments which until then had only been tested in the laboratory of economic textbook models. Because there was no consensus among policy makers, nor among academics for that matter, on how to respond to balance-of-payments disturbances caused by the oil crises, economic policies among countries diverged. These divergences reflected partly different degrees of tolerance for domestic price inflation, which in turn led to large exchange rate movements and external imbalances. The need to finance balance-of-payments deficits and to restore confidence in the exchange rate explains the larger IMF involvement in credit extension after the demise of the fixed exchange rate system.

The IMF As A Monetary Institution

Despite the fact that the IMF is not a lender of last resort in the traditional (central bank) sense of the word - indeed this was the role envisioned by Keynes - the financial structure of the Fund is uniquely suited to dealing with liquidity problems of its member states. The reason is that the IMF is in fact a club of members wishing to share responsibility for the stability of the international monetary system. This club is financed by the pooled resources of its members, mainly the foreign reserves of its member states' central banks, which can be temporarily lent out to another club member in times of crises. As these resources (quotas) continue to form part of a member state's foreign reserves while in use by the IMF, the member state maintains the right of immediate withdrawal of the foreign exchange inlay. As such, a member state's quota has to remain highly liquid, implying that money lent out not only has to be paid back (in its entire history the IMF, which has a preferred creditor status, has never written off a loan from its general resources), but it also has to be paid back relatively quickly (the loans need to have a revolving character). This implies that, in the absence of major crises, only a small portion of the resource pool will be lent out.

In principle, about 50% of the currencies laid in are considered liquid resources usable for lending; a logical reflection of the fact that against countries with a balance of payments deficit there are countries with a balance of payments surplus, whose reserves are available for lending to deficit countries via the IMF. In practice, the usable stock of liquid currencies is slightly smaller due to a downward adjustment to maintain working balances and to account for the possibility that the currencies of some members in relatively weak external positions could become unusable in financing Fund operations and transactions. At present, out of the IMF pool of US$210 billion, outstanding credit amounts to US$36 billion (excluding the concessional Enhanced Structural Adjustment Facility, which is financed separately, mostly by donors). An amount of US$48 billion of usable currencies is still readily available for credit extension. Under the General Arrangements to Borrow and the New Arrangements to Borrow another amount of US$47 billion is available from the Group of Ten and other countries, if the Fund's resources need to be supplemented to deal with exceptional circumstances that pose a threat to the stability of the system.

The IMF's monetary character and financial structure thus have an important implication. In cases where private capital flows are not forthcoming or reserves have been depleted, the IMF - with its pool of untapped resources - has the flexibility to respond quickly to unexpected shocks to the system (the Fund's resources have been the equivalent of about 5% of world imports over recent decades)[9]. Because the IMF is in the business of judging and helping design comprehensive macro-economic programmes for its member states (and has the economic expertise to do so), it is well placed for formulating an appropriate response to more systemic crises. This pivotal role is derived in part from the almost universal membership of the institution and in part from the concentration of macro-economic expertise within the Fund. For example, a restructuring of debt in the London and Paris Club is usually made conditional on the existence of a track record under a Fund program.

Interestingly enough, this leverage comes at relatively little cost to the IMF's creditor members; the only real cost of operating the Fund is the lost income resulting from the interest rate differential between the market rate of interest and the rate of remuneration (a minimum of 80% of the SDR-interest rate) paid by the IMF to member states over the holdings of their reserve position. A back-of-the-envelope calculation for the Netherlands indicates that, based on the current interest rate differential of 200 basis points, this lost income is in the order of US$27 million per annum. By comparison, if this operating cost were a budgetary item this would amount to less than 1% of the Ministry of Foreign Affairs' development cooperation budget. Similar calculations for the United Kingdom and France yield an annual cost of US$25 million and US$40 million per annum, respectively. The differences in lost income between countries reflect relative quota size and use by the Fund of respective currencies[10]. Of course, the lost income comes at the expense of the central bank's profits and thus ultimately lowers the transfer of central bank profit to the Ministry of Finance. The debtor countries of the IMF benefit from this: otherwise they would have to borrow at much higher interest rates in the financial markets assuming that they would have access. For some poor member countries the finance made available by multilateral institutions is the only external source of capital available.

The Rationale For Fund Involvement In Financial Crises

As in other areas of government intervention, the general rationale for the IMF's role is vested in the inadequate provision of public goods or in the existence of market imperfections, both of which IMF lending can help to remedy[11]. Free trade is such a public good. By providing exceptional finance in the event of adverse balance of payments problems, be it a trade shock or a sudden reversal of capital flows, the IMF can provide countries with insurance for orderly adjustment on reasonable terms. History shows that private financial markets are unable to provide such insurance, either because the interest rate charged is prohibitively high, or because they are simply unwilling to lend altogether This access to additional financing in times of crises is welfare-enhancing. By allowing countries to smooth out their adjustment process over time, economic disruption is minimized and the country is enabled to stay current in its international obligations without resorting to (capital) restrictions. The latter would not only be painful for the country itself, but would also generate unfavorable externalities for other countries.

Another public good is exchange rate stability. Even though the par value system no longer exists, the IMF still has a role to play in preventing competitive devaluations by promoting adjustment of domestic policies toward sustainable exchange rate stability and by stimulating policy coordination among major industrial countries. Furthermore, an understanding about the workings of the international monetary system, and knowledge about what constitutes healthy economic policy are also public goods, both of which the IMF seeks to address through its technical assistance and surveillance activities.

The IMF's policy advice can help alleviate market imperfections. If there is a mismatch between borrowers and investors due to a lack of information about a country's creditworthiness or the viability of its economic policies, the commitment of IMF resources in support of an adjustment program can signal a seal of approval of a member's policies and, as such, catalyze other sources of finance. A lack of information can also lead to sudden shifts in investor sentiment. A recent example is the large inflow of capital into Latin America in the late 1980s and early 1990s and the sudden reversal in the case of Mexico. Through its surveillance the IMF can encourage a more timely and comprehensive flow of statistics to financial markets, thus reducing the likelihood of sudden and disruptive market reactions.

FOUR POST-BRETTON WOODS CRISES

The unique financial structure of the IMF has not only put it in a perfect position to deal with financial crises in the period covered in this book (1970-1995), but it has also used these crises to bolster its legitimacy as an overseer of the international monetary system; even after the fall of the Bretton Woods system. Figure 1 illustrates this point.

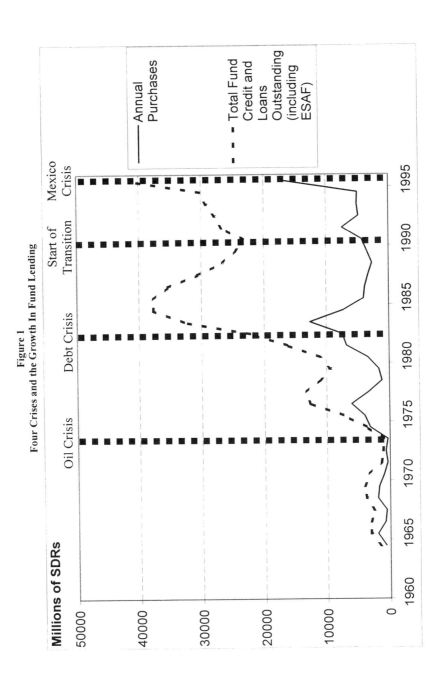

Figure 1
Four Crises and the Growth In Fund Lending

Prior to the fall of the par value system, Fund lending was relatively subdued; but the IMF's importance within the international monetary system was undisputed. Following the breakdown of the fixed rate agreement, however, (and failed efforts to revive some sort of exchange rate system) Fund lending fell to historic lows while at the same time uncertainty arose as to what role the IMF should continue to play. This uncertainty abruptly came to an end when the Fund was catapulted into leadership in four major crises. The precise role of the IMF in these crises, and the connected explosion in Fund lending, will be the focus of the remainder of this paper.

The Oil Crises

The announcement by the Organization of Petroleum Exporting Countries (OPEC) of a sharp price increase of oil (December 1973), evoked a sense of economic crisis that had been absent for several decades[12]. A key factor in the good economic growth performance of industrial countries - the availability of cheap and abundant energy - was suddenly removed. Imbalances in international payments on an unprecedented scale were expected, as well as a substantial drop in world demand for goods and services[13]. In the absence of agreed rules for international behavior under the floating exchange rate regime, there was a real danger of beggar-thy-neighbor policies.

The marked shifts in the pattern of world payments radically altered the concept of what constituted a sustainable international balance of payments structure. In the past, the modest current account deficits of developing countries were financed by modest capital account deficits of industrial countries. Now that these latter countries would also have current account deficits, it was unclear as to how the small group of OPEC countries would finance the combined non-OPEC current account deficit. Given the small population in OPEC countries it was unlikely that their increased imports could offset more than a very small portion of the substantial deficits. The asymmetry between the country groups seemed to indicate a structural problem rather than a financial one; basic changes in the patterns of consumption and production of oil importing countries would be necessary. Resort to traditional monetary and fiscal responses or a devaluation of currencies would risk only shifting the deficits between non-OPEC countries.

The key question, was how to ensure appropriate financing of the enlarged current account deficits by recycling surplus OPEC revenues. Although it was recognized that the international financial markets, such as the Eurodollar market, had an important role to play, there seemed to be distinct limits on the ability of private markets to borrow from oil exporters on short-term and re-lend to oil importers on medium-term. There was no guarantee that surplus funds would find their way to oil importing countries that needed them most, particularly developing countries. In addition, lending to governments was a wholly new development in international private banking. Thus, the international financial system was faced with a clear case of a market coordination problem, requiring some sort of official facility to bridge the transition period in which long-term solutions could be worked out.

On January 3, 1974, only eleven days after the OPEC announcement, IMF Managing Director Witteveen proposed that a special temporary facility to finance oil deficits be set up in the Fund; the proposal was approved on January 17th. This decision was made amidst considerable uncertainty and opposition. The US administration, in particular, viewed the establishment of such a facility as tantamount to underwriting the OPEC cartel's higher prices (which they refused to accept). Moreover, Treasury Secretary Schultz was worried that developing countries without alternative sources of financing, which would have to borrow for several years, would be unable to repay the loans. Loans to these countries would endanger the revolving nature of the Fund's financial resources. The Fund would, in effect, be substituting its own high credit standing in international financial markets for the low credit standing of many very poor developing members, it was feared.

Since the Fund's resources had been little used in the early 1970s, it would have been possible to use the Fund's own resources for the oil facility. However, this would have tied up the Fund's resources for one particular purpose and pre-empted alternative uses. In addition, the initial main-stream reaction to the oil crisis was Keynesian in character, with the aim to finance and thus counteract the immediate drop in demand rather than adjust. An oil facility with such low conditionality[14] would have conflicted with the Fund's established policy on credit facilities. Consequently, it was decided that the Fund would borrow the funds. The IMF's own resources could then be used to finance more comprehensive economic programs (with stricter conditionality) in the medium-term; notable examples among industrialized countries were Italy and the U.K. in 1974-75 and again in 1976-77. As the Fund would have to pay a market interest rate over the loans, it set up a separate subsidy account to reduce developing countries' interest rates. The subsidy account was an innovative step in the Fund's evolution. Constrained by the principle of uniformity of treatment in its normal operations (i.e. no differentiation between member states is allowed), the subsidy account was set up outside the Fund's general resources. It was the first account for which the Fund served as a trustee; in this way it laid the basis for establishment of future concessional facilities for developing countries (the Trust Fund in 1976, the Structural Adjustment Facility in 1986, and the Enhanced Structural Adjustment Facility in 1987).

At the end of 1974, when a decision had to be made to extend the oil facility by another year, commercial banks had vastly increased their international lending operations and were in effect recycling the OPEC surpluses. Nevertheless, two factors seemed to warrant continuance of the oil facility. In the first place, following the failure of the Herstatt Bank in June, concern had arisen that commercial banks might be endangering their liquidity positions and becoming overexposed. At the same time, there was some concern that policy makers focused too much on the financing of large deficits, rather than on adjusting the level of oil imports. An extension of the IMF oil facility - with envisioned stricter conditionality - could alleviate both these concerns.

In all, between September 1974 and May 1976, when the oil facility was ended, 55 members drew a total of almost US$10 billion in 156 transactions. Thus, the amount of money made available under the oil facility was small compared to the huge payments imbalances eventually financed. Nevertheless, because the money was made available so shortly after the onset of the oil crisis and continued until alternative financial arrangements took hold, it served as a bridge between the old era of cheap oil and the new era of expensive oil[15]. This was particularly true for developing countries which formed the vast majority of those countries drawing on the oil facility. The facility was also the first time the IMF undertook to help finance massive balance of payments deficits for its members. At a time when relations between many countries were strained, the arrangement succeeded in managing the consequences of the oil price increase in a multilateral framework, without countries resorting to destructive trade measures (16 countries had lent money to the oil facility while 25 countries contributed to the subsidy account). Despite these successes, however, it is questionable whether the Fund's reaction to the first oil shock - with its emphasis on finance rather than adjustment - was entirely appropriate. In the end, the accommodation of price rises helped fuel inflationary expectations and helped finance increased budget deficits and, as such, contributed to the stagflationary experiences of many countries. No oil facility was created to combat the second oil crises in 1978. In a way, the second oil shock itself evidenced the lack of adjustment that had taken place after 1974 and 1975. Attention had to shift from financing deficits to adjustment, for which the IMF's regular facilities would prove to be adequate.

The Debt Crisis In The 1980s

In retrospect, it is fair to say that the way in which the oil crisis was handled was a major determinant of the debt crisis. Many countries which borrowed heavily after the first oil shock (due to a combination of surplus dollars and negative real interest rates) did not use the capital flows for productive investments. In 1978 the total debt of non-oil developing countries had increased to US$336 billion, two and a half times its 1973 level (US$130 billion). Many projects were initiated not because they were economically sound but because they had found external commercial financing which, directly or indirectly, was guaranteed by a sovereign debtor[16]. When the well of petrodollars suddenly dried up and debt service obligations increased (due to a combination of floating-rate contracts and rising US interest rates), the debt became unserviceable[17].

Despite the fact that Mexico's default may have been an accident waiting to happen, Mexico's announcement in August 1982 that it could no longer service its US$86 billion of external debt came as a surprise. The world had not been fully aware of the high concentration of the less-developed countries' (LDC) debt within a small group of countries (of total LDC debt of US$700 billion nearly half was owed by eight countries) and the dramatic shortening of maturities. This debt was, in turn, highly concentrated in the loan portfolios of American banks and accounted for 70% of US banks' claims on the LDCs. Fear emerged that debt defaults or moratoria by two or three large debtor nations could seriously damage the financial positions of the world's largest banks and therewith put the stability of the global financial system at risk[18]. The 69% drop in net international bank lending to LDCs between 1982-83 was similar to the international liquidity squeeze suffered by debtor nations after the 1929 catastrophe. Bank failures in the US rose from an average of 8 in 1977-79 to 42 in 1982, 48 in 1983 and 79 in 1984. By the end of 1986, more than 40 countries in Latin America, Africa and elsewhere had encountered severe external financing problems.

In a rescue operation by the US Government in cooperation with the other G-10 countries, a series of short-term bridging loans were provided to allow time for an IMF-program to be arranged. However, it quickly became clear that even the approved SDR 3.6 billion Fund package for Mexico in December 1982 would not be enough. As Managing Director de Larosière put it: "it is simply not possible for borrowing countries to go from a situation in which they were absorbing US$50 billion a year of net new lending from commercial banks to one where inflows are zero or negative without disastrous consequences for both current welfare and future development prospect.[19]" In this sense the IMF viewed the crisis at least in part as a liquidity crisis and it was of the opinion that net new financing would also have to come from commercial banks which up till then had been the main providers of capital.

Circumstances at the time did not encourage lenders to provide further resources to indebted countries, and this situation called for an important innovation in IMF policies and procedures, the introduction of "concerted" lending packages. In a radical departure from past practice the IMF began to require creditors to provide firm assurances of the availability of external financing before it would move with its own support of the debtor adjustment program. A critical mass of commitments of external assistance thus became a prerequisite for the completion of an arrangement with the IMF. The Fund staff worked out how much the developing countries could afford to pay their creditors and compared this with the debt-service that was due. The resulting "financing-gap" was to be filled by new loans. For Mexico alone the Fund succeeded in arranging a US$5 billion financing package involving 530 commercial banks and by February 1983 the Fund approved a similar SDR 5 billion package for Brazil.

In this way, the IMF moved to catalyze capital flows toward countries willing and able to undertake an adjustment in their economies; stand-by arrangements from the Fund became the center-piece of all rescheduling agreements (during 1985 and 1986 almost two thirds of total net bank lending to developing countries took the form of concerted lending). At the same time, the IMF also increased its possibilities to finance debtor countries by introducing the policy of enlarged access to the Fund's resources. Cumulative access limits of a member's quota were raised from 100 or 165% of quota (the limit for stand-by and extended fund facilities respectively) to a cumulative total of 607% of quota[20].

Concerted lending was intended as a stopgap measure meant to buy time for countries to resume growth. Indeed, by 1985 Fund programs in Latin America had been successful at turning a combined 1982 US$51 billion trade deficit into a US$7 billion trade surplus. The weakness of the strategy was that it depended on a rapid resumption of production growth in the debtor countries - on the idea that the capacity to repay debt would start to grow faster than the debt itself. By 1985, however, growth had not yet resumed and, due to the obligation to ensure the revolving nature of its resources, the IMF's wings were clipped: the Fund was receiving more in debt-service from the heavily indebted developing countries than it was extending in new loans. Fund financing could not be continued at the levels of the beginning of the debt crisis, and its involvement was in some cases limited to "enhanced surveillance" and monitoring of a country's policies[21].

The Brady plan of 1989 signaled the failure of the "muddling through" strategy, i.e. the Baker plan (1985-1989) with its emphasis on sustained lending in exchange for adjustment. A central feature of the new approach was that the IMF and World Bank were urged to provide funding for debt service reduction - as opposed to rescheduling - purposes. In addition, the IMF was urged to modify its practice of delaying its own disbursements to debtors until commercial bank creditors had agreed to reschedule their own lending commitments. The original rationale for this IMF practice was the institution's desire to overcome a market coordination problem and push banks into concerted lending, but, by 1989, IMF financing had turned into a bargaining chip used by the banks against the debtors. This required a number of adjustments in IMF policies. A modification of its financing policy, so that arrangements with the IMF could become effective even before the completion of negotiations with creditors on a financing package; the lengthening and increase of funds available under the Extended Fund Facility (a credit facility with a longer duration than a normal stand-by program and with more focus on structural policies); the expansion and adaptation of a financial facility to deal with unforeseen contingencies (Compensatory and Contingency Financing Facility); and a cautious tolerance of arrears, typically linked to a well-defined plan for their eventual elimination.

In the end, the debt crises turned out to be much more a question of getting development back on track than one of providing temporary liquidity. This is not to say that the role of the IMF was not pivotal in staving off the imminent danger of widespread defaults in the years immediately following Mexico's default - it was. However, when the combination of short term financing and adjustment proved insufficient to alleviate the solvability problem, the Fund was unable to provide the leadership necessary for the eventual (required) reduction of the debt burdens of its membership (although the IMF played an important role in propagating the notion of debt reduction). With regard to the Fund's own claims on its membership, this inability logically followed from the IMF's special mandate as a monetary institution; debt reduction would be equivalent to giving away other member states' reserves. Even if individual member states, i.e. the owners of Fund capital, voted in favor of such a give-away scheme, this would in all likelihood be to the detriment of countries' future willingness to provide the IMF with new financing[22].

The Transition From Centrally Planned To Market Oriented Economies (1989-)

The fall of the Berlin wall and the subsequent shift in economic focus in the former centrally planned economies constituted a momentous event, but perhaps not a crisis in the sense of the oil and debt crises described above. Nevertheless, the systemic transformation provided an historic opportunity for over 25 countries to cast off the shackles of communism and embark on a more promising future. Indeed, not just for economic reasons; life expectancy in Eastern Europe and the Soviet Union had been declining since the mid-1960s; unprecedented for developed countries in peacetime. With the application for membership by the former Soviet bloc countries, the IMF was getting close to being a universal institution.

Coming to the aid of the transforming economies was (and is) within the mandate of the Fund: CMEA trade collapsed and, due to the systemic inefficiencies in production, the former centrally planned economies were likely to experience a sustained period of balance of payments imbalances. More practically, however, the centralized systems of microeconomic management would need to be replaced with macroeconomic management through fiscal and monetary policies. Economic agents now had to react to market signals instead of executing instructions from the center. Due to the general lack of expertise in these areas in transition countries, the Fund initiated a spectacular rise in its technical assistance, particularly in the area of monetary control, tax administration, banking legislation and supervision, reform of the payments and settlements systems, and statistical systems. As a result, between 1989/90 and 1993/94 technical assistance missions doubled[23]. In addition, normal Fund programs were initiated, and in 1993 the Executive Board of the IMF created a new temporary facility, the Systemic Transformation Facility, "specifically designed to extend financial assistance to members experiencing severe disruptions in their trade and payments arrangements due to a shift from significant reliance on trading at non-market prices to multilateral, market-based trade.[24]" This facility was available in addition to other Fund credit facilities and was drawn on by almost all transition countries for a total of roughly SDR 4 billion. All in all, annual Fund lending to these countries (mostly in Central and Eastern Europe) increased from a low of SDR 50 million in 1989 to SDR 5.3 billion in 1995. As a percentage of total IMF lending this constituted a rise from 1.4% in 1989 to 31.5% in 1995 (with a high of 63.8% in 1994).

The unique nature of the problems in transition economies implies that the Fund itself - like the former centrally planned economies - is engaged in a 'learning by doing' process. For instance, while discussions initially focused on the relative benefits of shock therapy versus gradualism (with a predominantly macro-economic focus), present discussions have shifted more to the underlying aspects of transition.

In particular, the Fund seems to have underestimated somewhat the need for an adequate legal system (and its enforcement) and for the strengthening of countries' institutional capacity to carry out reforms. In the fiscal field, for instance, government revenues in many countries often account for no more than 10% of GDP. Inefficiencies in tax collection (and a lack of tax collectors), loop holes in tax legislation, and the slow pace of privatization (leaving public enterprises exempt from paying taxes), have often led to sequestration by governments. In many cases, due to the excessive weight put on monetary measures, the policy mix has been unsustainable while, at the same time, governments have been unable to direct scarce resources to productive uses. Another area which has, belatedly, assumed central importance in Fund programs is the fragility of the financial sector, particularly of banks. By now, however, these more micro-economic reforms have received the attention they deserve. Generally speaking, Fund involvement in those countries which embraced comprehensive and speedy reform has been a success.

The Mexico Crisis (December 1994)

The most surprising feature of the second Mexico crisis was probably not the nature of the economic problems but the speed with which the problem developed. Three days prior to the exchange rate crisis, an auction of dollar denominated bonds ('tesobonos') had been four times oversubscribed at 14% interest. Two weeks later, at an interest rate of 31%, only half of the bonds found buyers. Again two weeks later, the IMF approved a US$17.8 billion IMF adjustment package, the largest ever approved in the history of the Fund. What triggered these events?

Although Mexico's stabilization policies of the 1980s had been relatively successful in controlling inflation, domestic price increases remained significantly higher than that of its largest trading partner, the US, thus undermining Mexico's competitive position. Nevertheless, the Banco de Mexico maintained its tight monetary policies, in particular the peso-dollar peg which was achieved by way of high interest rate spreads over the US dollar. At the same time, Mexico's star performance as an emerging market (conclusion of the NAFTA agreement and admission to the OECD) made it an attractive investment, enabling it to run a current account deficit of almost 8% of GDP in 1994. When confidence waned and reserves dropped, however, President Zedillo devalued the peso by 15% on December 22nd. Although, initially the aim had been to re-peg the peso after the devaluation, the peso went into a free fall: within the space of three months the peso lost half of its value.

The immediate danger of the fall of the peso was a second Mexican default (as in 1982); US$10 billion in dollar denominated bonds was due in the first quarter while the central bank held only US$6.3 billion in foreign reserves. To avert the danger of default and possible "monsoonal" effects on other countries, the IMF, on February 1st, announced the approval of a US$17.8 billion stand-by program under its "exceptional circumstances clause.[25]" The US, which had initially announced a US$40 billion aid package but ran into opposition from Congress, contributed

US$20 billion through its Exchange Stabilization Fund (for which Congressional approval was not necessary). In addition, a credit line of US$10 billion was provided by other industrial and Latin American countries through the Bank of International Settlements, which eventually was never used. The resulting US$50 billion financing package was roughly equal to the sum of debt service payments on principal falling due in 1995; total debt service in 1995, including interest payments, amounted to US$60 billion. Thanks to the financing package and appropriate adjustment policies (the trade balance swung into surplus) Mexico remained current on its debt service obligations.

The role of the IMF in handling the acute financial problems of Mexico in 1995 was distinctly different from the role of the Fund in dealing with that other Mexican crisis, in 1982. One major difference, of course, was the state of the Mexican economy itself. While at the beginning of the 1980s the economic fundamentals had been weak, the economic fundamentals in 1995 were considerably stronger; in large part due to the decade of adjustment and reform which had taken place after the first crisis. Government finances had been brought in order, inflation had declined, the external debt had been restructured, the economy was more open, and an extensive privatization program had been completed. Therefore, the crisis in 1995 was much more a crisis of liquidity than one of solvency. A second distinction lies in the composition of the capital flows. Most of the external obligations of Mexico in 1982 had been to banks. In contrast, in 1995 the largest part of the payments obligations consisted of short-term bonds, mostly in the hands of investors in the US. As such, market sentiment played a much larger role than in the beginning of the 1980s.

Of primary concern to the Fund, therefore, was the restoration of confidence in the Mexican economy. In this respect, the substantial size of the financing provided played an important role (although it could be argued that the size of the IMF stand-by arrangement was excessively large: only three quarters of the available amount was actually drawn). Within a year, the current account deficit had moved into surplus, economic growth and employment growth had recovered, and Mexico's access to international financial markets had been restored. In addition, the aid package for Mexico seems to have successfully mitigated contagion effects on other emerging market economies. Immediately following the fall of the Mexican stock market, stock markets in, for instance, Brazil, Hong Kong and Malaysia plummeted while at the same time spreads on Brady bonds rose sharply. As soon as the Mexican economy had stabilized, however, stock markets in these countries recovered and capital flows resumed.

Apart from these beneficial effects of the IMF's involvement, there may have been a potentially damaging moral hazard effect. First, on the part of debtor countries, moral hazard may have occurred if countries conclude that they can relax their policy discipline on the assumption that, should things go wrong, they will be bailed out by the IMF. This type of moral hazard seems unlikely, however. Mexico not only suffered political damage from the economic crisis but also had to swallow some bitter economic medicine in the form of IMF conditionality; hardly an invitation to repeat past mistakes. The second, more important, moral hazard effect is on the part of the creditors, who may now judge the risk of non-payment by debtor countries considerably smaller. As such, the disciplinary influence of financial markets may have been reduced, thereby increasing the likelihood of renewed crises. Although this effect is difficult to quantify, the rapid decline in Brady bond spreads, and the quick resumption of capital flows to emerging markets seem to suggest that this effect may indeed be of legitimate concern.

LESSONS FOR THE IMF

After the demise of the Bretton Woods system, the IMF has managed to carve out a continued central position in the international financial system. Although its role in the industrial world as a provider of credit has diminished - and therewith its ability to influence policies of those countries - its presence in the developing countries, if anything, has increased and the Fund has found a new field of work in the containment of financial crises. It has proven to be the only multilateral institution with the intellectual capacity to react quickly and with the financial capacity to underpin its words with quickly disbursed resources. In fact, where in many countries restrictions have been placed on the financing of governments by central banks, the IMF stands out as a central bankers' bank which can prime liquidity in the system. It can take decisions relatively quickly and, thus, can sway sentiments in the financial markets.

Although the IMF's role in the four crises described above generally has been a positive one, some critical observations can be made. In the debt crises, for instance, years of intensive IMF involvement was not enough to put many African and Western Hemisphere countries back on a sustainable growth path (contrary to most Asian economies), and debt forgiveness was eventually necessary. In fact, one could even argue that in some cases painful economic adjustment was prolonged because the IMF itself was constrained by its own monetary character to take the initiative in debt reduction. This is also a criticism heard in relation to the more current debt problems of its poorest member states.

Another interesting question is how far the IMF is stretching its mandate to lend money to the transition economies. The IMF Articles dictate that resources may only be used temporarily to correct balance of payments imbalances. In many Eastern European countries, IMF programs (with a limited duration) are stacked on to each other to extend the Fund's presence in this region. In Hungary, for instance, a stand-by program (SBA) in 1988 was followed by another SBA in 1990, an Extended Fund Facility in 1991, a new SBA in 1993, and yet another SBA in 1996; although the current program is of a precautionary nature only. It should be noted, however, that all these programs are implemented at the request of the particular member state involved. The Fund is fulfilling a legitimate need for macroeconomic expertise for which no alternative institution is available. In any case, the Fund's involvement in this region has given renewed impetus to the IMF's role as an international economic institution.

Despite successful IMF efforts to combat financial crises, they keep reoccurring. This may be seen as implying inadequacies in the Fund's surveillance function. A more straightforward, and perhaps fairer explanation, however, is that the possibility of financial crises is inherent in the working of the present liberalized international monetary system and that the IMF does not have miracle solutions to the world's economic problems. Its member states are sovereign and are thus entitled to make their own policy mistakes. The Fund can exercise its influence, directly through its surveillance activities, but also indirectly, by enhancing transparency and thus adding the discipline of the judgement of the financial markets. The approach of the Fund itself in the various crises has been very much one of learning by doing, both in its relations with member states as well as in its policy messages to financial markets. In this regard, several steps have been taken to improve the Fund's capacity to prevent and resolve crises.

Surveillance And Special Data Dissemination Standards

The first initiative concerns the development of a special data dissemination standard. At the April 1995 meeting of the Interim Committee, it was recommended that "timely publication by members of comprehensive data would give greater transparency to their economic policies" and "requested the Executive Directors to work toward the establishment of standards to guide members in the provision of data to the public." In general a major problem for modern policy making and for financial markets alike, involves information and its availability. In the 1980s, the worst cases of mismanagement (and the failure of surveillance) occurred in cases where proper information was lacking and the IMF had not the technical capacity to correct nor the political ability to protest against the insufficiency of information[26]. For a number of countries there is still no country page in International Financial Statistics. The regular release of information is a way of de-politicizing its supply and leaving thousands of market participants rather than any one political body to make judgments about the appropriateness of policy.

Emergency Financing Mechanism

A second way in which the Fund has been active is the improvement of its own internal decision making procedures. Seven weeks after the Mexican peso embarked on its nosedive, an IMF-program was put in place; this is fast, but perhaps not fast enough in case of future crises. Moreover, the rapid conclusion of the stand-by agreement was primarily due to severe pressure from the US, while normal IMF-policies and procedures were thwarted. In order to ensure a more orderly (and faster) procedure in the event of future financial crises, the Fund has developed an Emergency Financing Mechanism; a procedure in which the Fund can react to liquidity crises within two weeks.

Financial Sector Stability

The third initiative concerns the improvement of surveillance itself. By more closely monitoring the circumstances leading to financial crises, the IMF can detect problems in a timely manner. To this end, increased attention has recently been given to the problems of overheating in emerging markets. The Executive Board of the IMF has also increasingly focused on the composition of financing flows to countries and possible contagion effects emerging from increasingly integrated economies. At the basis of this heightened attention lies the analysis that emerging markets differ markedly from the industrialized countries: they must develop their economies in a world where capital transactions are already of major significance, due not least to the liberalization effected earlier in the industrialized countries.

This has several important implications, as the case of Mexico has illustrated. First, this means that in their liberalization attempts, emerging markets are immediately faced with vast and volatile capital flows, at the same time when they must also undertake the necessary macroeconomic reforms. In addition, the demand for money tends to be unstable owing to the relatively major effect of confidence factors, attributable in part to the sometimes still fragile political stability in these often young democracies. Furthermore, capital flows to and from emerging markets are highly sensitive to movements in international interest rates. Such a volatile environment complicates sound credit risk assessment by banks. Finally, due to the often limited product mix, growth of GDP may vary markedly, thus making the economy highly dependent on price movements in certain markets, causing heavy fluctuations in the terms of trade as well.

Financial markets in emerging economies often have not yet reached the degree of sophistication of those in industrialized countries. Banks usually still play a dominant role, not only in payments but also in providing liquidity; liquid substitutes for bank deposits are barely available, if at all. Moreover, the available capital is often in the hands of only a few banks, thus enhancing the risk of a systemic crisis in the event of problems at one of these banks. Hence, the volume of net capital inflows may be vast relative to the size of the financial system. Another characteristic of emerging markets is the vulnerability of the banking system. In a volatile economic environment, as outlined above, the maturity mismatch in their balance sheets, given the traditional role of banks in the transformation of maturity, gains an added dimension. Banking practices may not invariably have been sound, as lending often takes place on the basis of personal relations and the proportion of bad loans is high. Finally, the institutional framework is often inadequate. Cases in point are the legal framework for, among other things, financial contracts, disclosure standards, and requirements for publication of risk exposure. Notably in the transition countries in Central and Eastern Europe, the institutional framework has to be built up from scratch, often hampering banks' operations.

What is clear from this assessment, is the pivotal role which supervision has to play in safeguarding the stability of the financial system. Indeed, adequate supervision is a precondition for markets to function properly, not just a complement. The relative fragility of emerging markets implies that supervision in these countries will have to be especially strong, although the current state of affairs in several industrial countries' banking systems indicates that this is by no means an exclusive characteristic of emerging markets. In addition, it is imperative that problems in banking and financial systems are detected at an early stage. More deep-seated problems tend to have significant ripple-effects and can contaminate other parts of the economy.

The Fund's role in this area is to support the efforts of the local authorities through its surveillance activities and to ensure timely detection of weak spots in member states' financial systems. The main vehicle in this regard is the annual article IV consultation. The logical path to follow seems to be for the IMF to adopt the existing prudential standards already developed by the Basle Committee as the minimum-standard against which member states' banking systems are evaluated. In doing so, the Fund should focus on financial sector issues that hold a potential for macroeconomic disturbances. At the same time, the G-10 countries have established a 'working party on financial stability in emerging market economies' consisting of experts from the emerging market economies, G-10 countries, and representatives from the Bretton Woods institutions. Its task is to compile evidence on the key sources of vulnerability of emerging financial systems and map out the critical features for a robust financial system. More importantly, however, it provides a framework for arriving at a division of labor between the various international organizations. By distinguishing norm-setting institutions (such as the Basle Committee and IOSCO) from institutions primarily concerned with surveillance (like the IMF), overlap is prevented and emerging economies are provided with a clear benchmark for the development of their own standards.

Capital Convertibility

The fourth initiative concerns the possible expansion of the Fund's mandate (Articles of Agreement) to explicitly include the aim of capital account convertibility. The Articles were, of course, predominantly written in 1944, at a time when capital restrictions were viewed as a vital economic policy instrument to shield the countries from speculative and disruptive capital flows. Consequently, the IMF mandate only includes the aim of current account convertibility and, in fact, explicitly allows for the introduction of capital restrictions. This seems hopelessly out of date with economic reality and market developments.

The tremendous surge in international capital flows in recent decades and the achieved level of liberalization has not only changed the world economy, but also our capacity to control it. Excessive capital inflows can impede economic stability, even though macroeconomic policy itself may be adequate. Moreover, excessive outflows may exacerbate a balance of payments problem and sharp fluctuations in capital flows may lead to increased volatility in interest and exchange rates. At the same time, the integration of financial markets has resulted in a more rapid transmission of changes in economic policy and economic shocks. In a world of increasingly integrated financial markets capital restrictions have proven to be a largely ineffective response. Although restrictions may provide temporary breathing space in the event of large and disruptive capital flows, these restrictions become increasingly ineffective the longer they are kept in place. Instead, heightened attention should be given to those factors which can prevent disruptive capital flows: market-based interest and exchange rates, a robust and well-developed financial sector (with adequate supervision), political stability and a balanced policy mix. As the institution primarily concerned with safeguarding stability in the international monetary system, it seems only natural to assign a greater role to the Fund in capital transactions.

This does not imply an overhaul of the international monetary system. Rather, it requires that the Fund's charter be brought in line with the economic realities of our time. The Fund's staff now often finds themselves operating in a jurisdictional void, encouraging the removal of capital restrictions as part of a package of healthy economic policies, but lacking the legal backing to do so. This is to the detriment of Fund credibility and the effectiveness of its policy advice. To provide the IMF with the necessary legal backing an amendment will most likely have to be comprehensive. Most fundamentally, Article I, in which the purposes of the IMF are laid out, and which so far has endured all previous amendments unimpaired, should be changed. A strong statement of principle should be included clarifying the role of the Fund in the international monetary system. Specifically, an amendment to section (iv) may be envisioned, where the Fund's role is expanded to: "assist in the establishment of a multilateral system in respect of current and capital transactions."

But this will not be enough. To provide the Fund with legal backing it will be necessary to stipulate more precisely what the scope of this expanded role is. In this regard, the passage in article VI, which allows for the imposition of capital controls, will have to be replaced by a passage stating that, without the approval of the Fund, members shall not impose restrictions on international capital transactions and related payments and transfers. Note that such a formulation is broader than the one used for the liberalization of current transactions, which is restricted to 'payments and transfers'. This is necessary as capital restrictions are often placed not on the capital flows themselves but on the underlying transaction. Furthermore, contrary to the liberalization of underlying transactions for the current account, where the WTO (formerly GATT) plays an important role, there is no such organization to watch over the capital account. To confine the amendment to the 'making of payments and transfers' would risk dealing with the shadow rather than the substance.

As the Fund is often called in to repair the resulting economic damage of disruptive flows, there is a case for more intensive IMF involvement, particularly in its surveillance activities. In fact, the Fund seems uniquely placed to promote capital liberalization given its macroeconomic expertise and almost universal membership. Moreover, Fund practice of engaging in a dialogue with its member states in the context of surveillance, technical assistance or adjustment programs, enables it to make a well-balanced assessment and, if necessary, to persuade countries to remove restrictions. This allows the Fund to be bold in ambition but cautious in implementation; a more appropriate method than the often more rigid legal approach followed in trade treaties.

CLOSING REMARKS

Despite its institutional constraints, the IMF has been remarkably successful in providing an adequate response to financial crises. It has done so by neatly balancing the need for a flexible interpretation of its mandate (e.g. the creation of new facilities and enlarged access), while at the same time remaining faithful to its principles.

Five main determinants of success seem to stand out. First, the Fund has shown that it is able to react rapidly and creatively to unexpected shocks to the system. Indeed, in the case of the oil crises and the Mexico crises, proposals to deal with the problem had been worked out within a matter of days. Because of this ability to react quickly, the Fund has placed itself in a position of leadership on more than one occasion. As a result, the IMF has also been well positioned to act as an intermediary, whether it has been between oil-exporting and oil-importing countries, between rich and poor countries, or between creditors and debtors. The objectivity with which this coordinating-role was fulfilled (e.g. in the concerted lending packages and the recycling of petrodollars), strengthened by the universal character of the institution, are a second source of the Fund's success. The third determinant is the Fund's financial structure which enables the IMF to "put its money where its mouth is." This provides it with the financial clout needed to back up ambitious plans. Moreover, because of its quota structure and the revolving nature of its resources, adequate financing has been available to provide the Fund with the necessary flexibility to react to crises (e.g. the Mexico crises). A fourth determinant is derived from its macro-economic focus. Crises necessarily require some combination of financing and adjustment. The word "crises" by itself, however, indicates that an imbalance has occurred between the two. IMF adjustment programs have served to bridge the gap between debtors and creditors. The fifth and final determinant has been the expertise of the IMF-staff. By assembling a staff of highly trained professionals, the Fund has not only been able to educate policy makers in other countries in the course of its technical assistance and surveillance activities, it has also made the IMF uniquely suited to extinguish the economic fires of the last 25 years.

NOTES

[1] The authors wish to thank Greetje Frankena, Lex Hoogduin, Aerdt Houben, Henk Huisman and Coen Voormeulen for their comments on an earlier version of this paper. The opinions expressed in the paper are those of the authors and do not necessarily reflect the views of De Nederlandsche Bank.

[2] Horsefield K.J. ed., International Monetary Fund 1945-65, Vol.3 Documents (1969), p.405.

[3] Guitián M., The Unique Nature of the Responsibilities of the International Monetary Fund, IMF Pamphlet Series No. 46.

[4] The view had developed that speculative movements across national borders might jeopardize the goal of free trade based on fixed exchange rates and thus lead to instability. By insisting on convertibility for current account transactions only, the designers of the Bretton Woods system hoped to facilitate free trade while avoiding the possibility that private capital flows might tighten the external constraints faced by policy makers.

[5] By construction the Bretton Woods system required the US to run persistent current account deficits to provide global liquidity; at the same time however, these deficits undermined the stability of the dollar and with it the stability of the international monetary system (the so-called Triffin dilemma).

[6] This was also evident in the design of Fund programmes. While exchange rate action was included in only 32 percent of the Fund programs agreed in 1963-1972, this figure rose to 59% in the period 1973-1980, to 82% from 1981-83, and nearly 100% in the late 1980s. See Polak J., Exchange Rate Research and Policy at the IMF, IMF Staff Papers, Vol. 42 No.4 (December 1995), p.753.

[7] In 1989 global foreign exchange trading was estimated at US$650 billion daily, almost forty times the average daily value of world trade. By mid 1995 this figure had risen to US$1.190 billion daily. See 66th Annual Report, Bank of International Settlements, June 1996.

[8] IMF, Annual Report 1978.

[9] See A.F.P. Bakker, International Financial Institutions, p.28. This figure is dependant, of course, on the timing and frequency of quota increases. For instance, in 1992 immediately before the ninth quota increase took effect, this ratio was 3.4%. In 1993, after the quota increase, the ratio had increased to 5.1% while by 1995 it had again declined to 4.0%.

[10] It is notable that the calculations for the United Kingdom and the Netherlands yield similar annual cost estimates, despite the fact that the quota of the U.K. is more than twice as large as the quota of the Netherlands. Although this can partly be explained by the Fund's use of respective currencies, an additional factor is the relatively large gold component in the reserve tranche position of the United Kingdom, over which the IMF does not remunerate its member states. This has been left out of the calculation; if it were taken into consideration the lost income of the U.K. would be higher than that of the Netherlands.

[11] Masson P. & Mussa M., The role of the IMF: financing and its interactions with adjustment and surveillancxe, IMF Pamphlet Series, No.50.

[12] For a complete decade (1960-1970) the posted price of Arabian light crude oil remained a constant US$1.80 per barrel. By October 1, 1973, however, this price had risen to US$3.01 and a scarce three months later the price increased almost fourfold to US$11.65 per barrel.

[13] Fund staff calculations show that the current account surplus of oil exporting countries increased from US$6.7 billion in 1973 to US$68.3 billion in 1974. Approximately half of this increase was incurred by industrial countries and half by non-oil primary producing countries. The combined current account deficit for non-oil developing countries increased from -US$11.3 billion in 1973, to -US$37.0 in 1974 (and -US$46.3 in 1975).

[14] Only two requirements existed; the requirement of a balance of payments need and the expectation that a member drawing on the facility would cooperate with the Fund to find appropriate solutions for overcoming its balance of payments deficit. While the first was obviously met by every single non-oil producing country, the latter was only to be filled in after resources under the oil facility had been disbursed (the immediate need of members was too urgent and the situation too unclear to permit working out a full plan). One condition for access to the oil facility proved important from a signalling standpoint, however. Member states drawing on the oil facility were to state that they would refrain from imposing new, or intensifying, restrictions on payments without the prior approval of the Fund.

[15] See De Vries M.G., The International Monetary Fund 1972-1978: cooperation on trial, (1985) Vol.1, p.358

[16] "All those shopping centers in fashionable areas of Santiago could never generate the foreign exchange needed to service their external debts." See Diaz-Alejandro C.F., Latin American Debt: I don't think we are in Kansas anymore, Brookings Papers on Economic Activity (1984), p.340.

[17] This is of course an oversimplification of the events that actually led to the crisis. However, for the purpose of his article, we will not attempt to provide a complete overview of the wide range of contributing factors. Many others have done so (excellently) before us. Examples include: Anne Krueger (1987) "The International Debt Crisis," AEA Papers and Proceedings, Vol.77, No.2; William Cline (1985), "The World Debt Problem: analysis, experience and prospects," in "The Debt Problem," Journal of Development Planning, No.16 (United Nations).

[18] See Cheng H., International Financial Crises, Past and Present, "Economic Review," Federal Reserve Bank of San Francisco (fall 1986).

[19] Remarks to the American Enterprise Institute, Washington, December 5, 1983, as quoted from De Vries, Balance of Payments Adjustment 1945-1986, IMF, p.221.

[20] Given an estimated long-term sustainable ratio of around 250% of quota (staff calculations), the intention was that the policy of enlarged access would have a temporary nature, for the duration of the crisis (although the cumulative total at present is still 300%).

[21] The approach followed by the IMF - to scale down past levels of expenditure and concentrate scarce resources on more productive uses - had helped reduce current account deficits, cut government subsidies, raise taxes, cut wages, and increase prices of publicly supplied goods and services. Indeed, Mexico's government expenditure fell from 34% of GDP in 1982 to 21% of GDP in 1989. At the same time, however, public sector investment had fallen from 10% to 4.5% in the same period. See Van Wijnbergen (1991), "Debt Relief and Economic Growth in Mexico," The World Bank Economic Review, Vol.5, No.3, p.437-55.

[22] At first sight the difference between contributing to a debt reduction scheme directly (using budgetary resources) or indirectly (using the equivalent amount of resources stalled at an international institution) seems oblique. However, in the case of an IMF transfer, a country's outlay (i.e. a quota increase) has already passed through the political appropriation process, and is thus politically less painful.

[23] See IMF Survey, "IMF Technical Assistance Takes on a Higher Profile," May 30 1994, p.169.

[24] IMF Annual Report, 1993, p.60. The STF was phased out in 1995.

[25] Under the enlarged access policies (see note 20) a country can borrow no more than a cumulative total of 300% of its quota from the IMF. For Mexico this quota was approximately US$2.5 billion. However, this limit may be surpassed in case of exceptional circumstances. The actual loan to Mexico amounted to almost 700% of its quota, thereby being the largest credit ever approved by the IMF.

[26] James H., Principle of Surveillance, IMF Staff Papers Vol.42, No.4 (December 1995), p.788-789.

REFERENCES

Bakker A.F.P. en Rijsdijk J.P., "The Monetary Character of the International Monetary Fund," Quarterly Bulletin, No.3, De Nederlandsche Bank N.V. (Amsterdam, December 1984).

Bakker A.F.P., International Financial Institutions (London/New York, 1996).

"Balance of Payments Adjustment 1945 to 1986: the IMF experience," International Monetary Fund, Washington, D.C., 1987.

Bird G., "From Bretton Woods to Halifax and Beyond: the Political Economy of International Monetary Reform," The World Economy, Vol.19 No.2 (March 1996).

Boughton J.M. and Lateef S.K. ed. Fifty Years After Bretton Woods, the future of the IMF and the World Bank, Proceedings of a conference held in Madrid Spain September 29-30, 1994, International Monetary Fund & World Bank Group, Washington, D.C., 1995.

Buira A., "Reflections on the International Monetary System," Essays in International Finance, No.195 January 1995, Department of Economics Princeton, New Jersey, 1995.

Cheng H., "International Financial Crises, Past and Present," Economic Review, No.4, Federal Reserve Bank of San Francisco (Fall 1986).

Cline W., "The World Debt Problem: analysis, experience and prospects," in The Debt Problem, Journal of Development Planning, No.16, United Nations, NY.

de Larosière J., "The Debt Situation," IMF Survey, International Monetary Fund, Washington D.C., June 2, 1986.

de Vries, M.G., The International Monetary Fund 1972-1978: cooperation on trial, Vol. 1 & 2 (narrative and analysis), IMF, Washington, D.C., 1985.

Diaz-Alejandro, Carlos F., "Latin American Debt: I don't think we are in Kansas anymore," Brookings Papers on Economic Activity, 1984, pp.335-403.

Do We Need an International Lender of Last Resort," paper presented at Princeton University, April 20, 1995.

Frenkel J.A., Goldstein M. ed., "International Financial Policy: Essays in Honor of Jacques Polak," International Monetary Fund & De Nederlandsche Bank, Washington D.C., 1991.

Goldstein M., Isard P., Masson P. and Taylor M., "Policy Issues in the Evolving International Monetary System," Occasional Paper, No.96, IMF, Washington, D.C., 1992.

Guitián M., "The Unique Nature of the Responsibilities of the International Monetary Fund," Pamphlet Series, No.46, International Monetary Fund, Washington, D.C., 1992.

Henning R.C., "Political Economy of the Bretton Woods Institutions: Adapting to Financial Change," The World Economy, Vol. 19 No.2 (March 19, 1996)

Horsefield K.J., "The International Monetary Fund 1945-1965: twenty years of international monetary cooperation," Vol. III Documents, IMF, Washington, D.C., 1969.

IMF, "IMF Technical Assistance Takes on a Higher Profile," IMF Survey," May 30 1994.

IMF Under H.J. Witteveen: World Economic Cooperation Sustained in Years of Crisis," IMF Survey, IMF, Washington, D.C., June 19, 1978.

James H., "Principle of Surveillance," IMF Staff Papers, Vol.42 No.4, IMF, Washington, D.C., 1995.

Krueger A., "The International Debt Crisis," AEA Papers and Proceedings, American Economic Review, Vol.77, No.2, May 1987.

Krugman P., Obstfeld. International Economics-Theory and Policy, Third Edition, Harper Collins, New York, 1994.

Mussa M., Goldstein M., Clark P., Mathieson D. and Bayoumi T., "Improving the International Monetary System: constraints and possibilities," Occasional Paper, No. 116, IMF, Washington, D.C., 1994.

Masson P.R., Mussa M., "The Role of the IMF: financing and its interactions with adjustment and surveillance," Pamphlet Series, No. 50, International Monetary Fund, Washington, D.C., 1996.

Polak J., "Exchange Rate Research and Policy at the IMF," IMF Staff Papers, Vol.42 No.4, December, 1995.

Rules and Discretion in International Economic Policy," Occasional Paper, No.97, IMF, Washington, D.C., 1992.

Sachs J., "Alternative Approaches to Financial Crisis in Emerging Markets," Discussion paper prepared for meetings in Basel, SZ, December 9-10, 1995.

"The IMF in a Changing World 1945-85," International Monetary Fund, Washington, D.C., 1986.

Wijnbergen van S., "Debt Relief and Economic Growth in Mexico," The World Bank Economic Review, Vol.5, No.3, World Bank, Washington, D.C., 1991.

Witteveen H.J., "Belangentegenstellingen en het Internationale Monetaire Fonds," Maandschrift Economie, Jrg 60, 1996.

16

The Role Of The International Monetary Fund In Promoting Stability In The Global Economy

PHILIPPE MAYSTADT
Vice-Prime Minister and Minister of Finance and Foreign Trade, Belgium and Chairman, Interim Committee of the IMF

INTRODUCTION

What is the role of the International Monetary Fund (IMF)? How does the IMF adapt to the new challenges of a world environment that is changing at such a fast pace? What is the progress still to be made in order that, in the next century, the IMF can carry out its missions effectively? Those are the questions I would like to address here.

As the starting-point, I have chosen the financial crisis that hit Mexico in December 1994. This was a new type of crisis, which Michael Camdessus, the Managing Director of the IMF, called "the first crisis of the XXIst Century." Indeed, this crisis revealed the irreversible way in which we have entered a new world, which, in the space of a few months, has induced the IMF to really plunge into the XXIst century, the century of globalization. Consequently, the IMF had no choice but to draw lessons from the Mexican crisis and the globalization of the international capital markets for its role in the world economy.

When I say that the IMF has drawn lessons from the Mexican crisis, I use a general term, which refers in fact to the Management of the IMF, its staff, its

Executive Board, and its Interim Committee. I would like to specify that the Interim Committee -- which I have chaired since October 1993 -- consists of 24 members, just like the Executive Board of the Fund, the only difference being that those members are Finance Ministers and Central Bank Governors, who are appointed by each member or group of members of the Fund that elects an Executive Director.

The Interim Committee, which was created in 1974 to assist the Board of Governors of the IMF in managing the crisis situation caused by the collapse of the Bretton Woods regime, usually meets twice a year. It has come to play a key policy-making role in the IMF, and there is a close and mutually reinforcing collaboration among the Committee, IMF management, the Executive Board, and IMF staff. Its principal role is to try to reach a consensus on delicate questions which can only be resolved at the ministerial level. The decisions of the Board are then based on the consensus reached within the Committee.

THE MEXICAN FINANCIAL CRISIS OF DECEMBER 1994

In the early 1990s Mexico, like other developing countries of Latin-America and Asia, managed to increase its access to international capital markets in order to finance its investments and sustain its development.

This positive development results from many factors, i.e. the liberalization of capital movements, the technological revolution in communications, the drive towards portfolio diversification by institutional investors, and the structural reforms which transformed the financial markets of many developing countries during the 1980s.

The combination of these factors has furthered the continued expansion of the international financial markets, the emergence of stock markets in many developing countries and their greater participation in the bond and equity markets. Thus, very powerful driving forces have emerged to boost the development and growth of the developing countries.

Between 1990 and 1993, Mexico made the most of this; actually, during those years, capital inflows to Mexico averaged over 6 per cent of GDP.

However, the Mexican crisis has shown us the potential dangers inherent in unchecked recourse to capital markets. In the space of a few months, capital inflows declined dramatically, as the investor community was losing confidence in Mexico's macroeconomic performance. Consequently, the value of the peso dropped by 50 per cent, the Mexican stock market crumbled and the Mexican economy sank into a deep recession, causing a near 7 per cent drop in real GDP in 1995.

Abandoned by private investors, the Mexican government was left no choice but to adopt strict stabilization measures to bring back the current account deficit to a level close to balance within a few months.

You can imagine that the deflationary effect of these measures demanded considerable sacrifices from the Mexican population. That was the condition for winning back the confidence of the investors and regaining access to the international capital markets. And, in fact, six months after the crisis, Mexico succeeded in returning to the markets.

I have commented at length about the Mexican crisis to illustrate how the world economy is evolving in such a way as to give the financial markets a growing role in the international monetary system.

Like many others, I believe that globalization brings chances and opportunities, especially for the developing countries which have been able to increase their access to the international capital markets. However, it is also clear that it is a phenomenon which must be property understood and managed for it to be really a chance for all.

This is an enormous challenge for the IMF, which it has been addressing since the Mexican crisis by setting itself three objectives; reinforcing its mission of surveillance, increasing its global financial resources, and facilitating the integration of the poorest countries into the global economy. I would like to have a closer look at the progress made in those three areas during the last two years.

PROGRESS MADE TO STRENGTHEN THE ROLE OF THE IMF

Progress Made In The Area Of Surveillance

Let me first turn to the progress made in the area of surveillance.

Even if the severity of the Mexican crisis can be explained by the globalization of financial markets, which have made capital movements far more sudden, unexpected and violent, it is also true that the slippage in Mexico's economic performance, especially in 1994, played an important role in these events.

Consequently, one can ask oneself why the services of the IMF have not tried to convince the Mexican authorities to take corrective measures to win back the confidence of the investors. Indeed, the surveillance of the economic performances of its member countries is one of the essential missions of the IMF, its aim being precisely to encourage the authorities to take measures so as to avoid a balance of payments crisis.

If the IMF did not fully carry out its surveillance mission, it is because it had not anticipated, to the right extent, the slippage in Mexico's economic performance and its effects on market confidence. This happened because of problems in the communication of data by Mexico to the IMF and because the Fund did not wish to complicate further the task of the authorities by questioning their economic policies.

As a reaction to this, the Interim Committee concluded in April 1995 that it was important to tighten up the surveillance by the IMF by:

1. requesting the **member countries** to regularly communicate to the IMF economic data -- complete, up-to-date and relevant -- and to publish these data, thus giving greater transparency to their economic policies;

2. urging **investors** to properly evaluate the economic situation so as to be more risk-aware;

3. encouraging the IMF to establish a closer and more continuous dialogue with its member countries, to strengthen its analysis, to be frank and candid in its recommendations, and to give greater attention to the soundness of their financial sector with a view to detecting the emerging tensions at an early stage.

This approach to surveillance not only enables national authorities to benefit from the Fund's advice, but also enriches the IMF staff's knowledge with lessons drawn from the totality of the countries' experiences. It is thus a self-reinforcing process with both short-term and long-term benefits for the national authorities as well as for the Fund itself. Such surveillance leads to better understanding and permits drawing lessons with global application.

With respect to each of the objectives, concrete progress has been made in the last few months. I would like to pay particular attention to two of them.

First of all, as far as the communication of data to the markets is concerned, in March 1996 the IMF established a **Special Data Dissemination Standard** for the members having or seeking access to capital markets. Up to now about 40 countries, amongst which Mexico, the Philippines, Turkey and India, have subscribed to this standard, and have committed themselves to follow very specific rules regarding the dissemination of their economic and financial data.

This is a first example of concrete response which the IMF has given to promote further stability in the global economy.

The second example I would like to mention concerns the Declaration, endorsed by the Interim Committee in September 1996, of a **"Partnership for Sustainable Global Growth."**

This Declaration replaces the October 1994 Madrid Declaration, which emphasized sound domestic policies and ambitious structural reforms. Although these guidelines remain valid, the Interim Committee saw a need to update and broaden the Madrid Declaration, in light of the new challenges of a changing global environment. Three of the recommendations put forward in this new Declaration, deserve a closer look, because they are new to documents of the IMF.

Firstly, the Declaration recognizes that "the sustainability of economic growth depends on development of human resources," and that it is essential to reduce unproductive spending to improve education and training, to enable the provision of effective health care, and to alleviate poverty.

Secondly, the governments must promote good governance in all its aspects, including "by ensuring the rule of law" and "tackling corruption," as "essential elements of a framework within which economies can prosper."

Thirdly, the new Declaration stresses the necessity to ensure the soundness of banking systems through strong prudential regulation and supervision.

Like Michel Camdessus, I am convinced that this is not just another declaration, another call to action. This is a keynote statement of sound policy principles, which the Interim Committee has endorsed, taking into account the lessons learned from the recent strengthening of Fund surveillance and the new challenges facing our countries in a changing global environment. I would also like to add that these principles are universal; they provide an additional proof that globalization has brought people of the world closer together in a way that would have been unthinkable only a few years ago. This is why governments in all industrial, developing, and transition economies should attach particular importance to their implementation. In this context, it is worth noting that the Interim Committee will keep members' efforts at promoting the principles set in the new Declaration under review.

Progress Made Towards The Consolidation Of The IMF's Financial Basis

The second important lesson drawn from the Mexican crisis, concerns the IMF's financial resources.

In order to help Mexico in the beginning of last year, the IMF agreed to an 18 billion dollar loan.

This was an exceptional financial support -- its size unprecedented in the IMF's history. The basic goal was to support the stabilization program of the Mexican government and help it surmount its difficulties without resorting to exchange controls. Indeed, taking that road involved the risk of provoking a deep loss of confidence in the financial markets, which would inevitably have had a negative impact on all the developing countries.

As I mentioned before, the capital inflows towards Mexico were resumed pretty fast and "the tequila effect" -- that is, the transmission of the Mexican crisis to other countries of Latin America and Asia -- could be limited. Those were the objectives of the IMF.

This experience has shown that the IMF must, within a short time, be able to mobilize financial resources to meet the exceptional needs with which countries can be confronted in markets of a planetary dimension. From now on, the stability of the world economy requires means of intervention at the level of the destabilizing forces which can arise at any moment.

Therefore, I am very pleased with the progress made in establishing the New Arrangements to Borrow, which will double -- to SDR 34 billion -- the supplementary resources available to the IMF for coping with serious financial emergencies.

A sign of the new world environment which is taking shape -- while up to now only the G-10 countries and Saudi-Arabia were prepared to provide loans to the IMF through the General Arrangements to Borrow, a larger group of countries or institutions will participate in the New Arrangements, including several emerging economies. This will be a recognition of the important role played by those economies in the international financial community.

The broadening of the General Arrangements to Borrow is also justified with regard to another important decision which was taken in October 1995, namely the establishment of an exceptional procedure, **the Emergency Financing Mechanism,** to enable the IMF to respond promptly in the event of serious financial crises. However this new instrument is no hidden promise that the IMF and the international community contemplate systematically saving those investors who are the victims of liquidity crises of sovereign States. Actually, the current reform of the functioning of the international monetary system aims at making not only the countries more aware of their responsibilities, but also the investors of the private sector. That is why the IMF will resort to the Emergency Financing Mechanism with the greatest caution, on a case by case basis, and by imposing strong conditionality.

Progress Made In Helping The Poorest Countries

Although it is true that, more and more, countries like Mexico can finance their development by resorting to international capital markets, we cannot help noticing that too many of the poorest countries do not reap the benefits of globalization. As a matter of fact, there is a serious risk of marginalization of many of these countries, perhaps even of whole regions in the world.

Conscious of this reality - unacceptable from the viewpoint of equity and potentially dangerous for the stability of the international economic system - the Interim Committee reaffirmed in September 1996 its objective to encourage all the countries, including low-income countries, to integrate fully in the world economy. We have also wanted to show our strong commitment by endorsing a new initiative to ensure that the Heavily Indebted Poor Countries (HIPCs) that have established a sound track record of economic adjustment can restore a sustainable debt situation over the medium term.

This initiative will bring together the three main actors concerned with development aid, in a **partnership marked by a new solidarity:**

- firstly, **the governments of the poor countries,** which are expected to adhere to the principles of the new Declaration I have just mentioned, i.e., by conducting sound domestic policies and by improving the quality of government spending and promoting the development of human resources;

- secondly, **the community of creditors,** who must be prepared to provide exceptional financial support to ensure that all the heavily indebted poor countries which undertake the necessary reforms, can arrive at a viable debt situation over the medium term.

  With regard to this, I am pleased that the Paris Club creditors have announced that they are ready to provide debt reduction of up to 80 per cent for countries qualifying for additional relief within the Initiative.

- and, thirdly, **the IMF and the World Bank,** which will also have to participate in the financing of the new initiative from their own resources and support the adjustment and reform programs of the eligible countries.

As far as the IMF is concerned, it has been decided that the Fund's participation in the HIPC Initiative would be through special operations under the Enhanced Structural Adjustment Facility (ESAF), which is the instrument allowing the Fund to lend at concessional conditions to low-income counties. Those operations will take the form of a reduction in the net present value of the debt owed by a country to the Fund, through the provision of grants or loans on extended maturities. This commitment required that the Interim Committee agree on the financing of the continuation of ESAF. In this regard, I am particularly happy that we were able to come to an agreement on the financing of the ESAF, which will be based on bilateral contributions and, if needed, on the optimization of the management of the Fund's reserves.

This decision is important: apart from the fact that it has been a key element which has allowed the launch of the new initiative, it also confirms that the **IMF will, in the next century, continue to play an important role in providing support for the poorest developing countries.**

ELEMENTS OF A STRATEGY TO ADAPT THE IMF MORE TO THE FAST GLOBALIZING ECONOMY

Although the progress made in the last few months to adapt the IMF to the globalization of the world economy has been considerable. I am nevertheless convinced that there is still a lot of work to be done to help the Fund successfully carry out its missions in the next century.

I would like to mention three points.

Greater Responsibilities With Regard To Surveillance

To continue strengthening the surveillance role of the Fund, both in the industrial and in the developing and transition countries, is, in my opinion, an essential challenge for the IMF. The new Declaration of the Interim Committee gives to the IMF and to the Interim Committee the task of overseeing the efforts which member countries make to implement the principles of the new Declaration. In fact, this surveillance will contribute to ensure that this Declaration be not just a catalogue of good intentions.

The fact that, in the last few years, the Interim Committee has reinforced its role with regard to surveillance is a positive development, which allows the IMF to have a great, and thus, more efficient influence on the economic policies of its member countries. However, it would be useful to start a new era by giving the IMF the **power** -- which it does not have at present -- **to start special consultations in order to be able to counteract the risks of a balance-of-payment crisis by corrective measures.** In other words, as soon as such a risk would appear, the IMF should be able to take the initiative and send a mission to the country concerned to try and convince the authorities to react. If necessary, these consultations could include the authorities of several countries concerned.

Modest in appearance, this phase would contribute to a greater prevention of crises. Indeed, backed-up by the "peer-pressure" of the international community these consultations would, as a rule, convince the authorities of the countries concerned to react.

I also think that the IMF should not limit its surveillance to just member countries' policies. It is also essential that the Fund enhance its surveillance of financial markets and of exchange rate movements.

With regard to **financial markets,** it is clear that they have become very powerful and that they do pose challenges of their own, so they should be submitted to an appropriate IMF surveillance. The Interim Committee, aware of this question, had asked the Executive Board of the IMF to continue its analysis of the capital movements and of their consequences, and to report on this at its Spring 1997 meeting.

As far as **the evolution of the exchange rates** is concerned, it would be very disappointing if the objectives set out in the new Declaration of the Interim Committee could not be realized because of excessive exchange rate fluctuations, at local as well as global levels. Against this background, it is essential that the Fund display great vigilance against the use of the exchange rate as a protectionist weapon. Indeed, exchange rate stability, in particular real exchange rate stability, is desirable so as to avoid competitive distortions and reduce uncertainty in trade relations between countries.

Exchange rate stability is also important at the global level. In this regard, it is well established that the variability of real exchange rates has been far greater under the present system of generalized floating exchange rates than under the Bretton Woods regime. Cumulative swings in the key reserve currencies have been considerable at time, and have contributed to the view that the international monetary system should be reformed. However, practical and political obstacles have not allowed us to find the degree necessary to support a broad reform effort. I would hope that the adoption of the Euro, on January 1, 1999, will make it possible to re-address this question, in consultation with the IMF. The fusion of the European currencies in a single currency will indeed allow the Euro to have a place in world trade and currency portfolios which matches the relative importance of Europe in the world economy. Thus the balance of power between the United States and Europe will be more in equilibrium and Europe will be in a stronger position to negotiate a reform of the international monetary system.

There Is An Urgent Need To Increase The IMF's Quotas

The second area in which progress must be made in the next few months concerns the IMF's financial resources.

As I have already emphasized, the perspective of a doubling of the resources available to the Fund under the General Arrangements to Borrow, is reassuring. But the new arrangements must only be seen as a safety-net to cope with exceptional circumstances. In other words, they will not be used to finance regular Fund operations. These will continue to be financed through resources provided to the Fund.

In a way, the IMF's quotas constitute its capital. They are subscribed for the first time when joining the Fund, and after that at every general revision of the quotas. These revisions make it possible to maintain the capital of the monetary Fund proportionally adequate in relation to the size of the world economy, and to the tasks it must carry out there.

Today this capital amounts to 145 billion SDR, i.e. over 200 billion dollars. In the eyes of most of my colleagues of the Interim Committee, this level of the IMF's "own resources" is no longer adequate in light of the weakening of the Fund's liquidity and the changes in the world economy since the approval of the last increase, agreed in 1990. Therefore, they would like to see an increase of the quotas as soon as possible.

I share this opinion. Accordingly, I hope that we make progress on that score in the coming months. Taking into account the time that is necessary for parliamentary ratification, the increase could be effective from 1999 and determine the Fund's basic financial strength for the first few years of the XXIst century.

The IMF Must Take More Into Account The Social Dimension

Allow me to mention again the new Declaration of the Interim Committee, which stresses the importance of the valorization of the human resources and the fight against poverty "by implementing social protection mechanisms which are correctly targeted and which the countries can afford." This recommendation shows very well that the social aspect is winning ground in the so-called doctrine of the IMF, which forms the basis of the advice it gives to the member countries. This also clearly emerges from the Program of Action proposed by the Managing Director of the Fund and the President of the World Bank to assist the HIPCs. It is envisaged that programs under the Initiative will insist on "a policy of social progress."

How should we proceed?

In my view, the most appropriate way is for the IMF to enhance its dialogue and coordination with the international organizations which have established competence and responsibilities in the social field. In this perspective, I took the initiative to invite the Director General of the International Labor Office (ILO), Michel Hansenne, to a working lunch of the Interim Committee. This meeting, which took place in October 1995, has made it possible to re-launch the collaboration between the two institutions, in particular by asking the services of the ILO to help Fund missions to acquire a better understanding on labor markets and social protection issues.

The adoption of the new Declaration of the Interim Committee is another reason to strengthen the collaboration between the ILO and the IMF. Indeed, I think that the ILO has a role to play in helping implement the strategy set out in the Declaration. With regard to this, I would like to put forward an idea which could work towards this objective. The missions of the IMF in the member countries, in the context of Article IV consultations of programme negotiations, could meet the social partners more systematically so as to examine with them the efforts the country concerned has to prepare to make to meet the common objectives of the new Declaration of the Interim Committee. In the countries where the ILO is represented, these meetings could be prepared by the services of the ILO.

It would also be useful for the IMF to strengthen its on going dialogue with the other organizations of the United Nations which have a role to play in assisting countries to promote sustainable economic and social development. In this respect, the breaking up of responsibilities among the UN organizations makes it difficult for the IMF to broaden its dialogue with these organizations. That is why, like Michel Camdessus and Michel Hansenne, I would like to see the creation of a credible "social and humanitarian pillar" with which the three other great economic and financial institutions - the IMF, the World Bank and the World Trade Organization (WTO) - could exchange views and cooperate so as to better integrate the social dimension in their actions.

CONCLUSION

Progress made since last year to strengthen the role of the Fund in the area of surveillance, consolidate its financial basis, and make the Fund's facility for financing the poorest countries permanent and self-sustaining in the long term, will help the Fund to continue to perform its tasks in the global economy.

The agenda to adapt the Fund to the process of globalization is, however, not yet complete. Indeed, the search for economic and financial stability in the next century calls for intensifying the responsibilities of the Fund in surveillance, adjusting its financial resources to the global economy, and developing appropriate mechanisms to enable its staff to formulate its recommendations in a framework that looks more effectively at the interrelationship between economic and social development.

I hope that progress in these areas will be accomplished this year. This would contribute to maximizing the benefits of globalization and reducing the risks this process poses, especially with regard to financial stability and the exclusion of certain groups in nearly all regions of the world.

PART VII

SUMMARY AND CONCLUSIONS

Summary And Conclusions

SCHEHERAZADE S. REHMAN (editor)
Assistant Professor of International Finance and Director, Joint International MBA-MA Degree Programs, The George Washington University

SUMMARY

Global and regional financial crises are not a new international economic phenomenon. But their nature has changed over the last few years. The growing integration of global financial markets i.e. the increased size and more rapid relatively unfettered movement of private capital across national boundaries, the disposition of the participating investors and the instruments they use have altered the process. The world economy is also characterized by a variety of exchange rate systems ranging from fixed through semi-fixed to flexible arrangements. This poses a heretofore unknown set of challenges to national governments, financial market participants and multilateral organizations. The challenges, among others, limit national sovereignty in setting and implementing economic policies. Moreover, there are no global or regional financial crisis "managers" that are up to the task of quickly and efficiently moderating or resolving the crises when they occur.

One of the major causes of regional financial crises are the fixed or narrow band- based exchange rate systems introduced by regional economic blocs such as the EMS/ERM of the European Union. Under such a system, calls for symmetry are inconsistent with the presence of a strong anchor currency. Moreover, only domestic price stability, timely central realignments and flexibility can prevent financial crises such as those that affected the ERM in 1992 and 1993. However, such an exchange rate system provides for only one domestic price level and interest rate structure that is consistent with the price levels and interest rate structures of the rest of the world that generates balance of payments equilibria and full employment. Usually, the strongest central bank in the system sets interest rate and monetary policy without concern for the interests of the other participating nations. The result is postponed structural and macroeconomic adjustments, foregone output and high levels of unemployment which unless addressed and resolved, could lead to major financial crises.

The single currency, the Euro, of the European Union, can provide economic benefits through the reduction of, for example, transaction costs. But it is also likely to increase the already high level of economic policy differences among the potential members of the Economic and Monetary Union (EMU) planned for 1999. Thus the real issue in preventing future financial crises in the EMU may not be realization of the Maastricht Treaty convergence criteria but the strict enforcement of the post-EMU "Fiscal Stability and Growth Pact" and the proper management of the economic relations between the EMU "ins" and "outs." If the financial markets decide that the Euro is a credible new currency, small open economies such as Switzerland could benefit from its introduction. Moreover, if it becomes a major trade, investment and reserve currency, together with the US dollar it could contribute to the establishment of a more stable global financial environment.

The state of public finances and the net external financial position of the member nations of a fixed or narrow band based exchange rate system are also important considerations. Problems in these areas can lead to disinvestment, currency depreciation and long-term interest rate differentials which together can generate a financial crisis. When this happens, reality does not matter; what is decisive is the perception of the financial market participants. It takes credible governments to modify their beliefs, curb their reactions and guide their expectations so as to moderate or even undo the financial crises once they happen.

The 1994 Mexican crisis raised number of new issues. It had occurred in a country that was undergoing a set of successful economic reforms during the early 1990s and it involved a capital "flow" and "stock" as well as asymmetric information problems. At the outset of the crisis, bank balance sheets deteriorated because of loan losses due to rapid financial sector deregulation and credit expansion based on poor risk analysis by the banks and monitoring of bank performance by the regulatory authorities. The resulting asymmetric information (lack of reliable information) problem was reinforced by the increase in U.S. interest rates in the spring of 1994 that put a great deal of pressure on Mexican rates. Increasing political uncertainty in Mexico, a low savings rate and a shift from investment to consumption combined with an eventually foreign-currency denominated short-term debt (tesobonos) and a volatile inflow of portfolio investments as well as a political commitment to a fixed exchange rate resulted in declining reserves and a growing current account deficit. Due to a weakening of economic policy measures put in place earlier, the Mexican government could no longer sustain investor confidence and a reversal of capital flows occurred.

The much dreaded "Tequila Effect" i.e. spillover of the Mexican financial crisis, particularly in Latin America, did not occur. As the case of Argentina illustrates, financial discipline imposed by the convertibility (currency board) plan together with higher bank reserve requirements, a credible "no bail-out" (moral hazard) policy and the publication of information to prevent information asymmetry together with assistance received from multilateral organizations, prevented a major financial crisis originating in the "Tequila Effect." To the extent that there was a spillover, it manifested itself in the speeding up of the bank restructuring processes under way (failures and mergers) caused by increased competition.

The role of a strong, well structured, regulated and prudentially managed banking sector supported through multilateral assistance in preventing financial crises in the emerging market countries in general and in the transforming economies in particular is illustrated by the consolidation experience of the Russian banking industry. Stronger supervisory boards, more effective merger, bankruptcy and liquidation rules and procedures together with International Monetary Fund (IMF) stand-by-loan arrangements prevented a financial crisis that could have significantly constrained the already difficult and complicated Russian economic transformation process.

The transforming Central and East European economies are subject to a variety of political and economic strains and uncertainties. The experience of the now Czech Republic confirms that financial crises may be generated by major macroeconomic stabilization policy measures, systemic changes and political shocks such as the breakup of a country. Under such circumstances information asymmetry increased and thus the expectations of financial market participants had to be modified, curbed and guided. With the assistance of the IMF, the Czech government managed to do so and thus prevented a major financial crisis.

The management of internal and external disequlibria together with the large scale introduction of systemic changes can quickly generate major financial crises unless prevented through the establishment of a high level of market discipline and the provision of multilateral financial assistance. This is well illustrated by the experience of Hungary, a "premature social welfare" state whose vast array of social services could not be supported by the nation's economic performance. Following an initially rational growth strategy during the early 1990s, the country quickly reverted to an unsustainable growth path marked by undisciplined economic policies introduced for political reasons. By 1994, Hungary faced the potential of an extensive internal and external disequilibrium that could have resulted in a major financial crisis. The newly elected government introduced a comprehensive macroeconomic stabilization package that included a modified, crawling peg exchange rate system, revenue enhancement measures and a sharp reduction in welfare expenditures. The crisis was avoided, but real income and the standard of living declined.

War may also cause financial crises. The experience of Kuwait shows that only a strong financial infrastructure i.e. good working relations between the central bank and the commercial banking sector, the honoring of all financial obligations through a strong international network and an accurate assessment of the situation can prevent a financial crisis under such circumstances. The development of a post-liberation macroeconomic stabilization plan as well as the availability of foreign assistance were additional factors enabling the Kuwaiti government to quickly reestablish economic conditions conducive to the effective and efficient functioning of the financial system in general and of the banking sector in particular.

CONCLUSIONS

Based on the lessons learned from the analysis of the various regional financial crises several conclusions can be drawn with respect to the possible ways of preventing and managing such crises. First, the causes of financial crises are multiple, complex and interrelated, thus, the definition of systemic risk varies. The discussions in the relevant literature are a case in point. Nonetheless, it is possible to identify some common characteristics that are present in all types of financial crises such as erroneous policy measures introduced by the authorities, excessive actions and/or reactions of financial market participants, anticipated or unanticipated political and/or economic events, lack of reliable information (information asymmetry), uncertainty, confusions and panic. This commonality allows for a number of general observations concerning the causes, possible methods of prevention and management of financial crises.

Additional potential causes include inefficient monetary policy caused by the inability of banks in trouble to respond to interest rate changes and the reluctance of central banks to pursue tough policy measures because of their concerns for a weak banking sector. Premature domestic financial deregulation, the introduction of not well understood new financial products and the hasty removal of external capital controls are also potential sources of financial crisis.

Although macroeconomic policy cooperation is essential to the stability of any regional exchange rate mechanism, experience shows that such cooperation is extremely difficult to achieve because economic and political power usually is unevenly distributed among the participating nations. Moreover, the effects and signs of macroeconomic policy multipliers are not always well understood, thus, cooperation based on the wrong macroeconomic policy model can be welfare reducing.

Both the "flow" and "stock" characteristics of capital inflows into emerging market countries are critical issues that have to be carefully considered. Portfolio rather than direct investment flows, extensive short-term foreign currency denominated debt accompanied by a switch from investments to consumption together with a strong commitment to a fixed exchange rate, may quickly reduce reserves and generate a current account deficit, thereby creating a major financial crisis. Under such circumstances the manner and speed of exiting a fixed exchange rate system as well as the availability of a large cushion of owned or borrowed reserves, provided either through regional monetary arrangements or multilateral assistance programs, is of critical importance.

Every emerging market and transforming economy must integrate with the globalizing capital markets. However, the exposure of such nations to financial vulnerability and, thus, to financial crises should be minimized through a more careful management of the public debt and of the scope, sequencing and speed of financial market deregulation. Central banks should be prepared to deal with crisis through well planned strategies that include bank mergers, closures or restructuring, as necessary. Such measures should be reinforced through credible and sustainable macroeconomic policies insuring price stability, at least in the medium-term. Banking sectors must also be strengthened through the introduction of more prudential operating standards. The current international banking agreements as, for example, the 1988 Basle Capital Adequacy Accord, do not address the major sources of banking crises in the emerging market and transforming economies. Countries with weak banking systems are at a disadvantage in trying to deal with financial crises, particularly those caused by large shifts in international capital flows. Thus, international banking guidelines need to be developed that require the full disclosure of economic and financial data, thereby moderating information asymmetry and enhancing market discipline so that the policy measures and actions of borrowers' are more consistent with their solvency requirements. Additional measures that should be required include a functioning legal system in general and clear and efficient property rights as well as bankruptcy rules and procedures in particular. However, the strengthening of regulatory frameworks should be subjected to a careful cost-benefit analysis. In particular, unintended consequences that weaken market discipline must be considered. The moral hazard issue is an especially critical consideration in this respect.

All of these measures would enable national governments and financial sector participants to obtain more credibility, a quality that is essential in crisis prevention and management. In its 65th Annual report published in 1995, the Bank of International Settlements (BIS) pointed out other dimensions of credibility. It emphasized the importance of a well defined legislative mandate for the primary objective of monetary policy, central bank independence, the adoption of formal inflation control, monetary policy and exchange rate targets to oversee central bank performance, the consistency of intermediate and final policy targets and transparency. The Basle Committee of central banks' 25 "core principles" of banking supervision published in April 1997 can also aid in raising standards in emerging markets and, thus, strengthen credibility.

The globalization of capital markets together with the sharp increase in private capital flows under conditions described above has resulted in relatively frequent regional financial crises in recent times. Thus, the International Monetary Fund (IMF) has developed new surveillance, credit extension and technical assistance programs to prevent and/or manage such crises. Yet, the IMF is constrained in what it can do. It cannot, for example, publish the results of its surveillance of national economies because governments insist on confidentiality. Nor can it act as a central bank and become a lender of last resort. Thus, its ability to reduce information asymmetry or to provide financial stability is limited. But it can provide temporary liquidity and technical assistance through which it can influence the perception of financial market participants and thus provide some credibility to governments engaged in the management of financial crises.

The IMF performed well during the energy crisis of the 1970s, the external debt crisis of the 1980s and provided useful assistance to the transforming economies in the early 1990s as well as to Mexico in 1994. But its present-day "tool-kit" is not effective enough to prevent and/or manage future regional financial crises. There is a "Paris-Club" to address the issues related to the management of sovereign debt and there is also a "London-Club" to deal with matters arising out of commercial debt arrangements. But there is no formal or informal institution in place to provide a forum for discussions between governments and, for example, mutual fund managers who are managing emerging market investments on a large scale. The IMF's 1996 recommendation that nations that want access to private international capital markets should promote human resources, reduce and eventually eliminate corruption and strengthen their banking sectors through prudential supervision, is good advice. The IMF Interim Committee's 1997 decision to give the IMF the mandate to promote the free flow of capital worldwide is also a step in the right direction. Yet, these measures are not enough. The IMF should be authorized to increase its capital, raise its allocation of SDRs to member nations, consult with individual countries in advance of balance of payment problems, survey international capital markets, promote more exchange rate stability and, perhaps, even develop country-bankruptcy procedures as proposed in recent times. The development and application of such new policy tools raises difficult, complex and controversial issue. At the same time, their use could reduce the enormous political, economic and social cost that the various regional financial crises are regularly causing.

Index

A

CFA involvement, 127, 128
in EMS, 40, 45, 118
French referendum, 68
monetary policy of, 44
promoting MU, 34—35
Franc Fort Policy, 32—33, 119, 122, 129
Franc (France), 95—99, 116
Franc (Switzerland), EMU effect on,
109—112
Free Democratic Alliance, 250
Free market approach, crisis recovery, 10
Fugger family, 11
Fund. *see* International Monetary Fund
(IMF)

G

Gabon, 127
GCC. *see* Gulf Cooperation Council
(GCC)
G-5 countries, 14
G-7 countries, 14, 15—19
G-10 countries, 13, 14, 317
General Agreement on Tariffs and Trade
(GATT), 22, 25, 300
General Agreement on Trade in Services
(GATS), 22, 25
General Arrangements to Borrow (IMF),
303, 328, 332
George, Eddie, 100
Gerashchenko, Viktor, 216
Germany. *see also* Bundesbank
conditions for MU, 35—36
in EMS, 118
interest rates (1991-1996), 76
long-term forward rates (1992-1996),
74
public debt, 277—278
reunification, effect of, 48, 56
Gold-exchange standard, 12
Gold-pool agreement (1961), 12
Government action method, crisis
recovery, 10
Greece, 42, 96, 118, 121

Greenspan, Alan, 16, 155
Gross domestic product (Europe), 58,
133
Gulf Cooperation Council (GCC), 124—
127, 132
benefits of membership, 124
currencies per US dollar, 140
exchange rate policies, 116, 125—126
Kuwait, support during occupation,
126, 284
members in, 124
real GDP growth rates, 140
resource depletion in, 124—125

H

Hansenne, Michel, 332
Heavily Indebted Poor Countries
(HIPCs), 329
Hong Kong, 24, 31
House of Bardi, 10
House of Peruzzi, 10
Hungary, 337
communistic history of, 241—244
future tasks, 259—260
IMF involvement in, 314
monetary policy relaxation
(1992-1995), 248—250
recession/supply side adjustment,
246—248
short-term achievements of
stabilization, 257—259
stabilization program (1995), 250—
257
transition adjustment needs, 244—245

I

IMF. *see* International Monetary Fund
(IMF)
Import surcharges, 252—254
Inflation, 14, 17, 168, 258
Interest rates, 17, 115